SKILL DEVELOPMENT IN BIOINFORMATICS FOR FREE

Ajit Kumar Roy

Copyright :akroy@2016

ISBN-13:978-1536873719

ISBN-10:1536873713

Dedication:

Dedicated to my granddaughter 'ANGANA'

PREFACE

The idea of writing this book came as a result of over a decade long teaching, research and development activities in the field of Bioinformatics to fill the gap of demand of students/researchers engaged in the field. With the arrival of genomics and genome sequencing projects, biology has been transformed into an incredibly data-rich science. The vast amount of information generated has made computational analysis critical and has increased demand for skilled bioinformaticians. There are already thousands of online bioinformatics resources available but the limiting factors of the field is the difficulty in navigating the vast array of resources to identify the most appropriate tool one need. However, trying to find the right resource and learn how to use the often complex features and functions is difficult. The book explores ways that you can quickly find and effectively learn how to use resources. It will include a tour of example resources, organized by categories such as Algorithms and Analysis tools, expression resources, genome browsers Literature and text mining resources, and resources focused on nucleotides, proteins, pathways, disease and variation. Advent of the Internet and the rise of Web-based tools and technologies, resources, web content, blog posts, videos, webinars, and web sites that will facilitate easy access and use that saves time and effort avoiding massive generalized searches or hunting and pecking through lists of databases. The purpose of the book is to bridge the gap between the rising information needs of biological and medical researchers and the rapidly growing number of online bioinformatics resources. The freely available, searchable database arranges resources by categories and sub-categories such as Databases and Analysis Tools, Proteomics Resources, and Enzymes and Pathways. Key programming tools and technologies used in bioinformatics and molecular evolutionary research are provided. Those interested in learning basic biocomputing skills will find links to selected tutorials. A comprehensive list of web tools, public sequence databases and open source software and technologies are provided. The book is divided into the following chapters and within each chapter a number of subchapters for quick access to desired material.

Chapter 1:   BASICS OF BIOLOGY AND BIOINFORMATICS

Chapter 2:   TERMINOLOGIES RELATED TO BIOINFORMATICS

Chapter 3:   EDUCATIONAL RESOURCES

Chapter 4:   BIOINFORMATICS, INTERNET AND LINKS

Chapter 5:   APPLIED BIOINFORMATICS FOR RESEARCH

Chapter 6:   BIOLOGICAL DATABASES ON THE WEB

Chapter 7:   TECHNIQUES OF SEARCHING AND ACCESS TO WEB RESOURCES

Chapter 8:   WEB RESOURCES AT EDUCATIONAL INSTITUTES AND COURSES

Chapter 9:   BIOLOGICAL DATABASES, GATEWAYS AND PORTALS

Chapter 10: APPLICATION OF BIOINFORMATICS TOOLS AND SOFTWARE

Chapter 11: BIOINFORMATICS LINKS DIRECTORY

Chapter 12: INVALUABLE ACCESS TO TIME SAVING WEB TUTORIALS, TOOLS AND RESOURCES 369

Chapter 13: TUTORIALS AND VIDEOS

Chapter 14: BIOINFORMATICS RESOURCES FOR REVOLUTIONARY GENOMICS

Chapter 15: BIOINFORMATICS WEB PRACTICAL AT UMBER

Chapter 16: PATH CASE SYSTEMS BIOLOGY

Chapter 17: IMPORTANT WEBINAR AND BLOGS ON BIOINFORMATICS

Chapter 18: BIOINFORMATICS IN SOCIAL MEDIA

Chapter 19: BIOINFORMATICS FREQUENTLY ASKED QUESTIONS

Chapter 20: CENTERS OF BIOINFORMATICS ACTIVITY

Today's bioinformatician are in high demand. With a seemingly endless stream of biological data being generated across sectors, there is high demand for talented, experienced professionals at the crossroads of biology, statistics, and computer science. Scientists who can analyze large amounts of information and present it in a clear manner to decision makers are finding the sky is the limit in terms of jobs and career pathways, especially in the big pharma and biotech sectors.

It is an essential one-stop guide for researchers, graduate & post graduate students in bioinformatics, computer science, mathematics, statistics, and biological sciences as current online resources and learning technologies will continue to impact bioinformatics education programs. Thanks are due to all those who originally developed and conceived the idea of spreading the tools and techniques for the benefits of future generation of students and researchers.

AJIT KUMAR ROY

Contents

Chapter 1: BASICS OF BIOLOGY AND BIOINFORMATICS — 1

Preliminaries of Biology — 1
Definitions of Bioinformatics — 5
Activities in Bioinformatics — 8
Aims of Bioinformatics — 8
Tasks of Bioinformatics — 10
Bioinformatics and its scope — 12
The Potential of Bioinformatics — 13
Bioinformatics - Industry Overview — 15

Chapter 2: TERMINOLOGIES RELATED TO BIOINFORMATICS — 16

Bioinformatics and Computational Biology — 16
Genomics — 18
Proteomics — 19
Transcriptomics — 19
Pharmacogenomics — 19
The Central Dogma — 20
Five domains of Bioinformatics — 20
Development of Algorithms for Sequence Comparison — 22
Major breakthroughs in Bioinformatics through Algorithm — 23

Chapter 3: EDUCATIONAL RESOURCES — 24

Bioinformatics — 24
Next Generation Sequencing — 25

Machine Learning	26
Biostatistics	27
Biological Databases	28
Scientific Computing	29
Bioinformatics and Computational Biology Guide Tags	30
Web Tutorials, Tools, and Resources	34
Web Links for Bioinformatics	35
Bioinformatics Resources	35

Chapter 4: BIOINFORMATICS, INTERNET AND LINKS — 43

Internet educational resources for Bioinformatics	45
Web Sites in the News	47
NCBI: Bioinformatics Resources for Biosciences Researchers	47
Sequence Analysis Tools	61

Chapter 5: APPLIED BIOINFORMATICS FOR RESEARCH — 72

Mission of NCBI / EBI / DDBJ	72
Databases	74
Downloads	88
Submissions	94
How to submit sequences, download, retrieve, find display etc. from NCBI	109

Chapter 6: BIOLOGICAL DATABASES ON THE WEB — 112

Categories of Databases	112
Meta Databases	113
Genome Databases	114
Protein sequence Databases	118

Metabolic pathway Databases	118
General nucleotide databases	120
General protein databases	120
Specialized databases	121
Introduction to Molecular Biology Databases	122

Chapter 7: TECHNIQUES OF SEARCHING AND ACCESS TO WEB RESOURCES — 123

Searching the Web	123
Web Access to Bioinformatics Resources	124
Core Bioinformatics Organizations	125
Important websites that all biologists should know for Biocomputing & Analysis	126
Bioinformatics Web Sites & General Biocomputing Services	127
Alignments and similarity searches on-line	128
Genomics and Bioinformatics centers	132
Bioinformatics Resources	136
Nucleotide Sequence Databases (the principal ones)	136
Database Searching by Sequence Similarity	137
Phylogeny & Taxonomy	141
Gene Prediction	142
Gene List Annotation Tools	145
Computational Resources	146
Introduction to bioinformatics and computational biology	147
Algorithms	148
Science and Technology Sources on the Internet - University of California	149
Sequence Retrieval System (SRS) database descriptions	158

Software Directories: Bioinformatics Software Resource (BISR)	168
Tools in Specific Programming Languages	169
Large-Scale Gene Expression and Microarray Links and Resources	171
Nature's Genome Gateway	172
Southwest Biotechnology and Informatics Center (SWBIC)	172
NCBI: Education Page	175
Protein Data Bank (PDB): Education Resources	176

Chapter 8: WEB RESOURCES AT EDUCATIONAL INSTITUTES AND COURSES — 177

School of Biological Sciences, Bioinformatics Website	177
Columbia University: Web resources for Bioinformatics	179
University of Pittsburgh-Health Science Library System	183
Cornell University: Bioinformatics: Web-Based Resources & Computational Approaches to Biological Sciences	186

Chapter 9: BIOLOGICAL DATABASES, GATEWAYS AND PORTALS — 198

BioTools.info: Molecular Biology Gateways & Tools	198
Biomed Central Gateways	207
Links to Expasy Databases	220
Species specific databases	229
Human mutation databases / resources	257
Gene(s) / protein(s) specific databases / resources	262
Post-translational modifications databases and resources	270
Phylogenetics and taxonomy databases & resources	271
Gene expression databases and resources	273
Biological software and databases catalog servers	274

Biocomputing server's homepages	275
International Nucleotide Sequence Database Collaboration	282
Primary nucleotide sequence databases	283
RNA databases	294
Carbohydrate structure databases	296
Protein-protein and other molecular interactions	296
Signal transduction pathway databases	297
Metabolic pathway and Protein Function databases	298
Microarray databases	299
Specialized databases	301
Taxonomic databases	306
List of biological databases	308

Chapter 10: APPLICATION OF BIOINFORMATICS TOOLS AND SOFTWARE — 310

List of Bioinformatics Tools at International Bioinformatics Centers	313
Free Online Bioinformatics Tools	314
List of software developed by BGI	318
Links of University of Michigan Medical School	320
LGTC - Next-generation Sequencing Analysis	321
Bio Tools Info	326
Tools & Protocols	328
Primer Design	330
Finding Genes	331
Align Two Sequences	334
BLAST	335
Access to computing servers for high-throughput bioinformatics	335

Websites related to motif search	337
Genetic Databases	338
Genome Projects	339

Chapter 11: BIOINFORMATICS LINKS DIRECTORY — **340**

Human Genome Source	347
Model Organisms	349
Protein Source	352
Sequence Comparison	356
DNA	358
RNA	361
Other Molecules	362
Expression	364
Literature	366

Chapter 12: INVALUABLE ACCESS TO TIME SAVING WEB TUTORIALS, TOOLS AND RESOURCES — **369**

Web Tutorials	369
Find, Learn and Deliver	370
The most effective and efficient way to leverage genomics resources	371
Invaluable access to time saving content	372
Washington University, USA - List of all Open Helix Tutorials	373

Chapter 13: TUTORIALS AND VIDEOS — **395**

Tutorials	395
Bioinformatics Tutorials	397
Practical Bioinformatics: Other lists of Bioinformatics Tutorials: More Tutorials Websites:	403

VIDEOS	405
Foundation Tutorials for Bioinformatics Aspirants: Computer Tutorials for Science Stream Students	405
Science Tutorials for Computer Stream Students	409
Video Tutorials	413
Important Tutorial Videos	413
Tutorial videos of bioinformatics	414
Video Repositories	415
Examples of tutorial videos in Togo TV	422
Chapter 14: BIOINFORMATICS RESOURCES FOR REVOLUTIONARY GENOMICS	**425**
The primers4clades web server	425
Other useful PCR-related sites and WebPages	426
Alignment, Phylogeny and Evolutionary Analysis Tools	433
Expression Data	440
Protein predictions	441
Functional genomics	442
Primer Design	444
Chapter 15: BIOINFORMATICS WEB PRACTICAL AT UMBER	**445**
University of Manchester Bioinformatics Education and Research	445
Chapter 16: PATH CASE SYSTEMS BIOLOGY	**451**
Chapter 17: IMPORTANT WEBINAR AND BLOGS ON BIOINFORMATICS	**454**
What is Web-Based Seminar (Webinar)?	454
Bioinformatics Webinar / Seminar available at the web link	455
Biology & Bioinformatics Recorded Webinars by DNA Learning Center	456

BLAST Webinar	457
Recorded Webinars	460
Webinar Series: What about Privacy and Progress in Whole Genome Sequencing?	462
The Importance of Bioinformatics in NGS	462
Webinar: World Tour of Genomics Resources	463
Wiki Pathways	464
Tutorial	464
NIH Video casts	464
Bioinformatics Tutorials	465
Free online training from GeneGo	466
National Library of Medicine update	466
EBI Bioinformatics Roadshow	468
NCBI 3D Structure Help	470
BioSystems Database	471
Blogroll	476
List of Other Bioinformatics Blogs	477
Chapter 18: BIOINFORMATICS IN SOCIAL MEDIA	**510**
Social Media	510
News and Information on Bioinformatics	512
Bioinformatics-related medical blogs	513
Bioinformatics Podcasts and Interviews	513
Bioinformatics Community Sites, Face Book Groups and Forums	513
Micro-blogging: Twitter and Friend-feed in Bioinformatics	513
Bioinformatics Wikis	513
Bioinformatics videos, animations and video casts	514
Bioinformatics on Mobile	514

Social Bookmarking in Bioinformatics 514
Medical Search Engines in Bioinformatics 514
Slideshows about Bioinformatics 514

Chapter 19: BIOINFORMATICS FREQUENTLY ASKED QUESTIONS **515**

Bioinformatics FAQ 515
Fields related to Bioinformatics 516
Answers to Frequently Asked Questions 521
Definition of Bioinformatics: What is Bioinformatics? 526
Applying bioinformatics to biological research 534

Chapter 20: CENTERS OF BIOINFORMATICS ACTIVITY **536**

Research centers 536
Sequencing centers 537
Standard centers 537

GLOSSARY **538**

Chapter 1: BASICS OF BIOLOGY AND BIOINFORMATICS

Preliminaries of Biology

Biology is in the middle of a major paradigm shift driven by computing technology. Although it is already an informational science in many respects, the field has been rapidly becoming much more computational and analytical. Rapid progress in genetics and biochemistry research combined with the tools provided by modern biotechnology has generated massive volumes of genetic and protein sequence data.

Biotechnology involves the scientific manipulation of living organisms to produce products conducive to improving the lives and health of plants, animals, and humans, such as DNA diagnosis, fingerprinting, and genetic mapping.

Molecular Biology: Brief introduction to the basic notions of molecular biology presented. An overview can be found in any modern textbook on biology, biochemistry or molecular biology is a short review of computational methods in biological sequence analysis and recently several books summarizing problems and methods have been published. DNA (deoxyribonucleic acid) and proteins are biological macromolecules built as long linear chains of chemical components. In the case of DNA these components are the so-called nucleotides, of which there are four different ones, each denoted by one of the letters A, C, G and T. Proteins are made up of 20 different amino acids (or "residues") which are denoted by 20 different letters of the alphabet.

Table 1: the nucleotides

DNA	adenine	guanine	cytosine	thymine
	A	**G**	**C**	**T/U**
RNA	adenine	guanine	cytosine	uracil

Table 2: the twenty amino acids

	One-letter code	Three-letter-code	Name
1	A	Ala	Alanine
2	C	Cys	Cysteine
3	D	Asp	Aspartic Acid
4	E	Glu	Glutamic Acid
5	F	Phe	Phenylalanine
6	G	Gly	Glycine
7	H	His	Histidine
8	I	Ile	Isoleucine
9	K	Lys	Lysine
10	L	Leu	Leucine
11	M	Met	Methionine
12	N	Asn	Asparagine
13	P	Pro	Proline
14	Q	Gln	Glutamine
15	R	Arg	Arginine
16	S	Ser	Serine
17	T	Thr	Threonine
18	V	Val	Valine
19	W	Trp	Tryptophan
20	Y	Tyr	Tyrosine

DNA plays a fundamental role in the processes of life in two respects. First it contains the templates for the synthesis of proteins, which are essential molecules for any organism. Though being summarized under that one name there is a wide variety of proteins. What they have in common are their building blocks, the amino acids. Each of the 20 amino acids is coded for by one or more triplets of the nucleotides making up DNA. The end of a chain is coded for by another set of triplets (or codons, as they are also called). Based on this translation table (the genetic code) the linear string of DNA is translated into a linear string of amino acids, i.e. a protein. Here is an example:

$$\underbrace{GAA}_{E}\ \underbrace{CTA}_{L}\ \underbrace{CAC}_{H}\ \underbrace{ACG}_{T}\ \underbrace{TGT}_{C}\ \underbrace{AAC}_{N}$$

The amino acid sequence of a protein, also called its primary structure, is only one level at which it can be looked at. To fulfill its natural role a protein assumes a certain three dimensional structure, which is referred to as its tertiary structure. The term "secondary structure" refers to the local folding of the amino acid chain into small regular elements. The major classes of secondary structure are called beta strands and alpha helices. The three dimensional (tertiary) structure of a protein is usually built up of elements of alpha and/or beta structure together with loop regions in between them. It is the three dimensional folding of the chain which determines the biological function of a protein.

The second role in which DNA is essential to life is as a medium to transmit information (namely the building plans for proteins) from generation to generation. Watson and Crick in 1953 found the double helical structure of DNA. The linear chain does not really occur on its own but is paired to a complementary strand. The complementarily stems from the ability of the nucleotides is to establish specific pairs (A-T and G-C). The pair of complementary strands then forms the famous double helix. Each strand therefore carries the entire information and the biochemical machinery guarantees that the information can be copied over and over again even when the "original" molecule has long since vanished.

During this process of copying, changes (known as mutations) are introduced into the DNA sequence. The kinds of mutations which are important to sequence comparison are base changes, insertions of nucleotides into the chain and deletions from the chain. The elementary operations allowed in the definition of sequence similarity are chosen to correspond to these events. To visualize the relationship between two similar sequences they are represented in the form of an alignment:

```
V-LSPADKTNVKAAWGKVGAHAGEYGAEALERMFLSFPTTKTYFPHF-DL   HAHU
VHLTPEEKSAVTALWGKV--NVDEVGGEALGRLLVVYPWTQRFFESFGDL   HBHU
SH----GSAQVKGHGKKVADALTNAVAHVDDMPNALSALSDLHAHKLRV    HAHU
STPDAVMGNPKVKAHGKKVLGAFSDGLAHLDNLKGTFATLSELHCDKLHV   HBHU
DPVNFKLLSHCLLVTLAAHLPAEFTPAVHASLDKFLASVSTVLTSKYR     HAHU
DPENFRLLGNVLVCVLAHHFGKEFTPPVQAAYQKVVAGVANALAHKYH     HBHU
```

The two amino acid sequences compared here are the alpha chain of human hemoglobin (abbreviated HAHU) and its beta chain (HBHU). With the sequences being approximately 150 amino acids long, each block of lines contains part of the first sequence in the upper and of the second sequence in the lower line. Residues on top of each other in one block are equivalence. Some residues are conserved (the amino acids in the column are identical), some have been exchanged and part of the chain has been deleted from the one sequence or (equivalently) inserted in the other. Insertions or deletions are indicated by a letter paired with a dash, the gap-character. An alignment can also be interpreted as representing the operations necessary to transform a sequence into another one using the same operations as evolution does.

Definitions of Bioinformatics

a. Many names, for instance, *bioinformatics, biocomputing, biological computing, computational biology, computational genomics, biological data mining* ...

b. **No formal definition** of bioinformatics

c. Field of science in which biology, computer science and information technology merge into a single discipline

d. Development and application of computing, mathematical and statistical methods to **analyze biological, biochemical and biophysical data**

e. Employs computers to store, retrieve, analyze and assist in understanding biological information

f. **Multidisciplinary field** required in-depth knowledge of e.g. mathematics, algorithms, statistics, data mining, natural language processing, genome science, sequence analysis, molecular biology, pharmacology, biophysics, hardware engineering and software programming

Definitions: Bioinformatics has been defined as a means for analysing, comparing, graphically displaying, modelling, storing, systemising, searching, and ultimately distributing biological information, which includes sequences, structures, function, and phylogeny. Thus bioinformatics may be defined as a discipline that generates computational tools, databases, and methods to support genomic and post genomic research. It comprises the study of DNA structure and function, gene and protein expression, protein production, structure and function, genetic regulatory systems, and clinical applications. Bioinformatics needs the expertise from Computer Science, Mathematics, Statistics, Medicine, and Biology. Bioinformatics proceeds research, development, or application of computational tools and approaches for expanding the use of biological, medical, behavioural or health data, including those to acquire, store, organize, archive, analyze, or visualize such data. Further Bioinformatics is the study of how information is represented and transmitted in biological systems for myriad practical applications. These applications include creating new drugs, discovering cures for genetic diseases, cloning threatened species, creating new biomaterials for military and civilian applications, and creating high-yield and disease-resistant crops to feed the world's growing population. The ultimate goals of bioinformatics will be to abstract knowledge and principles from large-scale data, to present a complete representation of the cell and the organism, and to predict computationally systems of higher complexity, such as the interaction networks in cellular processes and the phenotypes of whole organisms.

Bioinformatics is the application of computational and analytical methods to biological problems and that is a rapidly evolving scientific discipline. Genome sequencing projects are producing vast amounts of biological data for many different organisms, and, increasingly, storing these data in public databases. Such biological databases are growing exponentially, along with the biological literature. Most of the large biology databases are based on traditional relational databases architectures; whereas others, especially systems dealing with images and other multimedia, are based on object-oriented designs.

Bioinformatics, like virtually every other knowledge-intensive field, is dependent on a robust information technology infrastructure that includes the Internet, the World Wide Web, intranets, and wireless systems. These and other network technologies are applied directly to sharing, manipulating, and archiving genetic sequences and other bioinformatics data. For example, the majority of resources available for researchers in the bioinformatics are Web-based systems such as GenBank, which is maintained by the National Centre for Biological Information (NCBI), the National Institutes of Health (NIH), and other government agencies. The issues and challenges associated with providing an adequate network infrastructure are related to selecting and implementing the appropriate communications models, selecting the best transmission technology, identifying the most effective protocols, dealing with limited bandwidth, selecting the most appropriate network topologies, and contending with security and privacy. Because of the computational requirements associated with bioinformatics, the field serves as a test-bed for many of the leading-edge networking technologies, such as the Great Global Grid (GGG), which distributes not only data but supercomputing-level processing power to PCs and workstations as well.

Bioinformatics has evolved into a full-fledged multidisciplinary subject that integrates developments in information and computer technology as applied to Biotechnology and Biological Sciences. Bioinformatics uses computer software tools for database creation, data management, data warehousing, data mining and global communication networking. Bioinformatics is the recording, annotation, storage, analysis, and searching/retrieval of nucleic acid sequence (genes and RNAs), protein sequence and structural information. This includes databases of the sequences and structural information as well methods to access, search, visualize and retrieve the information. Bioinformatics concern the creation and maintenance of databases of biological information whereby researchers can both access existing information and submit new entries. Function genomics, biomolecular structure, proteome analysis, cell metabolism, biodiversity, downstream processing in chemical engineering, drug and vaccine design are some of the areas in which Bioinformatics is an integral component.

Sub-disciplines within Bioinformatics: There are three important sub-disciplines within bioinformatics involving computational biology -

1) The development of new algorithms and statistics with which to assess relationships among members of large data sets.

2) The analysis and interpretation of various types of data including nucleotide and amino acid sequences, protein domains, and protein structures.

3) The development and implementation of tools that enable efficient access and management of different types of information.

Activities in Bioinformatics

We can split the activities in bioinformatics in two areas-

1) The organization.
2) The analysis of biological data.

Aims of Bioinformatics

The aims of bioinformatics are basically three-fold-

1) Organization of data in such a way that it allows researchers to access existing information & to submit new entries as they are produced. While data-creation is an essential task, the information stored in these databases is useless unless

analysed. Thus the purpose of bioinformatics extends well beyond mere volume control.

2) To develop tools and resources that help in the analysis of data. For example, having sequenced a particular protein, it is with previously characterized sequences. This requires more than just a straightforward database search. As such, programs such as FASTA and PSI-BLAST much consider what constitutes a biologically significant resemblance. Development of such resources extensive knowledge of computational theory, as well as a thorough understanding of biology.

3) Use of these tools to analyse the individual systems in detail, and frequently compared them with few that are related.

4) To use this data to analyze and interpret the results in a biologically meaningful manner.

5) To help researchers in the Pharmaceutical industry in understanding the protein structures to make the drug design easy.

Three levels of Bioinformatics:

1) <u>Analysis of a single gene (protein) sequence</u>. For example :
    i. *Similarity with other known genes*
    ii. *Phylogenetic trees ; evolutionary relationships*
    iii. *Identification of well-defined domains in the sequence*
    iv. *Sequence features (physical properties, binding sites, modification sites)*
    v. *Prediction of sub cellular localization*
    vi. *Prediction of secondary and tertiary structure*

2) <u>Analysis of complete genomes</u>. For example :
   i. *Which gene families are present, which missing*
   ii. *Location of genes on the chromosomes, correlation with function or evolution*
   iii. *Expansion / duplication of gene families*
   iv. *Presence or absence of biochemical pathways*
   v. *Identification of "missing" enzymes*
   vi. *Large-scale events in the evolution of organisms*

3) <u>Analysis of genes and genomes with respect to functional data</u>. For example :
   i. *Expression analysis ; microarray data ; mRNA conc. measurements*
   ii. *Proteomics ; protein conc. measurements, covalent modifications*
   iii. *Comparison and analysis of biochemical pathways*
   iv. *Deletion or mutant genotypes vs. phenotypes*
   v. *Identification of essential genes, or genes involved in specific processes*

Tasks of Bioinformatics

The tasks of Bioinformatics involve the analysis of sequence information. This involves the following activities.

   i. *Identifying the genes in the DNA sequences from various organisms.*
   ii. *Identifying families of related sequences and the development of models.*
   iii. *Aligning similar sequences and generating Phylogenetic trees to examine evolutionary relationships.*

iv. *Finding all the genes and proteins of a genome from a given sequence of amino acids.*
v. *Predicting active sites in the protein structures to attach drug molecules.*
vi. *Gene ontology, a semantic framework could be used to underpin a range of important bioinformatics tasks, such as the querying of heterogeneous bioinformatics sources or the systematic annotation of experimental results (Baker et al., 1999).*

Application Areas of Bioinformatics:

a) Post-genome applications
b) Sequence analyses
c) Protein structure prediction
d) Data processing, data management
e) Database searches
f) Phylogentic analyses
g) Gene expression, expression data analysis
h) Recognition of genes and regulatory elements
i) Visualization, modeling and simulation of metabolic pathways and regulatory networks
j) Software tools
k) *Computational biology* has found its applications in many areas. It helps in providing practical tools to explore Proteins and DNA in number of other ways.
l) *Bio-computing* is useful in recognition techniques to detect similarity between sequences and hence to interrelate structures and functions.
m) Another important application of Bioinformatics is the direct prediction of protein 3-Dimensional structure from the linear amino acid sequence.

n) It also simplifies the problem of understanding complex genomes by analyzing simple organisms and then applying the same principles to more complicated ones. This would result in identifying potential drug targets by checking homologies of essential microbial proteins.

o) Bioinformatics is useful in designing drugs.

Bioinformatics and its scope

Bioinformatics uses advances in the area of computer science, information science and computer and information technology, communication technology to solve complex problems in life sciences and particularly in biotechnology. Data capture, data warehousing and data mining have become major issues for biotechnologists and biological scientists due to sudden growth in quantitative data in biology such as complete genomes of biological species including human genome, protein sequences, protein 3-D structures, metabolic pathways databases, cell line & hybridoma information, biodiversity related information. Advancements in information technology, particularly the Internet, are being used to gather and access ever-increasing information in biology and biotechnology. Functional genomics, proteomics, discovery of new drugs and vaccines, molecular diagnostic kits and pharmacogenomics are some of the areas in which bioinformatics has become an integral part of Research & Development. The knowledge of multimedia databases, tools to carry out data analysis and modelling of molecules and biological systems on computer workstations as well as in a network environment has become essential for any student of Bioinformatics. Bioinformatics, the multidisciplinary area, has grown so much that one divides it into molecular bioinformatics, organal bioinformatics and species bioinformatics. Issues related to biodiversity and environment, cloning of higher animals such as Dolly and Polly, tissue culture and cloning of plants have brought out that Bioinformatics is not only a support branch of science but is also a subject that directs future course of research in biotechnology and life sciences. The importance and usefulness of Bioinformatics is realized in last few years by many industries. Therefore, large Bioinformatics R & D divisions are being established in many pharmaceutical companies, biotechnology companies and even in other conventional industry dealing with biological. Bioinformatics is thus rated as number one career in the field of biosciences.

In short, Bioinformatics deals with database creation, data analysis and modelling. Data capturing is done not only from printed material but also from network resources. Databases in biology are generally in the multimedia form organized in relational database model. Modelling is done not only on single biological molecule but also on multiple systems thus requiring a use of high performance computing systems.

Bioinformatics involves the analysis of biological data and randomness is inherent in both the biological processes themselves and the sampling mechanisms by which they are observed. This subject first introduces stochastic processes and their applications in Bioinformatics, including evolutionary models. It then considers the application of classical statistical methods including estimation, hypothesis testing, model selection, multiple comparisons, and multivariate statistical techniques in Bioinformatics.

The Potential of Bioinformatics

The potential of Bioinformatics in the identification of useful genes leading to the development of new gene products, drug discovery and drug development has led to a paradigm shift in biology and biotechnology-these fields are becoming more & more computationally intensive. The new paradigm, now emerging, is that all the genes will be known "in the sense of being resident in database available electronically", and the starting point of biological investigation will be theoretical and a scientist will begin with a theoretical conjecture and only then turning to experiment to follow or test the hypothesis. With a much deep understanding of the biological processes at the molecular level, the Bioinformatics scientist have developed new techniques to analyse genes on an industrial scale resulting in a new area of science known as *'Genomics'*.

The shift from gene biology has resulted in the development of strategies-from lab techniques to computer programmes to analyse whole batch of genes at once. Genomics is revolutionizing drug development, gene therapy, and our entire approach to health care and human medicine.

The genomic discoveries are getting translated in to practical biomedical results through Bioinformatics applications. Work on proteomics and genomics will continue using highly sophisticated software tools and data networks that can carry multimedia databases. Thus, the research will be in the development of multimedia databases in various areas of life sciences and biotechnology. There will be an urgent need for development of software tools for data mining, analysis and modelling, and downstream processing. Security of data, data transfer and data compression, auto checks on data accuracy and correctness will also be major research area of bioinformatics. The use of virtual reality in drug design, metabolic pathway design, and unicellular organism design, paving the way to design and modification of muticellular organisms, will be the challenges which Bioinformatics scientist and specialist have to tackle. It has now been universally recognized that Bioinformatics is the key to the new grand data-intensive molecular biology that will take us into 21 century.

Bioinformatics - Industry Overview

The bioinformatics market is expected to grow to $12.86 billion by 2020 with a CAGR of 21.2% during 2014-2020. Bioinformatics is an interdisciplinary field that is used in the development and storage of data, thus helping in the analysis, organization and retrieval of the biological data. Bioinformatics has various applications and thus forms part of almost all the fields in biology. Bioinformatics form a part of agriculture, animal breeding, molecular medicine, preventive medicine, etc. (source: http://www.prnewswire.com).Now it has demand for individuals capable of doing bioinformatics is soaring. Industry's demand for scientists with skills in Bioinformatics far exceeds the supply of qualified specialists in the field. Therefore, companies are developing methods of spotting potential Bioinformatics experts and then training them on the job.

Chapter 2: TERMINOLOGIES RELATED TO BIOINFORMATICS

Bioinformatics and Computational Biology

Bioinformatics and computational biology each maintain close interactions with life sciences to realize their full potential. Bioinformatics applies principles of information sciences and technologies to make the vast, diverse, and complex life sciences data more understandable and useful. Computational biology uses mathematical and computational approaches to address theoretical and experimental questions in biology. Although bioinformatics and computational biology are distinct, there is also significant overlap and activity at their interface.

Computational Biology is termed as development and application of data-analytical and theoretical methods, mathematical modelling and computational simulation techniques to the study of biological, behavioural, and social systems. Computational biology encompasses all areas of biology that involve computation for better understanding of a living cell and how it functions at a molecular level.

Computational Biology is application of core technology of computer science (eg. algorithms, artificial intelligence, databases etc) to problems arising from biology. Computational biology is particularly exciting today because the problems are large enough to motivate the efficient algorithms and moreover the demand of biology on computational science is increasing. The most pressing tasks in bioinformatics involve the analysis of sequence information.

Computational Biology is the name given to this process, and it involves the following:

1) Finding the genes in the DNA sequences of various organisms

2) Developing methods to predict the structure and/or function of newly discovered proteins and structural RNA sequences.

3) Clustering protein sequences into families of related sequences and the development of protein models.

4) Aligning similar proteins and generating phylogenetic trees to examine evolutionary relationships.

Biocomputing: Biocomputing is often used as a catch-all term covering all this area at the intersection of Biology and Computation, although many other terms are used to name the same area. We can distinguish in to (non-disjoint) sub-fields:

1) Bioinformatics - this includes management of biological databases, data mining and data modeling, as well as IT-tools for data visualization

2) Computational Biology - this includes efforts to solve biological problems with computational tools (such as modeling, algorithms, heuristics)

3) DNA computing and nano-engineering - this includes models and experiments to use DNA (and other) molecules to perform computations

4) Computations in living organisms - this is concerned with constructing computational components in living cells, as well as with studying computational processes taking place daily in living organisms.

Genomics

Genomics is any attempt to analyze or compare the entire genetic complement of a species or species (plural). It is, of course possible to compare genomes by comparing more-or-less representative subsets of genes within genomes.

Structural Genomics or Structural Bioinformatics: Refers to the analysis of macromolecular structure particularly proteins, using computational tools and theoretical frameworks. One of the goals of structural genomics is the extension of idea of genomics, to obtain accurate three-dimensional structural models for all known protein families, protein domains or protein folds. Structural alignment is a tool of structural genomics.

Functional Genomics: The biological role of individual genes, mechanisms underlying the regulation of their expression, and regulatory interactions among them. Functional genomics uses high throughput/global methods to simultaneously study the functions of large numbers or all the genes of an organism. Functional genomics refers to the use of molecular biology tools to understand the function of genes identified in sequencing projects. While sequencing projects yield static results, functional genomics focuses on dynamic aspects including regulation of gene expression. Functional genomics is a way to test and extend hypotheses that emerge from the analysis of sequence data.

Computational genomics: Computational genomics is the application of statistical analysis to the vast arrays of data generated by structural and functional genomics research. Even the smallest plant genome is comprised of over 100,000,000 base pairs of DNA. Extracting useful information from this large amount of sequence data requires significant computational ability and sophisticated analysis algorithms. Current functional genomics research depends heavily on computational tools which allow access to various information depositories as well as tools for mathematical and statistical modelling of data obtained by modern experimental technologies such as DNA microarrays, 2D gels, mass spectrometry, etc. Next generation sequencing technologies expected to generate ~1 TB image data per run (~every few days) and to keep a small compute cluster running nonstop just to assemble the sequence data.

Proteomics

Proteomics is the study of proteins – their location, structure and function. It is the identification, characterization and quantification of all proteins involved in a particular pathway, organelle, cell, tissue, organ or organism that can be studied in concert to provide accurate and comprehensive data about that system. Proteomics is the study of the function of all expressed proteins. The study of the proteome, called proteomics, now evokes not only all the proteins in any given cell, but also the set of all protein is forms and modifications, the interactions between them, the structural description of proteins and their higher-order complexes, and for that matter almost everything 'post-genomic'.

Transcriptomics

Study the collection of all the gene transcripts in a cell / tissue / organism. DNA microarrays.

Pharmacogenomics

Pharmacogenomics is the application of genomic approaches and technologies to the identification of drug targets.

Pharmacogenomics is using genetic information to predict whether a drug will help make a patient well or sick. It Studies how genes influence the response of humans to drugs, from the population to the molecular level.

The Central Dogma

The Central Dogma of Molecular Biology was originally defined by the American biochemist James Watson who, together with the British physicist Francis Crick, first described the now famous right-handed double helix of DNA (deoxyribonucleic acid) in 1953. The Central Dogma is deceptively simple: DNA defines the synthesis of protein by way of an RNA intermediary. What isn't so simple is documenting, controlling, and modifying this process which is the focus of much of bioinformatics. The Central Dogma: DNA is transcribed to RNA, which is translated to **protein.**

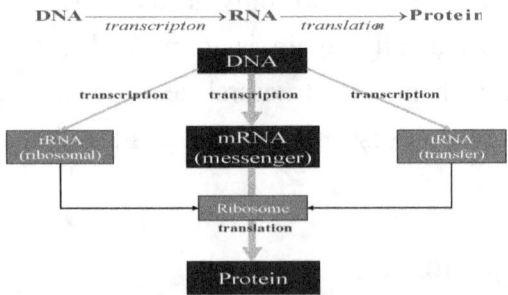

Figure: The central dogma of molecular biology

Five domains of Bioinformatics

Large-scale biological data can be represented in different forms for different computation and analysis. The common ones are:
♦ Sequence ♦ Structure ♦ Interaction ♦ Expression ♦ Function.

Biology Core Concept: ♦ Molecular biology ♦ Systems biology ♦ Evolutionary theory ♦ Sequence comparison ♦ Phylogenetic analysis.

Computer Science Core Concepts: ♦ Programming ♦ Database querying ♦ Data mining ♦ Machine learning ♦ Visualization ♦ Modelling.

Biostatistics Core Concepts: ♦ Biometry ♦ Descriptive statistics ♦ Multivariate analysis ♦ Evolutionary distance ♦ Phylogenetic inference.

Molecular Biology: Molecular Biology takes care of the following:

i. *Cell function*
ii. *Nucleic acids, DNA, RNA, chromosomes, genes*
iii. *Amino acids, proteins*

New Biology: In post genomic era a new language has been created for new biology which is as follows:

i. *Genomics*
ii. *Functional Genomics*
iii. *Proteomics*
iv. *cDNA microarrays*
v. *Global Gene Expression Patterns*

To deal with the abovementioned new biology, new **computational tools are applied for Biology that is as follows:**

i. *Sequencing*
ii. *Analyzing experimental data*
iii. *Representing vast quantities of information*
iv. *Searching*
v. *Pattern matching*

vi. Data mining
vii. Gene discovery
viii. Function discovery

Bioinformatics concern and Goals are the following:

i. *Classify*
ii. *Identify patterns/ Pattern Recognition*
iii. *Make predictions*
iv. *Data Modelling, Creation of models & Prediction*
v. *Assessment and Comparison*
vi. *Optimization*
vii. *Better utilize existing knowledge*

There is a need for computers and algorithms that allow Access, Processing, Storing, Sharing, Retrieving, Visualizing, Annotating etc. in order to reach the above mentioned goals.

Development of Algorithms for Sequence Comparison

1) Phylogenetic Algorithm
   a) Complex mathematical formula used to determine sequence homology
   b) All possible ways a large number of sequences can be compared to one another
2) Fitch and Margoliash
   a) Sequence comparisons to determine evolutionary trees
   b) Computer calculates the minimum number of steps to convert one sequence to another and builds possible trees
3) Needleman and Wunsch

a) Similarities in protein sequences

Most of the major breakthroughs in Bioinformatics arose through innovations in Mathematics or Statistics (FASTA, BLAST, Phred / Phrap, BLOSUM, GenScan, PSI-BLAST, Threading, GRAIL etc).

Therefore it is essential to gain an awareness of importance of mathematics and statistics in bioinformatics as because the same underlie nearly every aspect of Bioinformatics.

Major breakthroughs in Bioinformatics through Algorithm

Major breakthroughs in Bioinformatics have taken place through innovations in Mathematics or Statistics and development of the following computational tools:

1) FASTA,
2) BLAST,
3) Phred/Phrap,
4) BLOSUM,
5) GenScan,
6) PSI-BLAST,
7) Threading,
8) GRAIL etc.
9) PAM (Percent Accepted Mutation): for evolutionary studies. For example in PAM1, 1 accepted point mutation per 100 amino acids is required.
10) BLOSUM (BLOcks amino acid SUbstitution Matrix): for finding common motifs.

Chapter 3: EDUCATIONAL RESOURCES

Bioinformatics | Next Generation Sequencing | Machine Learning | Biostatistics | Biological Databases | Scientific Computing

Bioinformatics

(http://devbio.eu/bioinformatics?lang=en#Bioinformatics)

AG Bioinformatik Uni Potsdam (http://www.uni-potsdam.de/ibb/arbeitsgruppen/ordentliche-professuren/bioinformatik.html) - Arbeitsgruppevon Prof. Dr. Joachim Selbig a der Universität Potsdam, Golm Uni Potsdam.

Bioclipse (http://www.bioclipse.net/) - Java-based, open source, visual platform for chemo- and bioinformatics based on the Eclipse Rich Client Platform (RCP).

Bioconductor (http://www.bioconductor.org/) - Bioconductor provides tools for the analysis and comprehension of high-throughput genomic data. Bioconductor uses the R statistical programming language, and is open source and open development.

Biojs (http://code.google.com/p/biojs/) - A library of Java Script components to represent biological data graphically.

BioPerl (http://www.bioperl.org/wiki/Main_Page) - A community effort to produce Perl code for application in biology.

Bioservices (https://pypi.python.org/pypi/bioservices/) - Access to Biological Web Services from Python.

BioStar (http://www.biostars.org/) - An Online Question & Answer Resource for the Bioinformatics Community. BioStar Team.

ExPASy (http://www.expasy.org/) - ExPASy Proteomics Server. Swiss Institute of Bioinformatics; Schweiz.

Expression Profiler (http://www.bioinf.ebc.ee/EP/EP/) - European Bioinformatics Institute.

Expression Profiler NG EBI Expression Profiler - "Next Generation" European Bioinformatics Institute.

ExtOmics (http://extomics.com/) - Dienstleister im Feld der Bioinformatik: Analysenentwicklung, Softwareentwicklung, Datenbanken, Beratung Extomics.

Mathematical Modelling and Systems Biology Group, MPIMP Golm (http://www.mpimp-golm.mpg.de/13175/6nikoloski) - Head: Dr. Zoran Nikoloski Max Planck Institute of Molecular Plant Physiology.

Online Analysis Tools (http://molbiol-tools.ca/) - Ontario, Canada.

PSORT (http://www.psort.org/) - Tools for sub cellular localization prediction.

Next Generation Sequencing

(http://devbio.eu/bioinformatics?lang=en#NextGenerationSequencing)

454 Life Sciences (http://www.454.com/) - a Roche company.

CLC bio (http://www.clcbio.com/) - software made "for biologists by biologists".

DNASTAR (http://www.dnastar.com/) - software for life scientists.

Illumina (http://www.illumina.com/) - sequencing and array-based solutions for genetic research.

Life Technologies Corporation (http://www.lifetechnologies.com/in/en/home.html) - home of Applied Biosystems.

Next Generation Sequencing (NGS) - (http://en.wikibooks.org/wiki/Next_Generation_Sequencing_%28NGS%29) on Wiki Books.

OmicsMaps.com (http://omicsmaps.com/) - Next Generation Genomics: World Map of High-throughput Sequencers.

SEQanswers (http://seqanswers.com/) - Next Generation Sequencing (NGS) community Eric Olivares.

Machine Learning
(http://devbio.eu/bioinformatics?lang=en#MachineLearning)

Matlab MLTOOLS Toolbox (http://staffwww.dcs.shef.ac.uk/people/N.Lawrence/mltools/).

Mloss (http://mloss.org/software/) - Machine Learning Open Source Software.

Orange Toolbox (http://orange.biolab.si/) - Open source data visualization and analysis for novice and experts. Data mining through visual programming or Python scripting. Extensions for bioinformatics and text mining.

RapidMiner (http://sourceforge.net/projects/rapidminer/) - a machine learning toolbox *rapid-i.com*

Shogun Toolbox (http://www.shogun-toolbox.org/) - SHOGUN machine learning toolbox.

WEKA (http://www.cs.waikato.ac.nz/~ml/weka/) - Weka 3: Data Mining Software in Java.

Wikipedia on ML (http://en.wikipedia.org/wiki/Machine_learning).

Biostatistics (http://devbio.eu/bioinformatics?lang=en#Biostatistics)

Biostatistics (http://en.wikipedia.org/wiki/Biostatistics) - Wikipedia entry

Biostatistics (journal) (http://biostatistics.oxfordjournals.org/) - by Oxford Journals

Department of Biostatistics (http://www.hsph.harvard.edu/biostatistics/) - Harvard School of Public Health

R (http://www.r-project.org/) - The R Project for Statistical Computing

Rmagic (http://ipython.org/ipython-doc/dev/config/extensions/rmagic.html) - Easy access to R functionality in Python, filling in Python's gaps in statistics packages *Ipython developers*

SAS (http://support.sas.com/rnd/app/da/stat.html) - Software for Statistical analysis and much more *SAS Institute Inc.*

SPSS (http://www-01.ibm.com/software/analytics/spss/) - Software package for statistical analysis and more by IBM, *IBM Corporation*

Biological Databases
(http://devbio.eu/bioinformatics?lang=en#BiologicalDatabases)

BDGP (http://www.fruitfly.org/) - Berkeley Drosophila Genome Project *Drosophila Genome Center/Howard Hughes Medical Institute; USA*

BioProject (http://www.fruitfly.org/) - A collection of genomics, functional genomics, and genetics studies and links with their resulting datasets. This resource describes project scope, material, and objectives and provides a mechanism to retrieve datasets that are often difficult to find due to inconsistent annotation, multiple independent submissions, and the varied nature of diverse data types which are often stored in different databases. *NCBI*

ChromDB (http://www.ncbi.nlm.nih.gov/bioproject) - The Chromatin Database *University of Arizona; USA*

dbSNP (http://www.ncbi.nlm.nih.gov/SNP/) - Short Genetic Variations Database *NCBI*

DDBJ (http://www.ddbj.nig.ac.jp/) - DNA Data Bank of Japan, *Japan*

EBI (http://www.ebi.ac.uk/): European Bioinformatics Institute *European Bioinformatics Institute*

FlyBase (http://flybase.bio.indiana.edu/): A Database of Drosophila Genes & Genomes. *The Genetics Society of America, USA*

Forschungsportal.net (http://forschugsportal.net/) - Wie finden Sie Forschung in Deutschland? Suchmaschine des BMBF (Bundesministerium für Bildung und Forschung) *Bundesministerium für Bildung und Forschung; Deutschland*

Gene Index Project - TGI (http://compbio.dfci.harvard.edu/tgi/) - The goal of The Gene Index Project is to use the available EST and gene sequences, along with the reference genomes wherever available, to provide an inventory of likely genes and their variants and to annotate these with information regarding the functional roles played by these genes and their products. *Dana Farber Cancer Institute*

Gene Ontology (http://www.geneontology.org/) - The Gene Ontology project is a major bioinformatics initiative with the aim of standardizing the representation of gene and gene product attributes across species and databases. *The GO Consortium*

INSDC (http://www.insdc.org/) - International Nucleotide Sequence Database Collaboration *DDBJ, EMBL und GenBank (NCBI)*

MaizeGDB (http://www.maizegdb.org/): Maize Genetics and Genomics Database.

NCBI (http://www.ncbi.nlm.nih.gov/) - The National Center for Biotechnology Information advances science and health by providing access to biomedical and genomic information. *National Center for Biotechnology Information; USA*

WormBase (http://www.wormbase.org/#01-23-6) – Caenorhabditis elegans and friends

wwPDB (http://www.wwpdb.org/) - Worldwide Protein Data Bank

Scientific Computing

(http://devbio.eu/bioinformatics?lang=en#ScientificComputing)

Aptana Studio (http://www.aptana.com/products/studio3) Develop and test your entire web application using a single environment With support for the latest browser technology specs such as HTML5, CSS3, JavaScript, Ruby, Rails, PHP and Python, *Aptana.*

Eclipse (http://www.eclipse.org/) Multi-language Integrated development environment (IDE) *Eclipse Foundation*.

gnuplot (http://www.eclipse.org/) command-line driven graphing utility for Linux, Windows and many other platforms.

IPython (http://ipython.org/) Interactive Python, my favourite python shell.

MATLAB (http://ipython.org/) The Language of Technical Computing.

matplotlib (http://matplotlib.org/) famous python plotting library.

NumPy (http://www.numpy.org/) Numerical Python.

SciLab (http://www.scilab.org/) Free open source software for numerical computation and simulation, *Scilab Enterprises*.

SciPy (http://www.scipy.org/) Scientific Python.

Visual Studio (http://www.microsoft.com/visualstudio/eng) Entwicklungsumgebung von Microsoft, *Microsoft Corporation*.

WolframAlpha (http://www.wolframalpha.com/) computational knowledge engine

Bioinformatics and Computational Biology Guide Tags : bcb (http://libguides.wpi.edu/searchtags.php?iid=1333&tag=bcb), **computational biology** (http://libguides.wpi.edu/searchtags.php?iid=1333&tag=computational%20biology).

Resources for bioinformatics and computational biology (Last Updated : Jun 21, 2013) URL : (http://libguides.wpi.edu/bioinformatics) **Print Guide** (http://libguides.wpi.edu/print_content.php?pid=219585&sid=1837428&mode=g) **RSS Updates** (http://libguides.wpi.edu/content.php?pid= 219585&sid=1837428)

Web resources for bioinformatics (http://www.cs.columbia. edu/~cleslie/cs4761/resources.html)

a) MAGNet - Multiscale Analysis of Genomic and Cellular Networks (http://magnet.c2b2.columbia.edu/?q=node/1)

b) COGs - Phylogenetic classification of proteins encoded in complete genomes (http://www.ncbi.nlm.nih.gov/COG/)

c) Computational Biology or Bioinformatics references (http://users.soe.ucsc. edu/~karplus/compbio_pages.html)

d) The ORBIT Project (http://www.orbitproject.org/) - Online registry of Biomedical Informatics tools

e) Bioinformatics Links Directory (http://bioinformatics.ca/links_directory/)

f) GenBank (http://www.ncbi.nlm.nih.gov/genbank/) - NIH genetic sequence database, an annotated collection of all publicly available DNA sequences

g) KEGG : Kyoto Encyclopedia of Genes and Genomes (http://www.genome. jp/kegg/) - Integrated database resource consisting of 16 main databases, broadly categorized into systems information, genomic information, and chemical information.

h) Map Viewer (http://www.ncbi.nlm.nih.gov/mapview/) - Map Viewer provides a wide variety of genome mapping and sequencing data

i) UniProt (Universal Protein Resource) (http://www.uniprot.org/) - A comprehensive, high-quality and freely accessible resource of protein sequence and functional information.

UCSC Bioinformatics (Computational Biology) Home Page

a) (http://www.cbse.ucsc.edu/research/bioinf_compbio) for information about bioinformatics research at UCSC.

b) (http://www.bme.ucsc.edu/) for information about the Biomolecular Engineering Department.

c) (http://www.bme.ucsc.edu/graduate) for information about the graduate program in Bioinformatics.

d) (http://www.bme.ucsc.edu/bioinformatics) for information about the undergraduate program in Bioinformatics.

e) (http://www.cbse.ucsc.edu/) for information about the Center for Biomolecular Science and Engineering.

Learn about Genetics & Genomics

a) 123 Genomics (http://123genomics.homestead.com/index.html)

b) Cytogenetics Gallery (http://www.pathology.washington.edu/galleries/ Cytogallery/main.php?file=intro)

c) Dolan DNA Learning Center (http://www.dnalc.org)

d) Genomics & Chemical Genetics - Howard Hughes Medical Institute (http://www.hhmi.org/biointeractive/genomics/index.html)

e) Genomics.Energy.Gov (http://genomics.energy.gov/)

f) GOLD: Genomes Online Database (http://www.genomesonline.org/cgi-bin/ GOLD/index.cgi)

g) Human Chromosome Launchpad (https://public.ornl.gov/hgmis/launchpad/ default.cfm)

h) Learn Genetics: Genetic Science Learning Center (http://learn.genetics.utah.edu/)

i) MGI - Mouse Genome Informatics (http://www.informatics.jax.org/)

j) NCBI Genome Resource Guides (http://www.ncbi.nlm.nih.gov/genome/guide/)

k) PRIMER : Genomics and Its Impact on Science and Society : The Human Genome Project and Beyond (2008) (http://www.ornl.gov/sci/techresources/HumanGenome/publicat/printer/index.shtml)

l) Public Health Genomics - CDC (http://www.cdc.gov/genomics/default.htm)

m) Talking Glossary of Genetic Terms (http://www.genome.gov/Glossary/)

[Source: (http://libguides.bodleian.ox.ac.uk/content.php?pid=264386&sid=2187124)]

Molecular Biology

a) Computational Molecular Biology (http://nihlibrary.nih.gov/ResearchTools/pages/default.aspx)

b) Library of 3-D Molecular Structures (http://www.nyu.edu/pages/mathmol/library/index.html)

c) MMDB (Molecular Modeling DataBase) (http://www.ncbi.nlm.nih.gov/Structure/MMDB/mmdb.shtml)

d) BioMolecular Explorer3D (http://www.umass.edu/molvis/bme3d/materials/explore.html)

Web Tutorials, Tools, and Resources

Selected Internet Resources Molecular Biology and Bioinformatics

a) WEB TUTORIALS, TOOLS, AND RESOURCES (http://www.loc.gov/rr/scitech/selected-internet/molecular.html#tutorials)

b) GENETIC DATABASES (http://www.loc.gov/rr/scitech/selected-internet/molecular.html#databases)

c) GENOME PROJECTS (http://www.loc.gov/rr/scitech/selected-internet/molecular.html#projects)

d) Highly replicated polytene chromosomes of a fly's salivary glands (stained blue) and antibodies (stained red) (http://intramural.niddk.nih.gov/research/faculty.asp?People_ID=1699): From the the National Institute of Diabetes and Digestive and Kidney Diseases (NIDDK) Web site.

e) BioMedNet Research Tools (http://research.bmn.com/)

f) CMS Molecular Biology Resource (http://mbcf.dfci.harvard.edu/cmsmbr/)

g) Genetics Tutorials (http://science.nhmccd.edu/biol/genetics.html)

h) Health Web / Genetics (http://healthweb.org/browse.cfm?subjectid=42)

i) Morgan--Genetic Tutorial (http://morgan.rutgers.edu/morganWebFrames/How-to-use/HTU-Frameset.html)

j) Online Mendelian Inheritance in Men (NCBI) (http://www.ncbi.nlm.nih.gov/sites/entrez?db=nucleotide)

k) Protein Information Resource (http://pir.georgetown.edu/)

l) Talking Glossary of Genetic Terms (http://www.genome.gov/glossary.cfm)

m) WWW Virtual Library-Genetics (http://www.ornl.gov/sci/techresources/Human Genome/genetics.shtml)

Web Links for Bioinformatics

Trainonline : These online bioinformatics tutorials demonstrate how to use tools and databases supplied by EMBL-EBI to carry out a range of bioinformatics tasks.

CBRG : The Computational Biology Research Group is based at Oxford and provides the University with a range of bioinformatics resources and support services.

NCBI : The National Centre for Biotechnology Information is a central provider of bioinformatics resources and services in the US. Their extensive website provides guides and reference to all the services they support.

Bioinformatics Resources

Bioinformatics: (http://www.ebi.ac.uk/2can) is a broad subject which covers the application of computer technology to storing, searching, processing and retrieving biological data. Bioinformatics resources often take the form of on-line databases or applications which you can use to access and analyse data contributed by researchers from all over the world. The data can be of many different types including but not limited too -

a) Nucleic acid sequences.

b) Protein sequences.

c) Protein structures.

d) Data from Microarray studies.

e) Data from protein interaction studies.

Bioinformatics applications available on-line can help you with aspects of searching, analysing and comparing bioinformatics data. For example -

- a) Primer design tools (http://www.ncbi.nlm.nih.gov/guide/howto/design-pcr-primers/) - identify optimal regions on a given DNA sequence to create primers for applications such as PCR or sequencing.
- b) Sequence alignment tools (http://www.ebi.ac.uk/2can/tutorials/nucleotide/ align.html) - create alignments of multiple sequences and build phylogenetic trees.

Information Resources for Bioinformatics: Bioscientists working in many fields are often required to use bioinformatics resources of some kind. There are a range of different resources available to help you find out more about using bioinformatics tools -

- a) Introductory and advanced textbooks covering a range of bioinformatics techniques.
- b) On-line tutorials and reference material provided by respected bioinformatics organisations and universities.
- c) Bioinformatics journals.

You can find links to some examples of bioinformatics information resources in the other boxes on this page.

Genetic Databases

- a) BLAST- Basic Local Alignment Search Tool (NCBI) (http://www.ncbi.nlm.nih.gov/BLAST/)

b) Cancer Genome Anatomy Project (http://cgap.nci.nih.gov/)

c) DNA Data Bank of Japan (DDBJ) (http://www.ddbj.nig.ac.jp)

d) Entrez, The Life Sciences Search Engine (Entrez) (http://www.ncbi.nlm. nih.gov/Entrez/)

e) Entrez Genome (http://www.ncbi.nlm.nih.gov/sites/entrez?db=genome)

f) ExPASy Molecular Biology Server (Expert Protein Analysis System) (http://au.expasy.org)

g) Nucleic Acid Database (US Department of Energy) (http://ndbserver. rutgers.edu)

h) Nucleotide (GenBank) (http://www.ncbi.nlm.nih.gov/sites/entrez?db=nucleotide)

i) Nucleotide Sequence Database (EMBL) (http://www.ebi.ac.uk/embl/)

Genome Databases

a) Ensembl Genome Browser (http://www.ensembl.org/index.html) : assembled and annotated vertebrate genomes

b) EnsemblGenomes (http://ensemblgenomes.org/) : invertebrate, protist, plant, fungi and bacterial genomes

c) Pre!Ensembl (http://pre.ensembl.org/index.html) : draft assemblies of vertebrate genomes

d) JGI Genome Portal (http://genome.jgi-psf.org/) : large collection of genome ref. sequences, some assembled

e) NCBI Genomic Map Viewer (http://www.ncbi.nlm.nih.gov/mapview/) : search and browse reference sequences for a large collection of genomes

f) NCBI Genomic Trace Archive (http://www.ncbi.nlm.nih.gov/Traces/home/) UCSC Genome Bioinformatics (http://genome.ucsc.edu/) : ref. sequences and draft assemblies of various genomes

g) HGSC Genome Data : includes invertebrate genomes not available on other browsers

h) Elephant Shark Genome Project (http://esharkgenome.imcb.a-star.edu.sg/)

i) Vertebrate TimeCapsule (http://transcriptome.cdb.riken.go.jp/vtcap/index.htm) : Transcriptome database - bichir, hagfish and cloudy dogfish ESTs

j) SalmonDB (http://genomicasalmones.dim.uchile.cl/) : Genome resources for salmonid species

k) Oikopleura Genome Browser (http://www.genoscope.cns.fr/externe/GenomeBrowser/Oikopleura/)

l) SpBase (http://www.spbase.org/SpBase/) : Purple sea urchin genome database

m) StellaBase (http://evodevo.bu.edu/stellabase/) : Sea anemone genome database

n) Silkworm Genome Database (http://silkworm.swu.edu.cn/silkdb/)

o) BeeBase (http://hymenopteragenome.org/beebase/) : Honey bee genomic resources

Evolutionary Resources

a) TimeTree :: The Timescale of Life (http://www.timetree.org/) : Extensive resource that allows you to search for divergence times between taxa - includes updated sources from the scientific literature as well as book chapters

b) Tree of Life Web Project (http://tolweb.org/tree/) : Less focus on phylogeny and divergence times, but with summarized info pages on the different taxa

Synteny Databases

a) Genomicus (http://www.genomicus.biologie.ens.fr/genomicus-60.01/cgi-bin/search.pl) : integrated synteny genome browser

b) SyntenyDB (http://syntenydb.uoregon.edu/synteny_db/): offers several graphical comparisons of Ensembl genome data

c) Cinteny (http://cinteny.cchmc.org/) : fast identification of syntenic chromosome blocks

d) Chromhome (http://www.chromhome.org/) : Chromosome homology mapping (mammals)

Sequence Manipulation and Alignment Web Tools

a) The Sequence Manipulation Suite (http://biology.hpcf.upr.edu/sms/): Direct translation or show translation in all reading frames, ORF finder, reverse complement etc.

b) ClustalW Multiple Sequence Alignment (http://www.genome.jp/tools/clustalw/) : Online execution of the ClustalW alignment algorithm

c) Sequence and phylogeny data format converter (http://www.phylogeny.fr/version2_cgi/data_converter.cgi): Convert files between Newick, Nexus, Phylip, Clustal and Fasta formats.

d) BEAUti (http://beast.bio.ed.ac.uk/BEAUti) : Convert Nexus files into XML

Sequence Analysis and Alignment Software

a) ClustalX (http://www.clustal.org/): The most quick & useful sequence alignment and phylogenetic (NJ, UPGMA) tree application.

b) MAFFT (http://mafft.cbrc.jp/alignment/software/index.html): Sequence alignment and phylogenetic (NJ, UPGMA) software, both download and online execution.

c) CLC Sequence Viewer (http://www.clcbio.com/products/clc-sequence-viewer/): Very versatile and complete sequence manipulation, alignment (multiple methods) and phylogenetic tree (NJ, UPGMA) application.

d) JalView (http://www.jalview.org/) : Sequence analysis and alignment application incorporating the JABAWS 2 (http://www.compbio.dundee.ac.uk/jabaws/) package of multiple sequence alignment tools as well as some phylogenetic tree functions

e) eBioX (http://www.ebioinformatics.org/ebiox/): Very versatile and easy to use sequence analysis and alignment tool for Mac

f) Se-Al (http://tree.bio.ed.ac.uk/software/seal/): Simple sequence analysis and alignment application (doesn't run on Mac OS X 10.7).

g) BioEdit (Win only) (http://www.mbio.ncsu.edu/BioEdit/bioedit.html) : Versatile, if a bit complex, sequence analysis application with a greater variety of functions

Phylogeny Software

a) MolecularEvolution.org (http://molecularevolution.org/) : Includes updated links to a selection of commonly used bioinformatic software for molecular evolution, including PAML, PAUP*, PHYLIP and others

b) Felsenstein lab - Phylogeny Programs (http://evolution.genetics.washington.edu/phylip/software.html): A huge selection of most, if not all, commonly used phylogeny software

c) The Phylogenetic Handbook Software (http://www.kuleuven.be/aidslab/phylogenybook/Software.html): Another extensive selection of phylogeny software

d) MEGA 4 (Win/Linux only) (http://www.megasoftware.net/) : Phylogenetic tree software (NJ, MP)

e) TreePuzzle (http://www.tree-puzzle.de/) : Phylogenetic tree software (QPML)

f) PhyML 3.0 (http://atgc.lirmm.fr/phyml/) : Phylogenetic Maximum Likelihood algorithm application, both web-based and executable

g) BEAST (http://beast.bio.ed.ac.uk/Main_Page) : Bayesian analysis of molecular sequences/phylogenies

h) MrBayes (http://mrbayes.sourceforge.net/) : Bayesian inference of molecular phylogenies

i) Phycas (http://hydrodictyon.eeb.uconn.edu/projects/phycas/index.php/ Phycas_Home) : Bayesian inference of phylogeny from nucleotide sequences

j) RAxML BlackBox (http://embnet.vital-it.ch/raxml-bb/): Online execution of the Randomized Axelerated Maximum Likelihood program

k) Garli Web Service v2.0 (http://www.molecularevolution.org/software/phylogenetics/garli/garli_create_job) : Online execution of Genetic Algorithm for Rapid

l) Likelihood Inference / download version (https://code.google.com/p/garli/)

m) ProtTest (http://darwin.uvigo.es/software/prottest.html) : Calculates the best amino acid substitution model for phylogenetic analyses

n) jModelTest (http://darwin.uvigo.es/software/jModelTest.html) : Calculates the best nucleotide substitution model for phylogenetic analyses

Phylogenetic Tree Viewers and Editors

a) FigTree (http://tree.bio.ed.ac.uk/software/figtree/) : The best phylogenetic tree viewer

b) TreeView X (http://darwin.zoology.gla.ac.uk/~rpage/treeviewx/) and

c) TreeView (older version) (http://taxonomy.zoology.gla.ac.uk/rod/treeview.html) : Phylogenetic tree viewer

d) TreeThief : Manual phylogenetic tree entry

e) TreeSnatcher Plus (http://www.cs.hhu.de/): Phylogenetic tree capturing.

(http://www.devbio.eu/bioinformatics)

Chapter 4: BIOINFORMATICS, INTERNET AND LINKS

Internet facilitates linking to current programs and initiatives utilizing the Internet to form clearing-houses and distributed networks of biological information. Some are integrated system for agricultural genome analysis, including databases, conferences, publications, courses, and a particularly good plant genome online database tutorial. Links to many tools and programs are available from the National Institutes of Health for sequence analysis and molecular biology, including databases, protocols and tutorials. Many a pages include links to a number of model organism databases, banks and tables, and to a number of genetic databases, Department of Molecular and Cellular Biology.

Searching: Various ways are available to search; a text-based query can be submitted through the system like Entrez system. A sequence query can be submitted through the program. To search a particular type of database or item, it should be selected from the menu. Various lists include a number of databases. The list can be accessed by category/type of database or alphabetically by title. By clicking on the short description of each database, a paragraph-long description can be accessed from the database. Another system, Sequence Retrieval System interface provides links to sites that allow web based searching and retrieval of nucleotide and protein sequence. With the **facility** to query most of the major **Bioinformatics** databases and retrieve textual information but it is not the complete list.

Like other fields of knowledge, **Bioinformatics** has grown and seeing the researches going on in the genetic scenario, nobody can ignore the increasing impact of **Bioinformatics**. We can relate it with the increasing impact of Internet in information scenario. The future holds the ever increasing dependability on information and information technology so it can be said that Internet is an efficient tool for accessing the Bio-information in the form of **Bioinformatics**. The need is to know, explore and exploiting it.

1. (www.cats.ucsc.edu)
2. (www.cato.com/biotech/)
3. (www.the-scientist.com)
4. (www.nbif.org/links/1.20.php)
5. (www.genomics.phrma.org/today/)
6. (www.gnn.tigr.org/main.shtml)
7. (www.ebi.ac.uk/ismb-97/papers2.html)
8. (www.cgl.ucsf.edu/psb/)
9. (www.Biosis.org.zrdocs/zoolinfo/biol_inf.htm)
10. (www.ars-genome.cornell.edu/)
11. (www.molbio.info.nih.gov/molbio/)
12. (www.golgi.harvard.edu/Biolinks.html)
13. (www.molbio.info.nih.gov/cgi-bin/pdb)
14. (www.oup.co.uk/bioinformatics/contents/)
15. (www.cgb.indiana.edu/bioinformatics/resources)
16. (www.genome.ucsc.edu/)
17. (www.ebi.ac.uk/index.html)
18. (www.atcc.org)

19. (www.bio.org/welcome.html)

20. (www.biotech-register.com/)

21. (www.nbif.org)

22. (www.proteome.com/services/index.html)

23. (www.rcsb.org/pdb/)

24. (www.sciewb.com)

25. (www.bioinfo.com/fbdhome.html)

26. (www.bioinformatics.org)

27. (www.yahoo.com)

28. (www.cbt.org)

29. (www.unipune.ernet.in)

30. (www.mcrcr0.med.nyu.edu/rcr/molbio/syllabus-98.html)

31. (www.ncbi.nlm.nih.gov/Entrez/index.html)

32. (www.ncbi.lm.nih.gov/BLAST)

Internet educational resources for Bioinformatics

NCBI: sequence data repository, US **Bioinformatics** center. (http://www.ncbi.nlm.nih.gov/)

EBI: sequence data repository, European **Bioinformatics** center. (http://www.ebi.ac.uk/)

Pasteur: France bioinfo. center, Bio Netbook is an excellent database of Internet information for biosciences, **Bioinformatics**. (http://bioweb.pasteur.fr/intro-uk.html) Bio Netbook

ExPASy/SWISSPROT: protein sequence data center. (http://www.expasy.ch/) good list of bioinfo resources

Sanger: European sequencing, **Bioinformatics** center. (http://www.sanger.ac.uk/)

Weizmann: Israel **Bioinformatics** center. (http://bioinformatics.weizmann.ac.il/)

GenomeWeb: Bioinformatics resources. (http://www.hgmp.mrc.ac.uk/ GenomeWeb/)

CSHL: US sequencing, **Bioinformatics** center. (http://www.cshl.org/)

WUSTL: US sequencing, **Bioinformatics** center. (http://www.ibc.wustl.edu/)

Stanford genome center US sequencing, **Bioinformatics** center. (http://genome-www.stanford.edu/)

TIGR: US sequencing, **Bioinformatics** center. (http://www.tigr.org/)

Celera: US commercial sequencing, **Bioinformatics** center. (http://www.celera.com/)

GenomeNet: Japan **Bioinformatics** center (http://www.genome.ad.jp/)

Bionet: Usenet network news for biology. (http://www.bio.net/)

BioMedNet: Bioinformatics resources including HMS Beagle, (http://www.bmn.com/)

BioInform mostly commercial news, services - good list of companies in **Bioinformatics**. (http://www.bioinform.com/)

Web Sites in the News

a) ***Bioinformatics** via D'Trends* : A good place to begin your research on the field, because it provides all of the background information by the person who coined the term himself --Dr. Hwa A. Lim (aka HAL)

b) *Human Genome Project Information Web Site:* A government source and a great place to go for most of the information relating to current genome research. Sponsored by the U.S. Department of Energy Human Genome Program.

c) *The National Human Genome Research Institute (NHGRI):* Grant information, intramural research, ethical, legal and social implications, genomic and genetic resources. Also includes links to the policy and public affairs, workshops and conferences, and "The Genome Hub."

***Bioinformatics** homepage:* Internet Resources for **Bioinformatics** Coordinator: Dr. George Michaels. The aim of this page is to provide CSI students and researchers of **Bioinformatics** and Computational Biology an internet resource for their research as well as news, events, activities.

NCBI: Bioinformatics Resources for Biosciences Researchers

What is NCBI? NCBI is the National Center for Biotechnology Information. The Center was founded in 1988 as a division of the National Library of Medicine (NLM) at the National Institutes of Health (NIH). The NCBI website contains several free computerized information-processing methods of biological information.

NCBI not only conducts research on biomedical problems at the molecular level using mathematical and computational methods, but also provides numerous free databases and molecular search tools, with extensive support documentation for these resources.

Why Use NCBI? The Entrez search of NCBI allows a search across all databases: Genome, Gene, Protein, Nucleotide, even PubMed.

NCBI gives you real-time results for all searches

NCBI's multi-database management allows you to go from one database to another without having to re-enter your search terms

Using This Guide: This guide is the same as the handout used in the Introduction to NCBI's Bioinformatics Resources class (http://www.galter.northwestern.edu/) offered by Galter Library. The class is only offered twice a year, but you can always schedule a session by request, or use this online guide to learn at your own pace.

If you would like to follow the steps and examples described in this guide, it is recommended that you **open the NCBI website in another browser window** and re-size the browser windows so both the guide and the NCBI pages can be viewed simultaneously.

Currently there is one video tutorial contained in this guide, located in the MapViewer section (http://www.galter.northwestern.edu/guides-and-tutorials/ncbi-bioinformatics-resources-for-biosciences-researchers#MapViewerwithVideoTutorial). More videos are being developed and will be added to this guide as they are created.

Accessing NCBI's Cross-Database Search Page

Go to (http://www.ncbi.nlm.nih.gov/)

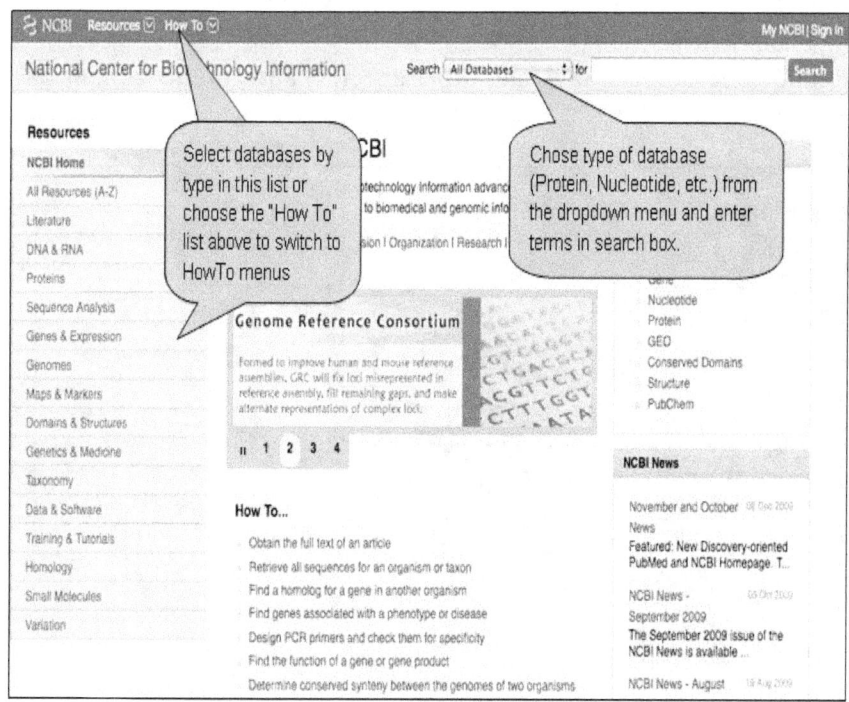

Navigation Hints: There are shortcuts and menus on all NCBI database pages:

1) Top-of-page menu bar shortcuts will take you to other major NCBI tools

2) Right-side pull-down menus for each entry will take you to related records

3) To get back to the NCBI home page at any time, just click the NCBI logo in the upper left of any screen

Start with a General Search: Search terms can be entered just as in PubMed:

1) You can use Boolean terms (AND, OR)

2) You can supply qualifiers in square brackets [au] = author, [organism], etc.

Try a search for "tubby" (a gene for obesity in mice with homologues in humans, rats, and other species) and "homo sapiens" as organism:

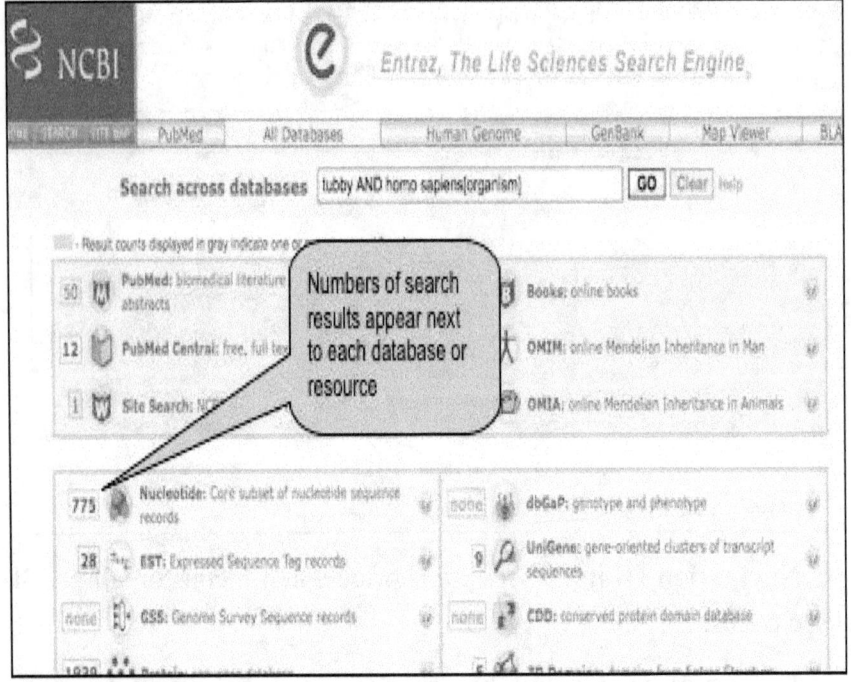

GenBank: NCBI's Genetic Information Repository and Entrez Nucleotide Database

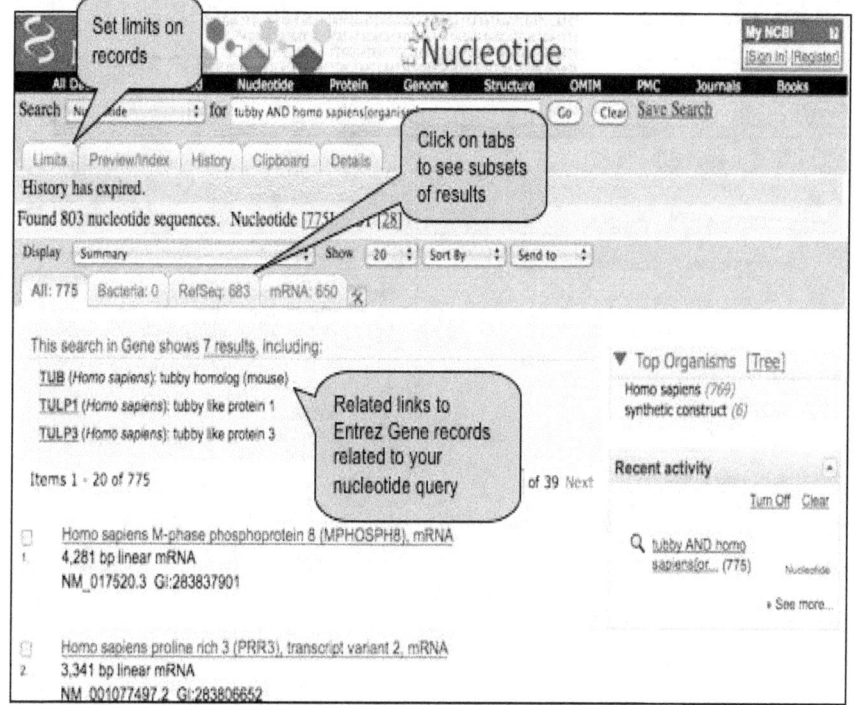

On this screen

1) **Display** allows you to view records as FASTA, GenBank or other styles

2) **Mark** a record by clicking the **checkbox** beside an entry

3) Set **limits** for a more defined search

4) View the full record for any entry by clicking its Name/title

None of the records on this first page appear to be tubby itself, but Entrez helpfully suggests links in the Entrez Gene database that may be related to your search, so **click on the link to the Entrez Gene record for "TUB" in the Gene results box at the top of the page.**

Entrez Gene

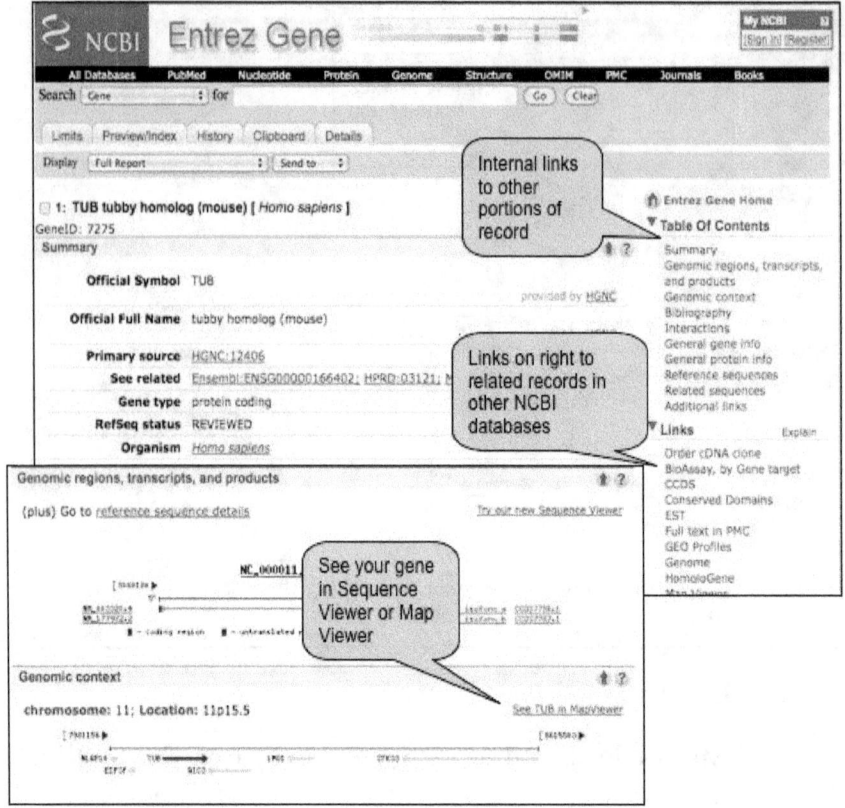

On this screen

1) **Link** to related records in other NCBI databases through menu on right

2) Jump to **Map Viewer** or **Sequence Viewer**

3) Read **GeneRIF**s (references from the literature supporting the genes function)

4) **View** transcript regions and protein products

5) See where the gene lies on the chromosome and its nearest neighbours

6) View information from other databases such as Gene Ontology

7) For more detail on the gene, its location on the chromosome and homologous genes in other species, go to Map Viewer

8) **Click** "See TUB in Map Viewer"

MapViewer (with Video Tutorial)

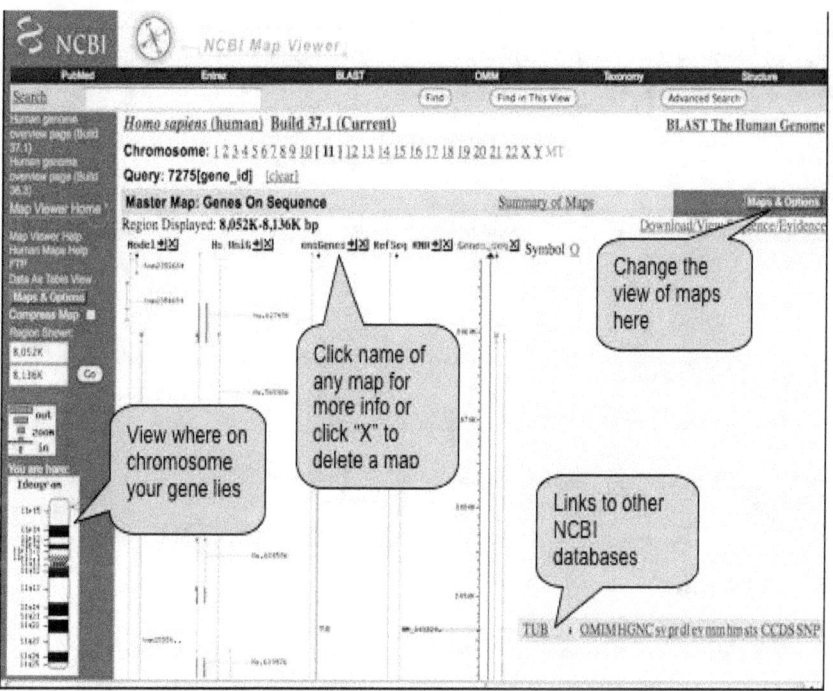

On this screen

1) Use **Maps & Options button** to view the genomic maps of other species in this region for interspecies homology or to add specific types of maps to view (CpG islands, etc.)

2) View contigs, coding sequences

3) View neighboring genes

4) **Zoom** in or zoom out

5) **BLAST** the human genome using the direct link to genomic BLAST

6) **Link** to other databases, such as OMIM, through the links in pinkish menu bar

7) **Click** on the **SNP** link in the pinkish label box

Entrez SNP

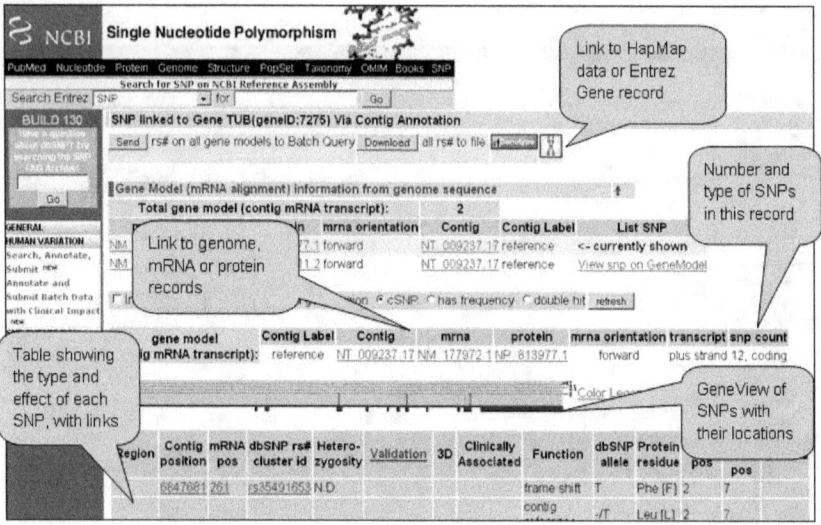

On this screen

1) View **location** and **type** of SNPs on a gene model, and **link** to each record in the Entrez SNP database

2) **Link** to HapMap data for variation in your gene or to Entrez Gene record

3) **Link** to records for genome contig, mRNA and protein records for your gene

4) View types of validation models for SNPs

5) **Click on the mRNA link** in the gene model box **(NM_177972)**

Entrez Nucleotide

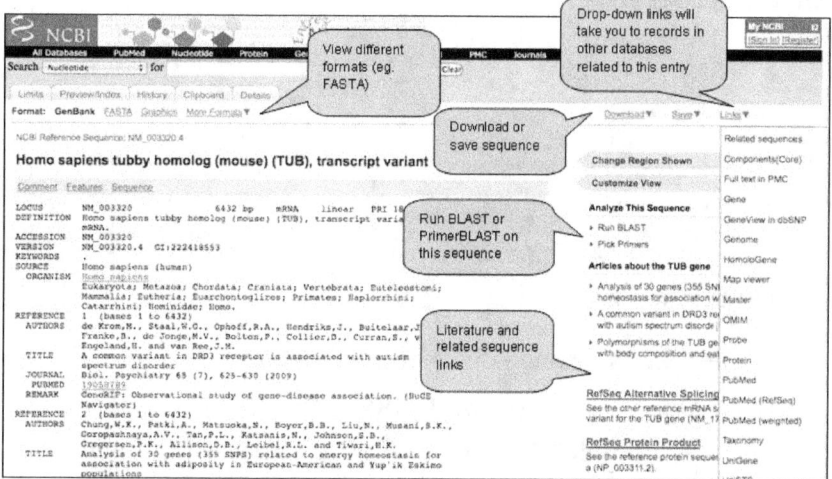

On this screen

1) **Links** pull-down menu to right allows you to link to related records for this entry in other NCBI databases

2) **Click Protein**

Entrez Protein

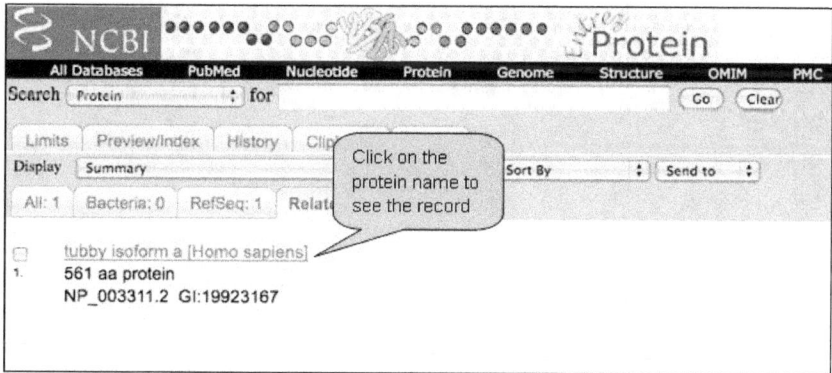

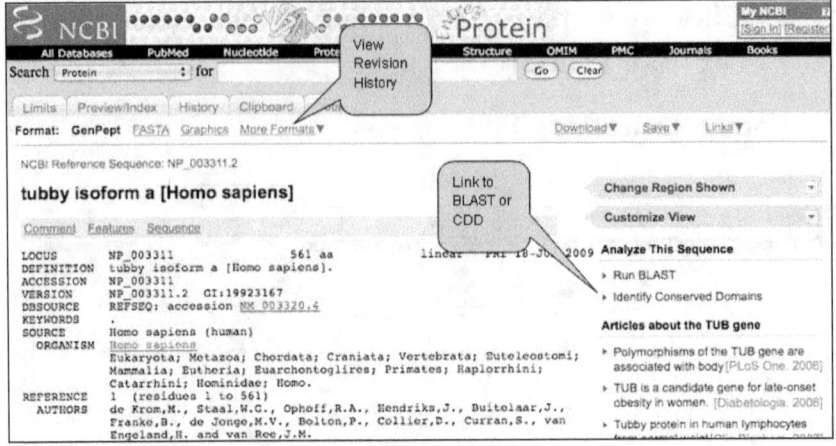

On this screen

a. Set **Limits**, change the **Display**
b. Through the drop-down **Links** menu:
   i. Do a quick **BLink** (BLAST Link) to get an automatic BLAST of similar proteins
   ii. Check the protein for **Conserved Domains**
c. Check the sequence **Revision History** (More Formats drop-down menu)
d. **Click BLink** (from the pull-down Links menu)

Viewing Related Sequences and Structures: Performing a BLAST through the BLAST interface requires you to enter the sequence as FASTA format. Clicking the **BLink link** from any protein record will take you to a **page of pre-run BLAST sequence similarities**.

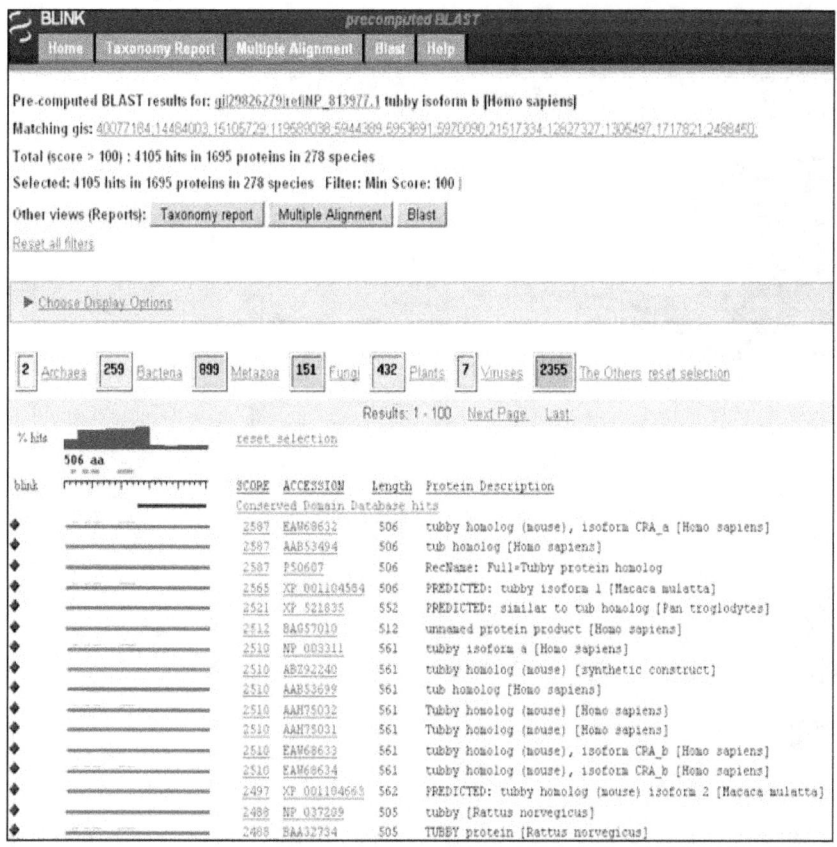

The MMDB and Viewing Structures with Cn3D: From your Protein view page, **check the links on the right** for a **Structure** or **Related Structure** link. If there are no solved structures or related structures for your protein, you won't see any structure links.

Alternatively, you can **go back to the NCBI home page** at (http://www.ncbi.nlm.nih.gov/) and search for your protein structure by setting the pull-down menu to **Structure** and typing your query protein in the search box (eg., tubby). This will give you a list of possible crystal structures for your protein. Select one by clicking on the Accession Number. This will take you to the **MMDB (Molecular Modelling Database)** structure page.

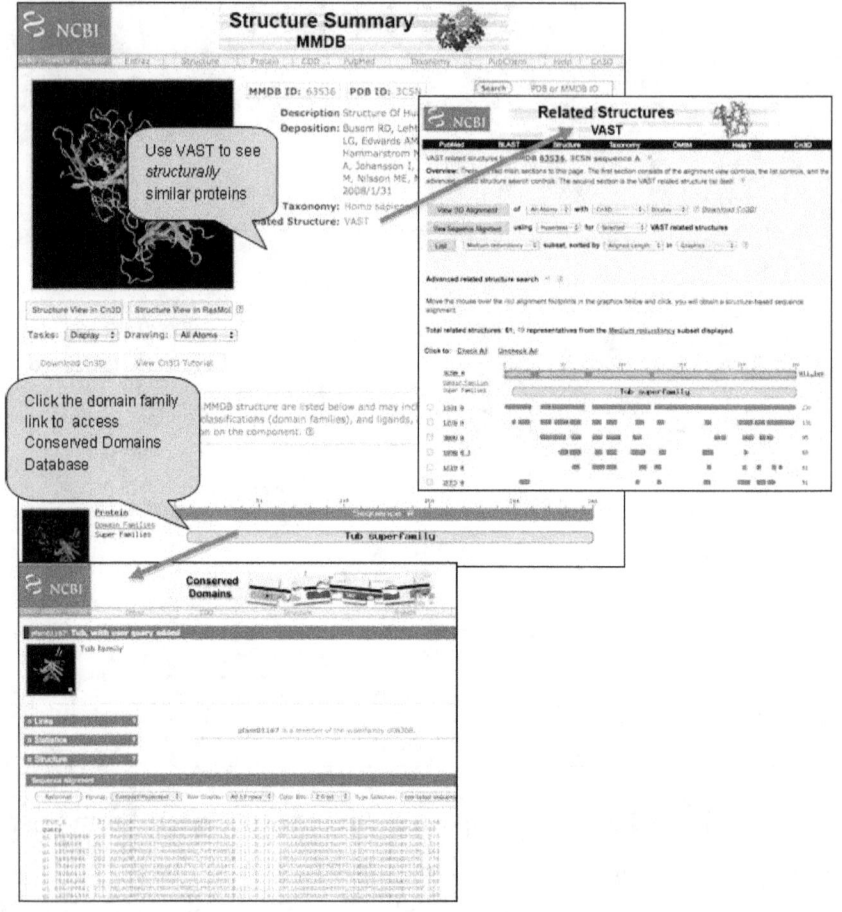

On the Structure Summary screen

1) View the **crystal structure** of the protein

2) Run a **structure similarity search (VAST)** which finds other proteins with similar 3D structures (different from BLAST, which finds sequence similarities) of any of the chains of the protein

3) View the **citation** in which the structure was first characterized

In order to view structures, you *must* install the Cn3D software on your computer. It is a free download from NCBI. You can access the download page from http://www.ncbi.nlm.nih.gov/Structure/CN3D/cn3d.shtml and follow the installation instructions.

Once you have Cn3D installed, you can open and view the crystal structure for your protein by clicking on the button **View 3D Structure** on any structure page. This will open a pop-up window that asks you to choose the program to open the molecule, with Cn3D as the default. Click **OK**.

This will open the molecule in a new window, laid over your MMDB structure page:

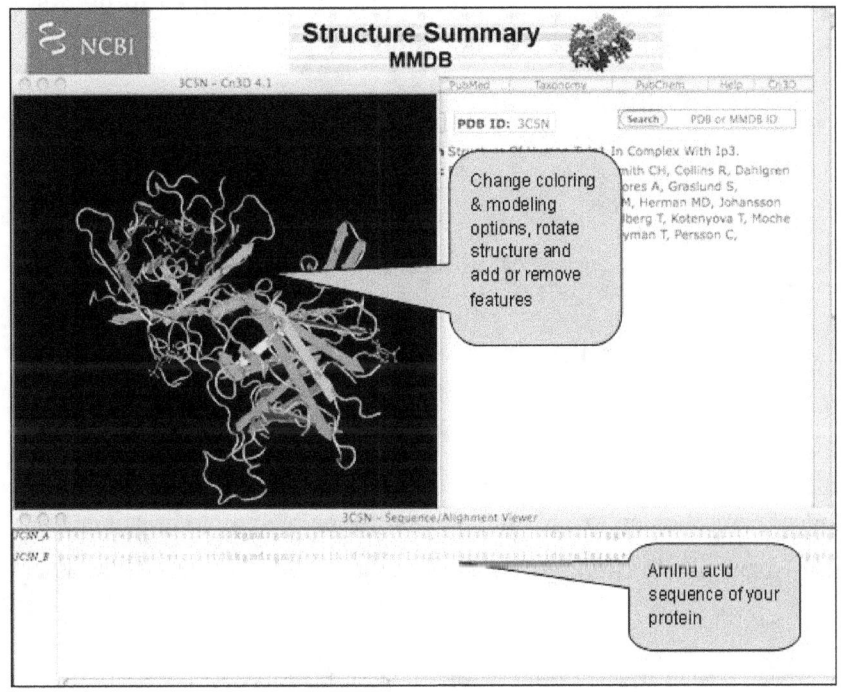

Other Useful Databases and Tools @ NCBI

1) <u>OMIM</u> – Online Mendelian Inheritance in Man (http://www.galter.northwestern.edu/signin)

2) Amino Acid Explorer (http://www.galter.northwestern.edu/signin)

3) PubChem (chemical database) (http://www.galter.northwestern.edu/signin)

4) NCBI Bookshelf (free online texts) (http://www.galter.northwestern.edu/signin)

5) Genome Workbench (download the desktop application) (http://www.galter.northwestern.edu/signin) and lots more ...

NCBI Educational Resources: The NCBI Education Page (http://www.galter.northwestern.edu/signin) includes links to all sorts of NCBI tutorials and materials including -

NCBI Handbook

BLAST Tutorial

BLAST Guide

Cn3D Structure tutorial

NCBI's Science Primer

Further Help

For assistance in using any of the NCBI tools and databases, email or call (312-503-8689) Pamela Shaw, Biosciences & Bioinformatics Librarian (http://www.galter.northwestern.edu/contact/Galter/Reference).

More organised collections of Web resources

BCM Search Launcher (http://searchlauncher.bcm.tmc.edu/) - The Baylor College of Medicine Search Launcher is an on-going project to organize molecular biology-related search and analysis services available on the WWW by function by providing a single point-of-entry for related searches.

SeWeR @ http://www.bioinformatics.org/sewer/ - SEquence analysis using WEb Resources. A unified interface for diverse web resources.

JustBio.com @ http://www.justbio.com/ - Contains some hosted tools not present on the other mega-sites.

Bioinformatics Servers

EBI Tools @ http://www.ebi.ac.uk/services - Blast, Fasta, Sequence Analysis, Homology Searches, Sequence Translation, Protein Annotation, Genomes, Proteomes, Sequence Alignments, **including Clustal** @ http://www.ebi.ac.uk/Tools/msa/

Expasy @ http://www.expasy.org/ - Proteomics server at Swiss Institute of Bioinformatics.

NCBI genomics Tools @ http://www.ncbi.nlm.nih.gov/guide/all/#tools - NCBI's tools for genomics

Sequence Analysis Tools

Other Analytical Tools

1) HOME (http://phobos.ramapo.edu/~pbagga/index.html)

2) Comparison & Alignments (http://phobos.ramapo.edu/~pbagga/binf/binf_res/ bioinfo_sat_comp.htm)

3) Functional Analysis (http://phobos.ramapo.edu/~pbagga/binf/binf_res/bioinfo_sat_func.htm)

4) Structural Analysis (http://phobos.ramapo.edu/~pbagga/binf/binf_res/bioinfo_sat_struc.htm)

5) Other Analytical Tools (http://phobos.ramapo.edu/~pbagga/binf/binf_res/bioinfo_sat_other.htm)

ACEDB : A. C. Elegans Data Base (http://www.sanger.ac.uk/resources/software/) - A software tool to manage and provide easy access to large collections of genomic data.

BCM Search Launcher (http://searchlauncher.bcm.tmc.edu/) - An on-going project to organize molecular biology-related search and analysis services available on the WWW by function by providing a single point-of-entry for related searches.

BCM ReadSeq (http://dot.imgen.bcm.tmc.edu:9331/seq-util/redseq.html) - Allows to convert Sequence Formats using ReadSeq method.

BIMAS: Bioinformatics & Molecular Analysis Section (http://bimas.dcrt.nih.gov/) - The BIMAS provides guidance, support and resources to scientists throughout the NIH in the genomic and genetic analysis fields of BioInformatics.

BIOLOGY WORKBENCH (http://workbench.sdsc.edu/) - Database searching integrated with access to a wide variety of analysis and modelling tools, all within a point and click interface that eliminates file format compatibility problems.

Biotoolkit (http://www.biosupplynet.com/btk08/) - Hundreds of advanced online tools for molecular biology data retrieval, analysis, and visualization. Also provides annotated links to web tools for the study of nucleic acid, genome, and protein structure.

CBRG: Computational Biochemistry Research Group (http://www.cbrg.ethz.ch/) - This server offers many free and helpful services and tools for Computational Biologists, Biochemists, and Molecular Evolutionists.

CBS distanceP (http://www.cbs.dtu.dk/services/distanceP/): The server predicts distance constraints between amino acids in proteins from the amino acid sequence.

Comparative Sequence Analysis (http://www.bork.embl-heidelberg.de/Frame/) - Here you can test your DNA sequence for sequencing errors.

CUBIC (http://cubic.bioc.columbia.edu/) - Columbia University Bioinformatics center services PredictProtein, META, PredictNLS, and EVA.

DARWIN: Data Analysis and Retrieval with Indexed Nucleotide/Peptide Sequences (http://cbrg.inf.ethz.ch/subsection3_1_7.html) - An interactive tool for peptide and nucleotide sequence analysis. A growing library of functions for sequence management and analysis, statistics, numerics, graphics, parallel execution and more.

DAS: Transmembrane Prediction Server (http://www.sbc.su.se/~miklos/DAS/) - Predicts transmembrane regions of a query sequence. A number of algorithms designed to identify putative transmembrane helices in the primary amino acid sequence have been developed, and current methods can identify around 90-95% of all true transmembrane segments with an over-prediction rate of only a few percent.

Divide-and-Conquer Multiple Sequence Alignment (http://bibiserv.techfak.uni-bielefeld.de/dca/) - A program for producing fast, high quality simultaneous multiple sequence alignments of amino acid, RNA, or DNA sequences.

DNA Primer Melt Calculator (http://www.strauss.lanl.gov/outgoing/DNAprimer/ DNAprimer.html) - A handy calculator of PCR primers for DNA Transformation in a nice justified layout of the sequence with codon numbering.

DOGS: Database Of Genome Sizes (http://www.cbs.dtu.dk/databases/DOGS/ index.php) - The purpose of this database is to provide a comprehensive list of estimated genome sizes for different organisms.

Dr. Tsong-Li Wang's Web Page (http://www.cis.njit.edu/~jason/) - A collection od sequence analysis tool.

Electronic PCR (http://www.ncbi.nlm.nih.gov/STS/) - PCR-based sequence tagged sites (STSs) have been used as landmarks for construction of various types of genomic maps. Using "electronic PCR" (e-PCR), these sites can be detected in DNA sequences, potentially allowing their map locations to be determined.

Embl Amino Acid Analysis Server (http://www.embl.heidelberg.de/aaa.html) - A server for protein and amino acid analysis.

EMBOSS (http://emboss.sourceforge.net/) - "The European Molecular Biology Open Software Suite". EMBOSS is a free Open Source software analysis package specially developed for the needs of the molecular biology (e.g. EMBnet) user community. The software automatically copes with data in a variety of formats and even allows transparent retrieval of sequence data from the web. Also, as extensive libraries are provided with the package, it is a platform to allow other scientists to develop and release software in true open source spirit. EMBOSS also integrates a range of currently available packages and tools for sequence analysis into a seamless whole. EMBOSS breaks the historical trend towards commercial software packages.

EMBOSS Sequence Analysis Servers (http://emboss.sourceforge.net/servers/) - A suite of free software tools for sequence analysis, including that of GCG. There are a wide variety of programs that make up the suite, ranging in application from database searching to presentation of sequence data.

ExPASy Proteomics Tools (http://www.expasy.org/tools/) - Provides tools from the ExPASy server as well as a few other servers.

ExPASy: Expert Protein Analysis System (http://www.expasy.org/) - This server is dedicated to the analysis of protein sequences and structures as well as 2-D PAGE.

ExPASy 3Dcrunch (http://swissmodel.expasy.org/) - The aim of 3Dcrunch is to submit all entries of the SWISS-PROT and trEMBL databases to SWISS-MODEL. Furthermore, all sequences of bacterial origin will be submitted to fold the recognition algorithm implemented in FoldFit. Taken together, these approaches will yield structural models for all sequences with clear similarities to proteins of know 3-D structure and a suggested fold class for all bacterial sequences.

FASTA Programs at the University of Virginia (http://alpha10.bioch.virginia.edu/fasta/) - This web page provides a table of FASTA programs at the University of Virginia.

Gcg: Genetics Computer Group (http://www.ggi.com/) - It enables scientists to analyze DNA and protein sequences by editing, mapping, comparing, and aligning them. Other programs facilitate RNA secondary structure prediction, DNA fragment assembly, and evolutionary analysis. GCG serves molecular biologists by building practical tools that implement the most important techniques of mathematical biology.

Genefisher (http://bibiserv.techfak.uni-bielefeld.de/genefisher2/) - An interactive PCR primer design program that will process aligned or unaligned sequences.

GENEMARK (http://genemark.biology.gatech.edu/GeneMark/index.html) - GeneMark, gene prediction algorithm, has been used for the analysis of EST sequences as well as for predicting rather long exons and designing RT-PCR primers.

Genetic Code Viewer (http://www.ebi.ac.uk/cgi-bin/mutations/trtables.cgi) - Genetic Code Viewer is a simple tool for showing different versions of genetic code used by various taxonomic groups.

GenomeAtlas (http://www.cbs.dtu.dk/services/GenomeAtlas/) - The DNA Structural Atlas is a method of visualizing structural features within large regions of DNA. It was originally designed for analysis of complete genomes, but can also be used quite readily for analysis of regions of DNA as small as a few thousand bp in length.

Jambw: Java-based Molecular Biology Workbench (http://www.embl-heidelberg.de/~toldo/JaMBW.html) - The programs and documentation have been put together in order to try to give a free access to the exploitment of the most common bioinformatics operations that a molecular biologist currently has.

LabOnWeb (http://www.labonweb.com/) - Life science research engine. A collection of gene discovery tools designed to accelerate work in the lab, improve the quality and accuracy of experiments, simplify the delivery of information and help researchers make more informed decisions throughout the discovery process.

Large Dot Plots (http://alces.med.umn.edu/rawdot.html) - This page accesses a very fast dot plot algorithm designed for large DNA sequences.

MODELLER (http://guitar.rockfeller.edu/modeller/modeller.html) - MODELLER is most frequently used for homology or comparative modelling of protein three-dimensional structure: the user provides an alignment of a sequence to be modelled with known related structures and MODELLER will automatically calculate a full-atom model. More generally, MODELLER models protein 3D structure by satisfaction of spatial restraints.

Nps@: Network Protein Sequence Analysis (http://npsa-pbil.ibcp.fr/cgi-bin/npsa_automat.pl?page=/NPSA/npsa_server.html): An interactive web server dedicated to protein sequence analysis and available for the biologist community.

PATSCAN (http://www-unix.mcs.anl.gov/compbio/PatScan/HTML/patscan.html) - A pattern matcher, which searches protein or nucleotide (DNA, RNA, tRNA etc.) sequence archives for instances of a pattern, which you input.

PCR Primer Selection (http://alces.med.umn.edu/rawprimer.html) - This page provides an interface to a PCR primer selection program based on xprimer.

PEDANT: Protein Extraction, Description, and Analysis Tool (http://pedant.mips.biochem.mpg.de/) - A software system for completely automatic and exhaustive analysis of protein sequence sets - from individual sequences to complete genomes.

Phylogeny Programs (http://evolution.genetics.washington.edu/phylip/software.html): A comprehensive compilation of available phylogeny programs

Primer 3 (http://www.genome.wi.mit.edu/cgi-bin/primer/primer3_www.cgi) - Designs PCR primers from a nucleotide sequence.

RasMol & Chime: Molecular Visualization Freeware (http://www.umass.edu/microbio/rasmol/) - RasMol is free software for looking at molecular structures. Chime shows molecules like RasMol, but unlike RasMol, Chime shows molecules inside a web page.

RDP: Ribosomal Database Project II (http://www.cme.msu.edu/RDP/html/index.html) - Provides ribosome related data services, including online data analysis, rRNA derived phylogenetic trees, and aligned and annotated rRNA sequences.

ReadSeq (at BCM) (http://dot.imgen.bcm.tmc.edu:9331/seq-util/readseq.html) - Allows to convert Sequence Formats using ReadSeq method.

Repeat Finder (http://www.proweb.org/Tools/selfblast.html/) - Finds a repeat in a DNA of protein sequence using BLAST.

Repeatmasker Web Server (http://ftp.genome.washington.edu/cgi-bin/RepeatMasker) - Repeatmasker screens DNA sequences in fasta format against a library of repetitive elements and returns a masked query sequence ready for database searches as well as a table annotating the masked regions.

RIFLE: Rapid Identification by Fragment Length Evaluation (http://bibiserv.techfak.uni-bielefeld.de/RIFLE/) - Compares restriction patterns of possibly unknown microorganisms against a database of theoretical restriction patterns generated from a 16S rDNA database. Restriction patterns of multiple restriction enzymes can be combined to improve the quality of identification; additional parameters allow the individual adaptation to laboratory processes.

RNA Movies (http://bibiserv.techfak.uni-bielefeld.de/rnamovies/) - A system for the visualization of RNA secondary structure spaces. Its input is a script consisting of primary and secondary structure information. From this script, the system generates animated graphical structure representations.

ROSE : Random-model of Sequence Evolution (http://bibiserv.techfak.uni-bielefeld.de/rose/) - Rose implements a new probabilistic model of the evolution of RNA, DNA, or protein-like sequences. The data created by *Rose* are suitable for the evaluation of methods in multiple sequence alignment computation and the prediction of phylogenetic relationships.

SBASE (http://www3.icgeb.trieste.it/~sbaserv/) - A protein domain library sequences that contain 237.937 annotated structural, functional, ligand-binding and topogenic segments of proteins, cross-referenced to all major sequence databases and sequence pattern collections.

SOM-BLOCK (http://www2.bioinf.mdc-berlin.de/block/home7.html) - A method based on self-organizing maps (SOMs) to find patterns in protein sequences.

SRPDB: Signal Recognition Particle Database (http://psyche.uthct.edu/dbs/SRPDB/SRPDB.html) - Provides Aligned, Annotated and Phylogenetically Ordered Sequences Related to Structure and Function of SRP.

TESS: Transcription Element Search System (http://www.cbil.upenn.edu/tess/): Searches a nucleic acid sequence for potential transcription factor binding sites from the Transfac database.

The Bio-Web Tools (http://cellbiol.com/Tools.html) - A comprehensive list of Sequence analysis tools.

The Gene Discovery Page (http://www3rdmill.com/discovery.htm) - If your sequence analysis needs are basic, you are invited to use The Gene Discovery Page for your Bioinformatics solutions. The Gene Discovery Page organizes select web-accessible bioinformatics tools in a coherent fashion.

The Genome Channel (http://compbio.ornl.gov/channel/index.html) - A tool for the comprehensive sequence-based view of genomes.

TRADAT: TRAnscription Databases and Analysis Tools) http://www.itba.mi.cnr.it/tradat/) - Databases that collect experimental relevant data such as TRANSFAC and EPD provide the basis for sequence analysis.

Virtual Genome Center (http://alces.med.umn.edu/VGC.html) - This website provides several bioinformatics tools ranging from database searches to a variety of sequence analysis tools.

Webcutter (http://tools.neb.com/NEBcutter2/) - A tool by New England Biollabs (NEB) to help restriction map nucleotide sequences. In addition to restriction site mapping, Webcutter 2 also performs degenerate digests, including the option of finding restriction sites that can be introduced into a sequence by silent mutagenesis ("silent cutters").

Back to the Top (http://phobos.ramapo.edu/~pbagga/binf/binf_res/bioinfo_sat_other.htm#top)	Bioinformatics Resources Home (http://phobos.ramapo.edu/~pbagga/binf/binf_res/binf_int_res.htm)	Contact me

HOME (http://phobos.ramapo.edu/~pbhaga/index.html)	Bioinf. Resources Home (http://phobos.ramapo.edu/~pbhaga/binf/binf_res/binf_int_res.htm)	Bioinformatics Center (http://phobos.ramapo.edu/~pbhaga/binf/binf_res/binf_center.htm)	DB Searching Tools (http://phobos.ramapo.edu/~pbagga/binf/binf_res/bioinfo_dbsearch.htm)
Genomic DBs (http://phobos.ramapo.edu/~pbhaga/binf/binf_res/bioinfo_gndb_gen.htm)	Taxonomic & Phylogenetic DBs (http://phobos.ramapo.edu/~pbhaga/binf/binf_res/bioinfo_taxo.htm)	Sequence Retrieval (http://phobos.ramapo.edu/~pbhaga/binf/binf_res/bioinfo_seqret.htm)	Sequence DBs (http://phobos.ramapo.edu/~pbagga/binf/binf_res/bioinfo_seqdb_na.htm)

Structural DBs (http://phobos.ramapo.edu/~pbhaga/binf/binf_res/bioinfo_struc_na.htm)	Specialized DBs (http://phobos.ramapo.edu/~pbhaga/binf/binf_res/bioinfo_specdb.htm)	Seq. Analysis Tools (http://phobos.amapo.edu/~pbhaga/binf/binf_res/bioinfo_sat_comp.htm)	Software (http://phobos.ramapo.edu/~pbagga/binf/binf_res/bioinfo_soft.htm)
Biblio. Resources (http://phobos.ramapo.edu/~pbhaga/binf/binf_res/bioinfo_biblio_db.htm)	Education/ Research (http://phobos.ramapo.edu/~pbhaga/binf/binf_res/bioinfo_edu_edu.htm)	Bioinformatics Servers (http://phobos.ramapo.edu/~pbhaga/binf/binf_res/bioinfo_serv.htm)	Misc. Resources (http://phobos.ramapo.edu/~pbagga/binf/binf_res/bioinfo_misc.htm)

[Source: (http://www.ccg.unam.mx/~vinuesa/Bioinformatics_resources_web.html)]

Chapter 5: APPLIED BIOINFORMATICS FOR RESEARCH

Mission of NCBI / EBI / DDBJ

a) To provide freely available data and bioinformatics services to all facets of the scientific community

b) To contribute to the advancement of biology through basic investigator-driven research

c) To provide advanced bioinformatics training to scientists at all levels

d) To help disseminate cutting-edge technologies to industry

e) To coordinate biological data provision throughout Europe.

Research (http://www.ebi.ac.uk/research): EMBL-EBI provides a unique environment for **bioinformatics research** (http://www.ebi.ac.uk/research) and our broad palette of research interests compliments our data resources. In the era of personal genomics, our research is increasingly translational and related to problems of direct significance to medicine and the environment. Our research leaders train emerging computational biologists in the **EMBL International PhD Programme** (http://www.ebi.ac.uk/research/eipp) and offer many different opportunities for **postdocs** (http://www.ebi.ac.uk/research/postdocs) and **visiting scholars** (http://www.ebi.ac.uk/about/jobs/visitors-and-scholars).

European coordination (http://www.elixir-europe.org/): EMBL-EBI is a pivotal partner in several of Europe's emerging **research infrastructures** (http://www.elixir-europe.org/). We play a key role in ELIXIR (http://www.elixir-europe.org/), the emerging infrastructure for biological information in Europe, and BioMedBridges, a project to build technical bridges between data and services in the biological, medical, translational and clinical domains. We are also pivotal partners in many other initiatives that impact the global scientific community.

Services (http://www.ebi.ac.uk/services): We maintain the world's most comprehensive range of freely available and up-to-date molecular databases (http://www.ebi.ac.uk/services). Developed in collaboration with our colleagues worldwide, our databases and tools span the full range of molecular biology, from nucleotide sequences to full systems. Our services let scientists share data, perform complex queries and analyse the results in different ways. Users can work locally by downloading our data and software, or use our web services (http://www.ebi.ac.uk/services) to access our resources programmatically. Our website serves millions of researchers, who are wet-lab and computational biologists in industry and academia working in all areas of the life sciences, from clinical biology to agri-food research.

Training ((http://www.ebi.ac.uk/training): We provide hands-on bioinformatics training courses (http://www.ebi.ac.uk/training/handson) in our purpose-built IT training suite to help experimental biologists get to grips with their data using our wide range of resources. We also bring our training to host institutions throughout the world with our Bioinformatics Roadshows (http://www.ebi.ac.uk/training/roadshow). You can train in your own time and at your own pace using our new Train online (http://www.ebi.ac.uk/training/online/) resource.

Industry: The Industry Programme (http://www.ebi.ac.uk/industry) is a forum for interaction between EMBL-EBI and the industrial life-science research sector. Our member organisations, which include pharmaceutical and agribusiness companies, engage with EMBL-EBI in the latest bioinformatics research, service and standards development as well as training and pre-competitive projects. We also support small and medium-sized enterprises through our SME Forum (http://www.ebi.ac.uk/industry/sme-forum).

Databases

The European Bioinformatics Institute is part of EMBL (http://www.embl.org/), Europe's flagship laboratory for the life sciences. EMBL-EBI provides freely available data from life science experiments (http://www.ebi.ac.uk/services) covering the full spectrum of molecular biology. While best known for the provision of bioinformatics services, about 20% of institute is devoted to basic research (http://www.ebi.ac.uk/research). Extensive training (http://www.ebi.ac.uk/training/) programme helps researchers in academia and industry to make the most of the incredible amount of data being produced every day in life science experiments. A non-profit, intergovernmental organisation funded by EMBL member states (http://www.embl.de/aboutus/general_information/organisation/member_states/index.html), located on the Wellcome Trust Genome Campus (http://www.ebi.ac.uk/about/travel) at Hinxton, Cambridge in the United Kingdom.

Databases listed below for researchers (http://www.ncbi.nlm.nih.gov/)

Assembly (http://www.ncbi.nlm.nih.gov/assembly): A database providing information on the structure of assembled genomes, assembly names and other meta-data, statistical reports, and links to genomic sequence data.

BioProject (formerly Genome Project) (http://www.ncbi.nlm.nih.gov/bioproject): A collection of genomics, functional genomics, and genetics studies and links to their resulting datasets. This resource describes project scope, material, and objectives and provides a mechanism to retrieve datasets that are often difficult to find due to inconsistent annotation, multiple independent submissions, and the varied nature of diverse data types which are often stored in different databases.

BioSample (http://www.ncbi.nlm.nih.gov/biosample): The BioSample database contains descriptions of biological source materials used in experimental assays.

BioSystems (http://www.ncbi.nlm.nih.gov/biosystems): Database that group's biomedical literature, small molecules, and sequence data in terms of biological relationships.

Bookshelf (http://www.ncbi.nlm.nih.gov/bookshelf): A collection of biomedical books that can be searched directly or from linked data in other NCBI databases. The collection includes biomedical textbooks, other scientific titles, genetic resources such as GeneReviews, and NCBI help manuals.

ClinVar (http://www.ncbi.nlm.nih.gov/clinvar): A resource to provide a public, tracked record of reported relationships between human variation and observed health status with supporting evidence. Related information in the NIH Genetic Testing Registry (GTR) (http://www.ncbi.nlm.nih.gov/gtr/), MedGen (http://www.ncbi.nlm.nih.gov/medgen/) Gene (http://www.ncbi.nlm.nih.gov/gene/), OMIM (http://www.omim.org/), PubMed (http://www.ncbi.nlm.nih.gov/pubmed/) and other sources are accessible through hyperlinks on the records.

CloneDB (formerly Clone Registry) (http://www.ncbi.nlm.nih.gov/clone): A database that integrates information about clones and libraries, including sequence data, map positions and distributor information.

Computational Resources from NCBI's Structure Group (http://www.ncbi.nlm.nih.gov/structure/): A centralized page providing access and links to resources developed by the Structure Group of the NCBI Computational Biology Branch (CBB). These resources cover databases and tools to help in the study of macromolecular structures, conserved domains and protein classification, small molecules and their biological activity, and biological pathways and systems.

Consensus CDS (CCDS) (http://www.ncbi.nlm.nih.gov/projects/CCDS/CcdsBrowse.cgi): A collaborative effort to identify a core set of human and mouse protein coding regions that are consistently annotated and of high quality.

Conserved Domain Database (CDD) (http://www.ncbi.nlm.nih.gov/cdd): A collection of sequence alignments and profiles representing protein domains conserved in molecular evolution. It also includes alignments of the domains to known 3-dimensional protein structures in the MMDB database.

Database of Expressed Sequence Tags (dbEST) (http://www.ncbi.nlm.nih.gov/nucst): A divison of GenBank that contains short single-pass reads of cDNA (transcript) sequences. dbEST can be searched directly through the Nucleotide EST Database.

Database of Genome Survey Sequences (dbGSS) (http://www.ncbi.nlm.nih.gov/nucgss): A division of GenBank that contains short single-pass reads of genomic DNA. dbGSS can be searched directly through the Nucleotide GSS Database.

Database of Genomic Structural Variation (dbVar) (http://www.ncbi.nlm.nih.gov/dbvar): The dbVar database has been developed to archive information associated with large scale genomic variation, including large insertions, deletions, translocations and inversions. In addition to archiving variation discovery, dbVar also stores associations of defined variants with phenotype information.

Database of Genotypes and Phenotypes (dbGaP) (http://www.ncbi.nlm.nih.gov/gap): An archive and distribution center for the description and results of studies which investigate the interaction of genotype and phenotype. These studies include genome-wide association (GWAS), medical resequencing, molecular diagnostic assays, as well as association between genotype and non-clinical traits.

Database of Major Histocompatibility Complex (dbMHC) (http://www.ncbi.nlm.nih.gov/gv/mhc/main.cgi?cmd=init): An open, publicly accessible platform where the HLA community can submit, edit, view, and exchange data related to the human major histocompatibility complex. It consists of an interactive Alignment Viewer for HLA and related genes, an MHC microsatellite database, a sequence interpretation site for Sequencing Based Typing (SBT), and a Primer/Probe database.

Database of Short Genetic Variations (dbSNP) (http://www.ncbi.nlm.nih.gov/snp): Includes single nucleotide variations, microsatellites, and small-scale insertions and deletions. dbSNP contains population-specific frequency and genotype data, experimental conditions, molecular context, and mapping information for both neutral variations and clinical mutations.

Epigenomics (http://www.ncbi.nlm.nih.gov/epigenomics): This resource enables users to explore and visualize richly-annotated epigenomics datasets. It provides a unique interface to search and navigate epigenomic data in the context of biological sample information, as well as tools to select, download and view multiple sets of epigenomic data as tracks on genome browsers.

GenBank (http://www.ncbi.nlm.nih.gov/genbank): The NIH genetic sequence database, an annotated collection of all publicly available DNA sequences. GenBank is part of the International Nucleotide Sequence Database Collaboration, which comprises the DNA DataBank of Japan (DDBJ), the European Molecular Biology Laboratory (EMBL), and GenBank at NCBI. These three organizations exchange data on a daily basis. GenBank consists of several divisions, most of which can be accessed through the Nucleotide database. The exceptions are the EST and GSS divisions, which are accessed through the Nucleotide EST and Nucleotide GSS databases, respectively.

Gene (http://www.ncbi.nlm.nih.gov/gene): A searchable database of genes, focusing on genomes that have been completely sequenced and that have an active research community to contribute gene-specific data. Information includes nomenclature, chromosomal localization, gene products and their attributes (e.g., protein interactions), associated markers, phenotypes, interactions, and links to citations, sequences, variation details, maps, expression reports, homologs, protein domain content, and external databases.

Gene Expression Omnibus (GEO) Database (http://www.ncbi.nlm.nih.gov/geo/): A public functional genomics data repository supporting MIAME-compliant data submissions. Array- and sequence-based data are accepted and tools are provided to help users query and download experiments and curated gene expression profiles.

Gene Expression Omnibus (GEO) Datasets (http://www.ncbi.nlm.nih.gov/gds): Stores curated gene expression and molecular abundance DataSets assembled from the Gene Expression Omnibus (GEO) repository. Dataset records contain additional resources, including cluster tools and differential expression queries.

Gene Expression Omnibus (GEO) Profiles (http://www.ncbi.nlm.nih.gov/geoprofiles/): Stores individual gene expression and molecular abundance Profiles assembled from the Gene Expression Omnibus (GEO) repository. Search for specific profiles of interest based on gene annotation or pre-computed profile characteristics.

GeneReviews (http://www.ncbi.nlm.nih.gov/books/NBK1116/): A collection of expert-authored, peer-reviewed disease descriptions on the NCBI Bookshelf that apply genetic testing to the diagnosis, management, and genetic counselling of patients and families with specific inherited conditions.

Genes and Disease (http://www.ncbi.nlm.nih.gov/books/NBK22183/): Summaries of information for selected genetic disorders with discussions of the underlying mutation(s) and clinical features, as well as links to related databases and organizations.

Genetic Testing Registry (GTR) (http://www.ncbi.nlm.nih.gov/gtr/): A voluntary registry of genetic tests and laboratories, with detailed information about the tests such as what is measured and analytic and clinical validity. GTR also is a nexus for information about genetic conditions and provides context-specific links to a variety of resources, including practice guidelines, published literature, and genetic data/information. The initial scope of GTR includes single gene tests for Mendelian disorders, as well as arrays, panels and pharmacogenetic tests.

Genome (http://www.ncbi.nlm.nih.gov/genome): Contains sequence and map data from the whole genomes of over 1000 organisms. The genomes represent both completely sequenced organisms and those for which sequencing is in progress. All three main domains of life (bacteria, archaea, and eukaryota) are represented, as well as many viruses, phages, viroids, plasmids, and organelles.

Genome Reference Consortium (GRC) (http://www.ncbi.nlm.nih.gov/projects/genome/assembly/grc): The Genome Reference Consortium (GRC) maintains responsibility for the human and mouse reference genomes. Members consist of The Genome Center at Washington University, the Wellcome Trust Sanger Institute, the European Bioinformatics Institute (EBI) and the National Center for Biotechnology Information (NCBI). The GRC works to correct misrepresented loci and to close remaining assembly gaps. In addition, the GRC seeks to provide alternate assemblies for complex or structurally variant genomic loci. At the GRC website (http://www.genomereference.org), the public can view genomic regions currently under review, report genome-related problems and contact the GRC.

HIV-1, Human Protein Interaction Database (http://www.ncbi.nlm.nih.gov/RefSeq/HIVInteractions): A database of known interactions of HIV-1 proteins with proteins from human hosts. It provides annotated bibliographies of published reports of protein interactions, with links to the corresponding PubMed records and sequence data.

HomoloGene (http://www.ncbi.nlm.nih.gov/homologene): A gene homology tool that compares nucleotide sequences between pairs of organisms in order to identify putative orthologs. Curated orthologs are incorporated from a variety of sources via the Gene database.

Influenza Virus (http://www.ncbi.nlm.nih.gov/genomes/FLU/FLU.html): A compilation of data from the NIAID Influenza Genome Sequencing Project and GenBank. It provides tools for flu sequence analysis, annotation and submission to GenBank. This resource also has links to other flu sequence resources, and publications and general information about flu viruses.

Journals in NCBI Databases (http://www.ncbi.nlm.nih.gov/nlmcatalog/journals): Subset of the NLM Catalog database providing information on journals that are referenced in NCBI database records, including PubMed abstracts. This subset can be searched using the journal title, MEDLINE or ISO abbreviation, ISSN, or the NLM Catalog ID.

MeSH Database (http://www.ncbi.nlm.nih.gov/mesh): MeSH (Medical Subject Headings) is the U.S. National Library of Medicine's controlled vocabulary for indexing articles for MEDLINE/PubMed. MeSH terminology provides a consistent way to retrieve information that may use different terminology for the same concepts.

MedGen (http://www.ncbi.nlm.nih.gov/medgen): A portal to information about medical genetics. MedGen includes term lists from multiple sources and organizes them into concept groupings and hierarchies. Links are also provided to information related to those concepts in the NIH Genetic Testing Registry (GTR), ClinVar, Gene, OMIM, PubMed, and other sources.

NCBI C++ Toolkit Manual (http://www.ncbi.nlm.nih.gov/toolkit/doc/book/): A comprehensive manual on the NCBI C++ toolkit, including its design and development framework, a C++ library reference, software examples and demos, FAQs and release notes. The manual is searchable online and can be downloaded as a series of PDF documents.

NCBI Education Page (http://www.ncbi.nlm.nih.gov/education/): Provides links to tutorials and training materials, including PowerPoint slides and print handouts.

NCBI Glossary (http://www.ncbi.nlm.nih.gov/books/NBK21106/): Part of the NCBI Handbook, this glossary contains descriptions of NCBI tools and acronyms, bioinformatics terms and data representation formats.

NCBI Handbook (http://www.ncbi.nlm.nih.gov/books/NBK143764/): An extensive collection of articles about NCBI databases and software. Designed for a novice user, each article presents a general overview of the resource and its design, along with tips for searching and using available analysis tools. All articles can be searched online and downloaded in PDF format; the handbook can be accessed through the NCBI Bookshelf.

NCBI Help Manual (http://www.ncbi.nlm.nih.gov/books/NBK3831/): Accessed through the NCBI Bookshelf, the Help Manual contains documentation for many NCBI resources, including PubMed, PubMed Central, the Entrez system, Gene, SNP and LinkOut. All chapters can be downloaded in PDF format.

NCBI Website Search (http://www.ncbi.nlm.nih.gov/ncbisearch/?item=all[sb]): A database of static NCBI web pages, documentation, and online tools. These pages include such content as specialized online sequence analysis tools, back issues of newsletters, legacy resource description pages, sample code, and other miscellaneous resources. Searching this database is equivalent to a site search tool for the whole NCBI web site, with the exception of the FTP directories.

National Library of Medicine (NLM) Catalog (http://www.ncbi.nlm.nih.gov/nlmcatalog): Bibliographic data for all the journals, books, audiovisuals, computer software, electronic resources and other materials that are in the library's holdings.

Nucleotide Database (http://www.ncbi.nlm.nih.gov/nuccore): A collection of nucleotide sequences from several sources, including GenBank, RefSeq, the Third Party Annotation (TPA) database, and PDB. Searching the Nucleotide Database will yield available results from each of its component databases.

Online Mendelian Inheritance in Man (OMIM) (http://www.ncbi.nlm.nih.gov/omim): A database of human genes and genetic disorders. NCBI maintains current content and continues to support its searching and integration with other NCBI databases. However, OMIM now has a new home at omim.org (http://omim.org/) and users are directed to this site for full record displays.

PopSet (http://www.ncbi.nlm.nih.gov/popset): Database of related DNA sequences that originate from comparative studies: phylogenetic, population, environmental and, to a lesser degree, mutational. Each record in the database is a set of DNA sequences. For example, a population set provides information on genetic variation within an organism, while a phylogenetic set may contain sequences, and their alignment, of a single gene obtained from several related organisms.

Probe (http://www.ncbi.nlm.nih.gov/probe): A public registry of nucleic acid reagents designed for use in a wide variety of biomedical research applications, together with information on reagent distributors, probe effectiveness, and computed sequence similarities.

Protein Clusters (http://www.ncbi.nlm.nih.gov/proteinclusters): A collection of related protein sequences (clusters), consisting of Reference Sequence proteins encoded by complete prokaryotic and organelle plasmids and genomes. The database provides easy access to annotation information, publications, domains, structures, external links, and analysis tools.

Protein Database (http://www.ncbi.nlm.nih.gov/protein) : A database that includes protein sequence records from a variety of sources, including GenPept, RefSeq, Swiss-Prot, PIR, PRF, and PDB.

PubChem BioAssay (http://www.ncbi.nlm.nih.gov/pcassay) : Consists of deposited bioactivity data and descriptions of bioactivity assays used to screen the chemical substances contained in the PubChem Substance database, including descriptions of the conditions and the readouts (bioactivity levels) specific to the screening procedure.

PubChem Compound (http://www.ncbi.nlm.nih.gov/pccompound): Contains unique, validated chemical structures (small molecules) that can be searched using names, synonyms or keywords. The compound records may link to more than one PubChem Substance record if different depositors supplied the same structure. These Compound records reflect validated chemical depiction information provided to describe substances in PubChem Substance. Structures stored within PubChem Compounds are pre-clustered and cross-referenced by identity and similarity groups. Additionally, calculated properties and descriptors are available for searching and filtering of chemical structures.

PubChem Substance (http://www.ncbi.nlm.nih.gov/pcsubstance): PubChem Substance records contain substance information electronically submitted to PubChem by depositors. This includes any chemical structure information submitted, as well as chemical names, comments, and links to the depositor's web site.

PubMed (http://www.ncbi.nlm.nih.gov/pubmed): A database of citations and abstracts for biomedical literature from MEDLINE and additional life science journals. Links are provided when full text versions of the articles are available via PubMed Central (described below) or other websites.

PubMed Central (PMC) (http://www.ncbi.nlm.nih.gov/pmc/): A digital archive of full-text biomedical and life sciences journal literature, including clinical medicine and public health.

PubMed Health (http://www.ncbi.nlm.nih.gov/pubmedhealth): A collection of clinical effectiveness reviews and other resources to help consumers and clinicians use and understand clinical research results. These are drawn from the NCBI Bookshelf and PubMed, including published systematic reviews from organizations such as the Agency for Health Care Research and Quality, The Cochrane Collaboration, and others (see complete listing). Links to full text articles are provided when available.

RefSeqGene (http://www.ncbi.nlm.nih.gov/refseq/rsg/): A collection of human gene-specific reference genomic sequences. RefSeq gene is a subset of NCBI's RefSeq database, and are defined based on review from curators of locus-specific databases and the genetic testing community. They form a stable foundation for reporting mutations, for establishing consistent intron and exon numbering conventions, and for defining the coordinates of other biologically significant variation. RefSeqGene is a part of the Locus Reference Genomic (LRG http://www.lrg-sequence.org/) Collaboration.

Reference Sequence (RefSeq) (http://www.ncbi.nlm.nih.gov/RefSeq/): A collection of curated, non-redundant genomic DNA, transcript (RNA), and protein sequences produced by NCBI. RefSeqs provide a stable reference for genome annotation, gene identification and characterization, mutation and polymorphism analysis, expression studies, and comparative analyses. The RefSeq collection is accessed through the Nucleotide and Protein databases.

Retrovirus Resources (http://www.ncbi.nlm.nih.gov/retroviruses/) : A collection of resources specifically designed to support the research of retroviruses, including a genotyping tool that uses the BLAST algorithm to identify the genotype of a query sequence; an alignment tool for global alignment of multiple sequences; an HIV-1 automatic sequence annotation tool; and annotated maps of numerous retroviruses viewable in GenBank, FASTA, and graphic formats, with links to associated sequence records.

SARS CoV (http://www.ncbi.nlm.nih.gov/genomes/SARS/SARS.html) : A summary of data for the SARS coronavirus (CoV), including links to the most recent sequence data and publications, links to other SARS related resources, and a pre-computed alignment of genome sequences from various isolates.

Sequence Read Archive (SRA) (http://www.ncbi.nlm.nih.gov/Traces/sra/sra.cgi?) : The Sequence Read Archive (SRA) stores sequencing data from the next generation of sequencing platforms including Roche 454 GS System®, Illumina Genome Analyzer®, Life Technologies AB SOLiD System®, Helicos Biosciences Heliscope®, Complete Genomics®, and Pacific Biosciences SMRT®.

Structure (Molecular Modeling Database) (http://www.ncbi.nlm.nih.gov/sites/entrez?db=structure): Contains macromolecular 3D structures derived from the Protein Data Bank, as well as tools for their visualization and comparative analysis.

Taxonomy (http://www.ncbi.nlm.nih.gov/taxonomy): Contains the names and phylogenetic lineages of more than 160,000 organisms that have molecular data in the NCBI databases. New taxa are added to the Taxonomy database as data are deposited for them.

Third Party Annotation (TPA) Database (http://www.ncbi.nlm.nih.gov/genbank/TPA.html): A database that contains sequences built from the existing primary sequence data in GenBank. The sequences and corresponding annotations are experimentally supported and have been published in a peer-reviewed scientific journal. TPA records are retrieved through the Nucleotide Database.

Trace Archive (http://www.ncbi.nlm.nih.gov/Traces/trace.cgi): A repository of DNA sequence chromatograms (traces), base calls, and quality estimates for single-pass reads from various large-scale sequencing projects.

UniGene (http://www.ncbi.nlm.nih.gov/unigene): A database that provides sets of transcript sequences that appear to come from the same transcription locus (gene or expressed pseudogene), together with information on protein similarities, gene expression, cDNA clone reagents, and genomic location.

UniGene Library Browser (http://www.ncbi.nlm.nih.gov/UniGene/lbrowse2.cgi): This database contains libraries of Expressed Sequence Tags (ESTs) organized by organism, tissue type and developmental stage.

Viral Genomes (http://www.ncbi.nlm.nih.gov/genomes/GenomesHome.cgi?) : A wide range of resources, including a brief summary of the biology of viruses, links to viral genome sequences in Entrez Genome, and information about viral Reference Sequences, a collection of reference sequences for thousands of viral genomes.

Virus Variation (http://www.ncbi.nlm.nih.gov/genomes/VirusVariation/) : An extension of the Influenza Virus Resource to other organisms, providing an interface to download sequence sets of selected viruses, analysis tools, including virus-specific BLAST pages, and genome annotation pipelines.

Downloads

BLAST (Stand-alone) (http://blast.ncbi.nlm.nih.gov/Blast.cgi?CMD=Web&PAGE_Type=BlastDocs&DOC_TYPE=Download): BLAST executables for local use are provided for Solaris, LINUX, Windows, and MacOSX systems. See the README file in the ftp directory for more information. Pre-formatted databases for BLAST nucleotide, protein, and translated searches also are available for downloading under the db subdirectory.

FTP: BLAST Databases (ftp://ftp.ncbi.nlm.nih.gov/blast/db/): Sequence databases for use with the stand-alone BLAST programs. The files in this directory are pre-formatted databases that are ready to use with BLAST.

FTP: CDD (ftp://ftp.ncbi.nlm.nih.gov/pub/mmdb/cdd/): This site provides full data records for CDD, along with individual Position Specific Scoring Matrices (PSSMs), mFASTA sequences and annotation data for each conserved domain. See the README file for full details.

FTP: ClinVar Data (ftp://ftp.ncbi.nlm.nih.gov/pub/clinvar): This site provides full data extractions in XML and summary data in VCF format. It contains files with information about standard terms used in ClinVar, MedGen, and GTR.

FTP: FASTA BLAST Databases (ftp://ftp.ncbi.nlm.nih.gov/blast/db/FASTA): Sequence databases in FASTA format for use with the stand-alone BLAST programs. These databases must be formatted using formatdb before they can be used with BLAST.

FTP: GenBank (http://www.ncbi.nlm.nih.gov/genbank/GenBankFtp.html): This site contains files for all sequence records in GenBank in the default flat file format. The files are organized by

GenBank division, and the full contents are described in the README.genbank file.

FTP: GenPept (ftp://ftp.ncbi.nlm.nih.gov/ncbi-asn1/protein_fasta/): The protein sequences corresponding to the translations of coding sequences (CDS) in GenBank are collected for each GenBank release. Please see the README file in the directory for more information.

FTP: Gene (ftp://ftp.ncbi.nlm.nih.gov/gene/): This site contains three directories: DATA, GeneRIF and tools. The DATA directory contains files listing all data linked to GeneIDs along with subdirectories containing ASN.1 data for the Gene records. The GeneRIF (Gene References into Function) directory contains PubMed identifiers for articles describing the function of a single gene or interactions between products of two genes. Sample programs for manipulating gene data are provided in the tools directory. Please see the README file for details.

FTP: Gene Expression Omnibus (GEO) Profiles and Datasets (ftp://ftp.ncbi.nlm.nih.gov/pub/geo/): This site contains GEO data in two formats: SOFT (Simple Omnibus in Text Format) and MINiML (MIAME Notation in Markup Language). Summary text files and supplementary data are also available. Please see the README.TXT file for more information.

FTP: Genome (ftp://ftp.ncbi.nlm.nih.gov/genomes/): This site contains genome sequence and mapping data for organisms in Entrez Genome. The data are organized in directories for single species or groups of species. Mapping data are collected in the directory Map View and are organized by species. See the README file in the root directory and the README files in the species subdirectories for detailed information.

FTP: Genome Mapping Data (ftp://ftp.ncbi.nlm.nih.gov/genomes/MapView): Contains directories for each genome that include available mapping data for current and previous builds of that genome.

FTP: HomoloGene (ftp://ftp.ncbi.nlm.nih.gov/pub/HomoloGene/current): This site contains data for each build of HomoloGene, beginning with build 35. Complete data for each build are provided in XML, and a data summary is provided in tab-delimited text format.

FTP: NCBI Field Guide Manual (ftp://ftp.ncbi.nlm.nih.gov/pub/FieldGuide/FGPlus/): Downloadable material for NCBI's previously offered Field Guide training course.

FTP: NCBI Structure Course Materials (ftp://ftp.ncbi.nlm.nih.gov/pub/sayers/Structure/): PowerPoint slides, handouts and exercises for the previously offered NCBI course "Exploring 3D Molecular Structures."

FTP: NCBI Taxonomy (ftp://ftp.ncbi.nlm.nih.gov/pub/taxonomy/): This site contains the full taxonomy database along with files associating nucleotide and protein sequence records with their taxonomy IDs. See the taxdump_readme.txt and gi_taxid.readme files for more information.

FTP: Protein Clusters (ftp://ftp.ncbi.nlm.nih.gov/genomes/Bacteria/CLUSTERS/): This site contains data from the Protein Clusters database arranged by release date. See the README files for more information.

FTP: PubChem (ftp://ftp.ncbi.nlm.nih.gov/pubchem/): This site provides data from the PubChem Substance, Compound and Bioassay databases for download via ftp. Full downloads of the databases are available along with daily, weekly and monthly updates for Substance and Compound. Substance and Compound data are provided in ASN.1, SDF and XML formats. See the README files for more information.

FTP: RefSeq (ftp://ftp.ncbi.nlm.nih.gov/refseq/release/): This site contains all nucleotide and protein sequence records in the Reference Sequence (RefSeq) collection. The ""release"" directory contains the most current release of the complete collection, while data for selected organisms (such as human, mouse and rat) are available in separate directories. Data are available in FASTA and flat file formats. See the README file for details.

FTP: SKY/M-Fish and CGH Data (ftp://ftp.ncbi.nlm.nih.gov/sky-cgh/): This site contains SKY-CGH data in ASN.1, XML and EasySKYCGH formats. See the skycghreadme.txt file for more information.

FTP: SNP (ftp://ftp.ncbi.nlm.nih.gov/snp/): Downloadable data for SNP.

FTP: Sequence Read Archive (SRA) Download Facility (http://www.ncbi.nlm.nih.gov/Traces/sra/sra.cgi?cmd=show&f=faspftp_runs_v1&m=downloads&s=download_sra): This site contains next-generation sequencing data organized by the submitted sequencing project.

FTP: Site (http://www.ncbi.nlm.nih.gov/Ftp/): FTP download site for NCBI databases, tools, and utilities.

FTP: Structure (MMDB) (ftp://ftp.ncbi.nlm.nih.gov/mmdb/): This site contains ASN.1 data for all records in MMDB along with VAST alignment data and the non-redundant PDB (nr-PDB) data sets. See the README file for more information.

FTP: Trace Archive (ftp://ftp.ncbi.nlm.nih.gov/pub/TraceDB): This site contains the trace chromatogram data organized by species. Data include chromatogram, quality scores, FASTA sequences from automatic base calls, and other ancillary information in tab-delimited text as well as XML formats. See the README file for details.

FTP: UniGene (ftp://ftp.ncbi.nlm.nih.gov/repository/UniGene/): This site contains individual directories for each organism with data in UniGene. The data for each species includes the unique sequence for each UniGene cluster, all sequences in each cluster in FASTA format and library information for the cluster. See the README file for further details.

FTP: UniVec (ftp://ftp.ncbi.nlm.nih.gov/pub/UniVec/): This site contains the UniVec and UniVec_Core databases in FASTA format. See the README.uv file for details.

FTP: Whole Genome Shotgun Sequences (ftp://ftp.ncbi.nlm.nih.gov/genbank/wgs): This site contains whole genome shotgun sequence data organized by the 4-digit project code. Data include GenBank and GenPept flat files, quality scores and summary statistics. See the README.genbank.wgs file for more information.

FTP: dbGAP Open-Access Data (ftp://ftp.ncbi.nlm.nih.gov/dbgap): Open-access data generally include summaries of genotype/phenotype association studies, descriptions of the measured variables, and study documents, such as the protocol and questionnaires. Access to individual-level data, including phenotypic data tables and genotypes, requires varying levels of authorization.

FTP: dbMHC Data (ftp://ftp.ncbi.nlm.nih.gov/pub/mhc): This site contains data in separate directories for the various projects and resources within the database of human major histocompatibility (dbMHC).

MEDLINE (Leasing) (http://www.nlm.nih.gov/databases/journal.html): NLM leases MEDLINE/PubMed to U.S. individuals or organizations.

NCBI Data Specifications (http://www.ncbi.nlm.nih.gov/data_specs): Specifications for NCBI data in ASN.1 or DTD format are available on the Index of data_specs page. The "NCBI_data_conversion.html" links to the conversion tool.

National Library of Medicine (NLM) DTDs (http://dtd.nlm.nih.gov/): A suite of tag sets for authoring and archiving journal articles as well as transferring journal articles from publishers to archives and between archives. There are four tag sets: Archiving and Interchange Tag Set - Created to enable an archive to capture as many of the structural and semantic components of existing printed and tagged journal material as conveniently as possible; Journal Publishing Tag Set - Optimized for archives that wish to regularize and control their content, not to accept the sequence and arrangement presented to them by any particular publisher; Article Authoring Tag Set - Designed for authoring new journal articles; NCBI Book Tag Set - Written specifically to describe volumes for the NCBI online libraries.

PubChem Download Service (http://pubchem.ncbi.nlm.nih.gov/pc_fetch/pc_fetch.cgi): This service allows users to download compound or substance records corresponding to a set of PubChem identifiers, which can be supplied manually or through a text file. Numerous download formats are available, including SDF, XML and SMILES.

PubMed Central (PMC) Open-Access Subset (http://www.ncbi.nlm.nih.gov/pmc/tools/openftlist/): The PMC Open-Access Subset is a relatively small part of the total collection of articles in PMC. Whereas the majority of articles in PMC are subject to traditional copyright restrictions, these articles are protected by copyright, but are made available under a Creative Commons or similar license that generally allows more liberal redistribution and reuse than a traditional copyright. Please refer to the license statement in each article for specific terms of use.

RSS Feeds (http://www.ncbi.nlm.nih.gov/feed/): Subscribe to Web/RSS feeds for updates about NCBI resources.

Submissions

BioProject Submission (https://submit.ncbi.nlm.nih.gov/subs/bioproject/): An online form that provides an interface for researchers, consortia and organizations to register their BioProjects. This serves as the starting point for the submission of genomic and genetic data for the study. The data does not need to be submitted at the time of BioProject registration.

ClinVar Submissions (http://www.ncbi.nlm.nih.gov/clinvar/docs/submit/): Guidelines and instructions for submitting assertions about the pathogenicity of human genetic variants. These submissions can include summary data about a variant (variant level/aggregate data); support for variants per case (case-level) is in development.

Database of Genotype and Phenotype (dbGaP) Data Submission Policies (http://www.ncbi.nlm.nih.gov/projects/gap/cgi-bin/about.cgi): Guidelines and requirements for submitting genotype and phenotype association data to dbGaP.

Database of Major Histocompatibility Complex (dbMHC) Microsatellite Markers Submission Template (http://www.ncbi.nlm.nih.gov/gv/mhc/xslcgi.fcgi?cmd=mssearch&user_id=0&probe_id=0&source_id=0&locus_id=0&locus_group=1&proto_id=0&kit_id=0&dummy=0#submt): Guidelines and template for submitting MHC region microsatellite data to dbMHC.

GenBank : BankIt (http://www.ncbi.nlm.nih.gov/WebSub/?tool=genbank): A web-based sequence submission tool for one or a few submissions to the GenBank database, designed to make the submission process quick and easy.

GenBank : Barcode (http://www.ncbi.nlm.nih.gov/WebSub/index.cgi?tool=barcode): Tool for submission to the GenBank database of Barcode short nucleotide sequences from a standard genetic locus for use in species identification.

GenBank : Sequin (http://www.ncbi.nlm.nih.gov/projects/Sequin/): A stand-alone software tool developed by the NCBI for submitting and updating entries to public sequence databases (GenBank, EMBL, or DDBJ). It is capable of handling simple submissions that contain a single short mRNA sequence, complex submissions containing long sequences, multiple annotations, segmented sets of DNA, as well as sequences from phylogenetic and population studies with alignments. For simple submission, use the online submission tool BankIt instead.

GenBank : tbl2asn (http://www.ncbi.nlm.nih.gov/genbank/tbl2asn2/): A command-line program that automates the creation of sequence records for submission to GenBank using many of the same functions as Sequin. It is used primarily for submission of complete genomes and large batches of sequences.

Gene Expression Omnibus (GEO) Web Deposit (http://www.ncbi.nlm.nih.gov/geo/info/submission.html): Submit expression data, such as microarray, SAGE or mass spectrometry datasets to the NCBI Gene Expression Omnibus (GEO) database.

GeneRIF (http://www.ncbi.nlm.nih.gov/gene/about-generif): GeneRIF provides a simple mechanism to allow scientists to add to the functional annotation of genes in the Gene database.

Genetic Testing Registry (GTR) Submissions (http://www.ncbi.nlm.nih.gov/gtr/docs/submit/): Guidelines and instructions for registering laboratories and submitting genetic test information including clinical and research tests for germline or somatic test targets. GTR welcomes registration of cytogenetic, biochemical, and molecular tests for Mendelian disorders, pharmacogenetic phenotypes and complex panels.

NIH Manuscript Submissions (NIHMS) (http://www.nihms.nih.gov/): The NIH Manuscript Submission (NIHMS) System is used to submit manuscripts that arise from NIH funding to the PubMed Central (http://www.ncbi.nlm.nih.gov/pmc/) digital archive, in accordance with the NIH Public Access Policy and the law it implements. The law and Public Access Policy are intended to ensure that the public has access to the published results of NIH-funded research.

PubChem Upload (http://pubchem.ncbi.nlm.nih.gov/upload/#welcome): This site enables users to submit data to the PubChem Substance and BioAssay databases, including chemical structures, experimental biological activity results, annotations, siRNA data and more. It can also be used to update previously submitted records.

SNP Submission Tool (http://www.ncbi.nlm.nih.gov/projects/SNP/): The SNP database tools page provides links to the general submission guidelines and to the submission handle request. The page has also two specific links for single- or batch submissions of the human variation data using Human Genome Variation Society nomenclature.

Sequence Read Archive Submission (http://www.ncbi.nlm.nih.gov/Traces/sra_sub/sub.cgi?) : This link describes how submitters of SRA data can obtain a secure NCBI FTP site for their data, and also describes the allowed data formats and directory structures.

Submission Portal (https://submit.ncbi.nlm.nih.gov/): A single entry point for submitters to link to and find information about all of the data submission processes at NCBI. Currently, this serves as an interface for the registration of BioProjects and BioSamples and submission of data for WGS and GTR. Future additions to this site are planned.

Trace Archive Submission (http://www.ncbi.nlm.nih.gov/Traces/trace.cgi?cmd=show&f=submit&m=doc&s=submit) : This link describes how submitters of trace data can obtain a secure NCBI FTP site for their data, and also describes the allowed data formats and directory structures.

Tools

1000 Genomes Browser (http://www.ncbi.nlm.nih.gov/variation/tools/1000genomes/): An interactive graphical viewer that allows users to explore variant calls, genotype calls and supporting evidence (such as aligned sequence reads) that have been produced by the 1000 Genomes Project (http://www.1000genomes.org/).

Amino Acid Explorer (http://www.ncbi.nlm.nih.gov/Class/Structure/aa/aa_explorer.cgi) : This tool allows users to explore the characteristics of amino acids by comparing their structural and chemical properties, predicting protein sequence changes caused by mutations, viewing common substitutions, and browsing the functions of given residues in conserved domains.

Assembly Archive (http://www.ncbi.nlm.nih.gov/Traces/assembly/assmbrowser.cgi): Links the raw sequence information found in the Trace Archive with assembly information found in publicly available sequence repositories (GenBank/EMBL/DDBJ). The Assembly Viewer allows a user to see the multiple sequence alignments as well as the actual sequence chromatogram.

BLAST Link (BLink) (http://www.ncbi.nlm.nih.gov/sutils/blink.cgi?mode=query) : A link option on protein records that displays the results of a pre-computed BLAST search of that protein against all other protein sequences at NCBI.

BLAST Microbial Genomes (http://blast.ncbi.nlm.nih.gov/Blast.cgi?_PAGE_TYPE=BlastSearch&PROG_DEF=blastn&BLAST_PROG_DEF=megaBlast&SHOW_DEFAULTS=on&BLAST_SPEC=MicrobialGenomes): Performs a BLAST search for similar sequences from selected complete eukaryotic and prokaryotic genomes.

BLAST RefSeqGene (http://blast.ncbi.nlm.nih.gov/Blast.cgi?PROGRAM=blastn&BLAST_PROGRAMS=megaBlast&PAGE_TYPE=BlastSearch&SHOW_DEFAULTS=on&BLAST_SPEC=RefseqGene): Performs a BLAST search of the genomic sequences in the RefSeqGene/ (http://www.ncbi.nlm.nih.gov/refseq/rsg/) LRG set. The default display provides ready navigation to review alignments in the Graphics display.

BLAST Tutorials and Guides (http://blast.ncbi.nlm.nih.gov/Blast.cgi?CMD=Web&PAGE_TYPE=BlastDocs): This page links to a number of BLAST-related tutorials and guides, including a selection guide for BLAST algorithms, descriptions of BLAST output formats, explanations of the parameters for stand-alone BLAST, directions for setting up stand-alone BLAST on local machines and using the BLAST URL API.

Basic Local Alignment Search Tool (BLAST) (http://blast.ncbi.nlm.nih.gov/Blast.cgi): Finds regions of local similarity between biological sequences. The program compares nucleotide or protein sequences to sequence databases and calculates the statistical significance of matches. BLAST can be used to infer functional and evolutionary relationships between sequences as well as to help identify members of gene families.

Batch Entrez (http://www.ncbi.nlm.nih.gov/sites/batchentrez): Allows you to retrieve records from many Entrez databases by uploading a file of GI or accession numbers from the Nucleotide or Protein databases, or a file of unique identifiers from other Entrez databases. Search results can be saved in various formats directly to a local file on your computer.

BioAssay Services (http://pubchem.ncbi.nlm.nih.gov/assay/assay.cgi): Tools that summarize the biological test results in the PubChem database and provide alternative ways to view bioassay results and structure-activity relationships. Users also can download their analyses and data tables.

CDTree (http://www.ncbi.nlm.nih.gov/Structure/cdtree/cdtree.shtml): A stand-alone application for classifying protein sequences and investigating their evolutionary relationships. CDTree can import, analyze and update existing Conserved Domain (CDD) records and hierarchies, and also allows users to create their own. CDTree is tightly integrated with Entrez CDD and Cn3D, and allows users to create and update protein domain alignments.

COBALT (http://www.st-va.ncbi.nlm.nih.gov/tools/cobalt/re_cobalt.cgi?): COBALT is a protein multiple sequence alignment tool that finds a collection of pair wise constraints derived from conserved domain database, protein motif database, and sequence similarity, using RPS-BLAST, BLASTP, and PHI-BLAST.

Cn3D (http://www.ncbi.nlm.nih.gov/Structure/CN3D/cn3d.shtml): A stand-alone application for viewing 3-dimensional structures from NCBI's Entrez retrieval service. Cn3D runs on Windows, Macintosh, and UNIX and can be configured to receive data from most popular web browsers. Cn3D simultaneously displays structure, sequence, and alignment, and has powerful annotation and alignment editing features.

Coffee Break (http://www.ncbi.nlm.nih.gov/books/NBK2345/) Part of the NCBI Bookshelf, Coffee Break combines reports on recent biomedical discoveries with use of NCBI tools. Each report incorporates interactive tutorials that show how NCBI bioinformatics tools are used as a part of the research process.

Concise Microbial Protein BLAST (http://www.ncbi.nlm.nih.gov/genomes/prokhits.cgi) : A specialized BLAST service in which the queried database consists of all proteins from complete microbial (prokaryotic) genomes. NCBI has precalculated clusters of similar proteins at the genus-level and one representative is chosen from each cluster in order to reduce the dataset, thereby reducing search time and providing a broader taxonomic view.

Conserved Domain Architecture Retrieval Tool (CDART) (http://www.ncbi.nlm.nih.gov/Structure/lexington/lexington.cgi?cmd=rps): Displays the functional domains that make up a given protein sequence. It lists proteins with similar domain architectures and can retrieve proteins that contain particular combinations of domains.

Conserved Domain Search Service (CD Search) (http://www.ncbi.nlm.nih.gov/Structure/cdd/wrpsb.cgi): Identifies the conserved domains present in a protein sequence. CD-Search uses RPS-BLAST (Reverse Position-Specific BLAST) to compare a query sequence against position-specific score matrices that have been prepared from conserved domain alignments present in the Conserved Domain Database (CDD).

Digital Differential Display (DDD) (http://www.ncbi.nlm.nih.gov/UniGene/ddd.cgi): A tool for comparing EST profiles in order to identify genes with significantly different expression levels.

E-Bench (http://www.ncbi.nlm.nih.gov/Class/wheeler/eutils/eu.cgi): This interactive tool allows users to build E-utility URLs, either from a form or by hand, and then view their raw output. The tool provides a simple environment for testing E-utility URLs before including them in applications.

E-Utilities (http://www.ncbi.nlm.nih.gov/books/NBK25501/): Tools that provide access to data within NCBI's Entrez system outside of the regular web query interface. They provide a method of automating Entrez tasks within software applications. Each utility performs a specialized retrieval task, and can be used simply by writing a specially formatted URL.

Ebot (http://www.ncbi.nlm.nih.gov/Class/PowerTools/eutils/ebot/ebot.cgi): A tool that allows users to construct an E-utility analysis pipeline using an online form, and then generates a Perl script to execute the pipeline.

Electronic PCR (e-PCR) (http://www.ncbi.nlm.nih.gov/tools/epcr/): A computational procedure that is used to identify sequence tagged sites (STSs) within DNA sequences. e-PCR looks for potential STSs in DNA sequences by searching for subsequences that closely match the PCR primers and have the correct order, orientation, and spacing that could represent the PCR primers used to generate known STSs.

Frequency-weighted Link (FLink) (http://www.ncbi.nlm.nih.gov/Structure/flink/flink.cgi): FLink is a tool that enables you to link from a group of records in a source database to a ranked list of associated records in a destination database based on frequency-weighted statistics.

Gene Expression Omnibus (GEO) BLAST (http://www.ncbi.nlm.nih.gov/Structure/flink/flink.cgi): Tool for aligning a query sequence (nucleotide or protein) to GenBank sequences included on microarray or SAGE platforms in the GEO database.

Gene Plot (http://www.ncbi.nlm.nih.gov/sutils/geneplot.cgi): A tool for pair wise comparison of two prokaryotic genomes that displays pairs of protein homologs that are symmetrical best hits between the two genomes.

Genetic Codes (http://www.ncbi.nlm.nih.gov/Taxonomy/taxonomyhome.html/index.cgi?chapter=cgencodes): Displays the genetic codes for organisms in the Taxonomy database in tables and on a taxonomic tree.

Genome BLAST (http://blast.ncbi.nlm.nih.gov/Blast.cgi): This tool compares nucleotide or protein sequences to genomic sequence databases and calculates the statistical significance of matches using the Basic Local Alignment Search Tool (BLAST) algorithm.

Genome ProtMap (http://www.ncbi.nlm.nih.gov/sutils/protmap.cgi): Genome ProtMap maps each protein from a COG, or in the case of viruses a VOG, back to its genome, and displays all the genomic segments coding for members of this particular group of related proteins. The view can be shifted to focus on an adjacent COG/VOG, and clusters can be searched by name, protein gi, or gene locus tag.

Genome Remapping Service (http://www.ncbi.nlm.nih.gov/genome/tools/remap): NCBI's Remap tool allows users to project annotation data and convert locations of features from one genomic assembly to another or to RefSeqGene sequences through a base by base analysis. Options are provided to adjust the stringency of remapping, and summary results are displayed on the web page. Full results can be downloaded for viewing in NCBI's Genome Workbench graphical viewer, and annotation data for the remapped features, as well as summary data, is also available for download.

Genome Workbench (http://www.ncbi.nlm.nih.gov/tools/gbench/): An integrated application for viewing and analyzing sequence data. With Genome Workbench, you can view data in publically available sequence databases at NCBI, and mix these data with your own data.

LinkOut (http://www.ncbi.nlm.nih.gov/projects/linkout/): A service that allows third parties to link directly from PubMed and other Entrez database records to relevant web-accessible resources beyond the Entrez system. Examples of LinkOut resources include full-text publications, biological databases, consumer health information and research tools.

Map Viewer (http://www.ncbi.nlm.nih.gov/mapview/): Provides special browsing capabilities of maps and assembled sequences for a subset of organisms. You can view and search an organism's complete genome, display maps, and zoom into progressively greater levels of detail, down to the sequence data for a region of interest.

NCBI News (http://www.ncbi.nlm.nih.gov/news/): Provides information on new and updated resources and NCBI research and development projects. The News site contains feature articles highlighting services, resource features and tools, as well as frequent postings describing important announcements regarding key datasets and services of interest to the user community. Links to NCBI's social media sites along and a list of available RSS feeds and Email listservs are provided.

NCBI Toolbox (http://www.ncbi.nlm.nih.gov/IEB/ToolBox/index.cgi): A set of software and data exchange specifications used by NCBI to produce portable, modular software for molecular biology. The software in the Toolbox is primarily designed to read records in

Abstract Syntax Notation 1 (ASN.1) format, an International Standards Organization (ISO) data representation format.

OSIRIS (http://www.ncbi.nlm.nih.gov/projects/SNP/osiris/): A public domain quality assurance software package that facilitates the assessment of multiplex short tandem repeat (STR) DNA profiles based on laboratory-specific protocols. OSIRIS evaluates the raw electrophoresis data using an independently derived mathematically-based sizing algorithm. It offers two new peak quality measures - fit level and sizing residual. It can be customized to accommodate laboratory-specific signatures such as background noise settings, customized naming conventions and additional internal laboratory controls.

Open Reading Frame Finder (ORF Finder) (http://www.ncbi.nlm.nih.gov/gorf/gorf.html): A graphical analysis tool that finds all open reading frames in a user's sequence or in a sequence already in the database. Sixteen different genetic codes can be used. The deduced amino acid sequence can be saved in various formats and searched against protein databases using BLAST.

PSSM Viewer (http://www.ncbi.nlm.nih.gov/Class/Structure/pssm/pssm_viewer.cgi): Allows users to display, sort, subset and download position-specific score matrices (PSSMs) either from CDD records or from Position Specific Iterated (PSI)-BLAST protein searches. The tool also can align a query protein to the PSSM and highlight positions of high conservation.

Phenotype-Genotype Integrator (PheGenI) (http://www.ncbi.nlm.nih.gov/gap/phegeni): Supports finding human phenotype/genotype relationships with queries by phenotype, chromosome location, gene, and SNP identifiers. Currently includes information from dbGaP, the NHGRI GWAS Catalog, and GTeX, which displays results on the genome, on sequence, or in tables for download.

Primer-BLAST (http://www.ncbi.nlm.nih.gov/tools/primer-blast/): The Primer-BLAST tool uses Primer3 to design PCR primers to a sequence template. The potential products are then automatically analyzed with a BLAST search against user specified databases, to check the specificity to the target intended.

ProSplign (http://www.ncbi.nlm.nih.gov/sutils/static/prosplign/prosplign.html): A utility for computing alignment of proteins to genomic nucleotide sequence. It is based on a variation of the Needleman Wunsch global alignment algorithm and specifically accounts for introns and splice signals. Due to this algorithm, ProSplign is accurate in determining splice sites and tolerant to sequencing errors.

PubChem Power User Gateway (PUG) (http://pubchem.ncbi.nlm.nih.gov/pug/pughelp.html): PUG provides access to PubChem services via a programmatic interface. PUG allows users to download data, initiate chemical structure searches, standardize chemical structures and interact with the E-utilities. PUG can be accessed using either standard URLs or via SOAP.

PubChem Standardization Service (http://pubchem.ncbi.nlm.nih.gov/standardize/standardize.cgi): Standardization, in PubChem terminology, is the processing of chemical structures in the same way used to create PubChem Compound records from contributors' original structures. This service lets users see how PubChem would handle any structure they would like to submit.

PubChem Structure Search (http://pubchem.ncbi.nlm.nih.gov/search/search.cgi): PubChem Structure Search allows the PubChem Compound Database to be queried by chemical structure or chemical structure pattern. The PubChem Sketcher allows a query to be drawn manually. Users may also specify the structural query input by PubChem Compound Identifier (CID), SMILES, SMARTS, InChI, Molecular Formula, or by upload of a supported structure file format.

PubMed Clinical Queries (http://www.ncbi.nlm.nih.gov/pubmed/clinical): A specialized PubMed search form targeted to clinicians and health services researchers. The page simplifies searching by clinical study category, finding systematic reviews and searching the medical genetics literature.

PubMed Commons (http://www.ncbi.nlm.nih.gov/pubmedcommons): A commenting system serving as a forum for open constructive criticism and discussion of scientific issues. All authors of publications in PubMed are eligible to become members and share opinions and information about publications listed in PubMed.

PubMed Tutorials (http://www.nlm.nih.gov/bsd/disted/pubmedtutorial/cover.html): A collection of web and flash tutorials on PubMed searching and linking, saving searches in MyNCBI, using MeSH and other PubMed services.

Related Structures (http://structure.ncbi.nlm.nih.gov/Structure/cblast/cblast.cgi): The Related Structures tool allows users to find 3D structures from the Molecular Modelling Database (MMDB) that are similar in sequence to a query protein. Although the query protein may not yet have a resolved structure, the 3D shape of a similar protein sequence can shed light on the putative shape and biological function of the query protein.

SNP Database Specialized Search Tools (http://www.ncbi.nlm.nih.gov/projects/SNP/): A variety of tools are available for searching the SNP database, allowing search by genotype, method, population, submitter, markers and sequence similarity using BLAST.

These are linked under ""Search"" on the left side bar of the dbSNP main page.

Sequence Viewer (http://www.ncbi.nlm.nih.gov/projects/sviewer/): Provides a configurable graphical display of a nucleotide or protein sequence and features that have been annotated on that sequence. In addition to use on NCBI sequence database pages, this viewer is available as an embeddable webpage component. Detailed documentation including an API Reference guide is available for developers wishing to embed the viewer in their own pages.

Splign (http://www.ncbi.nlm.nih.gov/sutils/splign/splign.cgi): A utility for computing cDNA-to-Genomic sequence alignments. It is based on a variation of the Needleman-Wunsch global alignment algorithm and specifically accounts for introns and splice signals. Due to this algorithm, Splign is accurate in determining splice sites and tolerant to sequencing errors.

TaxPlot (http://www.ncbi.nlm.nih.gov/sutils/taxik2.cgi): A tool for comparing genomes on the basis of the protein sequences they encode. To use TaxPlot, one selects a reference genome and two species for comparison. Pre-computed BLAST results are then used to plot a point for each predicted protein in the reference genome, based on the best alignment with proteins in each of the two genomes being compared.

Taxonomy Browser (http://www.ncbi.nlm.nih.gov/Taxopnomy/Browser/wwwtax.cgi?mode=Root): Supports searching the taxonomy tree using partial taxonomic names, common names, wild cards and phonetically similar names. For each taxonomic node, the tool provides links to all data in Entrez for that node, displays the lineage, and provides links to external sites related to the node.

Taxonomy Common Tree (http://www.ncbi.nlm.nih.gov/Taxonomy/CommonTree/wwwcmt.cgi): Generates a taxonomic tree for a selected group of organisms. Users can upload a file of taxonomy IDs or names, or they can enter names or IDs directly.

Taxonomy Statistics (http://www.ncbi.nlm.nih.gov/Taxonomy/taxonomyhome.html/index.cgi?chapter=STATISTICS&uncultured=hide&unspecified=hide): Displays the number of taxonomic nodes in the database for a given rank and date of inclusion.

Taxonomy Status Reports (http://www.ncbi.nlm.nih.gov/Taxonomy/TaxIdentifier/tax_identifier.cgi): Displays the current status of a set of taxonomic nodes or IDs.

Variation Reporter (http://www.ncbi.nlm.nih.gov/variation/tools/reporter): A tool designed to search human sequence variation data by location and to report matching variants found in dbSNP, dbVar and ClinVar. Individual variations or batch files can be submitted in HGVS, GVF, VCS or BED formats. Related information will be reported in a downloadable table containing variation identifiers, nucleotide and cytogenetic band locations on various genomic assemblies, allele type and minor allele frequencies, predicted functional consequences (missense, nonsense, frameshift, splice site, etc.), reported clinical significance, and relevant citations. For variants not present in the NCBI variation resources, the tool computes molecular consequences based on RefSeq transcripts.

Variation Viewer (http://www.ncbi.nlm.nih.gov/variation/view): A genomic browser to search and view genomic variations listed in dbSNP, dbVar, and ClinVar databases. Searches can be performed using chromosomal location, gene symbol, phenotype, or variant IDs from dbSNP and dbVar. The browser enables exploration of results in a dynamic graphical sequence viewer with annotated tables of variations.

VecScreen (http://www.ncbi.nlm.nih.gov/tools/vecscreen): A system for quickly identifying segments of a nucleic acid sequence that may be of vector origin. VecScreen searches a query sequence for segments that match any sequence in a specialized non-redundant vector database (UniVec).

Vector Alignment Search Tool (VAST) (http://www.ncbi.nlm.nih.gov/structure/VAST/vast.html): A computer algorithm that identifies similar protein 3-dimensional structures. Structure neighbours for every structure in MMDB are pre-computed and accessible via links on the MMDB Structure Summary pages. These neighbours can be used to identify distant homologs that cannot be recognized by sequence comparison alone.

Viral Genotyping Tool (http://www.ncbi.nlm.nih.gov/projects/genotyping/formpage.cgi): This tool helps identify the genotype of a viral sequence. A window is slid along the query sequence and each window is compared by BLAST to each of the reference sequences for a particular virus.

How to submit sequences, download, retrieve, find display etc. from NCBI

1) Save text searches and set up automated searches with E-mailed results
2) Find bioassays in which a given drug is active
3) Find bioassays that test a particular disease or protein target
4) Submit data to NCBI
5) Download NCBI Software
6) Submit sequence data to NCBI

7) Retrieve all sequences for an organism or taxon
8) Find the function of a gene or gene product
9) View all SNPs associated with a gene
10) Find genes associated with a phenotype or disease
11) Find expression patterns
12) Obtain genomic sequence for/near a gene, marker, transcript or protein
13) Find human variations associated with a phenotype or disease (clinical association)
14) Convert feature coordinates between genomic assemblies
15) View/download features around an object or between two objects on a chromosome
16) Compare protein homologs between two microbial genomes
17) Find sequenced genomes, including those in progress, for a taxonomic group
18) Download the complete genome for an organism
19) Display genomic annotation graphically
20) Determine conserved synteny between the genomes of two organisms
21) Find a homolog for a gene in another organism
22) Find articles about a topic similar to that in a given article
23) Obtain the full text of an article
24) View the 3D structure of a protein

25) Find a curated version of a sequence record (NCBI Reference Sequence)
26) Align two or more 3D structures to a given structure
27) Find published information on a gene or sequence
28) Find transcript sequences for a gene
29) Link from an object on a map to another resource
30) Run BLAST software on a local computer
31) Submit multiple query sequences in a single BLAST search
32) Design PCR primers and check them for specificity
33) Automate BLAST searches performed on NCBI servers
34) Compare your sequence to the RefSeqGene/LRG standard
35) Find the complete taxonomic lineage for an organism
36) Generate a Common Tree for a set of taxa
37) Find out what's new at NCBI
38) Learn about an NCBI resource
39) Learn about the basics of molecular biology and bioinformatics
40) View a mutation site in a 3D structure
41) View genotype frequency data for a gene, disease or short genetic variation
42) Download a large, custom set of records from NCBI

Source: (http://www.ncbi.nlm.nih.gov/guide/all/)

Chapter 6: BIOLOGICAL DATABASES ON THE WEB

Categories of Databases

1) Bibliography
2) Sequences (DNA, protein)
3) Genomics
4) Protein domain/family
5) Mutation/polymorphism
6) Proteomics (2D gel, MS)
7) 3D structure
8) Metabolic networks
9) Regulatory networks

Primary sequence databases: The **International Nucleotide Sequence Database** (INSD) (http://www.insdc.org/) consists of the following databases.

1) DDBJ (DNA Data Bank of Japan) (http://www.ddbj.nig.ac.jp/Welcome-e.html)
2) EMBL Nucleotide Sequence DB (**European Molecular Biology Laboratory**) (http://en.wikipedia.org/wiki/European_Molecular_Biology_Laboratory)
3) GenBank (**National Center for Biotechnology Information**) (http://en.wikipedia.org/wiki/National_Center_for_Biotechnology_Information)

The three databases, DDBJ (Japan), GenBank (USA) and EMBL Nucleotide Sequence Database (Europe), are repositories for nucleotide sequence data from all organisms. All three databases accept nucleotide sequence submissions, and then exchange new and updated data on a daily basis to achieve optimal synchronization between them. These three databases are primary databases, as they house original sequence data.

Meta Databases

In reality a Meta database can be considered a database of databases, rather than any one integration project or technology. They collect data from different sources and usually make them available in new and more convenient form, or with an emphasis on a particular disease or organism.

Entrez[2] (http://en.wikipedia.org/wiki/Entrez) (**National Center for Biotechnology Information**) (http://en.wikipedia.org/wiki/National_Center_for_Biotechnology_Information)

euGenes (**Indiana University**) (http://en.wikipedia.org/wiki/Indiana_University_Bloomington)

GeneCards (**Weizmann Inst.**) (http://en.wikipedia.org/wiki/Weizmann_Institute_of_Science)

SOURCE (**Stanford University**) (http://en.wikipedia.org/wiki/stanford_university)

mGen containing four of the world biggest databases GenBank, Refseq, EMBL and DDBJ - easy and simple program friendly gene extraction

Bioinformatics Harvester [3] http://en.wikipedia.org/wiki/Bioinformatic_Harvester (**Karlsruhe Institute of Technology**) (http://en.wikipedia.org/wiki/Karlsruhe_Institute_of_Technology) - Integrating 26 major protein/gene resources.

MetaBase [4] (http://en.wikipedia.org/MetaBase) (**KOBIC**) (http://en.wikipedia.org/KOBIC) - A user contributed database of biological databases.

ConsensusPathDB (http://en.wikipedia.org/wiki/ConsensusPathDB) - A molecular functional interaction database, integrating information from 12 other databases.

Pathogen Portal A repository linking to the **Bioinformatics Resource Centers** (http://en.wikipedia.org/wiki/Bioinformatics_Resource_Centers) (BRCs) sponsored by the National Institute of Allergy and Infectious Diseases (NIAID)

BioGraph (**University of Antwerp** (http://en.wikipedia.org/wiki/University_of_Antwerp), **Vlaams Instituut voor Biotechnologie** (http://en.wikipedia.org/wiki/Vlaams_Institute_voor_Biotechnology) A knowledge discovery service based on the integration of over 20 heterogeneous biomedical knowledge bases.

Genome Databases

These databases collect organism genome sequences, annotate and analyze them, and provide public access. Some add curation of experimental literature to improve computed annotations. These databases may hold many species genomes, or a single model organism genome.

Human Genome Databases

a) Draft Human Genome @ NCBI (http://www.ncbi.nlm.nih.gov/genome/guide/human/)

b) Draft Human Genome @ UCSC (http://genome.ucsc.edu/)

c) **Ensembl** (http://www.ensembl.org/index.html) - automatically annotated human genome. **The Data Mining (Mart View) is cool and very useful!**

d) GDB (http://gdbwww.gdb.org/) - Genome Database

e) Mammalian Gene Collection (http://mgc.nci.nih.gov/) - full-length (open reading frame) sequences for human and mouse

f) STACK (http://www.sanbi.ac.za/Dbases.html) - Sequence Tag Alignment and Consensus Knowledgebase

g) GeneCards (http://bioinformatics.weizmann.ac.il/cards/) - human genes, proteins and diseases

Databases of other Organisms

a) GOLD (http://wit.integratedgenomics.com/GOLD/) - Genomes on line Database, information on complete and ongoing genome projects

b) TIGR Comprehensive Microbial Resource (http://www.jcvi.org/cms/research/past-projects/cmr/overview/)

c) TIGR Microbial Database (http://www.jcvi.org/cms/research/projects/tdb/overview/)

d) The Proteome Databases (https://portal.biobase-international.com/cgi-bin/_portal/_login.cgi) - yeast, worm, & human, good annotation

e) Saccharomyces Genome Database (http://genome-www.stanford.edu/saccharomyces/)

f) WormBase (http://www.wormbase.org/) - C. elegans

g) FlyBase (http://flybase.org/)

h) Berkeley Drosophila Genome Project (http://www.fruitfly.org/)

i) Mouse Genome Informatics (http://www.informatics.jax.org/)

j) The Arabidopsis Information Resource (http://www.arabidopsis.org/)

k) ZFIN (http://zfin.org/) - Zebra fish Information Network

l) DictyBase (http://dictybase.org/) - Dictyostelium discoideum

m) EcoGene (http://bmb.med.miami.edu/EcoGene/EcoWeb/) - E. coli

n) HIV sequence database (http://www.hiv.lanl.gov/content/index)

Bioinformatics Harvester: (http://en.wikipedia.org/wiki/Bioinformatic_Harvester)

1) **SNPedia** (http://en.wikipedia.org/wiki/SNPedia)

2) CAMERA (http://camera.calit2.net/index.php/) Resource for microbial genomics and metagenomics

3) EcoCyc (http://ecocyc.org) a database that describes the genome and the biochemical machinery of the **model organism** (http://en.wikipedia.org/wiki/Model_organism) E. coli K-12

4) **Ensembl** (http://en.wikipedia.org/wiki/Ensemble) provides automatic annotation databases for human, mouse, other **vertebrate** (http://en.wikipedia.org/wiki/Vertebrate) and **eukaryote** (http://en.wikipedia.org/wiki/Eukaryote) genomes.

5) Flybase, genome of the **model organism Drosophila melanogaster** (http://en.wikipedia.org/wiki/Drosophila_melanogaster)

6) **Saccharomyces Genome Database** (http://en.wikipedia.org/wiki/Saccharomyces_Genome_Database), genome of the **yeast** (http://en.wikipedia.org/wiki/Yeast) model organism.

7) **Xenbase** (http://en.wikipedia.org/wiki/Xenbase), genome of the **model organism** *Xenopus tropicalis* and *Xenopus laevis*.

8) Wormbase, genome of the **model organism Caenorhabditis elegans** (http://en.wikipedia.org/wiki/Caenorhabditis_elegans)

9) **Zebra fish Information Network** (http://en.wikipedia.org/wiki/Zebrafish_Information_Network), genome of this **fish** (http://en.wikipedia.org/wiki/Fish) model organism.

10) TAIR (http://arabidopsis.org/), the Arabidopsis Information Resource.

11) **UCSC Malaria Genome Browser** (http://en.wikipedia.org/wiki/UCSC_Malaria_Genome_Browser), genome of malaria causing species (**Plasmodium falciparumata** and others)

12) Formidable ant genome database provides blast search and sequences.

13) Vector Base **The NIAID Bioinformatics Resource Center for Invertebrate Vectors of Human Pathogens** (http://en.wikipedia.org/wiki/Vectorbase).

Protein sequence Databases (http://en.wikipedia.org.wiki/Protein_Sequence)

1) **UniProt** (http://en.wikipedia.org/wiki/UniProt) : Universal **Protein** Resource (UniProt Consortium) : **EBI** (http://en.wikipedia.org/wiki/European_Bioinformatics_Institute), Expasy, **PIR** (http://en.wikipedia.org/wiki/Protein_Information_Resource)

2) PIR Protein Information Resource (**Georgetown University Medical Centre -GUMC**)

3) Swiss-Prot : Protein Knowledgebase (**Swiss Institute of Bioinformatics**)

4) PROSITE Database of **Protein Families** and Domains

5) DIP Database of Interacting Proteins (**Univ. of California**)

6) Pfam Protein families database of alignments and HMMs (Sanger Institute)

7) BIND Bimolecular Interaction Network Database

8) NetPro

Metabolic pathway Databases (http://en.wikipedia.org/wiki/Metabolic_pathway)

1) BioCyc Database Collection including **EcoCyc** (http://en.wikipedia.org/wiki/EcoCyc) and **MetaCyc** (http://en.wikipedia.org/wiki/MetaCyc)

2) KEGG PATHWAY Database [12] (http://www.genome.jp/kegg/pathway.html) (**Univ. of Kyoto** - http://en.wikipedia.org/wiki/Kyoto University)

3) **MANET database [13]** (http://www.manet.uiuc.edu/) (University of Illinois - http://en.wikipedia.org/wiki/University_of_Illinois_at_Urbana%E2%80%93Champaign)

4) **Reactome[14]** (http://www.reactome.org/) **Cold Spring Harbor Laboratory** (http://en.wikipedia.org/wiki/Cold_Spring_Harbor_Laboratory), **EBI** (http://en.wikipedia.org/wiki/European_Bioinformatics_Institute), Gene Ontology Consortium)

5) Microarray databases

6) Array Express (http://www.ebi.ac.uk/arrayexpress/) (**European Bioinformatics Institute**)

7) Gene Expression Omnibus (http://www.ncbi.nlm.nih.gov/geo/) (**National Centre for Biotechnology Information**)

8) GPX (Scottish Centre for Genomic Technology and Informatics)

9) Stanford Microarray Database (http://smd.princeton.edu/) (SMD) (**Stanford University**)

10) PCR / real time PCR **primer** (http://en.wikipedia.org/wiki/Primer%28molecular_biology%29) databases

11) PathoOligoDB (http://www.pathooligodb.com/) : A free QPCR oligo database for pathogens

12) **DiProDB** A database to collect and analyse thermodynamic, structural and other dinucleotide properties.

13) NCBI-UniGene (http://www.ncbi.nlm.nih.gov/unigene) (National Centre for Biotechnology Information)

14) **Oncogenomic databases** A compilation of databases that serve for cancer research.

15) OMIM Inherited Diseases (http://www.ncbi.nlm.nih.gov/omim) (Online Mendelian Inheritance in Man)

16) SNPSTR database A database of SNPSTRs - compound genetic markers consisting of a microsatellite (STR) and one tightly linked SNP - in human, mouse, rat, dog and chicken.

17) TreeBASE (http://treebase.org/treebase-web/home.html;jsessionid=2ADB6726D90770B69ACA9790150F9A83) - An open-access database of phylogenetic trees and the data behind them.

General nucleotide databases

a) EMBL (Hinxton, UK) (http://www.ebi.ac.uk./ebi_docs/embl_db/ebi/ topembl.html)

b) Genbank (Bethesda, USA) (http://www.ncbi.nlm.nih.gov/Genbank/ GenbankSearch.html)

c) DDBJ (Mishima, Japan) (http://www.ddbj.nig.ac.jp/)

General protein databases

a) SWISS-PROT (Geneva, Switzerland) (http://web.expasy.org/docs/swiss-prot_guideline.html)

b) PROSITE (Geneva, Switzerland) (http://prosite.expasy.org/)

c) PRODOM (Lyon, France) (http://prodom.prabi.fr/prodom/current/html/home.php)

d) PIR (Washington DC, USA) (http://pir.georgetown.edu/pirwww/)

e) PDB (San Diego, USA) (http://www.rcsb.org/pdb/home/home.do)

Specialized databases

a) **Prokaryotes**
   i. GenoList (Paris, France) (http://genolist.pasteur.fr/)
   ii. HGT-DB (Tarragona, Spain) (http://genomes.urv.es/HGT-DB/)
   iii. Genome division at NCBI (Bethesda, USA) (ftp://ftp.ncbi.nih.gov/genbank/genomes/Bacteria/)
   iv. Genome Information Broker (Mishima, Japan) (http://gib.genes.nig.ac.jp/)

b) **Eukaryotes**
   i. GDB (Baltimore, USA) (http://www.gdb.org/)
   ii. MGI (Bar Harbor, USA) (http://www.informatics.jax.org/)
   iii. IMGT (Montpellier, France) (http://imgt.cines.fr/)
   iv. OMIM (Bethesda, USA) (http://www.ncbi.nlm.nih.gov/omim)
   v. Ensembl (Hinxton, UK) (http://www.ensembl.org/index.html)

c) **Complete genomes projects**
   i. Genomes OnLine Database (Chicago, USA) (https://gold.jgi-psf.org/)

d) **Gene expression**
   i. Sage GENIE (Bethesda, USA) (http://cgap.nci.nih.gov/SAGE/)

Introduction to Molecular Biology Databases
(http://www.ebi.ac.uk/swissprot/Publications/mbd1.html):

Although not technically a directory, this article, written in 1999, is a very helpful introduction to the major databases, including many of the organism specific ones that are outside the scope of this guide - A good starting place for the non-specialist.

Chapter 7: TECHNIQUES OF SEARCHING AND ACCESS TO WEB RESOURCES

Searching the Web

Why should I use Web sites?

a) Web sites are a great source of information about organizations and institutions and government generated statistics and reports.

b) They are also useful for comparing popular perceptions to scientific research findings. The free Web contains a vast collection of resources - some worthwhile.

How do I find good Web sites?

Start by reviewing the Web Searching Guide (http://libguides.library.cofc.edu/websearching) for expert advice on the best search engines--both general and specialized.

Of particular note are the "academic web resources" (http://libguides.library.cofc.edu/ websearching) which includes a link to Google Scholar (http://scholar.google.co.in/) or (http://www.scholar.google.com) and other search engines that focus on, credible, scholarly information available on the Web.

No single search engine comes close to indexing the entire Web. Be sure to search two or three different search engines if you want to be thorough.

For every major, most minors, and other special topics, librarians have put together a subject guide (http://www.libguides.library.cofc.edu/content.php) with links to quality sites.

For quick and mainly free Web-based reference information such as encyclopedias, check out the on-line reference page (http://libguides.library.cofc.edu/ reference).

Web Access to Bioinformatics Resources

a) http://www.flickr.com/photos/24801682@N08/5110719318/
b) http://www.flickr.com/photos/24801682@N08/
c) http://creativecommons.org/licenses/by/2.0/

Web access to bioinformatics resources maintained by the platform: PipeAlign (file:///I:\PipeAlign), SRS (file:///I:\SRS) and EMBOSS (file://I:\EMBOSS) web interfaced software are made available for all and without any limit of use.

Access to remote bioinformatics resources that have been selected by the platform: The platform carries out a technical watch on bioinformatics resources on a wide-range of topics. Please visit our page of selected resources (http://bips.u.strasbg.fr/en/watchselection.php) to carry out tasks such as primer design, GO and pathway analysis, cross information using Venn diagrams, draw genomic circular maps, display read alignments on the genome, carry out a transcriptional similarity search in a pharmacogenomic database.

Access to computing servers for high-throughput bioinformatics: Computing servers of the bioinformatics platform are using the Linux/Unix operating system (OS). Connection to the servers can be carried out using a Ssh (secure shell) program. The connexion gives access to a personal zone which is secured by a login and password. Using the servers requires mastering the Linux/Unix OS, to know how to run command line programs and how to submit jobs to queues (qsub). The platform maintains bioinformatics databases (Swissprot, Trembl, PDB, transcripts ...) that can be accessed by SRS (Sequence Retrieval System) using the getz program. Further command-line programs (read mappers, blast tools, R ...) are also installed on the servers and shared between users. Server resources are limited (disk space, CPU and RAM) and good usage rules apply, such as deleting old files, monitoring RAM and submitting jobs to queues n order to dispatch CPU load on different machines. Every user is responsible for his information processing and should not do anything that could be a prejudice against the informatics network and the server integrity.

If you wish to have an access and a work environment on the servers, please make a request to us.

Technical Requirements: In order to access the platform servers you will need a personal computer (Windows or Linux PC, MAC) an internet connection; a connexion software (ssh) installed on your computer; a user account on the server (authenticated by login/password).

Core Bioinformatics Organizations

Each of these organizations provides access to a wealth of bioinformatics databases, software and reference literature. They can all be accessed freely over the web and do not require a subscription.

Important websites that all biologists should know for Biocomputing & Analysis

a) NCBI (http://www.ncbi.nlm.nih.gov/) The National Center for Biotechnology Information is a central provider of bioinformatics resources and services in the US. Their extensive website provides guides and reference to all the services they support.

b) EMBL/EBI (http://www.ebi.ac.uk/) The European Molecular Biology Laboratory and European Bioinformatics Institute These databases provide access to all the bioinformatics data held be EMBL/EBI.

c) The Canadian Bioinformatics Resource (http://www.cbr.nrc.ca/).

d) SwissProt/ExPASy (Swiss Bioinformatics Resource) (http://expasy.cbr.nrc.ca/sprot/) PDB (The Protein Databank) (http://www.rcsb.org/PDB/).

e) DDBJ (http://www.ddbj.nig.ac.jp/) The DNA Data bank of Japan provides access to databases, software tools and documentation provided by the DDBJ.

f) (http://libguides.bodleian.ox.ac.uk/content.php?pid=264386&sid=2187124) The following list of web resources was compiled by Prof. Bill Noble. Contact (cleslie@cs.columbia.edu) for any queries regarding URL.

Bioinformatics Web Sites & General Biocomputing Services

This list contains pointers to various information sources in computational molecular biology. This is not an exhaustive listing and it only reflects what we found useful here at PBIL.

a) ReNaBi (France) (http://www.renabi.fr/)

b) GenomeNet WWW Server (Kyoto, Japan) (http://www.genome.jp/)

c) Center for Information Biology (Mishima, Japan) (http://www.cib.nig.ac.jp/)

d) Pôle Bio-Informatique Lyonnais (Lyon, France) (http://doua.prabi.fr/)

e) European Bioinformatics Institute (Hinxton, UK) (http://www.ebi.ac.uk/)

f) DKFZ Theoretical Bioinformatics (Heidelberg, Germany) (http://ibios.dkfz.de/tbi/)

g) ExPASy Molecular Biology Server (Geneva, Switzerland) (http://www.expasy.org/)

h) National Center for Genome Resources (Santa Fe, USA) (http://www.ncgr.org/)

i) National Center for Biotechnology Information (Bethesda, USA) (http://www.ncbi.nlm.nih.gov/)

j) Swiss Institute for Experimental Cancer Research (Lausanne, Switzerland) (http://www.ch.embnet.org/)

k) Mobyle Portal at Pasteur Institute (Paris, France) (http://mobyle.pasteur.fr/cgi-bin/portal.py)

Retrieval systems

a) DBGET (Kyoto, Japan) (http://www.genome.jp/dbget/dbget.html)

b) WWW-Query (Lyon, France) (http://pbil.univ-lyon1.fr/search/query_fam.php)

c) Public SRS servers (Cambridge, UK) (http://downloads.lionbio.co.uk/publicsrs.html)

Alignments and similarity searches on-line

Similarity searches

a) BLAST at NCBI (Bethesda, USA) (http://blast.ncbi.nlm.nih.gov/Blast.cgi)

b) BLAST at PBIL (Lyon, France) (http://pbil.univ-lyon1.fr/BLAST/blast.html)

c) BLAST at ISREC (Lausanne, Switzerland) (http://www.ch.embnet.org/error.html)

d) WU-BLAST at EMBL (Hinxton, UK) (http://www.ebi.ac.uk/blast2/)

e) FASTA and SSEARCH at EBI (Hinxton, UK) (http://www.ebi.ac.uk/Tools/sss/fasta/)

Pair wise alignments

a) LFASTA at PBIL (Lyon, France) *Local alignments* (http://doua.prabi.fr/software/lfasta)

b) SIM4 at PBIL (Lyon, France) *Aligns cDNA and genomic DNA* (http://doua.prabi.fr/software/sim4)

c) WISE2 at Pasteur (Paris, France) *Aligns protein and genomic DNA* (http://doua.prabi.fr/software/sim4)

d) SIM at ExPASy (Geneva, Switzerland) (http://web.expasy.org/sim/)

e) BLAST two sequences at NCBI (Bethesda, USA) (http://blast.ncbi.nlm.nih.gov/Blast.cgi?PAGE_TYPE= BlastSearch&PROG_DEF=blastn&BLAST_PROG_DEF= megaBlast&BLAST_SPEC=blast2seq)

f) SIM, GAP, NAP and LAP at Michigan Tech. Univ. (Houghton, USA) (http://genome.cs.mtu.edu/align/align.html)

g) JAligner (Alexandria, Egypt) *Java implementation of the Smith-Waterman algorithm*

Multiple alignments

a) BLAST+ClustalW at EMBL (Heidelberg, Germany) *Multiple alignment of homologous sequences detected by BLAST* (http://dove.embl-heidelberg.de/ Blast2e/)

b) ClustalW2 at EBI (Hinxton, UK) (http://www.ebi.ac.uk/ Tools/msa/clustalw2/) *Display and edit alignments with JalView* (http://www.ebi.ac.uk/~michele/jalview/contents.html)

c) ClustalW at DDBJ (Mishima, Japan) (http://www.ddbj.nig.ac.jp/searches-e.html)

d) ClustalW at GenomeNet (Kyoto, Japan) (http://align.genome.jp/)

e) ClustalW at Pasteur (Paris, France) (http://mobyle.pasteur.fr/ cgi-bin/portal.py?# forms::clustalw-multialign)

f) ClustalW at PBIL (Lyon, France) (https://npsa-prabi.ibcp.fr/ cgi-bin/npsa_ automat.pl?page=npsa_clustalw.html) *Colored alignments and secondary structure predictions*

g) Multalin at PBIL (Lyon, France) (https://npsa-prabi.ibcp.fr/cgi-bin/npsa_automat.pl?page=npsa_multalin.html) *Colored alignments and secondary structure predictions*

h) Multalin at INRA (Toulouse, France) *Colored alignments* (http://multalin.toulouse.inra.fr/multalin/)

i) MAFFT at MiB (Fukuoka, Japan) (http://align.bmr.kyushu-u.ac.jp/mafft/online/server/)

j) MUSCLE at EBI (Hinxton, UK). (http://www.ebi.ac.uk/muscle/)

k) DIALIGN2 at Pasteur (Paris, France) (http://mobyle.pasteur.fr/cgi-bin/portal.py?#forms::dialign)

l) DIALIGN2 at BiBiServ (Bielefeld, Germany) (http://bibiserv.techfak.uni-bielefeld.de/dialign/submission.html)

m) DCA at BiBiServ (Bielefeld, Germany) (http://bibiserv.techfak.uni-bielefeld.de/dca/submission.html)

n) MAP at Michigan Tech. Univ. (Houghton, USA) (http://genome.cs.mtu.edu/map.html)

o) T-COFFEE at SIB (Lausanne, Switzerland) (http://tcoffee.vital-it.ch/cgi-bin/Tcoffee//tcoffee_cgi/index.cgi)

p) MATCH-BOX at MBR (Namur, Belgium) (http://www.fundp.ac.be/sciences/biologie/bms/matchbox_submit.html)

q) MAVID/AMAP at UCB (Berkeley, USA) (http://baboon.math.berkeley.edu/mavid/)

r) BlastAlign at BioAfrica (Pretoria, South Africa) *Aligns nucleotide sequences that have large indels* (http://www.bioafrica.net/blast/BlastAlign.html)

s) [Kalign at the Karolinska Institute](http://msa.sbc.su.se/cgi-bin/msa.cgi) (Stockholm, Sweden) (http://msa.sbc.su.se/ cgi-bin/msa.cgi)

Motif / Pattern / Profile searches

a) PIMA II at BMERC (Boston, USA) (http://bmerc-www.bu.edu/protein-seq/pimaII-new.html)

Gene recognition

a) GeneMark at GeorgiaTech (Atlanta, UK) (http://exon.gatech.edu/GeneMark/)

b) GrailEXP at ORNL (Oak Ridge, USA) (http://grail.lsd.ornl.gov/grailexp/)

c) GenScan at MIT (Boston, USA) (http://genes.mit.edu/GENSCAN.html)

d) GenScan at Pasteur (Paris, France) (http://mobyle.pasteur.fr/cgi-bin/portal.py? #forms::genscan)

DNA analysis

i. Repeat Masker (Seattle, USA) (http://www.repeatmasker.org/cgi-bin/WEBRepeatMasker)

ii. Bend.it at ICGEB (Trieste, Italy) (http://hydra.icgeb.trieste.it/dna/bend_it.html)

iii. Signal scan service (Bethesda, USA) (http://bimas.dcrt.nih.gov/molbio/signal/)

iv. Promoter scan service (Bethesda, USA) (http://www-bimas.cit.nih.gov/molbio/proscan/)

v. Dragon promoter finder (Singapore) (http://research.i2r.a-star.edu.sg/promoter/)

vi. Elements of transcription (Neuherberg, Germany) (http://www.gsf.de/biodv/index.html)

RNA analysis

i. ESSA RNA software (Toulouse, France) (http://www-bia.inra.fr/T/essa/Doc/essa_home.html)

ii. The RNA world at IMB (Jena, Germany) (http://www.rna.uni-jena.de/rna.php)

Protein analysis

i. SignalP server (Lyngby, Denmark) (http://www.cbs.dtu.dk/services/SignalP/)

ii. ExPASy protein analysis tools (Geneva, Switzerland) (http://www.expasy.org/tools/)

Downloadable software

a) CodonW (Oxford, UK) (http://codonw.sourceforge.net//culong.html)

Genomics and Bioinformatics centers

a) National Center for Biotechnology Information home page (http://libguides.bodleian.ox.ac.uk/content.php?pid=264386&sid=2187124/)

b) NCBI's ENTREZ browser for biosequence databases (not available)

c) NCBI's BLAST biosequence database search tool (http://blast.ncbi.nlm.nih.gov/Blast.cgi)

d) Computational Molecular Biology at NIH (https://www.google.co.in/#q=computational+molecular+biology+at+nih)

e) European Moloecular Biology Laboratory WWW services (http://www.embl.de/services/index.html/)

f) EMBL's SRS browser for biosequence databases (not available)

g) EMBL's PHD program to predict protein secondary structure (https://www.predictprotein.org/)

h) European Bioinformatics Institute home page (http://www.ebi.ac.uk/)

i) Sanger Centre home page (http://www.sanger.ac.uk/)

j) Protein Bata Bank (PDB) (http://www.rcsb.org/pdb/home/home.do)

Other Important Organizations

a) American Crystallographic Association (ACA) - http://aca.hwi.buffalo.edu/

b) Bioinformatics.org - http://bioinformatics.org/

c) The Center for Information Biology and DNA Data Bank of Japan - http://www.cib.nig.ac.jp/Welcome.html

d) European Bioinformatics Institute (EBI) - http://www.ebi.ac.uk/

e) European Molecular Biology Laboratory (EMBL) – http://www.embl.de/

f) Federation of American Societies for Experimental Biology (FASEB) – http://www.faseb.org/

g) The Human Genome Organization (HUGO) - http://www.hugo-international.org/

h) International Society for Computational Biology (ISCB) - http://iscb.org/

i) National Center for Biotechnology Information (NCBI) - http://www.ncbi.nlm.nih.gov:80/

j) National Center for Genome Resources - http://www.ncgr.org/

k) National Human Genome Research Institute (NHGRI) - http://www.nhgri.nih.gov/

l) National Library of Medicine (NLM) - http://www.nlm.nih.gov/

m) Swiss Institute of Bioinformatics (SIB) - http://www.isb-sib.ch/

1. **NCBI (National Centre for Biotechnology Information) (http://www.ncbi.nlm.nih.gov/)**
    a. Entrez (http://www.ncbi.nlm.nih.gov/entrez)
    b. Blast (http://www.ncbi.nlm.nih.gov/BLAST/)
    c. PubMed (http://www.ncbi.nlm.nih.gov/pubmed/html)
        i. Basic (http://www.ncbi.nlm.nih.gov/PubMed/)
        ii. Advanced (Old PubMed) (http://www.ncbi.nlm.nih.gov/PubMedOld/medline.html)
    d. EBI (European Bioinformatics Institute) (http://www.ebi.ac.uk/)
    e. Software Tools (http://www.ebi.ac.uk/services)
    f. The Ensembl Project (Eukaryotic genome annotation) (http://www.ensembl.org/)
    g. Search the draft human genome

  i. via the Ensembl Blast Server (http://www.ensembl.org/Data/blast.html)

  ii. via the Human Blast Server at the Sanger Centre (http://www.Sanger.ac.uk/HGP/blast_server.shtml)

 h. Databases (http://www.ebi.ac.uk/databases/index.html)

 i. Ftp archive (http://www.ebi.ac.uk/FTP/index.html)

2. **EXPASY (Swiss Institute of Bioinformatics) (http://www.expasy.org/)**

 a. SWISS-PROT and TrEMBL databases (http://www.expasy.ch/sprot/)

 b. PROSITE database (http://www.expasy.ch/prosite)

 c. SWISS-2DPAGE (http://www.expasy.ch/ch2d/)

 d. Links to many resources (http://www.expasy.ch/alinks.html)

 e. Sequence analysis tools (http://www.expasy.ch/tools)

3. **Protein Information Resource (http://www-nbrf.georgetown.edu/pirwww/pirhome.shtml)**

 a. In collaboration with:

  i. MIPS - The Munich Information Center for Protein Sequences (http://www.mips.biochem..mpg.de)

  ii. JIPID - The Japanese International Protein Sequence Database (file:///I:\JIPID)

4. **The DNA Data Bank of Japan (http://www.ddbj.nig.ac.jp/)**

5. **RCSB (Research Collaboratory for Structural Bioinformatics) (http://www.rcsb.org/index.html)**

a. New PDB (http://www.rcsb.org/pdb/home/home.do)
    i. PDB Search Lite - Simple keyword search (http://www.rcsb.org/pdb/searchlite.html)
    ii. PDB Search Fields - Advanced search (http://www.rcsb.org/pdb/search/advSearch.do)
b. The Nucleic Acid DataBase (http://ndbserver.rutgers.edu/)

6. **IUBIO Archive at Indiana University (http://iubio.bio/indiana.edu/)**

Bioinformatics Resources
(https://anil.cchmc.org/BioInfoRes.html)

• Nucleotide Databases • Protein Databases • Sequence Similarity Searching • Sequence Alignment • Human Genome • Other Genomes • Genome-scale Analysis • Protein Domain Families • Motif Finding • Protein 3D Structure • Phylogeny & Taxonomy • Gene Prediction • Gene Expression • Gene Regulation • Biomolecular Networks • Systems Biology • Other Databases • Miscellaneous Tools • Computational Resources • Bioinformatics On-line Courses & Tutorials • Information • Other Lists • Sequence Manipulation

Nucleotide Sequence Databases (the principal ones)

a) NCBI - National Center for Biotechnology Information (http://www.ncbi.nlm.nih.gov/)

b) EBI - European Bioinformatics Institute (http://www.ebi.ac.uk/)

c) DDBJ - DNA Data Bank of Japan (http://www.ddbj.nig.ac.jp/)

Database Searching by Sequence Similarity

a) BLAST @ NCBI (http://blast.ncbi.nlm.nih.gov/Blast.cgi)

b) PSI-BLAST @ NCBI

c) FASTA @ EBI (http://www.ebi.ac.uk/Tools/sss/fasta/)

d) **BLAT** (http://genome.ucsc.edu/) Jim Kent's Blat is just superb in terms of speed and the integrated view you get for viewing the results (My Personal favourite!)

Sequence Alignment

a) USC Sequence Alignment Server (http://www-hto.usc.edu/software/seqain/seqain-query.html) - align 2 sequences with all possible varieties of dynamic programming

b) T-COFFEE -multiple sequence alignment (http://igs-server.cnrs_mrs.fr/~cnotred/projects_home_page/t_coffee-_home_page.html)

c) ClustalW @ EBI (http://www.ebi.ac.uk/Tools/msa/) multiple sequence alignment

d) MSA 2.1 - (http://www.ibc.wustl.edu/ibc/msa.html) optimal multiple sequence alignment using the Carrillo-Lipman method

e) BOXSHADE (http://mobyle.pasteur.fr/cgi-bin/portal.py?#forms::boxshade) - pretty printing and shading of multiple alignments

f) Splign (http://www.ncbi.nlm.nih.gov/sutils/splign/splign.cgi) - Splign is a utility for computing cDNA-to-Genomic, or spliced sequence alignments. At the heart of the program is a global alignment algorithm that specifically accounts for introns and splice signals. **New!**

g) Spidey (http://www.ncbi.nlm.nih.gov/IEB/Research/Ostell/Spidey/index.html) - an mRNA-to-genomic alignment program

h) **SIM4** - (http://biom3.univ-lyon1.fr/sim4.html) a program to align cDNA and genomic DNA (My Personal favourite!)

i) Wise2 (http://www.sanger.ac.uk/resources/software/) - align a protein or profile HMM against genomic sequence to predict a gene structure, and related tools

j) **PipMaker** (http://pipmaker.bx.psu.edu/pipmaker/) - computes alignments of similar regions in two (long) DNA sequences (Yet another of my favourites!)

k) VISTA (http://genome.lbl.gov/vista/index.shtml) - align + detect conserved regions in long genomic sequences

l) myGodzilla (http://pipeline.lbl.gov/cgi-bin/mygodzilla) - align a sequence to its ortholog in the human genome

Genome-wide Analysis

a) MBGD (http://mbgd.genome.ad.jp/) - comparative analysis of completely sequenced microbial genomes

b) COGs (http://www.ncbi.nlm.nih.gov/COG/) - phylogenetic classification of orthologous proteins from complete genomes

c) STRING (http://string.embl.de/) - detect whether a given query gene occurs repeatedly with certain other genes in potential operons

d) Pedant (http://web.expasy.org/translate/) - automatic whole genome annotation

e) GeneCensus (http://bioinfo.mbb.yale.edu/genome/) - various whole genome comparisons

Protein Domains: Databases and Search Tools

a) InterPro (http://www.ebi.ac.uk/interpro/) - integration of Pfam, PRINTS, PROSITE, SWISS-PROT + TrEMBL

b) PROSITE (http://prosite.expasy.org/) - database of protein families and domains

c) Pfam (http://genome.wustl.edu/Pfam/) - alignments and hidden Markov models covering many common protein domains

d) SMART (http://smart.embl-heidelberg.de/) - analysis of domains in proteins

e) ProDom (http://www.toulouse.inra.fr/infos/404) - protein domain database

f) PRINTS Database (http://www.biochem.ucl.ac.uk/bsm/dbbrowser/PRINTS/ PRINTS.html) - groups of conserved motifs used to characterise protein families

g) Blocks (http://www.blocks.fhcrc.org/) - multiply aligned ungapped segments corresponding to the most highly conserved regions of proteins

h) Protein Domain Profile Analysis @ BMERC (http://bmerc-www.bu.edu/ bioinformatics/profile_request.html) - search a library of profiles with a protein sequence

i) TIGRFAMs (http://www.jcvi.org/cgi-bin/tigrfams/index.cgi) - yet more protein families based on Hidden Markov Models

Motif and Pattern Search in Sequences

a) Gibbs Motif Sampler (http://ccmbweb.ccv.brown.edu/gibbs/gibbs.html) - identification of conserved motifs in DNA or protein sequences

b) AlignACE Homepage (http://atlas.med.harvard.edu/) - gene regulatory motif finding

c) MEME (http://www.sdsc.edu/MEME/meme/website/) - motif discovery and search in protein and DNA sequences

d) SAM (http://compbio.soe.ucsc.edu/sam.html) - tools for creating and using Hidden Markov Models

e) Pratt (http://www.ii.uib.no/~inge/Pratt.html) - discover patterns in unaligned protein sequences

f) Motivated Proteins (http://motif.gla.ac.uk/motif/index.html) - a web facility for exploring small hydrogen-bonded motifs

Protein 3D Structure

a) PDB (http://www.rcsb.org/pdb/home/home.do) - protein 3D structure database

b) RasMol / Protein Explorer (http://www.umass.edu/microbio/rasmol/) - molecule 3D structure viewers

c) SCOP (http://scop.mrc-lmb.cam.ac.uk/scop/) - Structural Classification Of Proteins

d) UCL BSM CATH classification (http://www.cathdb.info/)

e) The DALI Domain Database (http://www.ebi.ac.uk/msd-srv/ssm/)

f) FSSP (http://www.ebi.ac.uk/msd-srv/ssm/) - fold classification based on structure-structure alignment of proteins

g) SWISS-MODEL (http://swissmodel.expasy.org/) - homology modeling server

h) Structure Prediction Meta-server (http://www.bioinfo.pl/meta/)

i) K2 (http://zlab.bu.edu/k2/) - protein structure alignment

j) DALI (http://www.ebi.ac.uk/msd-srv/ssm/) - 3D structure alignment server

k) DSSP (http://mobyle.pasteur.fr/cgi-bin/portal.py?#forms::dssp) - defines secondary structure and solvent exposure from 3D coordinates

l) HSSP Database (http://swift.embl-heidelberg.de/hssp/) - Homology-derived Secondary Structure of Proteins

m) PredictProtein & PHD (http://cubic.bioc.columbia.edu/predictprotein) - predict secondary structure, solvent accessibility, transmembrane helices, and other stuff

n) Jpred2 (http://jura.ebi.ac.uk:8888/) - protein secondary structure prediction

o) PSIpred (& MEMSAT & GenTHREADER) (http://insulin.brunel.ac.uk.psipred/) - protein secondary structure prediction (& transmembrane helix prediction & tertiary structure prediction by threading)

Phylogeny & Taxonomy

a) The Tree of Life (http://phylogeny.arizona.edu/tree/phylogeny.html)

b) Species 2000 (http://www.sp2000.org/) - index of the world's known species

c) TreeBASE (http://www.herbaria.harvard.edu/treebase/) - a database of phylogenetic knowledge

d) PHYLIP (http://evolution.genetics.washington.edu/phylip.html) - package of programs for inferring phylogenies

e) TreeView (http://taxonomy.zoology.gla.ac.uk/rod/treeview.html) - user friendly tree displaying for Macs & Windows

Gene Prediction

a) Genscan (http://genes.mit.edu/GENSCAN.html) - eukaryotes

b) GeneMark (http://opal.biology.gatech.edu/GeneMark/)

c) Genie (http://users.soe.ucsc.edu/~dkulp/cgi-bin/genie) - eukaryotes

d) GLIMMER (http://ccb.jhu.edu/software/glimmer/index.shtml) - prokaryotes

e) tRNAscan - SE 1.1 (http://www.genetics.wustl.edu/eddy/tRNAscan-SE/) - search for tRNA genes in genomic sequence

f) GFF (General Feature Format) Specification (http://www.sanger.ac.uk/resources/software/gff/spec.html) - a standard format for genomic sequence annotation

Gene Expression Databases

a) HuGE (http://zlab.bu.edu/HugeSearch/nph-HugeSearch.cgi?action=start) - database of human gene expression using arrays

b) ExpressDB (http://arep.med.harvard.edu/ExpressDB/) - yeast and E. coli RNA expression data

c) SAGE @ NCBI (http://www.ncbi.nlm.hih.gov/SAGE/) - Serial Analysis of Gene Expression

d) Stanford Microarray Database (http://genome-www4.stanford.edu/MicroArray/ SMD/)

e) Gene Expression Omnibus (GEO) (http://www.ncbi.nlm.nih.gov/geo/)

Gene Regulation

a) <u>**TRAFAC**</u> - For identifying conserved and shared cis regulatory elements between a pair of genes.

b) <u>**CisMols**</u> (http://cismols.chmcc.org/) - For identifying conserved and shared cis regulatory elements between a set of co-expressed genes.

c) <u>TRANSFAC</u> (http://transfac.gbf.de/TRANSFAC/) - database of eukaryotic cis-acting regulatory DNA elements and trans-acting factors

d) <u>EPD</u> (http://epd.vital-it.ch/) - eukaryotic promoter database

e) <u>DBTSS</u> (http://elmo.ims.u-tokyo.ac.jp/dbtss/) - DataBase of Transcriptional Start Sites (human)

f) <u>SCPD</u> (http://cgsigma.cshl.org/jian/) - Saccharomyces cerevisiae promoter database

g) <u>DCPD</u> (http://labs.biology.ucsd.edu/Kadonaga/DCPD.html) - Drosophila Core Promoter Database

h) <u>RegulonDB</u> (http://tula.cifn.unam.mx:8850/regulondb/regulon_intro.frameset) - a database on transcriptional regulation in E. coli

i) <u>DPInteract</u> (http://arep.med.harvard.edu/dpinteract/) - protein binding sites on E. coli DNA

j) PromoterInspector (http://genomatrix.gsf.de/cgi-bin/promoterinspector/promoterinspector.pl.) prediction of promoter regions in mammalian genomic sequences

k) MatInspector (http://genomatrix.gsf.de/cgi-bin/matinspector/matinspector.pl) - search for transcription factor binding sites

l) Cister (http://zlab.bu.edu/~mfrith/cister.shtml) - cis-element cluster finder

m) Gene regulatory Tools (http://zlab.bu.edu/zlab/gene.shtml)

n) microRNA.org: microRNA Targets & Expression Profiles (http://www.microrna.org/microrna/home.do)

o) miRBase (http://www.mirbase.org/)

p) TarBase (http://www.diana.pcbi.upenn.edu/tarbase.html) - Provides a means of searching through a comprehensive set of experimentally supported microRNA targets in at least 8 organisms

q) microRNA resource ((http://www.ambion.com/techlib/resourses/miRNA/) - A gateway to all types of information about microRNAs, including articles, products, news, events, and other websites

Metabolic, Gene Regulatory & Signal Transduction Network Databases

a) KEGG (http://www.genome.ad.jp/kegg/) - Kyoto Encyclopaedia of Genes and Genomes

b) BioCarta (http://www.biocarta.com/)

c) **DAVID** (http://apps1.niaid.nih.gov/david/upload.asp) - Database for Annotation, Visualization and **I**ntegrated **D**iscovery - A useful server to for annotating microarray and other genetic data.

d) stke (http://www.stke.org/) - Signal Transduction Knowledge Environment

e) BIND (http://binddb.org/) - Biomolecular Interaction Network Database

f) EcoCyc (http://ecocyc.pangeasystems.com/ecosyc/ecosyc.html)

g) WIT (http://wit.mcs.anl.gov/)

h) **PathGuide** (http://www.pathguide.org/) - A very useful collection of resources dealing primarily with pathways

i) SPAD (http://www.grt.kyushu-u.ac.jp/spad/) - Signalling Pathway Database

j) CSNDB (http://geo.nihs.go.jp/csndb/) - Cell Signalling Networks Database

k) PathDB (http://www.ncgr.org/software/pathdb/)

l) Transpath (http://193.175.244.148/)

m) DIP (http://www.grt.kyushu-u.ac.jp/spad/) - Database of Interacting Proteins

n) PFBP (http://www.ebi.ac.uk/research/pfmp/) - Protein Function and Biochemical Networks

o) Alliance for Cellular Signalling (http://www.cellularsignaling.org/)

Gene List Annotation Tools

a) DAVID (http://apps1.niaid.nih.gov/david/upload.asp) - **D**atabases for **A**nnotation, **V**isualization and **I**ntegrated

Discovery - A useful server to for annotating microarray and other genetic data.

b) MSigDB (http://www.broad.mit.edu/gsea/msigdb/index.jsp) - Molecular Signatures Database

c) **ToppGene Suite New!** (http://toppgene.cchmc.org/) Gene list functional enrichment and candidate gene prioritization (My Personal favourite!)

d) Panther (http://www.pantherdb.org/)-**P**rotein **An**alysis **Th**rough **E**volutionary **R**elationships

e) L2L (http://depts.washington.edu/l2l/)

f) Babelomics (FatiGO+) (http://fitigo.bioinfo.cipf.es/)

g) OntoExpress (http://vortex.cs.wayne.edu/projects.htm)

Computational Resources

a) **SourceForge** (http://sourceforge.net/) - SourceForge.net is the world's largest Open Source software development website, with the largest repository of Open Source code and applications available on the Internet. SourceForge.net provides free services to Open Source developers.

b) W3C (http://www.w3.org/) - World Wide Web Consortium, definitive reference for HTML and other WWW stuff

c) Apache web server documentation (http://httpd.apache.org/docs-project/)

d) PHP information (http://php.net/)

e) Web Developer's Virtual Library (http://www.stars.com/) - encyclopedia of web design tutorials, articles and discussions

f) HTML Writers Guild (http://hwg.org/)

g) CPAN (http://www.cpan.org/) - PERL modules

h) bioperl (http://www.bioperl.org/wiki/Main_Page) - bioinformatics related PERL modules

i) C++ Standard Template Library Programmer's Guide (http://www.sgi.com/tech/ stl/)

j) C++ Annotations (http://www.icce.rug.nl/documents/cplusplus/)

k) Dinkum C Library Reference (http://www.dinkumware.com/htm_d/index.html)

l) GNU C Library Reference (http://www.gnu.org/manual/glibc-2.0.6/html_chapter/libc_toc.html)

m) C Tutorial (http://www.eskimo.com/~scs/cclass/cclass.html)

n) Java Tutorial (http://docs.oracle.com/javase/tutorial/)

o) Numerical Recipes in C and Fortran (http://www.ulib.org/webRoot/Books/Numerical_Receips/)

p) Dictionary of Algorithms, Data Structures, and Problems (http://hissa.ncsl.nist.gov/~black/DADS/)

q) The Linux Cookbook (http://www.ibiblio.org/obp/cookbook/)

r) Alphabetical Directory of Linux Commands (http://www.onlamp.com/ linux/cmd/)

Introduction to bioinformatics and computational biology

a) Introduction to Bioinformatics (Technion - Israel Institute of Technology) (http://www.cs.technion.ac.il/~cs236606/)

b) Introduction to Bioinformatics (UCSD) (http://elcapitan.ucsd.edu/bild94/)

c) A taste of bioinformatics (University College London) (http://www.biochem.ucl.ac.uk/bsm/dbbrowser/c32/contents.html)

d) Introduction to Computational Molecular Biology (Washington University in St. Louis) (http://bio5495.wustl.edu/)

e) Introduction to Bioinformatics (UCSD Extension) (http://www.bioinformaticscourses.com/index.html)

f) Computational Biology (University of Washington) (http://courses.cs.washington.edu/courses/cse527/01au/)

g) Introduction to Computational Biology (Carnegie Mellon University) (http://www.cmu.edu/bio/education/courses/03310/)

h) Introduction to Computational Molecular Biology (MIT) (http://people.csail.mit.edu/bab/class/01-18.417-home.html)

i) Introduction to Computational Molecular Biology: Genome and Protein Sequence Analysis (University of Washington) (http://bozeman.mbt.washington.edu/compbio/mbt599/)

Algorithms

a) Algorithms in Computational Biology (Technion -Israel Institute of Technology) (http://www.cs.technion.ac.il/~cs236522/)

b) Algorithms for Molecular Biology (School of Mathematical Sciences at Tel Aviv University) (http://www.math.tau.ac.il/~rshamir/algmb.html)

Science and Technology Sources on the Internet - University of California (**Guide to Selected Bioinformatics Internet Resources**)

Source: (http://www.istl.org/02-winter/internet.html#intro) (http://api.adlure.net/partner/click/771)

a. Introduction to Bioinformatics (http://www.istl.org/02-winter/ internet.html#intro)

b. Scope of this Guide (http://www.istl.org/02-winter/internet.html#scope)

c. Definitions, Glossaries, and Dictionaries (http://www.istl.org/02-winter/ internet.html#definitions)

d. News/Keeping Current (http://www.istl.org/02-winter/ internet.html#news)

e. Sequence and other Non-Bibliographic Databases (http://www.istl.org/02-winter/internet.html#sequence)

i. Introduction (http://www.istl.org/02-winter/internet.html#1)

ii. Database Directories and Lists (http://www.istl.org/02-winter/internet.html#2)

iii. Nucleotide Sequences (http://www.istl.org/02-winter/internet.html#3)

iv. Genome Databases (http://www.istl.org/02-winter/ internet.html#4)

v. Protein Sequences (http://www.istl.org/02-winter/ internet.html#5)

vi. Protein Structure (http://www.istl.org/02-winter/ internet.html#6)

- f. Software (http://www.istl.org/02-winter/internet.html#software)
    - i. Software Directories (http://www.istl.org/02-winter/internet.html#a)
    - ii. Tools in Specific Programming Languages (http://www.istl.org/02-winter/internet.html#b)
    - iii. Open Source Software Promoters (http://www.istl.org/02-winter/internet.html#c)
- g. Comprehensive Web Sites (http://www.istl.org/02-winter/internet.html#comprehensive)
- h. Bibliographic Databases (http://www.istl.org/02-winter/internet.html#bibliographic)
- i. Technical Reports and Preprints (http://www.istl.org/02-winter/ internet.html#techreports)
- j. Major Conferences and Symposia (http://www.istl.org/02-winter/internet.html#conferences)
- k. Important Organizations (http://www.istl.org/02-winter/internet.html#orgs)
- l. Guides, Tutorials and Primers (http://www.istl.org/02-winter/internet.html#guides)
- m. Recommended Reading (http://www.istl.org/02-winter/internet.html#reading)
- n. References (http://www.istl.org/02-winter/internet.html#references)

Introduction to Bioinformatics

See also Definitions, Glossaries, and Dictionaries (http://www.istl.org/02-winter/internet.html#definitions)

See also Recommended Reading (http://www.istl.org/02-winter/internet. html#reading)

The tremendous interest in bioinformatics, a new discipline at the intersection of molecular biology and computer science, is fuelled by the excitement surrounding the sequencing of the human genome and the promise of a new era in which genomic research dramatically improves the human condition. Advances in detection and treatment of disease and the production of genetically engineered foods are among the most often mentioned benefits. Bioinformatics is a fertile new area for programmers. As the eminent computer scientist Donald Knuth is often quoted as saying: "Biology easily has 500 years of exciting problems to work on" (Doernberg 1993) (http://www.istl.org/02-winter/internet.html#doernberg).

The National Center for Biotechnology Information (NCBI 2001) (http://www.istl.org/02-winter/internet.html#ncbi) defines bioinformatics as:"Bioinformatics is the field of science in which biology, computer science, and information technology merge into a single discipline...There are three important sub-disciplines within bioinformatics: the development of new algorithms and statistics with which to assess relationships among members of large data sets; the analysis and interpretation of various types of data including nucleotide and amino acid sequences, protein domains, and protein structures; and the development and implementation of tools that enable efficient access and management of different types of information."

Damian Counsell's Bioinformatics FAQ (2001) (http://www.istl.org/02-winter/internet.html#counsell) puts it more simply. "I would say most biologists talk about 'doing bioinformatics' when they use computers to store, retrieve, analyze or predict the composition or the structure of biomolecules. As computers become more powerful you could probably add simulate to this list of bioinformatics verbs. 'Biomolecules' include your genetic material---nucleic acids---and the products of your genes: proteins."

While the terms bioinformatics and computational biology are often used interchangeably, medical informatics is another field entirely. "Medical informatics generally deals with 'gross' data that is information from super-cellular systems, right up to the population level, while bioinformatics tends to be concerned with information about cellular and biomolecular structures and systems." (Counsell 2001) (http://www.istl.org/02-winter/internet.html#counsell).

For more information, see the Definitions, Glossaries and Dictionaries and the Recommended Reading sections of this guide.

Scope of this Guide

Because of the potential for this field to sweep a great deal of both computer science and molecular biology under its wing, this guide is by necessity very selective rather than comprehensive. There is a focus on human rather than plant or animal data sources and the ethical, business, political and legal aspects of bioinformatics and genomics are completely ignored (except for their appearance in the news sites). The resources selected are aimed at the college and research level. Furthermore, due to the large number of databases and web-based resources on the subject only the best or most well known in each category was chosen. (For an idea of the size of the problem, consider that the January 1, 2002 issue of *Nucleic Acids Research* lists 335 molecular biology databases that might be considered relevant to bioinformatics.) And although not intentional, the author's American academic perspective may have colored the selection of data sources. Bioinformatics is a particularly international subject, with a notably high degree of information sharing among researchers in different countries (not to mention a strong tradition of making this information freely available to the public). The human genome project was a particularly good example of this multinational collaboration. In fact, the same data is often available from similar but slightly differing databases located in different countries. For example, GenBank (at the National Center for Biotechnology Information), together with the DNA DataBank of Japan and the European Molecular Biology Laboratory (EMBL) comprise the International Nucleotide Sequence Database Collaboration. These three organizations exchange data on a daily basis. While this sharing is highly admirable from a scientific standpoint it does add to the sense of information overload and confusion for non-specialist librarians who approach this subject.

To find the resources listed in this webliography, the author read the books and articles listed in the Recommended Reading section of this guide, and consulted with graduate students and faculty in the bioinformatics program at the University of California Santa Cruz and with other academic librarians with interests in the field. The resources that bioinformatics faculty web pages point to were reviewed, as were the search results from the prominent search engines such as Google using the most likely keywords. Many of the resources listed by the Comprehensive Web Sites (http://www.istl.org/02-winter/internet.html#comprehensive) themselves were also assessed. The annual list of molecular biology databases from the journal *Nucleic Acids Research* was reviewed. In November 2001 the author also attended the day-long Medical Librarian Association's "Molecular Biology Information Resources" continuing education course [see - (http://www.ncbi.nlm.nih.gov/Class/MLACourse/)] which was taught by a specialist from the National Library of Medicine in order to better understand the NCBI databases in particular.

Definitions, Glossaries, and Dictionaries

Introduction to Bioinformatics (http://www.istl.org/02-winter/internet.html#intro)

Guides, Tutorials and Primers (http://www.istl.org/02-winter/internet.html#guides)

Definitions

A quick review of the basic genetic terms and concepts will help in understanding the sequence databases. The NCBI Genetics Review site is highly recommended reading since it provides a particularly good overview of the concepts as well as listing some good references for additional information (http://www.ncbi.nlm.nih.gov/Class/MLACourse/Original8Hour/Genetics/). The following terms are central to understanding bioinformatics.

Nucleotide: One of the structural components, or building blocks, of DNA and RNA. A nucleotide consists of a base (one of four chemicals: adenine, thymine [uracil instead of thymine for RNA], guanine, and cytosine) plus a molecule of sugar [ribose for RNA, deoxyribose for DNA] and one of phosphoric acid (from the National Human Genome Research Institute (NHGRI) Glossary of Genetic Terms (http://www.genome.gov/glossary.cfm).

Gene: A length of DNA which codes for a particular protein or in certain cases a functional or structural RNA molecule (from PhRMA Genomics Lexicon (http://genomics.phrma.org/lexicon/). Less than 5% of the human genome codes for genes. The rest are non-coding sequences which may have other functions.

Genome: The complete gene complement of an organism, contained in a set of chromosomes (in eukaryotes), in a single chromosome (in bacteria), or in a DNA or RNA molecule (in viruses) -

from Academic Press Dictionary of Science and Technology (http://www.harcourt.com/dictionary/).

Genomics: Operationally defined as investigations into the structure and function of very large numbers of genes undertaken in a simultaneous fashion (from What is Genomics? {http://www.genomecenter.ucdavis.edu/what.html}). Genetics looks at single genes, one at a time, as a snapshot. Genomics is trying to look at all the genes as a dynamic system, over time, and determine how they interact and influence biological pathways and physiology, in a much more global sense (from Basic Genetics & Genomics (http://www.genomicglossaries.com/content/Basic_Genetic_Glossaries.asp).

Proteome: The complement of proteins expressed by an organism, tissue or cell type (from Proteomes and Proteomics {http://www.mrc-dunn.cam.ac.uk/pages/proteomes.html}). The concept of the proteome is fundamentally different to that of the genome: while the genome is virtually static and can be well defined for an organism, the proteome continually changes in response to external and internal events (from Thinking Big: Proteome Studies in a Post- Genome Era (http://www.abrf.org/ABRFNews/1996/December1996/Proteome.html).

Proteomics: The study of the full set of proteins encoded by a genome (from the Human Genome Project Information Glossary (http://www.ornl.gov/sci/techresources/Human_Genome/glossary/).
The characterization of patterns of gene expression is at the protein level or the link between proteins and genomes. Proteomics encompasses many different approaches to protein study, from bioinformatics of protein content of genomes to large scale direct protein analysis of complicated protein mixtures, and the definition of a protein's properties, their interactions and modifications [from

Proteomes and Proteomics (http://www.mrc-dunn.cam.ac.uk/pages/proteomes.html)].

Glossaries and Dictionaries

Science Magazine: Functional Genomics Resources: "Finding the right word: A guide to some useful online glossaries" Post-genomics, biotech and bioinformatics - (http://www.sciencemag.org/site/feature/plus/sfg/education/glossaries.xhtml#postgenomics).

Access Excellence Graphics Gallery (http://www.accessexcellence.org/AB/GG/): "Graphics Gallery is a series of labeled diagrams with explanations representing the important processes of biotechnology. Each diagram is followed by a summary of information, providing a context for the process illustrated."

Genomics Glossary (http://www.genomicglossaries.com/): Actually a collection of several glossaries and taxonomies, including a Bioinformatics Glossary at (http://www.genomicglossaries.com/content/Bioinformatics_gloss.asp). The Scout Report and Science Magazine give this resource very high praise, but this author found the site to be cluttered and difficult to navigate, although the content is very good.

Human Genome Project Information Glossary (http://www.ornl.gov/sci/techresources/Human_Genome/glossary/): A useful glossary of genetics terms from the DOE Human Genome Program that you can both browse and search.

National Human Genome Research Institute (NHGRI) Glossary of Genetic Terms (http://www.genome.gov/glossary.cfm): This is sometimes called the "talking glossary" since audio clips allow you to hear definitions and longer explanations given by an expert. Try it with the word "nucleotide." Illustrations are also sometimes available.

PhRMA Genomics Lexicon (http://genomics.phrma.org/lexicon/): This extensive glossary is sponsored by the Pharmaceutical Research and Manufacturers of America. Also provides links to other dictionaries and glossaries.

Southwest Biotechnology and Informatics Center (SWBIC) News (http://www.nbif.org/links/1.20.php): Annotated directory of news sites, many focusing in bioinformatics (scroll down past the long table of contents to see the content). A good "launch pad" to news sites.

Genomics Today (http://genomics.phrma.org/today/): A daily headline news service that provides links to genomics news in other sites. It culls the relevant headlines from a wide variety of sources including wire services, newspapers, Yahoo, selected web sites, and university news sites, sponsored by the Pharmaceutical Research and Manufacturers of America.

GNN (Genome News Network) (http://www.genomenewsnetwork.org/index.php): Good source for news on scientific, as opposed to business, aspects of bioinformatics. Bioinformatics news is clearly marked. The short news summaries are to be commended for giving the full citation to the original scientific article at the end of each news piece. In addition to news there are also featured articles and a few educational links.

The Scientist (http://www.the-scientist.com/): Frequent coverage of bioinformatics news. Registration is free, after which you will automatically be sent via e-mail the tables of contents for each biweekly issue.

Sequence Retrieval System (SRS) database descriptions (http://downloads.lionbio.co.uk/publicsrs.html)

This database of database descriptions can be accessed in a number of ways. From the Public SRS Servers List (http://downloads.lionbio.co.uk/publicsrs.html) you can view an alphabetical list of databases (scroll down past the list of servers at the top to see the list of databases or "libraries" in the middle of the page). Click on the link for the server that is hosting the database you are interested in to view the record for the version of that database as mounted on that server. Or, you can link to the database descriptions from the search interface of a particular server (for example, see the European Bioinformatics Institute server at (http://srs6.ebi.ac.uk/srs6bin/cgi-bin/wgetz?-page+top+-newId). This method is particularly helpful because here the databases are sorted by database type (e.g., sequence libraries, protein 3D structures, mutations, SNP, metabolic pathways, etc.). Click on the plus sign next to the type to expand the list, then click on the database name to access the description of that database as mounted on that server. You can also go one step further and actually initiate your search in those databases from this page as well.

Nucleotide Sequences

GenBank - (http://www.ncbi.nlm.nih.gov/Genbank/GenbankSearch.html), and **Entrez Nucleotides Database** - (http://www.ncbi.nlm.nih.gov/entrez/query.fcgi?db=Nucleotide)**:** GenBank is the nucleotide sequence database built and distributed by the National Center for Biotechnology Information (NCBI) at the National Institutes of Health. As of this writing, GenBank contains more than 13 billion bases from over 100,000 species, and is growing exponentially [see (http://www.ncbi.nlm.nih.gov/Genbank/

genbankstats.html)]. The data are obtained through direct submission of sequence data from individual laboratories, from large-scale sequencing projects, and from the US Patent and Trademark Office. A little more than half of the total sequences in the database are from *Homo sapiens*.

There are two ways to search GenBank. A text-based query can be submitted through the **Entrez** system at (http://www.ncbi.nlm.nih.gov/Entrez/index.html), or a sequence query can be submitted through the BLAST family of programs [see (http://www.ncbi.nlm.nih.gov/ BLAST/)]. To search GenBank through the Entrez system you would select the Nucleotides database from the menu. The **Entrez Nucleotides Database** is a collection of sequences from several sources, including GenBank, RefSeq, and the Protein Databank, so you don't actually search GenBank exclusively. Searches of the Entrez Nucleotides database query the text and numeric fields in the record, such as the accession number, definition, keyword, gene name, and organism fields to name just a few. So, for example, you could enter the terms Bacillus anthraces and you would be presented with many records that contain and describe nucleotide or protein sequences related to the anthrax bacteria. The accession number is very handy, because it is a unique and persistent identifier for the GenBank entry as a whole and doesn't change even if there is a later change or update to the sequence or annotation. Nucleotide sequence records in the Nucleotides database are linked to the Pub Med citation of the article in which the sequences were published. Protein sequence records are linked to the nucleotide sequence from which the protein was translated. To become an effective searcher of this database takes study. For starters, take the Nucleotides database online tutorial that starts at (http://www.ncbi.nlm.nih.gov/Database/tut1.html), and consult the other resources available from the NCBI Education Page at (http://www.ncbi.nlm.nih.gov/Education/). See also the Recommended

Reading (http://www.istl.org/02-winter/internet.html#reading) section of this guide.

If you have obtained a record through a text-based Entrez Nucleotides Database search you can read the nucleotide sequence in the record. However, most researchers wish to submit a nucleotide sequence of interest to find the sequences that are most similar to theirs. This is done using the BLAST (**B**asic **L**ocal **A**lignment **S**earch **T**ool) programs. You select the BLAST program you wish to use depending upon the type of comparison you are doing (nucleotide to nucleotide, or nucleotide to protein sequence, etc.) and then you select the database to run the query in (any of several nucleotide or protein databases). Many NCBI databases accept BLAST searches, as do many of the other databases covered elsewhere in this guide. The result is a detailed report that summarizes your query, provides a graphical overview of database matches, indicates the statistical significance of the matches and describes each significant alignment. From here you can link to the full database record for the individual matches. You can learn more about BLAST searching from the NCBI BLAST educational page at (http://www.ncbi.nlm.nih.gov/Education/BLASTinfo/information3.html) (read the online tutorial).

EMBL Nucleotide Sequence Database (http://www.ebi.ac.uk/embl/):

"The EMBL Nucleotide Sequence Database constitutes Europe's primary nucleotide sequence resource. Main sources for DNA and RNA sequences are direct submissions from individual researchers, genome sequencing projects and patent applications. The database is produced in an international collaboration with GenBank (USA) and the DNA Database of Japan (DDBJ). Each of the three groups collects a portion of the total sequence data reported worldwide, and all new and updated database entries are exchanged between the groups on a daily basis."

From the home page you can submit simple text searches to the EMBL Nucleotide Sequence Database or to the Protein Databank (what you search when you select protein structures from the menu) or to a protein sequence database called Swall. For more complex searches, they recommend accessing the databases through the Sequence Retrieval System (SRS) server (http://srs.ebi.ac.uk/). SRS is a database querying / navigation system, similar in function to the Entrez system. It allows you to simultaneously search across several databases and to display the results in many ways. SRS can be used to access a large number of databases, including EMBL, SWISS-PROT and the Protein Databank, depending upon the configuration of the particular SRS server you are using. The structure and content of an EMBL Nucleotide record is very similar to that of an NCBI Entrez Nucleotide database record.

Genome Databases

Entrez Genome (http://www.ncbi.nlm.nih.gov/entrez/query.fcgi?db=Genome): "The whole genomes of over 800 organisms can be found in Entrez Genomes. The genomes represent both completely sequenced organisms and those for which sequencing is in progress. All three main domains of life - bacteria, archaea, and eukaryota - are represented, as well as many viruses and organelles." Text searches can be done from the main page. Data can also be accessed alphabetically by species (http://www.ncbi.nlm.nih.gov:80/PMGifs/Genomes/ allorg.html), or hierarchically by drilling down through a taxonomic list to a graphical overview for the genome of that organism, then to specific chromosomes, then on to specific genes. At each level are maps, pre-computed summaries and analysis appropriate to that level, and links to related records from a variety of other Entrez databases. BLAST searches of some genomes are also possible.

Very useful pages for some of the most commonly studied species (e.g., human, mouse, fruit fly, malaria parasite) can be found on the Genomic Biology page under "organism-specific resources" (http://www.ncbi.nlm.nih.gov/Genomes/). These pages are so detailed that each could be classified as a comprehensive web site in itself. Each one brings together links to the genomic data, useful tools, related data sources and news about the genome of that species. The Human Genome Guide (http://www.ncbi.nlm.nih.gov/genome/guide/human/) is particularly rich.

Human Genome Browser from UCSC (http://genome.ucsc.edu/): "The sequence of the human genome is too big to see at all at once; few people want to look at raw DNA sequence anyway. The alternative is the Human Genome Browser for a quick display of any requested portion of the genome at any scale, along with more than two dozen tracks of information (genes, ESTs, CpG islands, assembly gaps, chromosomal band,) associated with the complete human genome sequence... Clicking on a displayed feature opens a second window providing protein sequence, coordinates and accession numbers, as appropriate. Clicking in the corner of the display calls up raw DNA sequence corresponding to the display window boundaries. This look-up feature is far more convenient than manual retrieval of a precise coordinate range from GenBank entries."

The Genome Database (GDB) (http://www.gdb.org/): The Genome Database is the official central repository for genomic mapping data resulting from the Human Genome Initiative. The database contains three types of data: (1) regions of the human genome, including genes, clones, and ESTs, (2) maps of the human genome, including cytogenetic maps, linkage maps, radiation hybrid maps, content contig maps, and integrated maps (these maps can be displayed graphically via the Web), and (3) variations within the human genome including mutations and polymorphisms, plus allele frequency data. There are options to browse genes by chromosome, genes by symbol name and genetic diseases by chromosome. There are multiple ways to search, including text-based searches for people, citations, segment names or accession numbers, and sequence searching via BLAST.

Kyoto Encyclopedia of Genes and Genomes (http://www.genome.jp/kegg/):

This database often appears in Google search results, so let's put it in context. Despite the name, this is actually a biochemical pathway database and gene catalog, not an encyclopedia in the book sense. "The primary objective of KEGG is to computerize the current knowledge of molecular interactions; namely, metabolic pathways, regulatory pathways, and molecular assemblies. At the same time, KEGG maintains gene catalogs for all the organisms that have been sequenced and links each gene product to a component on the pathway. Because we need an additional catalog of building blocks, KEGG also organizes a database of all chemical compounds in living cells and links each compound to a pathway component."

Protein Sequences

SWISS-PROT (http://web.expasy.org/groups/swissprot/) - "SWISS-PROT is a curate protein sequence database which strives to provide a high level of annotation (such as the description of the function of a protein, its domain structure, post-translational modifications, variants, etc.), a minimal level of redundancy and a high level of integration with other databases." "The data in Swiss-Prot are derived from translations of DNA sequences from the EMBL Nucleotide Sequence Database, adapted from the Protein Identification

Resource (PIR) collection, extracted from the literature and directly submitted by researchers. It contains high-quality annotations, is non-redundant, and cross-referenced to several other databases, notably the EMBL nucleotide sequence database, PROSITE pattern database and PDB."

From the home page, a quick text search can be done by accession or ID number, description, gene name, or organism. By searching SWISS-PROT through the Sequence Retrieval System (SRS) more sophisticated searches can be performed and the format of the results can be customized. Access to SWISS-PROT (directly or via SRS) and links to many other proteomics resources are available from the **ExPASy** (**E**xpert **P**rotein **A**nalysis **S**ystem) proteomics server of the Swiss Institute of Bioinformatics (SIB) at {http://us.expasy.org/}. The SWISS-PROT records are quite detailed. Be advised that other databases or search systems that import SWISS-PROT data may not always provide access to the entire SWISS-PROT record.

Entrez Protein Database (http://www.ncbi.nlm.nih.gov:80/entrez/query.fcgi?dB=Protein) - "The Protein database contains sequence data from the translated coding regions from DNA sequences in GenBank, EMBL and DDBJ as well as protein sequences submitted to PIR, SWISS-PROT, PRF, and the Protein Data Bank (PDB) (sequences from solved structures)." The native SWISS-PROT records usually contain more detailed annotations than will be obtained from Entrez Protein Database records derived from SWISS-PROT records. In typical Entrez fashion, results from a search of the Protein database link to PubMed, to the taxonomy database, to related sequences, and in some cases to pre-computed BLAST search results (look for BLink links).

Protein Information Resource - International Protein Sequence Database (PIR-PSD) (http://pir.georgetown.edu/) - In

1988 the Protein Information Resource (PIR), which is affiliated with Georgetown University Medical Center, established a cooperative effort with the Munich Information Center for Protein Sequences (MIPS) and the Japan International Protein Information Database (JIPID) to collect, publish and distribute the PIR-International Protein Sequence Database (PIR-PSD). They describe the database as "a comprehensive, non-redundant, expertly annotated, fully classified and extensively cross-referenced protein sequence database in the public domain". Text searches can be done in the title, species, author, citation, keyword, super family, feature and gene name fields. Gapped-BLAST sequence similarity searches are also an option. Note that both SWISS-PROT and the Entrez Protein database contain data adapted from the PIR.

Protein Structure - Protein Data Bank (PDB) (http://www.rcsb.org/pdb/) - The PDB was established at Brookhaven National Laboratories in 1971, making it the first public bioinformatics database. The PDB is now operated by the Research Collaborator for Structural Bioinformatics (RCSB) which is a collaborative effort of the San Diego Supercomputing Center, Rutgers University, and the National Institute of Standards and Technology (NIST). The PDB is a repository of experimentally determined three-dimensional structures of biological macromolecules (proteins, enzymes, nucleic acids, protein-nucleic acid complexes, and viruses) derived from x-ray crystallography and NMR experiments (see http://www.rcsb.org/pdb/experimental_methods.html for a helpful overview of these methods). Depositing structures obtained from theoretical models is discouraged. Data are deposited by the international user community and maintained by the RCSB PDB staff. Approximately 50-100 new structures are deposited each week. A variety of information associated with each structure is available, including "sequence details, atomic coordinates, crystallization conditions, 3-D structure neighbours computed using various methods, derived geometric data, structure factors, 3-D images, and a variety of links to other resources."

There are three ways to search the PDB. The SearchLite interface accepts text queries using Boolean operators, and searches the text fields such as the author, compound, molecule class, and keywords fields. The Search Fields interface is an advanced search option that allows you to choose specific fields in which to search and to apply various limits. It also allows you to customize the format of the results. The third search method requires leaving the PDB site, going to the NCBI Entrez site and performing a NCBI BLAST sequence search with "pdb" selected as the target database. See the notes on protein BLAST searching at (http://www.ncbi.nlm.nih.gov/blast/html/BLASThomehelp.html#AABLAST).

Since this is such an old database, historic inconsistencies in the way data are reported within PDB records may lead to unexpected or incomplete results when searching, particularly for text-based information. Certain keywords, like alpha, are not properly searchable. For example, looking for alpha hemolysin fails to find anything, but a search on hemolysin alone results in ten hits, including 7AHL, which is alpha hemolysin. The PDB file format itself also has numerous flaws, but remains the most widely accepted format for structural data. The database producers are aware of these problems and are working to solve them. Several software packages can be used to view PDB files in 3D, including the RasMol and Chime browser plug-ins and Deep-View. For more information see the PDB Query Tutorial at (http://www.rcsb.org/pdbstatic/tutorials/LargeBeta.swf) and the PDB Documentation and Information page at (http://www.rcsb.org/pdb/info.html#General_Information). See also the entry for the MMDB below, which is a subset of the PDB with some added features.

MMDB: Molecular Modeling Database (http://www.ncbi.nlm.nih.gov/Structure/MMDB/mmdb.shtml) - The MMDB is NCBI's structure database. It is a subset of three-dimensional structures obtained from the Protein Databank (PDB), excluding theoretical models. MMDB adds value through the addition of explicit chemical graph information and through the cross-linking of structural data to bibliographic information, to the sequence databases, and to the NCBI taxonomy. The explicit bond information makes for more consistent interpretation of the coordinate data by visualization software. MMDB can provide data for three different structure viewers: Cn3D, a viewer developed by the NCBI; RasMol; and MAGE. All three are available for a variety of platforms (Windows, MacOS, and UNIX). After installing the software, the 3-dimensional structure can be viewed by clicking the button labeled View/Save Structure close to the bottom of each structure summary.

The structure database may be queried directly, using accession numbers or text terms such as author names, protein names, species names or publication dates. The result will yield "Structure Query" pages, providing access to entries which matched the keywords. From the Structure Summary pages of an individual matching entry one may access amino acid and nucleic acid sequences, retrieve Pub Med documents, get taxonomy information, and launch the software to view the 3D image.

The MMDB documentation also notes that "The structure database is considerably smaller than Entrez's protein or nucleotide databases, but a large fraction of all known protein sequences have homolog in this set, and one may often learn more about a protein by examining 3-D structures of its homolog. Protein sequences from MMDB are extracted and available in the Entrez protein sequence database. They are linked to the 3-D structures; therefore it is possible to determine whether a protein sequence in Entrez has homologs amongst known structures by examining its Related Sequences or Protein Neighbours and checking whether this set has any Structure Links."

Software

1) <u>Software Directories</u> (http://www.istl.org/02-winter/internet.html#a)

2) <u>Tools in Specific Programming Languages</u> (http://www.istl.org/02-winter/internet.html#b)

3) <u>Open Source Software Promoters</u> (http://www.istl.org/02-winter/internet.html#c)

Software Directories: Bioinformatics Software Resource (BISR) (http://bioinfo.nist.gov/BISR/)

A catalog and clearinghouse of links to bioinformatics and computational biology software and resources. Over 400 packages are currently available, more than 70% of the software is free, and a variety of operating systems are supported. This database is maintained by the Chemical Science and Technology Laboratory of the National Institute of Standards and Technology (NIST).

Database Searching, Browsing and Analysis Tools (http://www.ebi.ac.uk/Tools/ index.html) - A list of software tools (programs) you can use via the web to submit queries to the sequence databases and to analyze the results of those queries. This list is from the European Bioinformatics Institute. See also the ExPASy Proteomics Tools list below.

ExPASy Proteomics Tools (http://www.expasy.org/links.html) - Tools for proteomics that may be used over the web, covering such categories as protein identification and characterization, similarity searches, secondary structure prediction, and sequence alignment.

Genomics Software Seek (http://genamics.com/software/index.htm) - A repository and database of over 1200 free and commercial tools for use in molecular biology and biochemistry. Windows, MS-DOS, Mac, Unix and Linux platforms are supported, as well as online tools that run through your Internet browser. You may browse by category (such as DNA sequence analysis, molecular modeling, or protein structure prediction) or you may search by platform, program name or keyword.

Freshmeat Open Source Software Repository (http://freshmeat.net/) - This database of UNIX and cross-platform open source software is a good source for molecular modeling and visualization programs and contains a smattering of bioinformatics applications. Each entry provides a history of the project's releases (very useful for spotting stale code) and a popularity ranking. See also Open Source Software Promoters.

Tools in Specific Programming Languages

Bioinformatics makes use of a number of programming languages, including C++, Perl, Java, Python, XML, Ruby and Lisp. Worth noting here is the development of the various Bio*.org projects that now cluster under the umbrella group called the **Open Bioinformatics Foundation** (http://www.open-bio.org/), which was incorporated in October 2001. Each of these projects is an international association of developers of open source tools (software programs or program modules) for bioinformatics, genomics and life science research written in their particular language. Each association attempts to archive, mirror or provide pointers to any and all biology-related code in their specific language that is freely available for download. **BioPerl.org** was the first projects.

1) **BioPerl** (http://www.bioperl.org/wiki/Main_Page)
2) **BioPython** (http://biopython.org/wiki/Main_Page)
3) **BioJava** (http://biojava.org/wiki/Main_Page)
4) **BioDAS** (http://www.biodas.org/wiki/Main_Page)

Open Source Software Promoters

Just as bioinformatics researchers have been remarkably open (some would say advanced) in making their sequence data freely available to the public, many bioinformatics programmers want to do the same with their program source code. In this regard they join many other computer scientists and programmers in supporting open source software. OpenSource.org (http://www.opensource.org/) puts the benefits of the open model this way: "When programmers can read, redistribute, and modify the source code for a piece of software, the software evolves. People improve it, people adapt it, people fix bugs. And this can happen at a speed that, if one is used to the slow pace of conventional software development, seems astonishing." In addition to the Open Bioinformatics Foundation (http://www.open-bio.org/wiki/Main_Page) mentioned in the previous section, Bioinformatics.org : The Open Lab (http://bioinformatics.org/) and OpenInformatics.org (http://www.openinformatics.org/) are two other organizations of note dedicated to promoting open source software among bioinformatics and life science researchers.

Comprehensive Web Sites: see also Database Directories and Lists (http://www.istl.org/ 02-winter/internet.html#2)

Human Genome Project: There are many sites on this topic. Here are three good ones in terms of their comprehensive nature and links to research at the university level:

1) Genome Hub (from the National Human Genome Research Institute) - (http://www.genome.gov/page.cfm?pageID=10001674)

2) The Human Genome (from the National Center for Biotechnology Information) - (http://www.ncbi.nlm.nih.gov/genome/guide/human/)

3) Human Genome Project Information (from the U.S. Department of Energy) - (http://www.doegenomes.org/)

Large-Scale Gene Expression and Microarray Links and Resources (http://industry.ebi.ac.uk/~alan/MicroArray/)

To put microarrays into context with bioinformatics consider this quote from Gene-Chips.com (http://www.gene-chips.com/): "It is widely believed that thousands of genes and their products (i.e., RNA and proteins) in a given living organism function in a complicated and orchestrated way that creates the mystery of life. However, traditional methods in molecular biology generally work on a "one gene in one experiment" basis, which means that the throughput is very limited and the "whole picture" of gene function is hard to obtain. In the past several years, a new technology, called DNA microarray, has attracted tremendous interests among biologists. This technology promises to monitor the whole genome on a single chip so that researchers can have a better picture of the interactions among thousands of genes simultaneously. Terminologies that have been used in the literature to describe this technology include, but not limited to: biochip, DNA chip, DNA microarray, and gene array."

Bioinformatics comes into play in a microarray experiment in terms of image processing, robotics control, and analysis of the resulting raw data. This site is particularly useful because, by its own admission, its view of the subject is biased towards the development and application of bioinformatics to the technology of microarrays.

Nature's Genome Gateway (http://www.nature.com/genomics/)

Produced by the journal Nature, access to all material at this site is free. It offers a nice collection of full text research articles from the Nature Publishing Group journals arranged by organism (the human category in this section is the richest). An additional section of the site is completely devoted to the human genome. A post-genomics section looks at the applications of sequencing research. A well organized site with good information.

SMD Microarray Resources (http://genome-www4.stanford.edu/MicroArray/SMD/ resources.html): Good content nicely arranged is presented here. Headings for microarray databases, software, companies and academic sites as well as a good list of starting points under the general information heading. SMD stands for the Stanford Microarray Database, which stores microarray data and images. Some of the SMD data is available to the public.

Southwest Biotechnology and Informatics Center (SWBIC)

Bioinformatics & Genomics (http://www.swbic.org/links/1.php): This is a site of stellar organization and considerable content. All the standard categories are well represented (e.g., Conferences, Databases, News, Online Journals) and the subject specific categories are outstanding (Hidden Markov Models, Genomics and DNA Sequence Analysis, Metabolic Pathway Databases, etc.). The quality of the entries is high, and each entry is annotated. A search capability is also offered as an alternative to browsing.

Visualization Awareness Pages (http://industry.ebi.ac.uk/~Alan/VisSupp/VisAware/index.html): "These pages aim to catalogue visualization sites, applications, techniques and papers that may be of interest to the Bioinformatics and Biological community." This is an extensive and varied directory created by Alan Robinson, a researcher at the European Bioinformatics Institute. Extensive data visualization resource directories are not common, so it's especially nice to find one that focuses on bioinformatics visualization in particular.

PubMed (http://www.ncbi.nlm.nih.gov/pubmed): For medical bibliographic citations this is the place to go. PubMed is the public interface to the medical literature database (MEDLINE) produced by the National Library of Medicine. PubMed provides access to over 11 million MEDLINE citations for articles and conference papers back to the mid-1960. There are links to many sites providing full text articles (some for free) and PubMed citations link to Entrez nucleotide, protein and structure records when available. Unfortunately, PubMed currently supports searching by Chemical Abstracts Service (CAS) Registry Numbers (RNs) in a very limited way. The dictionary of RNs supported in PubMed is limited and is not currently extended to sequences found in other parts of the Entrez system. The PubMed interface is a rich and somewhat complicated one that requires some study to use efficiently. PubMed with its Entrez links provides an almost one-stop-shopping experience, and is an amazingly rich resource for medical and genetics data.

INSPEC (http://www.theiet.org/publish/inspec/about/) [subscription required]: For citations to computer science literature, start with INSPEC (for noncommercial computer science articles freely available on the Internet, see Research Index below). Produced by the Institution of Electrical Engineers (IEE), INSPEC is the leading bibliographic information service providing access to conference papers and journal articles in computer science and information technology as well as electrical engineering and physics. The database covers literature from 1969-present, and is available from a variety of database vendors, most of which will also provide links to your library's online journals.

ISI Web of Science (http://apps.isiknowledge.com/) [subscription required]: This is a large, powerful and costly citation database. It is an index to scientific, commercially published journal articles from 1975 to the present that also allows you to search for citations to a particular article. You look up the reference to a work that you have identified to find other more recent journal articles that have cited it. Cited reference searching is a unique way to trace ideas and subjects from past research into the present day - searchable by author, keyword, and cited reference. Computer scientists and biologists are quite interested in citation data. Web of Science doesn't index conferences as a primary literature source, which is a disadvantage in bioinformatics where conferences are so important. See also Research Index below.

NCSTRL - Networked Computer Science Technical Reference Library (http://csetechrep.ucsd.edu/Dienst/htdocs/Welcome.html): NCSTRL (pronounced "ancestral") is an international collection of technical reports from a selection of participating computer science and computer engineering departments, industrial and government research laboratories made available for non-commercial and educational use - Searchable by keyword, author, or title.

Pre-Print Network from the Department of Energy (http://www.osti.gov/preprints/): The Department of Energy funds a great deal of bioinformatics research at US universities. They are particularly interested in protein structure, DNA repair of radiation damage, and bioremediation of polluted sites. The Preprint Network is the gateway to preprints in disciplines of interest to the DOE, including bioinformatics. The Network is a met search engine that searches across a number of preprint and technical report collections, including the Networked Computer Science Technical Reference Library (NCSTRL), among others. They also offer an update service that will e-mail you when new resources are added in your area of interest. "The Preprint Network is one leg of a triad of electronic products for the science information consumer. We also offer PubSCIENCE ({http://www.osti.gov/pubscience}), a gateway to journal literature, and the DOE Information Bridge (http://www.osti.gov/bridge), an on-line access route to full-text technical report literature of the Department of Energy."

The Bioinformatics Resource (TBR) Tutorials (http://www.hgmp. mrc.ac.uk/CCP11/directory_tutorials.jsp?Rp=20): This brand new database (launched January 25, 2002) covers a wide range of topics, contains substantial numbers of records, and is both searchable by keyword and brows able by topic. Sixty-three tutorials are currently catalogued. The list is very heavily weighted towards university course web pages, yet there are some real gems in here. TBR is the website of the CCP11project (Collaborative Computational Project 11). CCP11 was established to foster bioinformatics in the UK research community, thus explaining the high number of UK resources listed.

NCBI: Education Page (http://www.ncbi.nlm.nih.gov/Education):

Online education materials from the National Center for Biotechnology Information includes online tutorials for the BLAST search program and some of the Entrez Databases (PubMed,

Nucleotides, Structures), as well as a useful essay on similarity searching and glossary of terms related to sequence searching.

Protein Data Bank (PDB): Education Resources (http://www.rcsb.org/pdb/static.do?p=general_information/news_publi cations/newsletters/ educationcorner.html):

A nicely organized directory of high quality educational sites related to proteins and nucleic acids, as well as pointers to tutorials on using the PDB itself. There is a section called "protein documentaries" that lists multimedia sites (VRML, RealPlayer and/or Chime plug-ins required) and an excellent selection of molecular modeling resources in the section called "Other Educational Resources." Also worth visiting is the link to "Links" in the upper right under "Other Information Resources" that takes you to their "Macromolecular Structure Related Resources" page which is a comprehensive web directory of its own.

Science Magazine: Functional Genomics Educational Resources (http://www.sciencemag.org/feature/plus/sfg/education/ index.shtml): This site has a lot to recommend it. A "film festival" section provides Real-time movies and webcasts of press conferences and lectures. The glossary section has already been recommended earlier in this guide. There is an annotated list of "Ten Great Educational Websites" (which are very cool, though most seem to be aimed at the high school level) plus an education site of the month. And not to be missed are the three sites in the "A Little Base (Pair) Humor" section: Cartoonists' views of the Human Genome Project from Slate magazine, the DNA-O-Gram which allows you to send a nucleotide-encoded message to a friend, and Swiss-Jokes -- "The infamous random sampler of helvetian humor from ExPASy."

Source: (http://www.istl.org/02-winter/internet.html)

Chapter 8: WEB RESOURCES AT EDUCATIONAL INSTITUTES AND COURSES

School of Biological Sciences, Bioinformatics Website (http://computing.bio.cam.ac.uk/index.html), (http://www.bio.cam.ac.uk/)

List of helpful Bioinformatics websites, including those with interactive tutorials: The EBI (European Bioinformatics Institute) provides online training (http://www.ebi.ac.uk/training/online/). This is as good way to find out about which nucleotide and protein analyses are available and how they work. In these EBI tutorials you will be guided through a series of exercises using sample fragments of sequence. To gain more information about these sequences, you will use a variety of tools that are available at the EBI to compare the sequences to databases and analyze them.

The NCBI (America's National Center for Biotechnological Information) also provide very useful set of interactive bioinformatics tutorials (http://www.ncbi.nlm.nih.gov/education/) together with listings and definitions of various tools (http://www.ncbi.nlm.nih.gov/guide/all/#tools_). Also at the NCBI it is worth considering the Coffee Break archive (http://www.ncbi.nlm.nih.gov/books/NBK2345/) that provides a series of reports which are usually based on a real biomedical discovery reported in the published peer-reviewed literature. The result is an interactive tutorial using NCBI tools that tells a biological story. At various points in each report the reader can see the evidence and find further related information using predefined searches; like PubMed searches of MEDLINE, and BLAST searches of GenBank.

There are many bioinformatics tools and services available from Cambridge at the School of Biological sciences bioinformatics website (http://computing.bio.cam.ac.uk/ index.html). Of special note are the courses run locally at the university, which range from the use of individual programs and services to learning how to write computer programs for biology. If you need to draw up the structures of a protein or any homologues whose structures have been solved, a good place to start is at the Protein Data Bank website (http://www.rcsb.org/pdb/home/home.do). There is an online tutorial (http://www.openhelix. com/pdb) and various training materials on how to use the PDB. Also of interest are narrated screencasts (http://www.pdb.org/pdb/static.do?p=general_information/screencasts.jsp) that illustrate the RCSB PDB website. If you have a sequence and have no information about its structure, it's fun to submit the sequence to one of several fold-recognition or modeling programs such as PHYRE (http://www.sbg.bio.ic.ac.uk/phyre2/html/page.cgi?id=index), FUGUE (http://tardis.nibio.go.jp/fugue/prfsearch.html) and SWISS-MODEL (http://swissmodel.expasy.org/).

Finally, for the Part II Biochemistry PBL exercise and associated teaching there will be a significant focus on websites where you can perform multiple analyses across multiple databases without having to go to multiple websites. The most important of these are the Ensembl Genome browser (http://www.ensembl.org/) and the EBI Services (http://www.ebi.ac.uk/services).

*Source: (*http://www.bioc.cam.ac.uk/teaching/third-year/biochemistry/bioinformatics*)*

Columbia University: Web resources for Bioinformatics

The following list of web resources was compiled by Prof. Bill Noble. If you find dead links, please contact me (cleslie@cs.columbia.edu) to correct URL.

Genomics and bioinformatics centers

a. National Center for Biotechnology Information home page (http://www.ncbi.nlm.nih.gov/)
   i. NCBI's ENTREZ browser for biosequence databases (http://www3.ncbi.nlm.nih.gov/Entrez/)
   ii. NCBI's BLAST biosequence database search tool (http://www.ncbi.nlm.nih.gov/BLAST/)

b. Computational Molecular Biology at NIH (http://molbio.info.nih.gov/molbio)

c. European Moloecular Biology Laboratory WWW services (http://www.embl-heidelberg.de/services/index.html)
   i. EMBL's SRS browser for biosequence databases (http://www.embl-heidelberg.de/srs5/)
   ii. EMBL's PHD program to predict protein secondary structure (http://www.embl-heidelberg.de/predictprotein/predictprotein.html)

d. European Bioinformatics Institute home page (http://www.ebi.ac.uk/)

e. Sanger Centre home page (http://www.sanger.ac.uk)

f. Protein Bata Bank (PDB) (http://www.rcbs.org/)

Indexes of bioinformatics tools and genomics projects

1) BioCatalog: EBI's page listing sequence analysis programs worldwide (http://www.ebi.ac.uk/biocat/biocat.html)

2) DOE's Genome Channel (http://compbio.ornl.gov/channel/)

Home pages for other bioinformatics courses

1) Mark Craven : Bioinformatics (http://www.cs.wisc.edu/~craven/cs838.html)

2) Kevin Karplus : Computational Biology (http://www.cse.ucsc.edu/classes/cmps243)

3) David Haussler : Computational Biology (http://www.cse.ucsc.edu/classes/cmps243/Fall99)

4) Georg Fuellen : Full on-line Hypertext Biocomputing (http://merlin.mbcr.bcm.tmc.edu:8001/bcdusa/welcome.html)

5) States/Zuker/Eddy/Gish : Computational Molecular Biology (http://bio5495.wustl.edu/) (This course contains web pages to help students unfamiliar with UNIX and Perl get started).

6) Karp/Ruzzo/Tompa : Algorithms in Molecular Biology (http://www.cs. washington.edu/education/courses/590bi/) (Includes slides from all lectures).

7) Naor/Shamir : Algorithms for Moloecular Biology (http://www.math.tau.ac.il/~shamir/algmb.html) (Includes notes taken by student "scribes" from lectures).

8) Altman/Brutlag/Levitt: Algorithms and Representations for Molecular Biology (http://smi-web.stanford.edu/projects/helix/mis214/) (Includes lots of resources and lectures).

9) Mike Levitt : Computational Structural Biology: Protein Simulation and Structure Prediction (http://csb.stanford.edu/levitt/sb228/)

10) Doug Brutlag : Computer Applications in Molecular Biology (http://cmgm.stanford.edu/biochem218/)

11) Steven Salzberg : Computational Biology (http://www.cs.jhu.edu/~salzberg/cs439.html)

12) Rik Belew : Computational Biology (http://www.cse.ucsd.edu/~rik/courses/cse290-wpp/index.html)

13) ISCB's listing of on-line bioinformatics courses (http://www.iscb.org/olCourse.html)

Academic Programs in Bioinformatics / Biotech at Other Institutions

1) Center for Computational and Experimental Genomics, USC (http://searchguide.level3.com/search/?q=http%3A//www-hto.usc.edu/&r=&t=0)

2) BioMolecular Engineering Research Center, Boston U. (http://www.bu.edu/bmerc/)

3) Dept. of Molecular Biotechnology, University of Washington (http://www.mbt.washington.edu)

4) Medical Informatics at Stanford (http://camis.stanford.edu/)

5) Computational Molecular Biology Program at Washington Univ. (http://www.ibc.wustl.edu/CMB/)

6) Keck Center for Advanced Training in Computational Biology (University of Pittsburgh and Carnegie Mellon, and also Baylor, Rice and the University of Houston) (http://www.cs.pitt.edu/keck/Frames/Welcome.html)

7) Computational Biology and Informatics Program at U. Penn. (http://www.pcbi.upenn.edu/)

8) Bioinformatics and Computational Biology Ph.D. Program at George Mason (http://www.science.gmu.edu/~michels/Bioinformatics/)

9) MIT Whitehead Center for Genome Research (http://www-genome.wi.mit.edu/)

10) Berkeley-UCSF joint program in bioengineering (http://www.coe.berkeley.edu/bioengineering/index.html)

11) ISCB's list of academic programs in Computational Biology (http://www.iscb.org/univ.html)

Bibliographies for Bioinformatics Literature and on-line Primers

1) DOE: Nice on-line primer on molecular genetics and human genome project with figures (http://web.ornl.gov/sci/techresources/Human_Genome/redirect.shtml)

2) DOE: Glossary of molecular biology and genome informatics terms (http://www.gdb.org/Dan/DOE/prim6.html)

3) DOE: Home page for the Human Genome Project (http://web.ornl.gov/sci/TechResources/Human_Genome/home.shtml)

4) On-line primer on DNA structure (http://www.blc.arizona.edu/Molecular_Graphics/DNA_Structure/DNA_Tutorial.HTML)

5) On-line protein structure tutorial (requires free CHIME plugin) (http://www.kumc.edu/biochemistry/bioc800/frames.html)

6) Computational genefinding tutorial (http://www.cse.ucsc.edu/~haussler/genefindingpaper/paper.html)

7) Burkhard Rost review paper on protein structure prediction (http://www.embl-heidelberg.de/~rost/papers/sisyphus.html)

8) Index to on-line and regular journals in the biosciences (http://mcb.harvard.edu/BioLinks.html)

9) Bioinformatics Journal (http://www3.oup.co.uk/bioinformatics/)

10) Journal of Computational Biology (http://www-hto.usc.edu/jcb/jcbtoc.html)

11) Extensive bibliography of papers on computational genefinding (http://linkage.rockefeller.edu/wli/gene/)

12) Naor/Shamir: class page containing several bibliographies (http://www.math.tau.ac.il/~rshamir/algmb.html)

[Source: (http://www.cs.columbia.edu/~cleslie/cs4761/resources.html)]

University of Pittsburgh-Health Science Library System

OBRC: Online Bioinformatics Resources Collection (http://www.hsls.pitt.edu/obrc/)

Find molecular databases & software tools with a combined search of the **HSLS Online Bioinformatics Resource Collection (OBRC)**, Nucleic Acids Research, the BioMed Central Databases collection, and a filtered PubMed search.

1) **Search Examples** : keyword [CRISPR, SNP (http://search.hsls.pitt.edu/vivisimo/cgi-bin/query-meta?

query=crispr&v%3Aproject=obrc)] ; phrase [protein structure prediction (http://search.hsls.pitt.edu/vivisimo/cgi-bin/query-meta?query=protein+structure+prediction&v%3Aproject=obrc)]

2) The Online Bioinformatics Resources Collection (OBRC) contains annotations and links for 2457 bioinformatics databases and software tools.

3) DNA Sequence Databases and Analysis Tools (463) (http://www.hsls.pitt.edu/obrc/index.php?page=dna)

4) Enzymes and Pathways (242) (http://www.hsls.pitt.edu/obrc/index.php?page=enzymes_pathways)

5) Gene Mutations, Genetic Variations and Diseases (257) (http://www.hsls.pitt.edu/obrc/index.php?page=mutations_diseases)

6) Genomics Databases and Analysis Tools (636) (http://www.hsls.pitt.edu/ obrc/index.php?page=genomics)

7) Immunological Databases and Tools (49) (http://www.hsls.pitt.edu/obrc/ index.php?page=immunology)

8) Microarray, SAGE, and other Gene Expression (166) (http://www.hsls.pitt.edu/ obrc/index.php?page=gene expression)

9) Organelle Databases (25) (http://www.hsls.pitt.edu/obrc/ index.php?page=organelle)

10) Other Databases and Tools (Literature Mining, Lab Protocols, Medical Topics, and others) (147) (http://www.hsls.pitt.edu/ obrc/index.php?page=others)

11) Plant Databases (146) (http://www.hsls.pitt.edu/obrc/ index.php?page=plant)

12) Protein Sequence Databases and Analysis Tools (408) http://www.hsls.pitt.edu/obrc/index.php?page=protein_sequences

13) Proteomics Resources (58) (http://www.hsls.pitt.edu/obrc/index.php?page=proteomics)

14) RNA Databases and Analysis Tools (222) (http://www.hsls.pitt.edu/obrc/index.php?page=rna)

15) Structure Databases and Analysis Tools (384) (http://www.hsls.pitt.edu/obrc/index.php?page=structure)

Source: (http://www.hsls.pitt.edu/obrc/)

A few more important resources to be aware of

a. *Human Genome Working Draft* (http://genome.ucsc.edu/)

b. *TIGR (The Institute for Genomic Research)* (http://www.tigr.org/)

c. *Celera* (http://www.celera.com/)

d. *(Model) Organism specific information :*

   i. *Yeast* (http://www.yeastgenome.org/)

   ii. *Arabidopsis* (http://www.tair.org/)

   iii. *Mouse* (http://www.jax.org/)

   iv. *Fruitfly* (http://www.fruitfly.org/)

   v. *Nematode* (http://www.wormbase.org/)

e. *Nucleic Acids Research Database Issue* (http://nar.oupjournals.org/) *- First issue every year*

Genome Projects

a) Human Genome Resources (NCBI) (http://www.ncbi.nlm.nih.gov/genome/guide/human/)

b) National Human Genome Research Institute (NIH) (http://www.nhgri.nih.gov)

c) Stanford Genome Resource (http://genome-www.stanford.edu/)

d) The Genome Projects (TIGER) (http://www.tigr.org/tdb/)

e) The Human Genome Project (DOE) (http://www.ornl.gov/sci/techresources/Human_Genome/publicat/primer/index.shtml)

Cornell University: Bioinformatics: Web-Based Resources & Computational Approaches to Biological Sciences (http://www-users.med.cornell.edu/~jawagne/logic & experimental_desig.html).

Go to: **logic & exptl design (homepage)** | **dictionary** | **proteins** | **cDNAs** | **antibodies** | **DNA & genes** | **links to related sites** |

    a. Introduction to bioinformatics

    b. Relationship of Bioinformatics to other pages on this site

    c. Bioinformatics and Experimental approaches

        1. Bridging among protein, DNA, and RNA sequences

        2. Searching for related sequences in other organisms

        3. Searching for functional patterns in proteins and nucleic acids

        4. Determine if there are known interactions among proteins

        5. Structural studies and predictions

    d. Managing data

    e. Bioinformatics and Scientific communication

    f. Getting in touch with the scientific literature

g. Identifying reagents and protocols for their use from biotechnology companies
h. Becoming aware of meetings where scientists exchange information and ideas
i. Find funding opportunities for your ideas and find out what others are doing or want to do.
j. Make a killing on the market.

Introduction: Although the fundamental ideas of most experiments in biological science are straightforward, the shear amount of data that has been produced is mind boggling. It is beyond the ability (or the desire) of any of us to recall or make use of all this information, yet when efficiently used, these data provide a rich source of information. Luckily, the advent of computer technology has provided the means for the community to organize these data and make them available to the community. The need to accomplish this task has created a new discipline within the community of biological scientists to:

a) focus on how data can be efficiently made available to the community, and, perhaps more importantly,
b) develop new algorithms to extract information from these data.

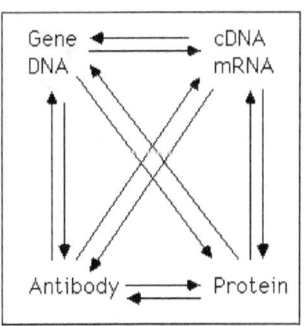

Specialists within the field of Bioinformatics work both independently and in collaboration with other scientists. Beyond the advances they make, the tools developed by this community can save you considerable time in your research. For example, in silica* (http://www-users.med.cornell.edu/~jawagne/dictionary_for_logic_and_e.html#I-dictionary) searches are much faster than corresponding experimental approaches. An afternoon at the computer can often save weeks of laboratory work. Beyond speed, in silica approaches can reveal important evidence for evolutionary and functional relationships between genes and proteins.

The relationship of Bioinformatics to other pages on this site: This site is organized around the idea that current experimental approaches allow scientists to use information to bootstrap themselves from information about one type of molecule (DNA, RNA, protein, or antibody) to another type of macromolecule (see the home page).

Likewise, once this type of information is obtained and organized, links among different types of information allow the scientist to move among information about DNA, RNA, proteins, genetics, biological structures, and other information as is illustrated by the Entrez databases (http://www.ncbi.nlm.nih.gov/Database/index.html), which are under constant development by NCBI (National Center of Biotechnology Information) (http://www.ncbi.nlm.nih.gov/) and collaborative scientists. Entrez's view of the relationship among databases and information is conceptualized by the following diagram, which was copied from their website. [OMIM (http://www.ncbi.nlm.nih.gov/omim) stands for On-Line Mendelian Inheritance in Man]:

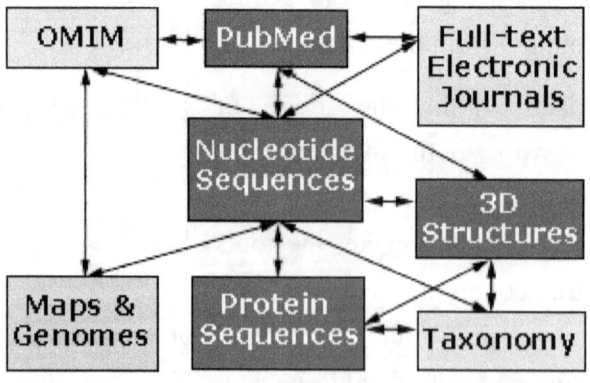

NCBI also has [advanced workshops for bioinformatics](http://www.ncbi.nlm.nih.gov/Class/NAWBIS/Test/modeules.html) and other [online tutorials](http://www.ncbi.nlm.nih.gov/Class/NAWBIS/Education/index.html) for many of their tools as well as tutorials in fundamental science concepts.

First, let's consider a few examples of the ways that using bioinformatics aids experimental approaches:

a) [Bridging among protein, DNA, and RNA sequences](http://www-users.med.cornell.edu/~jawagne/Bioinformatics.html#Bridgingmolbio)

b) [Searching for related sequences in other organisms](http://www-users.med.cornell.edu/~jawagne/Bioinformatics.html#otherorganisms)

c) [Searching for functional patterns in proteins and nucleic acids](http://www-users.med.cornell.edu/~jawagne/Bioinformatics.html#functionalpatterns)

d) [Determine if there are known interactions among proteins](http://www-users.med.cornell.edu/~jawagne/Bioinformatics.html#protein-interactions)

e) [Structural studies and predictions](http://www-users.med.cornell.edu/~jawagne/Bioinformatics.html#structuralpredictions)

f) [Managing data](http://www-users.med.cornell.edu/~jawagne/Bioinformatics.html#managingdata)

Then we will consider three additional ways that computer based approaches allow communication within the community and take advantages of commercial resources:

a) Getting in touch with the scientific literature (http://www-users.med.cornell.edu/~jawagne/Bioinformatics.html#science literature)

b) Identifying reagents and protocols for their use from biotechnology companies (http://www-users.med.cornell.edu/~jawagne/Bioinformatics.html#reagents&protocools)

c) Becoming aware of meetings where scientists exchange information and ideas (http://www-users.med.cornell.edu/~jawagne/Bioinformatics.html#meetings&organizations)

d) Find funding opportunities for your ideas and find out what others are doing or want to do. (http://www-users.med.cornell.edu/~jawagne/Bioinformatics.html#Funding%20&%20ideas)

e) Make a killing on the market. (http://www-users.med.cornell.edu/~jawagne/Bioinformatics.html#killingonmarket)

This page will also provide some links to resources, and we encourage users of this site to suggest additional links (http://www-users.med.cornell.edu/~jawagne/index.html#credits%20and%20additions) that may be of interest. There are several sites devoted to listing links to databases and computational research tools like Amos' WWW links page (http://www.expasy.org/links.html), the NCBI's Site Map (http://www.ncbi.nlm.nih.gov/Sitemap/index.html), or CMS Molecular Biology Resources (http://www.unl.edu/stc-95/ResTools/cmshp.html).

Bridging among protein, DNA, and RNA sequences

The central dogma predicts that the sequence of DNA predicts the sequence of RNA, which in turn determines the primary sequence of proteins.

a) There is extensive sequence information from a growing number of organisms, including the sequences of the complete genomes of a number of organisms. This information is rapidly becoming more extensive and is being annotated to include information about genes and their products and the presence of mutations and genetic markers within natural populations. See Ensembl & other information at the Sanger Institute or

b) The NCBI's Genomic Biology (http://www.ncbi.nih.gov/Genomes/) or

c) GOLD (http://wit.integratedgenomics.com/GOLD/) (Genome online database) or

d) NCBI's SNP database (http://www.ncbi.nlm.nih.gov/SNP/) (natural variations in humans) or

e) Celera's publication site (http://public.celera.com/cds/login.cfm) or

f) Stanford Genome Resources (http://genome-www.stanford.edu/) or Stanford's Genome Center (http://sequence-www.stanford.edu/) or

g) Likewise, there is extensive information about the sequence of RNAs, including the partial sequence information termed ESTs (expressed sequence tags). See NCBI's EST database (http://www.ncbi.nlm.nih.gov/dbEST/index.html) or The I.M.A.G.E. Consortium (http://image.llnl.gov/)

Thus, partial sequence information from a gene of interest can be used to search for either corresponding cDNAs or genomic DNAs which may reside in a publicly accessible database. This can lead to clues about:

a) Where else the gene might be expressed

b) The existence of overlapping cDNA clones that can be directly obtained rather than isolated from a library via a laborious screening process.

c) The sequences of flanking DNAs

d) The map position of the gene that gave rise to the original cDNA, which could reveal a potential association with genetic disorders or interesting phenotypes, etc.

e) The existence of orthologues* (http://www-users.med.cornell.edu/~jawagne/dictionary_for_logic_and_e.html#O-dictionary), or corresponding genes in other organisms BLAST (Basic Local Alignment Search Tool) (http://www.ncbi.nlm.nih.gov/BLAST). This type of data can be used to show evolutionary relationships among organisms and construct a 'Bush of Life.'

f) The existence of paralogues* (http://www-users.med.cornell.edu/~jawagne/dictionary_for_logic_and_e.html#P-dictionary) within the same organism, revealing a gene family. A database reviewing this type of information is found at COGs - Clusters of Orthologous Groups at NCMI.

Likewise, partial sequence information from a protein can be used design a probe to screen a cDNA library (http://www-users.med.cornell.edu/~jawagne/cDNA_clonning.html#_Screening), but it can also be used to query a nucleic acid data base for a protein with a related sequence.

Proteomic approaches produce a huge amount of data, and computational approaches can help manage that data. Algorithms can suggest the probable structure of protein fragments, including the complexity added by post-translational modifications as illustrated on the PROWL (http://prowl.rockefeller.edu/) site or the links on the ExPASy Proteomics tools page (http://www.expasy.org/tools/). Once sequences are determined, the relationship of partial sequence data can be compared to database information to identify the corresponding protein, RNA, or gene.

Searching for related sequences in other organisms: Knowledge of sequence information in one organism can be used to search for corresponding genes in another organism. For example, if genetic information suggests that a particular gene is associated with a human disease, an in silico search (a search of databases using silicon based chips) can identify candidates for the corresponding gene in other species at either the protein or nucleotide level (see BLAST). Phenotypes observed in one organism, are at least indications of possible functions for the orthologous genes in other organisms. See, for example, NCBI's OMIM data base (Online Mendelian Inheritance in Man) (http://www.ncbi.nlm.nih.gov/entrez/query.fcgi? db=OMIM).

Searching for functional patterns in proteins and nucleic acids: Very often, the function or activity of an unknown protein can be ascertained by identifying relationships to known functional domains within its amino acid sequence. Computers provide a powerful way to identify specific patterns in sequence information.

   a. For example, biochemical and molecular approaches have identified sequence specific DNA-binding proteins that can act as act as transcription factors. Once the preferred sequence recognized by these factors is known, DNA sequences can be searched for the existence of potential binding sites. One can query a database to determine the potential binding sites for a known factor in the entire genome or one can query for the presence of putative binding sites for any known protein within a DNA region of interest.

i. See the Transfac page (https://rcc.med.harvard.edu/hard_software/transfac/default.html) of Harvard's Research Computing Center.
ii. or TRADAT (TRAnscription Databases and Analysis Tools) (http://www.itba.mi.cnr.it/tradat/introduction.html).

b. Similarly, RNA's can be analyzed for the presence of known or possible structural or functional elements. See The RNA World (http://www.imb-jena.de/RNA.html) Web Site.

c. There are many examples of sites which use a variety of methods to predict the secondary and tertiary structures of a protein based solely on the primary sequence, including the predict protein (https://www.embl-heidelberg.de/predictprotein/predictprotein.html) server and the Swiss-model (http://www.expasy.org/swissmod/SWISS-MODEL.HTML).

d. Likewise, databases can be queried to determine if interesting patterns of primary or predicted secondary structure are present in a protein (or a predicted protein). The presence of such domains may provide evidence for the existence of a particular catalytic activity (e.g., the catalytic triad suggests a protein may be a protease) or a binding site (the bHLH structure suggests the possibility of a DNA binding domain while the L-hand suggests a calcium binding pocket, etc.). The ExPASy (Expert Protein Analysis System) (http://www.expasy.ch/) is devoted to analysis of protein sequence and structure. The scanprosite (http://www.expasy.org/tools/scanprosite/) program can search databases for the occurrence of patterns or profiles. Once an interesting pattern of protein sequence is determined (a motif), the database can be searched to determine if other proteins have the same motif, suggesting a relationship among proteins that can be explored. BLAST (Basic Local Alignment Search Tool) (http://www.ncbi.nlm.nih.gov/BLAST), includes algorithms to search for similarity at the protein or nucleic acid level.

e. Patterns within the nucleotide sequence are often able to predict the existence of genes, promoters, splice sites, etc within genomes. See ENSEMBL (http://www.ensembl.org/) or the NCBI's genebank (http://www.ncbi.nlm.nih.gov/entrez/query.fcgi?db=Nucleotide) or NCBI's Unigene (http://www.ncbi.nlm.nih.gov/UniGene) or NCBI's Map Viewer (http://www.ncbi.nlm.nih.gov/PMGifs/Genomes/MapviewerHelp.html#Overview). To search for patterns shared among DNA or protein sequences the CLUSTALW: Multiple Sequence Alignment site (http://clustalw.genome.ad.jp/) can be helpful.

Determine if there are known interactions among proteins: Frequently clues to the role of a protein can be developed by determining if a protein (or closely related proteins) is known to interact physically or interact indirectly as part of a known pathway. Databases, including known pathways and the proteins involved in those pathways, can provide a rapid way of developing testable models for a proteins function. Some databases also collect and update information as more information on signaling pathways emerges. Some sites that can facilitate this include:

a) DIP: the Database of Interacting Proteins (http://carrer.gnf.org/dbs/html/gkd005_gml.html)

b) BIND (http://www.blind.ca/) The Biomolecular Interaction Network Database.

c) DNA-Protein Interaction Data Base (http://www.dpidb.belozersky.msu.ru/)

d) Signaling Pathway Database (http://www.grt.kyushu-u.ac.jp/spad/)

e) Biocarta has sets of clickable signaling pathways (http://www.biocarta.com/genes/index.asp)

f) Cell Signaling Networks Database (http://geo.nihs.go.jp/csndb/)

g) TRANSFAC (http://www.biobase.de/pages/products/databases.html) includes databases that explain control of transcription

h) NucleaRDB (http://receptors.ucsf.edu/NR/) - An Information System for Nuclear Receptors

i) GPCRDB: (http://www.gpcr.org/7tm/) G protein-coupled Receptor Data Base

Structural studies and predictions: Web based computational programs and databases provide an accessible way of studying the structure and interactions of biological molecules. Programs can:

a) predict RNA secondary structure (e.g., see Computational approaches to RNA structure analysis (http://www-lecb.ncifcrf.gov/~bshapiro/RNAstructure.html) or Algorithms, Thermodynamics and databases for RNA Secondary Structure (http://bioinfo.math.rpi.edu/~zukerm/ma/).

b) compare the structure (or predicted structure) of related proteins (see predict protein, or Swiss-model, or Structural Classification of Proteins

c) model the binding of a ligand to a receptor,

d) model the interaction of a drug with an enzyme of receptor,

e) model the interaction of a protein with a membrane, or

f) model the interaction between two proteins.

The ability to visualize and model molecular interactions is an invaluable approach to understanding biological processes and it is often an essential element in experimental design. The interplay between structural/energetic studies and functional tests of these model helps refine both approaches.

Chapter 9: BIOLOGICAL DATABASES, GATEWAYS AND PORTALS

BioTools.info: Molecular Biology Gateways & Tools

a) Resources for the molecular biologist (http://www.biotools.info/tools.html)

b) Tools & Protocols (http://www.biotools.info/tools.html#b) - Genome Analysis, Sequence Analysis, Primer Design, Phylogeny, RNA Analysis

c) NCBI Resources for Genes & Genomes (http://www.biotools.info/links/ A1bioinfo.pdf)

d) From the Publishers (http://www.biotools.info/tools.html#c)

e) Science literature & dictionaries (http://www.biotools.info/education/literature.html)

f) Bioinformatics Support Service of the Max-Planck Society (http://www.biochem.mpg.de/en/facilities/ivs/SupportTraining/BioInfoSup/) with the Workshops on Bioinformatics Tools & Techniques\ Hand-outs (http://www.biochem.mpg.de/en/facilities/ivs/SupportTraining/Workshop/BioInfoWS/)

Resources @Biotools.info : (http://www.biotools.info/)

Gateways

a) BioinfoWiki (http://www.bioinfowiki.mpg.de/index.php/Main_Page) A Wiki on Bio Tools developed in the Max Planck Society.

b) European Bioinformatics Institute (EBI) (http://www.ebi.ac.uk/)
Center for research and services in bioinformatics. The Institute manages databases of biological data including nucleic acid, protein sequences and macromolecular structures.

c) ExPASy Life Science Directory (http://www.expasy.org/): A well organized collection of < 1000 web links from the Expert Protein Analysis System, a Proteomics and Molecular Biology Server for the analysis of protein sequences and structures as well as 2-D PAGE.

d) National Center for Biotechnology Information (NCBI) (http://www.ncbi.nlm.nih.gov/) Creates public databases, conducts research in computational biology, develops software tools for analyzing genome data, and disseminates biomedical information.

e) OBRC: Online Bioinformatics Resources Collection (http://www.hsls.pitt.edu/obrc/). The website of the UPMC (University of Pittsburgh Medical Center) contains annotations and links for more than 1600 open source bioinformatics databases and software tools.

f) WWW Virtual Library (http://vlib.org/)

Tools & Protocols

Genome Analysis

a) ENSEMBL Genome Server (http://asia.ensembl.org/index.html)

b) NCBI MapViewer (http://www.ncbi.nlm.nih.gov/mapview/)

c) UCSC Genome Bioinformatics (http://genome.ucsc.edu/)

Sequence Analysis

a) CLUSTAL W (http://www.ebi.ac.uk/Tools/msa/) - Multiple Sequence Alignments (EBI).

b) Genedoc (http://www.psc.edu/)

c) Sequence Manipulation Suite (http://bioinformatics.org/sms2/) Restriktionsanalyse im WWW

d) NEB Cutter (http://rebase.neb.com/rebase/rebtools.html)

e) Restrictionmapper (http://www.restrictionmapper.org/)

f) REBASE (http://rebase.neb.com/rebase/rebase.html) - The database of restriction enzymes.

g) Silent (http://mobyle.pasteur.fr/cgi-bin/portal.py?#forms::silent)

h) Mapper (http://arbl.cvmbs.colostate.edu/molkit/mapper/index.html) Primer Design

i) PCR Links (http://www.pcrlinks.com/)

j) Design PCR Primers (http://molbiol-tools.ca/PCR.htm)

k) Oligo Analyzer (http://eu.idtdna.com/analyzer/Applications/OligoAnalyzer/Default.aspx) (SciTools)

l) Primer3 (http://primer3.ut.ee/)

m) Primer BLAST (NCBI) (http://www.ncbi.nlm.nih.gov/tools/primer-blast/index.cgi?LINK_LOC=BlastHome)

n) Quantitative RT-PCR & PCR Array (http://www.sabiosciences.com/RTPCR.php?adwords=PCR) Phylogeny

o) Treeview (http://taxonomy.zoology.gla.ac.uk/rod/treeview.html)

p) Phylodendron (http://iubio.bio.indiana.edu/treeapp/)

q) MEGA (http://www.megasoftware.net/)

r) Phylogeny and Reconstructing Phylogenetic Trees (http://aleph0.clarku.edu/~djoyce/java/Phyltree/cover.html) - These few pages describe the problem of reconstructing phylogenetic trees.

s) Software products for phylogenetic analysis (http://aleph0.clarku.edu/~djoyce/java/Phyltree/cover.html)

DNA analysis tools

a) Gene Finding Format (GFF) tools and definition (http://www.sanger.ac.uk/ Software/GFF/)

b) C. elegans genes in GFF format (from 1998 Science paper) (http://www.sanger.ac.uk/Projects/C_elegans/Science98/)

c) Berkeley's Drosophila genome genefinding experiment (http://www.fruitfly.org/) (Look down the page a bit for the link. Contains tutorial, data, results comparing different genefinders)

d) Banbury cross genefinding benchmark data and international genefinding program results (now a bit out of date) (http://igs-server.cnrs-mrs.fr/igs/banbury/)

e) UCSC GENIE genefinding program (http://www.cse.ucsc.edu/research/compbio)

f) HMMgene genefinding program (http://www.cbs.dtu.dk/services/HMMgene/)

g) GRAIL genefinding program (http://avalon.epm.ornl.gov/Grail-bin/EmptyGrailForm)

h) GenScan genefinding program (http://ccr-081.mit.edu/GENSCAN.html)

i) PROCRUSTES genefinding program (http://www-hto.usc.edu/software/procrustes)

j) University of Wash. Genome Center RepeatMasker page (http://ftp.genome.washington.edu/cgi-bin/RepeatMasker)

k) Ewan Birney's Genewise package. (http://www.sanger.ac.uk/Software/Wise2/) HMMs for protein, EST and genomic DNA analysis.

l) Computational genefinding tutorial (http://www.cse.ucsc.edu/~haussler/genefinding_paper/paper.html)

RNA Analysis

a) Comparative RNA Web Site (http://www.rna.icmb.utexas.edu/)

b) RNA Modification Database (http://www.ma-mdb.cas.albany.edu/RNAmods/). From the Departments of Medicinal Chemistry and Biochemistry, Univ. of Utah.

c) RNA World (http://www.rna.icmb.utexas.edu/) - From the Institute of molecular biotechnology (Jena, Germany).

d) RNAi Technical Resources (http://www.lifetechnologies.com/in/en/home/brands/ambion.html) from Ambion (http://www.ambion.com/) - The RNA Company

Protein analysis tools

a) UCSC SAM-T98 (-T99) HMM applications server (http://www.cse.ucsc.edu/research/compbio/HMM-apps/HMM-applications.html)

b) UCSC SAM Hidden Markov Modeling program (http://www.cse.ucsc.edu/research/compbio/sam.html)

c) Sean Eddy's HMMer Hidden Markov modeling program (http://hmmer.wustl.edu/)

d) SWISSPROT database (http://www.expacy.ch/)

e) PFAM database (http://pfam.wustl.edu/) HMMs for protein families.

f) SMART database (http://coot.embl-heidelberg.de/SMART/) HMMs for protein families.

g) BLOCKS database (http://www.blocks.fhcrc.org/) Database of protein motifs.

h) UCLA/DOE protein structure prediction program (http://www.doe-mbi.ucla.edu/)

i) CASP protein structure prediction contest home page (http://predictioncenter.llnl.gov/)

j) Frontiers of Protein Structure Prediction (comparative analysis) (http://predict.sanger.ac.uk/irbm-course97/)

k) RASMOL and CHIME protein structure viewers (http://www.umass.edu/microbio/rasmol/)

l) CATH database of protein structure classification (http://www.biochem.ucl.ac.uk/bsm/cath/)

m) FSSP database of protein structure classification (http://www2.ebi.ac.uk/dali/fssp.html)

n) SCOP database of protein structure classification (http://scop.mrc-lmb.cam.ac.uk/scop/) (see also temp address of new version of SCOP database of protein structure classification (http://scop.mrc-lmb.cam.ac.uk:8000/scop/)

o) MOLMOL (http://www.mol.biol.ethz.ch/wuthrich/software/molmol/bruker/)

p) PHD. (http://www.public.iastate.edu/~pedro/pprotein_query.html) Prediction of protein secondary structure.

q) AAindex. (http://www.genome.ad.jp/dbget-bin/www_bfind?aaindex) Databases of amino acid properties.

Bioinformatics analysis tools, portals and sequence databases

a) Bioinformatics.org (http://www.bioinformatics.org/)

b) BioWeb@ Institute Pasteur (http://bioweb2.pasteur.fr/)

c) ClustalW online at EBI (http://www.ebi.ac.uk/Tools/msa/)

d) EMBL-EBI (http://www.ebi.ac.uk/)

e) EMBOSS (http://emboss.sourceforge.net/)

f) ExPASyProteomics Server (http://www.expasy.org/)

g) ExPASy - PROSITE (http://prosite.expasy.org/)

h) NCBI (http://www.ncbi.nlm.nih.gov/)

i) NCBI - BLAST (http://blast.ncbi.nlm.nih.gov/Blast.cgi)

j) Protal2dna (http://mobyle.pasteur.fr/cgi-bin/portal.py?#forms::protal2dna)

k) Psort (http://psort.hgc.jp/)

l) ReadSeq server (http://iubio.bio.indiana.edu/cgi-bin/readseq.cgi)

m) The Bioinformatics Links Directory (http://bioinformatics.ca/links_directory/index.php)

n) TMpred server (http://www.ch.embnet.org/software/TMPRED_form.html)

o) wEMBOSS (http://wemboss.sourceforge.net/) Home (http://www.ccg.unam.mx/~vinuesa/index.html) back to table of contents (http://www.ccg.unam.mx/~vinuesa/Bioinformatics_resources_web.html#table_of_contents)

Prediction Tools

PSIPRED Server (http://bioinf.cs.ucl.ac.uk/psipred/) : Protein structure prediction server - includes other prediction methods than just PSIPRED CBS Prediction Servers (http://www.cbs.dtu.dk/services/) : Includes the very useful TMHMM transmembrane domain prediction and SignalP (signal peptide) prediction, among others GenScan Web Server (http://genes.mit.edu/GENSCAN.html) : Predict gene structures from genomic sequence TMPro : Transmembrane helix prediction ADDA (http://ekhidna.biocenter.helsinki.fi/sqgraph/pairsdb/index_html) : Automatic Domain Decomposition Algorithm with several search functions JPred 3 (http://www.compbio.dundee.ac.uk/www-jpred/) : Secondary structure prediction server SplicePort : (http://www.spliceport.csumd.edu/) Splice site analysis and prediction tool Phobius (http://phobius.cbr.su.se/) : Combined transmembrane topology and signal peptide predictor PredictProtein (https://www.predictprotein.org/) : Protein prediction tool incorporating secondary structure, transmembrane helices, binding sites etc. InParanoid (http://inparanoid.sbc.su.se/cgi-bin/index.cgi): Eukaryotic orthology prediction tool MirrorTree Server (http://csbg.cnb.csic.es/mtserver/): Predict protein family co-evolution by sequences or trees.

Other Useful Applications and Tools

TextWrangler (Mac only) (http://www.barebones.com/products/textwrangler/) : Great general purpose text editor, transformer and manipulator - supports most alignment and phylogenetic tree formats Notepad++ (http://notepad-plus-plus.org/) : Versatile source-code and notepad application for Windows [PROSITE My Domains](http://prosite.expasy.org/ mydomains/) : Create and draw protein domain images [WebLogo](http://weblogo.berkeley.edu/ logo.cgi) : Create sequence logo images of conserved sequence motifs. ORIALS/GUIDES

Ensembl tutorials (http://www.ensembl.org/info/website/tutorials/index.html) : Guides to the Ensembl genome browser and its features [CLCbio Bioinformatics Explained](http://www.clcbio.com/support/application-notes/) : Basic bioinformatics background theory [Phylogenetic tree formats](http://molecularevolution.org/resources/treeformats) : Small tutorial on the commonly used Newick and Nexus formats. COMMENDED

Fernández-Suárez XM, Schuster MK: **Using the ensembl genome server to browse genomic sequence data.** Current Protocols in Bioinformatics 2010, Chapter 1: Unit 1.15. [PubMed](http://www.ncbi.nlm.nih.gov/pubmed/20521244).

Catchen JM, Braasch I, Postlethwait JH: **Conserved synteny and the zebra fish genome.** In Methods in Cell Biology Vol. 104 2011:259-85. [PubMed](http://www.ncbi.nlm.nih.gov/pubmed/21924168).

Catchen JM, Conery JS, Postlethwait JH: **Automated identification of conserved synteny after whole-genome duplication.** Genome Research 2009, 19:1497-505. [Full text at PubMed Central](http://www.ncbi.nlm.nih.gov/pmc/articles/PMC2720179/).

Lewin HA, Larkin DM, Pontius J, O'Brien SJ : **Every genome sequence needs a good map.** Genome Research 2009, 19:1925-8. [Full text at PubMed Central](http://www.ncbi.nlm.nih.gov/pmc/articles/PMC2775595/).

Philippe H, Brinkmann H, Lavrov DV, Littlewood DTJ, Manuel M, Wörheide G, Baurain D: **Resolving difficult phylogenetic questions: why more sequences are not enough.** PLoS Biology 2011, 9:e1000602. Full text at PLoS Biology (http://www.plosbiology.org/article/info%3Adoi%2F10.1371%2Fjournal.pbio.1000602).

Prosdocimi F, Linard B, Pontarotti P, Poch O, Thompson JD: **Controversies in modern evolutionary biology: the imperative for error detection and quality control.** BMC Genomics 2012, 13:5. Full text at BMC (http://www.biomedcentral.com/1471-2164/13/5).

Biomed Central Gateways

(http://www.biomedcentral.com/gateways/)

Some of the major bioinformatics web sites which contain many useful links are hereunder (http://www.csd.hku.hk/bruhk/iwantto.html).

Collections of content and resources from journals and sites published by BioMed Central, of interest to researchers in particular subject areas. The research articles in all journals published by BioMed Central are open access. Categories include:

a) Bioinformatics & Genomics Gateway (http://www.biomedcentral.com/gateways/bioinformaticsgenomics/)

b) Cancer Gateway (http://www.biomedcentral.com/gateways/cancer/)

c) China Gateway (http://www.biomedcentral.com/gateways/china/)

d) Microarrays Gateway (http://www.biomedcentral.com/gateways/microarrays/)

e) Neuroscience, Neurology & Psychiatry Gateway (http://www.biomedcentral.com/gateways/neuropshch/)

f) Respiratory Gateway (http://www.biomedcentral.com/gateways/respiration)

g) RNAi Gateway (http://www.biomedcentral.com/gateways/mai/)

h) Systems Biology Gateway (http://www.biomedcentral.com/gateways/systemsbiology/)

i) Nucleic Acid Research (http://nar.oxfordjournals.org/)

Each year, the first issue is devoted to **biological databases** and a later issue to relevant **web-based software resources**. Included is a collection of over 850 Molecular Biology Databases, divided into the following categories : Nucleotide sequence databases, RNA sequence databases, Protein sequence databases, Structure Databases, Genomics Databases (non-vertebrate), Metabolic and Signalling Pathways, Human and other Vertebrate Genomes, Human Genes and Diseases, Microarray Data and other Gene Expression Databases, Proteomics Resources, Other Molecular Biology Databases, Organelle databases, Plant databases, Immunological databases.

a) 2013 Database Issue (http://nar.oxfordjournals.org/content/41/D1.toc)

b) 2012 Web Server Issue (http://nar.oxfordjournals.org/content/40/W1.toc)

c) NAR Methods Online (http://www.oxfordjournals.org/our_journals/nar/new_nar_methods.html)

d) Omics Gateway (http://www.nature.com/omics/index.html) (Nature Publishing Group) (http://www.nature.com/omics/index.html) The Omics Gateway provides life scientists a convenient portal into publications relevant to large-scale biology from journals throughout NPG. Topics include :

  i. Cancer genomics (http://www.nature.com/omics/subjects/cancergenomics/2011.html)

  ii. Chemical genomics (http://www.nature.com/omics/subjects/checimalgenomics/2011.html)

  iii. Comparative, evolutionary and population genomics (http://www.nature.com/omics/subjects/comparativeevolutionaryandpopulationgenomics/)

  iv. Epigenomics (http://www.nature.com/omics/subjects/epigenomics/)

  v. Genetics of gene expression (http://www.nature.com/omics/subjects/geneticsofgeneexpression)

  vi. Genome sequence and analysis (http://www.nature.com/omics/subjects/genomesequenceandanalysis)

  vii. Glycomics (http://www.nature.com/omics/subjects/glycomics/)

  viii. Metabolomics / nomics (http://www.nature.com/omics/subjects/metabolomics/)

  ix. Pharmacogenomics (http://www.nature.com/omics/subjects/pharmacogenomics/)

  x. Proteomics (http://www.nature.com/omics/subjects/proteomics)

xi. Systems biology (http://www.nature.com/omics/subjects/systemsbiology/)

xii. Techniques and methods (http://www.nature.com/omics/subjects/techniquesandmethods/)

xiii. Transcriptomics (http://www.nature.com/omics/subjects/transcriptomics/)

xiv. Science NetWatch (http://www.nature.com/omics/index.html) Interesting science Web sites, selected from the Science Magazine. You can search the database or browse via the subject collections, e.g. Biochemistry (http://www.sciencemag.org/cgi/collection/nw_biochemistry?display=summary) Databases (http://www.sciencemag.org/cgi/collection/nw_databases?display=summary) or Molecular Biology (http://www.sciencemag.org/cgi/collection/nw_molec_biol?display=summary).

Examples of widely used Bioinformatics Database

a) Database interfaces
Genbank/EMBL/DDBJ, Medline, SwissProt, PDB …

b) Sequence alignment
BLAST, FASTA

c) Multiple sequence alignment
Clustal, MultAlin, DiAlign

d) Gene finding
Genscan, GenomeScan, GeneMark, GRAIL

e) Protein Domain analysis and identification
pfam, BLOCKS, ProDom,

f) Pattern Identification/Characterisation
Gibbs Sampler, AlignACE, MEME

g) Protein Folding prediction
PredictProtein, SwissModeler

EBI (http://www.ebi.ac.uk/):

a) SRS database interface
EMBL, SwissProt, and many more

b) Many server-based tools
ClustalW, DALI

SwissProt (http://expasy.cbr.nrc.ca/sprot/):

a) Curation!!!
Error rate in the information is greatly reduced in comparison to most other databases.

b) Extensive cross-linking to other data sources

SwissProt is the 'gold-standard' by which other databases can be measured, and is the best place to start if you have a specific protein to investigate.

Databases

Bioinformatics Resources and Tools

A database is a structured collection of records stored in a computer system. Genomic databases typically store DNA or protein sequences as well as annotated information about those sequences. Many databases also provide bioinformatics tools tools, such as BLAST, for finding specific sequences or annotations. There are hundreds of genomics databases: some are comprehensive, but are not carefully curated (GenBank), while others are carefully curated, but are narrow (FlyBase).

Bioinformatics and **Computational biology** are interdisciplinary (http://en.wikipedia.org/wiki/Interdisciplinarity) fields of research, development and application of algorithms (http://en.wikipedia.org/wiki/Algorithm), computational (http://en.wikipedia.org/wiki/Computer_science) and statistical (http://en.wikipedia.org/wiki/Statistics) methods for management and analysis of biological data, and for solving basic biological problems.

Bioinformatics tools are computer programs that analyze one or more sequences. There are dizzying arrays of bioinformatics tools that can analyze sequences to find protein domains (Pfam), or that can search through databases of millions of sequences to find ones that are similar (BLAST) or that can find potential protein-coding regions (ORF-Finder). Many are freely available over the web. It can be overwhelming to find and use bioinformatics tools because you need to know 1) what type of analysis you want performed 2) what type of tool to use 3) where to find the tool.

Biological databases are libraries of life sciences information, collected from scientific experiments, published literature, high-throughput experiment technology, and computational analyses. They contain information from research areas including genomics (http://en.wikipedia.org/wiki/Genomics), proteomics (http://en.wikipedia.org/wiki/Proteomics), metabolomics (http://en.wikipedia.org/wiki/Metabolomics), microarray (http://en.wikipedia.org/wiki/Microarray) gene expression, and phylogenetics (http://en.wikipedia.org/wiki/Phylogenetics). Information contained in biological databases includes gene function, structure, localization (both cellular and chromosomal), clinical effects of mutations as well as similarities of biological sequences and structures. Biological databases can be broadly classified into sequence and structure databases. Nucleic acid and protein sequences are stored in sequence databases and structure database only store proteins. These databases are important tools in assisting scientists to analyze and explain a host of biological phenomena from the structure of biomolecules (http://en.wikipedia.org/wiki/Biomolecule) and their interaction, to the whole metabolism (http://en.wikipedia.org/wiki/Metabolism) of organisms and to understanding the evolution (http://en.wikipedia.org/wiki/Evolution) of species (http://en.wikipedia.org/wiki/Species). This knowledge helps facilitate the fight against diseases, assists in the development of medications (http://en.wikipedia.org/wiki/Pharmaceutical_drug), predicting certain genetic diseases and in discovering basic relationships among species in the history of life (http://en.wikipedia.org/wiki/Timeline_of_evolutionary_history_of_life).

Biological knowledge is distributed among many different general and specialized databases. This sometimes makes it difficult to ensure the consistency of information. Integrative bioinformatics (http://en.wikipedia.org/wiki/Integrative_bioinformatics) is one field attempting to tackle this problem by providing unified access. One solution is how biological databases cross-reference to other databases with accession numbers (http://en.wikipedia.org/wiki/Accession_number_%28bioinformatics%29) to link their related knowledge together. Relational database (http://en.wikipedia.org/wiki/Relational_database) concepts of computer science (http://en.wikipedia.org/wiki/Computer_science) and Information retrieval (http://en.wikipedia.org/wiki/Information_retrieval) concepts of digital libraries (http://en.wikipedia.org/wiki/Digital_library) are important for understanding biological databases. Biological database design, development, and long-term management is a core area of the discipline of bioinformatics (http://en.wikipedia.org/wiki/Bioinformatics). Data contents include gene sequences, textual descriptions, attributes and ontology (http://en.wikipedia.org/wiki/Ontology_%28information_science%29) classifications, citations, and tabular data. These are often described as semi-structured data (http://en.wikipedia.org/wiki/Data_model), and can be represented as tables, key delimited records, and XML structures.

Bioinformatics has emerged into a discipline due to the availability of huge amount of data. The collection of biological information is very vast and as a result there are number of databases which are available online. Here's a list of major Biological databases:

Protein Sequences Databases

1. Primary Protein Sequence Databases:-The primary sequence databases currently hold over 300,000 non-redundant protein sequences. The most commonly-used are SWISS PROT and PIR.

2. Composite Databases:-There are a number of "composite" databases of protein sequences. These compile their sequence data from the primary sequence databases and filter them to retain only the non-redundant sequences. The best-known are OWL, NCBI.

3. Secondary Sequence Databases:-Secondary databases are those that contain information derived from the primary sequence databases like PROSITE, PRINTS and Pfam.

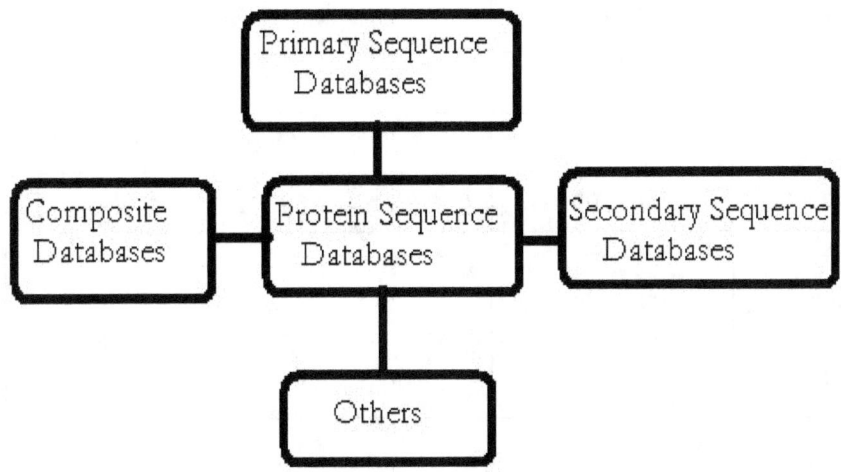

Still there are number of categories in which Protein Sequence Databases can be characterized, these databases are as follows:

Table: Protein Databases

Name	Type	Web Address
Swiss-Prot	Primary	www.expasy.ch
NCBI Protein database	Composite	http://www.ncbi.nlm.nih.gov/entrez/query.fcgi? db=Protein

Name	Type	Web Address
PIR-NREF	Primary	http://pir.georgetown.edu/
PROSITE	Pattern based secondary database	http://www.expasy.org/prosite
InterPro	Families/Domains	http://www.ebi.ac.uk/interpro
PRINTS	Family Fingerprints	http://www.bioinf.man.ac.uk/dbbrowser/PRINTS/

Name	Type	Web Address
Pfam	Protein families	http://www.sanger.ac.uk/Software/Pfam/
ProDom	Domains	http://www.toulouse.inra.fr/prodom.html
AAindex	Protein property	http://www.genome.ad.jp/aaindex/
PMD, Protein Mutant Database	Literature based information	http://pmd.ddbj.nig.ac.jp/
PRF/SEQDB	Amino acid sequences predicted from genes	http://www4.prf.or.jp/en/
OWL	Composite database	http://umber.sbs.man.ac.uk/dbbrowser/OWL/
SPTR	SWISS PROT+TrEMBL	http://www.hgmp.mrc.ac.uk/Bioinformatics/Databases/sptr-help.html

Table: Nucleotide Sequence Databases

Name	Web address
DNA Data Bank Of Japan, DDBJ	http://www.ddbj.nig.ac.jp
EMBL, EBI Databases	http://www.ebi.ac.uk/embl.html

Name	Web address
Genome Databases	http://www.ebi.ac.uk/genomes
UTRdb	http://bighost.area.ba.cnr.it/srs6/

RDP	http://rdp.cme.msu.edu/
Rrndb	http://rrndb.cme.msuedu/
REBASE	http://rebase.neb.com/rebase/rebase.html
DOGS	http://www.cbs.dtu.dk/databases/DOGS/index.html
NCBI	http://www.ncbi.nlm.nih.gov/
GenBank	http://www.ncbi.nih.gov/Genbank/GenbankOverview.html
Unigene	http://www.ncbi.nih.gov/UniGene/
Genomes	http://www.ncbi.nlm.nih.gov/entrez/query.fcgi?db=genome&cmd=search&term=

Structure based Databases

1. Protein Structure Databases

Name	Web Address
PDB, Protein Data Bank	http://www.rcsb.org/pdb
PDB-TM	http://www.enzim.hu/PDB_TM/
HOMSTRAD	http://www-cryst.bioc.cam.ac.uk/homstrad
Swiss-Model Repository	http://swissmodel.expasy.org/repository
ModBase	http://alto.compbio.ucsf.edu/modbase-cgi/index.cgi

Name	Web Address
NRL-3D	http://pir.georgetown.edu/pirwww/dbinfo/nrl3d.html
MMDB	http://www.ncbi.nlm.nih.gov/Structure

2. Nucleic Acid Structure Databases

Name	Web Address
NDB	http://ndbserver.rutgers.edu/
RNABase	http://www.rnabase.org/

3. Databases based on Structure based Classification

Name	Web Address
SCOP	http://scop.mrc-lmb.cam.ac.uk/scop
CATH	http://www.biochem.ucl.ac.uk/bsm/cath_new

Organism Specific Databases (Non-Human)

Name	Web Address
Rat	http://ratmap.gen.gu.se/
Sheep	http://ws4.niai.affrc.go.jp/dbsearch2/smap/
Mouse	http://www.informatics.jax.org/
Pig	http://www.genome.iastate.edu/ http://www.genome.iastate.edu/
Cow/Cattle	http://ws4.niai.affrc.go.jp/dbsearch2/cmap/ http://sol.marc.usda.gov/genome/cattle/cattle.html

Name	Web Address
Dog	http://mendel.berkeley.edu/dog.html
Zebra Fish	http://zfish.uoregon.edu/
Horse	http://www.vgl.ucdavis.edu/~lvmillon/
Puffer fish	http://fugu.hgmp.mrc.ac.uk/
Chicken	http://www.genome.iastate.edu/
Mosquito	http://klab.agsci.colostate.edu/
Drosophila	http://flybase.bio.indiana.edu/
E.coli	http://ecocyc.pangeasystems.com/ecocyc/ecocyc.html http://mol.genes.nig.ac.jp/ecoli/
Haemophilus influenzae	http://www.ai.sri.com/ecocyc/hincyc.html
Mycobacterium	http://probe.nalusda.gov:8300/cgi-bin/browse/mycdb
Streptococcus	http://dna1.chem.uoknor.edu/strep.html
Streptomyces	http://www.uea.ac.uk/nrp/jic/gstrgenome.htm
HIV	http://hiv-web.lanl.gov/
Virus Information Resource	http://life.anu.edu.au/./viruses/virus.html

Genome Databases (Human)

Name	Web Address
GDB, Genome Database	http://gdbwww.gdb.org/
GeneCards	http://bioinformatics.weizmann.ac.il/cards/

Name	Web Address
Gene Map'99	http://www.ncbi.nlm.nih.gov/genemap/
OMIM	http://www.ncbi.nlm.nih.gov/Omim/
TIGR	http://www.tigr.org/tdb/hgi/
GenAtlas	http://bisance.citi2.fr/GENATLAS/

Transcription Related Databases

Name	Web Address
TRANSFAC	http://transfac.gbf.de/TRANSFAC/index.html
TRANS Compel	http://www.gene-regulation.com/pub/databases.html#transcompel
TRED	http://rulai.cshl.edu/tred
JASPAR	http://jaspar.cgb.ki.se
TRRD	http://www.bionet.nsc.ru/trrd/
TESS	http://www.cbil.upenn.edu/tess

Links to Expasy Databases

Protein db | 3D structure db | 2DPAGE & MS db | DNA/RNA db | Carbohydrates db | Species specific db | Human mutation db | Genes/proteins specific db | PTM db | Phylogenetics db | Gene expression db | Patents | References | Dict., protocols & nomenclature | Biol. soft. & db catalogs | Gateways | Biol. journals & publishers | Biol. societies | Bio-computing servers | Biotech. Companies | Bioinformatics companies | Misc. medical ref. sites | Misc. scientific ref. sites

Source: (http://www.expasy.org/links.html)

Protein related databases

a. UniProt (http://www.uniprot.org/) - the universal protein resource (including UniProtKB -Swiss-Prot and TrEMBL, UniRef, UniParc)

b. **Around UniProtKB** (http://www.uniprot.org/) - links to related databases and portals

   i. **HAMAP** (http://hamap.expasy.org/) - Portal to microbial UniProtKB / Swiss-Prot entries

   ii. **SwissVar** (http://swissvar.expasy.org/) - Portal to human diseases and variant information in UniProtKB / Swiss-Prot

   iii. **UniPathway** (http://www.grenoble.prabi.fr/obiwarehouse/unipathway) - Metabolic pathways database

   iv. **ViralZone** (http://viralzone.expasy.org/) - Portal to viral UniProtKB / Swiss-Prot entries

   v. HPI (http://www.uniprot.org/program/Chordata) - Human Proteomics Initiative

   vi. PPAP (http://www.uniprot.org/program/Plants) - Plant Proteome Annotation Project

   vii. Tox-Prot (http://www.uniprot.org/program/Toxins) - Toxin Annotation Project

c. **Swiss Human Plasma protein dataset** (http://web.expasy.org/error/_removed.html?queryForm.html) - Novartis / Geneprot MicroProt2 dataset from Human Plasma samples

d. NCBI protein resources (http://www.ncbi.nlm.nih.gov/protein)

e. InterPro (http://www.ebi.ac.uk/interpro/) - Integrated Resources of Proteins Domains and Functional Sites

f. PROSITE (http://prosite.expasy.org/) - Database of protein families and domains

g. BLOCKS (http://blocks.fhcrc.org/) - BLOCKS db

h. Gene3D (http://gene3d.biochem.ucl.ac.uk/Gene3D/) - Structural and Functional Annotation of Protein Families

i. Panther (http://www.pantherdb.org/) - Functional classification system

j. Pfam (http://pfam.xfam.org/) - Protein families db (HMM derived) [Mirrors at JFRC (USA), CCBB (South Korea) Institute, UK, Karolinska Institutet (Sweden)]

k. PIRSF (http://pir.georgetown.edu/pirwww/dbinfo/pirsf.shtml) - Protein classification system

l. PRINTS (http://www.bioinf.manchester.ac.uk/dbbrowser/PRINTS/index.php) - Protein Motif fingerprint db

m. ProDom (http://prodom.prabi.fr/prodom/current/html/home.php) - Protein domain db (Automatically generated)

n. SBASE (http://hydra.icgeb.trieste.it/sbase/) - SBASE domain db

o. SMART (http://smart.embl-heidelberg.de/) - Simple Modular Architecture Research Tool

p. SUPERFAMILY (http://supfam.org/SUPERFAMILY/) - Library of profile HMMs representing all proteins of known structure

q. STRING (http://string.embl.de/) - Search Tool for the Retrieval of Interacting Genes/Proteins

r. TIGRFAMs (http://www.jcvi.org/cgi-bin/tigrfams/index.cgi) - TIGR protein families db

s. BIND (http://bond.unleashedinformatics.com/Action?) – Biomolecular Interaction Network Database

t. DIP (http://bond.unleashedinformatics.com/Action?) - Database of Interacting Proteins

u. MINT (http://160.80.34.4/mint/Welcome.do) - Molecular INTeraction database

v. HPRD (http://www.hprd.org/) - Human Protein Reference Database

w. IntAct (http://www.ebi.ac.uk/intact/)

x. BioGRID (http://thebiogrid.org/) - General Repository for Interaction Dataset

y. PPI (http://ppi.fli-leibniz.de/) - JCB Protein-Protein Interaction Website

z. PMD (http://pmd.ddbj.nig.ac.jp/) - Protein Mutant db

Protein 3D structure related databases

a. PDB (http://www.rcsb.org/pdb/home/home.do) - Protein Data Bank

b. PDBTM (http://pdbtm.enzim.hu/) - Protein Data Bank of Transmembrane Proteins

c. BioMagResBank (http://www.bmrb.wisc.edu/) - Repository for data on proteins, peptides, and nucleic acids from NMR spectroscopy

d. SWISS-MODEL Repository (http://swissmodel.expasy.org/repository/) - Automatically generated protein models db

e. ModBase (http://modbase.compbio.ucsf.edu/modbase-cgi/index.cgi) - Db of comparative protein structure models

f. CATH (http://www.cathdb.info/) - UCL BSM structural classification of proteins

g. SCOP (http://scop.mrc-lmb.cam.ac.uk/scop/) - Structural classification of proteins [Mirrors]

h. HCA (http://www2.ufp.pt/~pedros/HCA_db/) - Hydrophobic Cluster Database

i. Molecules To Go (http://helixweb.nih.gov/cgi-bin/pdb) - Molecules To Go (formerly known as Molecules R Us), browser for PDB

j. BMM Domain Fishing (http://www.bmm.icnet.uk/~3djigsaw/dom_fish/) – Bio-molecular Modeling Laboratory (ICRF) protein domain fishing

k. Relibase (http://relibase.ccdc.cam.ac.uk/account_utilities/login_form.php) - Receptor / ligand complexes db [Mirror in USA]

l. CCDC (http://www.ccdc.cam.ac.uk/pages/Home.aspx) - Cambridge Crystallo-graphic Data Center (Cambridge Structural Db (CSD))

m. HSSP (http://swift.cmbi.kun.nl/swift/hssp/) - Homology-derived secondary structure of proteins db

n. MutaProt (http://ligin.weizmann.ac.il/mutaprot/) - Comparison of PDB files which differ by point mutations

o. DisProt (http://www.disprot.org/) - Database of Protein Disorder

p. SWISS-3DIMAGE (ftp://ftp.expasy.org/databases/swiss-3dimage/ IMAGES/) - 3D images of proteins and other biological macromolecules

Proteomics databases and links

Gel-based data

a. MIAPEGelDB (http://miapegeldb.expasy.org/) - A public repository for MIAPE Gel electrophoresis documents

b. WORLD-2DPAGE List (http://world-2dpage.expasy.org/list/) - Links to known 2-D PAGE database servers, as well as to 2-D PAGE related servers and services

c. World-2DPAGE Repository (http://world-2dpage.expasy.org/repository/) - A public standards-compliant repository for gel-based proteomics data published in the literature

d. The World-2DPAGE Constellation (http://world-2dpage.expasy.org/) - Promote and publish gel-based proteomics data through the ExPASy server

e. Proteomics Links page (http://www.swissproteomicssociety.org/links.html) of the Swiss Proteomics Society (http://www.swissproteomicssociety.org/)

Mass spectrometry data

a. GPMdb (http://gpmdb.thegpm.org/) - Global Proteome Machine Database

b. OPD (http://www.marcottelab.org/index.php/OldBioinformaticsServerOPD/) - Open Proteomics Database (currently down)

c. PeptideAtlas (http://www.peptideatlas.org/) - peptides identified in tandem mass spectrometry proteomics experiments

d. PRIDE (http://www.ebi.ac.uk/pride/archive/) - PRoteomics IDEntifications database

e. Tranche (http://tranche.proteomecommons.org/) - Peer-to-peer distributed file system

Nucleotide and related databases

a. EMBL (http://www.ebi.ac.uk/embl) - EMBL Nucleotide sequence db (EBI)

b. Genbank (http://www.ncbi.nlm.nih.gov/genbank/) - GenBank Nucleotide Sequence db (NCBI)

c. DDBJ (http://www.ddbj.nig.ac.jp/) - DNA Data Bank of Japan

d. dbEST (http://www.ncbi.nlm.nih.gov/dbEST/) - dbEST (Expressed Sequence Tags) db (NCBI)

e. dbSTS (http://www.ncbi.nlm.nih.gov/dbSTS/) - dbSTS (Sequence Tagged Sites) db (NCBI)

f. Ensembl (http://www.ensembl.org/index.html) - Genome database for vertebrates and other eukaryotic species

g. UCSC Genome Browser (http://genome.ucsc.edu/)

h. AsDb (http://www.hgc.jp/~knakai/asdb.html) - Aberrant Splicing db

i. ACUTS (http://pbil.univ-lyon1.fr/acuts/ACUTS.html) - Ancient conserved untranslated DNA sequences db

j. Codon Usage Db (http://www.kazusa.or.jp/codon/)

k. EPD (http://epd.vital-it.ch/) - Eukaryotic Promoter db

l. HOVERGEN (http://pbil.univ-lyon1.fr/databases/hovergen.php) - Homologous Vertebrate Genes db

m. IMGT (http://imgt.cines.fr/) - ImMunoGeneTics db [Mirror at EBI]

n. RDP (http://rdp.cme.msu.edu/) - Ribosomal db Project

o. PLACE (http://www.dna.affrc.go.jp/PLACE/) - Plant cis-acting regulatory DNA elements db

p. PlantCARE (http://bioinformatics.psb.ugent.be/webtools/plantcare/html/) - Plant cis-acting regulatory DNA elements db

q. smiRNAdb (http://www.mirz.unibas.ch/cloningprofiles/) - Information about mammalian small RNAs

r. ssu rRNA (http://bioinformatics.psb.ugent.be/webtools/rRNA/ssu/) - Small ribosomal subunit at the European ribosomal RNA database

s. lsu rRNA (http://bioinformatics.psb.ugent.be/webtools/rRNA/lsu/) - Large ribosomal subunit at the European ribosomal RNA database

t. 5S rRNA (http://rose.man.poznan.pl/5SData/) - 5S ribosomal RNA db

u. greengenes (http://greengenes.lbl.gov/cgi-bin/nph-index.cgi) - 16S rRNA gene database and workbench

v. tmRNA Website (http://www.indiana.edu/~tmrna/)

w. tmRDB (http://www.ag.auburn.edu/mirror/tmRDB/) - tmRNA dB

x. tRNA (http://www.old.uni-bayreuth.de/departments/biochemie/sprinzl/_trna/) - tRNA compilation from the University of Bayreuth

y. RNA editing (http://dna.kdna.ucla.edu/rna/index.aspx) - RNA editing site

z. RNAmod db (http://biochem.ncsu.edu/RNAmods/) - RNA modification db

aa. MPDB (http://bioinformatics.istge.it/cldb/mpdb.html) - Molecular probe db

bb. VectorDB (http://life.nthu.edu.tw/~g854202/Vecdtb.html) - Vector sequence db

Carbohydrates resources

a. FCCA (http://www.fcca.gr.jp/FCCA-J/) - Forum Carbohydrates Coming of Age

b. GlycoSuiteDB (http://web.expasy.org/glycosuitedb.html) - Db of glycan structures

c. Monosaccharide browser (http://www.terravivida.com/vivida/monosaccharide/) or (http://celebdietsource.com/) - Space filling Fischer projection for monosaccharides

d. genomics resource for animal lectins (http://www.imperial.ac.uk/research/animallectins/)

Species specific databases

Human

1. OMIM (http://www.ncbi.nlm.nih.gov/sites/entrez?db=Omim/) - Online Mendelian Inheritance in Man

2. GENATLAS (http://genatlas.medecine.univ-paris5.fr/) - Human genes atlas

3. GeneTests (http://www.ncbi.nlm.nih.gov/sites/GeneTests/?db=GeneTests) - Medical genetics knowledge base

4. GeneCards (http://www.genecards.org/) - Db integrating information on human genes

5. GeneLoc (http://genecards.weizmann.ac.il/geneloc/index.shtml) - Integrated map of the human genome (ex- UDB)

6. Ensembl Human genome browser (http://www.ensembl.org/Homo_sapiens/Info/Index)

7. The Gene Index Project (http://compbio.dfci.harvard.edu/tgi/) - ex-TIGR Human Gene Indices

8. Hs UniGene (http://www.ncbi.nlm.nih.gov/UniGene/UGOrg.cgi?TAXID= 9606) - Human transcripts in GenBank (EST clusters)

9. STACK (http://www.sanbi.ac.za/Dbases.html) - Sequence Tag Alignment and Consensus Knowledgebase (Db of consensus human ESTs)

10. Allgenes.org (http://www.allgenes.org/) - Human predicted gene index / catalog

11. GeneLynx (http://www.genelynx.org/) - Portal to the human genome

12. HUGE (http://www.kazusa.or.jp/huge/) - Human Unidentified Gene-Encoded large proteins cDNA (KIAA...)

13. CGAP (http://cgap.nci.nih.gov/) - Cancer Genome Anatomy Project

14. MGC (http://mgc.nci.nih.gov/) - Mammalian Gene Collection

15. SCDb (http://stemcell.mssm.edu/v2/) - Stem cell db

16. Homophila (http://superfly/ucsd..edu/homophila/) - Human Disease to Drosophila gene db

17. Human Protein Atlas (http://www.proteinatlas.org/) - Displays the expression and localization of proteins in a large variety of normal human tissues and cancer cells

18. Progenetix CGH database (http://www.progenetix.net/) - Molecular Cytogenetics in Leukemia and Cancer

19. Contribution of the Sanger Centre to chromosomes 1,6,9,10,11,13,20,22 and X (http://www.sanger.ac.uk/about/history/hgp/)

20. Chr1 UniProtKB/Swiss-Prot (http://www.uniprot.org/docs/humchr01) - entries, gene names and cross-references to MIM

21. Chr2 UniProtKB/Swiss-Prot - entries, gene names and cross-references to MIM

22. Chr3 UniProtKB/Swiss-Prot - entries, gene names and cross-references to MIM

23. Chr4 UniProtKB/Swiss-Prot - entries, gene names and cross-references to MIM

24. Chr5 UniProtKB/Swiss-Prot - entries, gene names and cross-references to MIM

25. Chr6 UniProtKB/Swiss-Prot - entries, gene names and cross-references to MIM

26. Chr7 UniProtKB/Swiss-Prot - entries, gene names and cross-references to MIM

27. Chr8 UniProtKB/Swiss-Prot - entries, gene names and cross-references to MIM

28. Chr9 UniProtKB/Swiss-Prot - entries, gene names and cross-references to MIM

29. Chr10 UniProtKB/Swiss-Prot - entries, gene names and cross-references to MIM

30. Chr11 UniProtKB/Swiss-Prot - entries, gene names and cross-references to MIM

31. Chr12 UniProtKB/Swiss-Prot - entries, gene names and cross-references to MIM

32. Chr13 UniProtKB/Swiss-Prot - entries, gene names and cross-references to MIM

33. Chr14 UniProtKB/Swiss-Prot - entries, gene names and cross-references to MIM

34. Chr15 UniProtKB/Swiss-Prot - entries, gene names and cross-references to MIM

35. Chr16 UniProtKB/Swiss-Prot - entries, gene names and cross-references to MIM

36. Chr17 UniProtKB/Swiss-Prot - entries, gene names and cross-references to MIM

37. Chr18 UniProtKB/Swiss-Prot - entries, gene names and cross-references to MIM

38. Chr19 UniProtKB/Swiss-Prot - entries, gene names and cross-references to MIM

39. Chr20 UniProtKB/Swiss-Prot - entries, gene names and cross-references to MIM

40. Chr21 UniProtKB/Swiss-Prot - entries, gene names and cross-references to MIM

41. Chr22 at HGC - Human genome center for chromosome 22

42. Chr22 UniProtKB/Swiss-Prot - entries, gene names and cross-references to MIM

43. ChrX UniProtKB/Swiss-Prot - entries, gene names and cross-references to MIM

44. ChrY UniProtKB/Swiss-Prot - entries, gene names and cross-references to MIM

45. H-InvDB Database (http://www.h-invitational.jp/) - Human gene db, with cDNA clones available from six high throughput cDNA sequencing projects

46. Human Chromosome1 Launchpad (http://web.ornl.gov/sci/techresources/Human Genome/redirect.shtml)

47. Human Chromosome2 Launchpad

48. Human Chromosome3 Launchpad

49. Human Chromosome4 Launchpad

50. Human Chromosome5 Launchpad

51. Human Chromosome6 Launchpad

52. Human Chromosome7 Launchpad

53. Human Chromosome8 Launchpad

54. Human Chromosome9 Launchpad

55. Human Chromosome10 Launchpad

56. Human Chromosome11 Launchpad

57. Human Chromosome12 Launchpad

58. Human Chromosome13 Launchpad

59. Human Chromosome14 Launchpad

60. Human Chromosome15 Launchpad

61. Human Chromosome16 Launchpad

62. Human Chromosome17 Launchpad

63. Human Chromosome18 Launchpad

64. Human Chromosome19 Launchpad

65. Human Chromosome20 Launchpad

66. Human Chromosome21 Launchpad

67. Human Chromosome22 Launchpad

68. Human ChromosomeX Launchpad

69. Human ChromosomeY Launchpad

Vertebrates

1. OMIA (http://omia.angis.org.au/home/) - Online Mendelian Inheritance in Animals

2. MGI (http://www.informatics.jax.org/) - Mouse Genome Informatics (includes MGD)

3. Ensembl Mouse genome browser (http://www.ensembl.org/Mus_musculus/ Info/Index)

4. DFCI MGI (http://compbio.dfci.harvard.edu/tgi/cgi-bin/tgi/gimain.pl?gudb=Mouse) - TIGR Mouse Gene Index
5. Mm UniGene (http://www.ncbi.nlm.nih.gov/UniGene/UGOrg.cgi?TAXID=100900 - Mouse transcripts in GenBank (EST clusters)
6. MGC (http://mgc.nci.nih.gov/) - Mammalian Gene Collection
7. Mouse gene knockouts db (http://www.bioscience.org/knockout/knochrome.htm)
8. RGD (http://rgd.mcw.edu/) - Rat genome db
9. Ensembl Rat genome browser (http://www.ensembl.org/Rattus_norvegicus/Info/Index)
10. RatMAP (http://ratmap.gen.gu.se/) - Rat genome db
11. DFCI RGI (http://compbio.dfci.harvard.edu/tgi/cgi-bin/tgi/gimain.pl?gudb=Rat) - TIGR Rat Gene Index
12. Rn Unigene (http://www.ncbi.nlm.nih.gov/UniGene/UGOrg.cgi?TAXID=10116) - Rat transcripts in GenBank (EST clusters)
13. Ensembl Chimpanzee genome browser (http://www.ensembl.org/Pan_troglodytes/Info/Index/0
14. Ensembl Gorilla genome browser (http://www.ensembl.org/Gorilla_gorilla/Info/Index/)
15. Ensembl Cat genome browser (http://www.ensembl.org/Felis_catus/Info/Index/)
16. Ensembl Bovine genome browser (http://www.ensembl.org/Bos_taurus/Info/Index/)

17. Ensembl Dog genome browser (http://www.ensembl.org/Canis_familiaris/Info/Index/)
18. Ensembl Horse genome browser (http://www.ensembl.org/Equus_caballus/Info/Index/)
19. Ensembl Pig genome browser (http://www.ensembl.org/Sus_scrofa/Info/Index/)
20. Ensembl Rabbit genome browser (http://www.ensembl.org/Oryctolagus_cuniculus/Info/Index/)
21. BOVMAP (http://locus.jouy.infra.fr/cgi-bin/bovmap/intro2.pl) - Bovine genome db (in France)
22. NHGRI Dog Genome Project (http://research.nhgri.nih.gov/dog_genome/)
23. ArkDB (http://www.thearkdb.org/arkdb/) - Cat, Chicken, Cow, Deer, Horse, Pig, Quail, Sheep, Turkey genome databases
24. Ensembl Chicken genome browser (http://www.ensembl.org/Gallus_gallus/Info/Index/)
25. FishBase (http://www.fishbase.org/) - Global information system on fishes
26. Fugu genome project (http://www.fugu-sg.org/)
27. Fugu (http://fugu.biology.qmul.ac.uk/) - HGMP Resource Centre Fugu Project (Fugu rubripes)
28. Ensembl Fugu genome browser (http://www.ensembl.org/Takifugu_rubripes/Info/Index)
29. MEPD (http://ani.embl.de:8080/mepd/) - Medaka Expression Pattern Database

30. ArkDB (http://www.thearkdb.org/arkdb/) - Sea Bass, Salmon genome databases

31. ZFIN (http://zfin.org/) - Zebra fish Information Network

32. Ensembl Zebrafish genome browser (http://www.ensembl.org/Danio_rerio/ Info/Index)

Mitochondrion and chloroplast

1. GOBASE (http://gobase.bcm.umontreal.ca/) - Organelle Genome Database

2. MitoDat (http://www-immb.ncifcrf.gov/mitodat/) - Mendelian Inheritance and the Mitochondrion db

3. C.caldarium (http://genome.imb-jena.de/~gernot/cyanidium.html) - Cyanidium caldarium strain RK1 chloroplast genome

Insects

1. Drosophila_UniProtKB/Swiss-Prot (http://www.uniprot.org/docs/fly) entries, gene names and cross-references to FlyBase

2. FlyBase (http://flybase.org/) - Drosophila genetic and molecular db

3. BDGP (http://www.fruitfly.org/) - Berkeley Drosophila Genome Project

4. FlyView (http://flyview.uni-muenster.de/) - Drosophila image db

5. Homophila (http://superfly/ucsd..edu/homophila/) - Human Disease to Drosophila gene db

6. AnoDB (http://www.anobase.org/) - Anopheles gambiae db

7. Ensembl Anopheles gambiae genome browser (http://metazoa.ensembl.org/Anopheles_gambiae/Info/Index)

Invertebrates

1. WormBase (http://www.wormbase.org/) - C.elegans db [Mirror at Sanger]

2. C.elegans WWW server (http://elegans.swmed.edu/) - at University of Texas Southwestern

3. Ensembl C.elegans genome browser (http://www.ensembl.org/Caenorhabditis_elegans/Info/Index/)

4. NEXTDB (http://www.wormbase.org/) - The Nematode Expression Pattern DataBase

5. C.elegans UniProtKB/Swiss-Prot (http://www.uniprot.org/docs/celegans) entries, gene names and cross-references to WormPep

6. WormPep (http://www.sanger.ac.uk/Projects/C_elegans/WORMBASE/current/wormpep.shtml) - C.elegans proteins db

7. WorfDB (http://worfdb.dfci.harvard.edu/) - C. elegans ORFeome cloning project

8. Dictyostelium discoideum UniProtKB/Swiss-Prot (http://www.uniprot.org/docs/dicty) - entries, gene names and cross-references to DictyBase

9. DictyBase (http://dictybase.org/) - Dictyostelium discoideum db

10. DictyDb (http://glamdring.ucsd.edu/others/dsmith/dictydb.html) - Dictyostelium discoideum db

11. Dictyostelium Genome Sequencing project at BCM (http://dictygenome.bcm.tmc.edu/)

12. Cone shells Web site (http://grimwade.biochem.unimelb.edu.au/cone/)

13. Parasite genomes db and resources (http://www.ebi.ac.uk/parasites)

14. PlasmoDB (http://www.plasmodb.org/plasmo/home.jsp) - P.falciparum genome db

15. Malaria - WHO (http://www.wehi.edu.au/MalDB-www/who.html) - Malaria db (from WHO)

16. P.falciparum Sanger (http://www.sanger.ac.uk/resources/downloads/protozoa/plasmodium-falciparum.html) - P.falciparum genome project at Sanger

17. P.falciparum (http://parasite.vetmed.ufl.edu/) - Plasmodium falciparum Gene Sequence Tag project

18. Malaria parasite metabolic pathways (http://mpmp.huji.ac.il//)

19. GiardiaDB (http://giardiadb.org/giardiadb/)

20. LGN (http://www.sanger.ac.uk/resources/downloads/protozoa/leishmania-major. html) - Leishmania major Genome Project

21. ToxoDB (http://toxodb.org/toxo/) - Toxoplasma gondii genome project

22. Trypanosoma brucei genome project (http://www.sanger.ac.uk/resources/downloads/protozoa/trypanosoma-brucei.html)

23. Trypanosoma cruzi genome project (http://www.dbbm.fiocruz.br/genome/tcruzi/tcruzi.html)

24. kDNA (http://www.ebi.ac.uk/parasites) - Kinetoplast Minicircle Sequence db

Plants

1. NAL - AGIS (http://www.nal.usda.gov/) - Access to many plant genome databases at the National Agricultural Library

2. Mendel (http://www.mendel.ac.uk/) - Plant gene nomenclature database from CPGN

3. FLAGdb++ (http://urgv.evry.inra.fr/projects/FLAGdb++/HTML/index.shtml) - Integrative database around plant genomes

4. Arabidopsis UniProtKB/Swiss-Prot (http://www.uniprot.org/docs/arath) entries, gene names and WWW servers

5. TAIR (http://www.arabidopsis.org/) - The Arabidopsis Information Resource

6. MATDB (http://mips.gsf.de/proj/thal/db/) - MIPS Arabidopsis thaliana db

7. AMPL (http://wardlab.cbs.umn.edu/arabidopsis/) - Arabidopsis Membrane Protein Library

8. Arabidopsis at PlaCe (http://www.p450.kvl.dk/) - Site with info on P450, glucosyltransferases, etc.

9. Gramene (http://www.gramene.org/) - A comparative mapping resource for grains

10. Oryza sativa UniProtKB/Swiss-Prot (http://www.uniprot.org/docs/rice) entries, gene names and WWW servers

11. RGP (http://rgp.dna.affrc.go.jp/) - Rice Genome Research Program

12. Oryzabase (http://www.shigen.nig.ac.jp/rice/oryzabase/) - Japanese rice genome db

13. Rice genome annotation project (http://rice.plantbiology.msu.edu/) - at MSU (Michigan State University)

14. BeanGenes (http://beangenes.cws.ndsu.nodak.edu/) - Beans genome db

15. Brassica Genome Gateway (http://brassica.nbi.ac.uk/)

16. ChlamyDB (http://www.biology.duke.edu/chlamydb/) - Chlamydomonas reinhardtii genome db

17. CoffeeDNA (http://www.coffeedna.net/) - Coffee genomics web site

18. CottonDB (http://cottondb.org/) - Cotton genome db

19. MaizeDb (http://www.maizegdb.org/) - Maize genome db

20. Pisum sativum (pea) web site (in russian) (http://pisum.bionet.nsc.ru/)

21. TIGR Potato (http://www.jcvi.org/potato/) - TIGR Potato Functional Genomics project (at JCVI)

22. Snapdragon (A.majus) web site

23. DragonDB (http://www.antirrhinum.net/) - Snapdragon Database

24. SorghumDB (http://algodon.tamu.edu/sorghumdb.html) - Sorghum genome db

25. DFCI GmGI (http://compbio.dfci.harvard.edu/tgi/cgi-bin/tgi/gimain.pl?gudb=soybean) - DFCI Soybean Gene Index

26. SoyBase (http://soybase.ncgr.org/) - Soybean genome db
27. SoyBase metabolic db (http://cgsc.biology.yale.edu/metab.html) - Metabolic subset of the soybean genome db
28. DFCI LeGI (http://compbio.dfci.harvard.edu/tgi/cgi-bin/tgi/gimain.pl?gudb=tomato) - DFCI Tomato Gene Index
29. Dendrome (http://dendrome.ucdavis.edu/) - Forest trees genome db

Fungi

1. Ensembl Yeast (S.cerevisiae) genome browser (http://www.ensembl.org/Saccharomyces_cerevisiae/Info/Index/)
2. FGSC (http://www.fgsc.net/) - Fungal Genetics Stock Center
3. Genolevures (http://genolevures.org/) - Genomic Exploration of the Hemiascomycete Yeasts
4. FGI (http://www.broadinstitute.org/scientific-community/science/projects/fungal-genome-initiative/fungal-genome-initiative) - Fungal genome initiative at the Broad Institute
5. Fungal genome databases at MIPS (http://mips.gsf.de/projects/fungi/fungi_db.html)
6. Fungal genomes at the Sanger Institute (http://www.sanger.ac.uk/resources/downloads/fungi/)
7. FGR (http://gene.genetics.uga.edu/) - Fungal Genome Resource
8. MycoBank (http://www.mycobank.org/)
9. Yeast (S. cerevisiae) UniProtKB/Swiss-Prot (http://www.uniprot.org/docs/yeast) entries, gene names and cross-references to SGD

10. CYGD (http://mips.helmholtz-muenchen.de/genre/proj/yeast/) - MIPS Comprehensive Yeast Genome db

11. SGD (http://www.yeastgenome.org/) - Saccharomyces genome db

12. Yeast snoRNA (http://people.biochem.umass.edu/fournierlab/snornadb/main.php) - Yeast small nucleolar RNAs db

13. YTPdb (http://ytpdb.biopark-it.be/ytpdb/index.php/Main_Page) - Yeast Transport Protein db

14. YMPL (http://wardlab.cbs.umn.edu/yeast/) - Yeast Membrane Protein Library

15. YRC (http://depts.washington.edu/yeastrc/) - Yeast Resource Center

16. PROPHECY (http://prophecy.lundberg.gu.se/) - PROfiling of PHEnotypic Characteristics in Yeast

17. SCMD (http://yeast.gi.k.u-tokyo.ac.jp/datamine/) - Saccharomyces Cerevisiae Morphological db

18. GPofYPF (http://www.doe-mbi.ucla.edu/Services/GPofYPF/) - Global Profiling of Yeast Protein Function

19. Saccharomyces Genomes (http://www.genetics.wustl.edu/saccharomycesgenomes/) - Finding functional features in Saccharomyces Genomes by phylogenetic footprinting

20. Yeast Comparative Genomics (http://www.broadinstitute.org/annotation/fungi/comp_yeasts/)

21. S.pombe UniProtKB/Swiss-Prot (http://www.uniprot.org/docs/pombe) entries, gene names and WWW servers

22. GeneDB S.Pombe (http://www.pombase.org/) - Schizosaccharomyces pombe GeneDB

23. S.pombe genome project (http://www.pombase.org/)

24. PombeNet (http://www-bcf.usc.edu/~forsburg/) - Forsburg lab pombe pages

25. AGD (http://agd.vital-it.ch/) - Ashbya genome db

26. Aspergillus nidulans db (http://www.broadinstitute.org/annotation/genome/aspergillus_group/MultiHome.html)

27. The Aspergillus web site (http://www.aspergillus.org.uk/)

28. C. albicans UniProtKB/Swiss-Prot (http://www.uniprot.org/docs/calbican) entries gene names and WWW servers

29. CGD - Candida Genome db (http://www.candidagenome.org/)

30. C. albicans physical map (http://www.cbs.umn.edu/research/research-cbs/faculty-labs/albicansmap) - Candida albicans server at the Univ. of Minnesota

31. Candida albicans pages (http://candida.bri.nrc.ca/candida/) - Candida albicans at the NRC/BRI

32. CandidaDB (http://genodb.pasteur..fr/CandidaDB/) - Candida albicans GenoList browser at Institut Pasteur

33. Cryptococcus neoformans Genome Project (http://sequence-www.stanford.edu/group/C.neoformans/)

34. FGDB (http://mips.helmholtz-muenchen.de/genre/proj/fusarium/) - Fusarium graminearum Genome db

35. Kluyveromyces lactis annotation db (http://www-archbac.u-psud.fr/genomes/r_klactis/klactis.html)

36. MNCDB (http://mips.gsf.de/proj/neurospora/) - MIPS Neurospora crassa db

37. Neurospora crassa db (http://www.broadinstitute.org/annotation/genome/neurospora/MultiHome.html)

38. NGP (http://biology.unm.edu/biology/ngp/home.html) - Neurospora crassa genome project at New Mexico

39. Neurospora crassa Gene List (http://www.bioinf.leeds.ac.uk/~gen6ar/newgenelist/genes/gene_list.htm)

40. MUMDB (http://mips.helmholtz-muenchen.de/genre/proj/ustilago/) - MIPS Ustilago maydis db

41. PC (http://www.uky.edu/Projects/Pneumocystis/) - Pneumocystis carinii genome project

42. Phycomyces Web site (http://searchguide.level3.com/search/?q=http%3A//www.es.embnet.org/~genus/phycomyces.html&r=&t=0) - Resource site for scientists working on Phycomyces

Bacteria

1. WDCM (http://wdcm.nig.ac.jp/) - World Data Center for Microorganisms

2. List of Bacterial Names with Standing in Nomenclature (http://www.bacterio.net/)

3. List of complete bacterial proteomes in Swiss-Prot (HAMAP) (http://hamap.expasy.org/bacteria.html)

4. CBS (http://www.cbs.dtu.dk/services/GenomeAtlas/) - CBS Genome Atlas Database

5. CMR (http://www.jcvi.org/cms/research/past-projects/cmr/overview/) - TIGR Comprehensive Microbial Resource

6. GIB (http://gib.genes.nig.ac.jp/) - Genome information broker for Microbial genomes
7. GOLD Genomes On-line Database (https://gold.jgi-psf.org/)
8. HOBACGEN (http://pbil.univ-lyon1.fr/databases/hobacgen.html) - Homologous Bacterial Genes db
9. Comparison of the transport capabilities of bacterial genomes (http://www.membranetransport.org/) - from Ian Paulsen
10. BPGD (http://sydney.edu.au/science/molecular_bioscience/BPGD/default.htm) - Bacterial polysaccharide gene db
11. Bacterial quorum sensing (http://www.nottingham.ac.uk/quorum/)
12. MicrobeWorld (http://www.microbeworld.org/) - Educational site on microbes
13. E.coli UniProtKB/Swiss-Prot (http://www.uniprot.org/docs/ecoli) entries, gene names and cross-references to EcoGene
14. EcoWeb / EcoGene (http://www.ecogene.org/) - Very comprehensive E.coli db
15. ECCE - E.coli Cell Envelope Protein Data Collection
16. ECDC (http://www.uni-giessen.de/ecoli/ECDC/ecdc.html) - E.coli db collection
17. EcoCyc (http://www.ecocyc.org/) - Encyclopedia of E.coli genes and metabolism
18. EchoBASE (http://www.york.ac.uk/res/thomas/)

19. GenProtEC (http://genprotec.mbl.edu/) - E.coli genome and proteome db

20. Colibri (http://genolist.pasteur.fr/Colibri/) - E.coli GenoList browser at Institut Pasteur

21. ECGC (http://www.genome.wisc.edu/) - E.coli Genome Center at Wisconsin University

22. DDBJ E.coli (http://gib.genes.nig.ac.jp/single/index.php?spid=Ecol_K12_MG1655) - E.coli home page at DDBJ

23. Regulon DB (http://www.genome.wisc.edu/)

24. B.subtilis UniProtKB/Swiss-Prot (http://www.uniprot.org/docs/bacsu) entries, gene names and WWW servers

25. SubtiList (http://genolist.pasteur.fr/SubtiList/) - Bacillus subtilis GenoList browser at Institut Pasteur

26. NRSub (http://pbil.univ-lyon1.fr/nrsub/nrsub.html) - Bacillus subtilis non-redundant db

27. DBTBS (http://dbtbs.hgc.jp/) - Db of B.subtilis promoters and transcription factors

28. A.actinomycetemcomitans (http://www.genome.ou.edu/act.html) - Actinobacillus actinomycetemcomitans strain HK1651 genome project

29. B.stearothermophilus (http://www.genome.ou.edu/bstearo.html) - Bacillus stearothermophilus strain 10 genome project

30. Bordetella species genome projects at Sanger Institute (http://www.sanger.ac.uk/resources/downloads/bacteria/bordetella.html) - bronchiseptica strain RB50, parapertussis strain 1822 and pertussis strain Tohama I

31. BbDB (http://www.jcvi.org/cms/research/past-projects/cmr/overview/?database=gbb) - Borrelia burgdorferi B31 genome db at JCVI-CMR

32. Brucella abortus strain 2308 UniProtKB/Swiss-Prot (http://www.uniprot.org/docs/brua2) entries, gene names and WWW servers

33. Brucella abortus strain 9-941 UniProtKB/Swiss-Prot (http://www.uniprot.org/docs/bruab) entries, gene names and WWW servers

34. Brucella melitensis strain 16M UniProtKB/Swiss-Prot (http://www.uniprot.org/docs/brume) entries, gene names and WWW servers

35. Brucella suis strain 1330 UniProtKB/Swiss-Prot (http://www.uniprot.org/docs/brusu) entries, gene names and WWW servers

36. B.aphidicola (subsp. Acyrthosiphon pisum) UniProtKB/Swiss-Prot (http://www.uniprot.org/docs/bucai) entries, gene names and WWW servers

37. B.aphidicola (subsp. Schizaphis graminum) UniProtKB/Swiss-Prot (http://www.uniprot.org/docs/bucap) entries, gene names and WWW servers

38. C.jejuni (http://www.sanger.ac.uk/resources/downloads/bacteria/campylobacter-jejuni.html) - Campylobacter jejuni genome project

39. C.muridarum (http://www.jcvi.org/cms/research/past-projects/cmr/overview/?database=btc) - Chlamydia muridarum strain MoPn genome db at JCVI-CMR

40. C.pneumoniae AR39 - Chlamydia pneumoniae strain AR39 genome db at JCVI-CMR

41. C.pneumoniae J138 (http://www.jcvi.org/cms/research/past-projects/cmr/ overview/?database=bcp) - Chlamydia pneumoniae strain J138 genome db at JCVI-CMR

42. Chromobacterium violaceum (http://www.brgene.lncc.br/indexCV.html) - Brazilian Genome

43. C.michiganensis (http://www.sanger.ac.uk/resources/downloads/bacteria/clavibacter-michiganensis.html) Claviabacter michiganensis subsp. sepdonicus genome project at Sanger Institute

44. C.difficile (http://www.sanger.ac.uk/resources/downloads/bacteria/clostridium-difficile.html) - Clostridium difficile strain 630 genome project at Sanger Institute

45. C.diphtheriae (http://www.sanger.ac.uk/resources/downloads/bacteria/ corynebacterium-diphtheriae.html) - Corynebacterium diphtheriae strain NCTC 13129 genome project at Sanger Institute

46. Coxiella burnetii strain RSA 493 UniProtKB/Swiss-Prot (http://www.uniprot.org/docs/coxbu) entries, gene names and WWW servers

47. CyanoBase (http://genome.microbedb.jp/cyanobase/) - The Genome Database for Cyanobacteria

48. CyanoList (http://genolist.pasteur.fr/CyanoList/) - Synechocystis PCC6803 and Anabaena PCC7120 GenoList browser at Institut Pasteur

49. DrDB (http://www.jcvi.org/cms/research/past-projects/cmr/overview/?database=gdr) - Deinococcus radiodurans strain R1 genome db at JCVI-CMR

50. E.ruminantium (http://www.sanger.ac.uk/resources/downloads/bacteria/ehrlichia-ruminantium.html) - Ehrlichia ruminantium (formerly Cowdria ruminantium) genome project at Sanger Institute

51. H.influenzae UniProtKB/Swiss-Prot (http://www.uniprot.org/docs/haein) entries, gene names and WWW servers

52. HiDB (http://www.jcvi.org/cms/research/past-projects/cmr/overview/?database=ghi) - Haemophilus influenzae genome db at JCVI-CMR

53. H.pylori UniProtKB/Swiss-Prot (http://www.uniprot.org/docs/helpy) entries, gene names and WWW servers

54. HpDB (http://www.jcvi.org/cms/research/past-projects/cmr/overview/? database=ghp) - Helicobacter pylori strain 26695 genome db at JCVI-CMR

55. PyloriGene (http://genolist.pasteur.fr/PyloriGene/) - Helicobacter pylori GenoList browser at Institut Pasteur

56. L.lactis (http://spock.jouy.infra.fr/) - Lactobacillus lactis subsp. lactis strain IL1403 genome db

57. L.plantarum (http://www.cmbi.ru.nl/plantarum) - Lactobacillus plantarum genome project

58. LegioList (http://genolist.pasteur.fr/LegioList/) - Legionella pneumophila Paris strain and Legionella pneumophila Lens strain GenoList browser at Institut Pasteur

59. ListiList (http://genolist.pasteur.fr/ListiList/) - Listeria monocytogenes and Listeria innocua GenoList browser at Institut Pasteur

60. BoviList (http://genolist.pasteur.fr/BoviList/) - Mycobacterium bovis strain AF2122/97 GenoList browser at Institut Pasteur

61. Mycobacterium (http://www.sanger.ac.uk/resources/downloads/bacteria/mycobacterium.html) - Mycobacterium genome projects at Sanger Institute

62. Leproma (http://genolist.pasteur.fr/Leproma/) - Mycobacterium leprae strain TN genome db

63. TubercuList (http://genolist.pasteur.fr/TubercuList/) - Mycobacterium tuberculosis strain H37Rv GenoList browser at Institut Pasteur

64. MtDB (http://www.jcvi.org/cms/research/past-projects/cmr/overview/?database=gmt) - Mycobacterium tuberculosis strain Oshkosh genome db at JCVI-CMR

65. M.tuberculosis structural genomics consortium (http://www.doe-mbi.ucla.edu/TB/)

66. BuruList (http://genolist.pasteur.fr/BuruList/) - Mycobacterium ulcerans strain Agy99 GenoList browser at Institut Pasteur

67. M.genitalium UniProtKB/Swiss-Prot (http://www.uniprot.org/docs/mycge) entries, gene names and WWW servers

68. MgDB (http://www.jcvi.org/cms/research/past-projects/cmr/overview/?database=gmg) - Mycoplasma genitalium genome db at JCVI-CMR

69. M.pneumoniae UniProtKB/Swiss-Prot (http://www.uniprot.org/docs/mycpn) entries, gene names and WWW servers

70. M.pneumoniae (http://www.zmbh.uni-heidelberg.de/M_pneumoniae/genome/Results.html) - Mycoplasma pneumoniae genome project

71. MypuList (http://genolist.pasteur.fr/MypuList/) - Mycoplasma pulmonis GenoList browser at Institut Pasteur

72. Mycoplasma synoviae genome db (http://www.brgene.lncc.br/indexMS.html) - Brazilian Genome

73. Nesseria (http://www.sanger.ac.uk/resources/downloads/bacteria/ neisseria.html) - Neisseria genome projects at Sanger Institute

74. N.meningitidis B (http://www.jcvi.org/cms/research/past-projects/cmr/ overview/?database=gnm) - Neisseria meningitidis serogroup B strain MC58 genome db at JCVI-CMR

75. N.europaea (http://genome.jgi-psf.org/niteu/niteu.home.html) - Nitrosomonas europaea genome project

76. PhotoList (http://genolist.pasteur.fr/PhotoList/) - Photorhabdus luminescens strain TT01 GenoList browser at Institut Pasteur

77. P.marinus (http://genome.jgi-psf.org/prom9/prom9.home.html) - Prochlorococcus marinus genome project

78. P.aeruginosa project (http://www.pseudomonas.com/) - Pseudomonas aeruginosa genome project

79. R.solanacearum (https://iant.toulouse.inra.fr/bacteria/annotation/cgi/ralso.cgi) - Ralstonia solanacearum genome project

80. Rhizobium pNGR234a UniProtKB/Swiss-Prot (http://www.uniprot.org/docs/ngr234) entries, gene names and WWW servers

81. RhizoBase (http://genome.microbedb.jp/rhizobase/) - The Genome Database for Rhizobia

82. Rhizobium pNGR234a analysis (http://genome.imb.jena.de/other/cfreiber/pNGR234a2.html)

83. Rhodobacter sphaeroides genome db (http://www.jcvi.org/cms/research/past-projects/cmr/overview/?database=ntrs03)

84. R.palustris (http://genome.jgi-psf.org/rhopa/rhopa.info.html) - Rhodopseudomonas palustris genome project

85. RicBase (http://igs.server.cnrs-mrs.fr/mgdb/Rickettsia) - Rickettsia conorii strain Malish 7 genome project

86. R.bellii strain RML369-C UniProtKB/Swiss-Prot (http://www.uniprot.org/ docs/ricbr) entries, gene names and WWW servers

87. R.conorii strain Malish 7 UniProtKB/Swiss-Prot (http://www.uniprot.org/ docs/riccn) entries, gene names and WWW servers

88. R.felis strain URRWXCa12 UniProtKB/Swiss-Prot (http://www.uniprot. org/docs/ricfe) entries, gene names and WWW servers

89. R.prowazekii UniProtKB/Swiss-Prot (http://www.uniprot.org/docs/ricpr) entries, gene names and WWW servers

90. R.typhi strain Wilmington UniProtKB/Swiss-Prot (http://www.uniprot.org/ docs/ricty) entries, gene names and WWW servers

91. Salmonella (http://www.sanger.ac.uk/resources/downloads/bacteria/ salmonella.html) - Salmonella genome projects at Sanger Institute

92. S.meliloti (https://iant.toulouse.inra.fr//bacteria/annotation/cgi/rhime.cgi/) - Sinorhizobium meliloti genome project

93. AureoList (http://genolist.pasteur.fr/AureoList/) - Staphylococcus aureus strains N315 and Mu50 GenoList browser at Institut Pasteur

94. S.aureus (http://www.genome.ou.edu/staph.html) - Staphylococcus aureus strain NCTC 8325 genome project

95. SagaList (http://genolist.pasteur.fr/SagaList/) - Streptococcus agalactiae strain NEM316 GenoList browser at Institut Pasteur

96. StreptoPneumoList (http://genolist.pasteur.fr/StreptoPneumoList/) - Streptococcus pneumoniae strains R6 and Tigr4 GenoList browser at Institut Pasteur

97. S.mutans (http://www.genome.ou.edu/smutans.html) - Streptococcus mutans strain UAB159 genome project

98. S.pyogenes M1 (http://www.genome.ou.edu/strep.html) - Streptococcus pyogenes strain SF370 serotype M1 genome project

99. S.pyogenes (http://www.sanger.ac.uk/resources/downloads/bacteria/streptococcus-pyogenes.html) - Streptococcus pyogenes genome project at Sanger Institute

100. S.suis (http://www.sanger.ac.uk/resources/downloads/bacteria/streptococcus-suis.html) - Streptococcus suis genome project at Sanger Institute

101. S.uberis (http://www.sanger.ac.uk/resources/downloads/bacteria/streptococcus-uberis.html) - Streptococcus uberis genome project at Sanger Institute

102. S.coelicolor (http://www.sanger.ac.uk/resources/downloads/bacteria/streptomyces-coelicolor.html) - Streptomyces coelicolor genome project at Sanger Institute

103. S.avermitilis (http://avermitilis.ls.kitasato-u.ac.jp/) - Streptomyces avermitilis strain MA-4680 genome project

104. Synechocystis strain PCC 6803 UniProtKB/Swiss-Prot entries, gene names and WWW servers

105. TmDB (http://www.jcvi.org/cms/research/past-projects/cmr/overview/?database=btm) - Thermotoga maritima genome db at JCVI-CMR

106. TpDB (http://www.jcvi.org/cms/research/past-projects/cmr/overview/?database=gtp) - Treponema pallidum genome db at JCVI-CMR

107. T.whipplei (http://www.sanger.ac.uk/resources/downloads/bacteria/tropheryma-whipplei.html) - Tropheryma whipplei genome project at Sanger Institute

108. U.urealyticum (http://genome.microbio.uab.edu/uu/uugen.htm) - Ureaplasma urealyticum genome WWW site

109. VcDB (http://www.jcvi.org/cms/research/past-projects/cmr/overview/?database=gvc) - Vibrio cholerae genome db at JCVI-CMR

110. X.fastidiosa (http://aeg.lbi.ic.unicamp.br/xf/) - Xylella fastidiosa genome project

111. Yersinia (http://www.sanger.ac.uk/resources/downloads/bacteria/ yersinia.html) - Yersinia genome projects at Sanger Institute

Archaea

1. List of complete archaeal proteomes in Swiss-Prot (HAMAP) (http://hamap.expasy.org/archaea.html)

2. UCSC Archeal Genome Browser (http://archaea.ucsc.edu/)

3. A.pernix (http://www.bio.nite.go.jp/dogan/project/view/APE) -Aeropyrum pernix K1 genome db

4. AfDB (http://www.jcvi.org/cms/research/past-projects/cmr/overview/?database=gaf) - Archaeoglobus fulgidus genome db at JCVI-CMR

5. Halobacterium NRC-1 (http://halo4.umbi.umd.edu/cgi-bin/haloweb/nrc1.pl) - Halobacterium strain NRC-1 genome project

6. M.jannaschii UniProtKB/Swiss-Prot (http://www.uniprot.org/docs/metja) entries, gene names and WWW servers

7. MjDB (http://www.jcvi.org/cms/research/past-projects/cmr/overview/?database=arg) - Methanococcus jannaschii genome db at JCVI-CMR

8. Pyrococcus abyssi genome and re-annotation db (http://www-archbac.u-psud.fr/genomes/newpab/newpab. html)

9. Pyrococcus sp. OT3 (http://www.aist.go.jp/aist_j/aist_repository/riodb/ index.html)

10. Sulfolobus solfataricus P2 genome project (http://www-archbac.u-psud.fr/ Projects/Sulfolobus/Sulfolobus.html)

11. T.volcanium (http://www.aist.go.jp/aist_j/aist_repository/riodb/index.html) - Thermoplasma volcanium genome project

Viruses and phages

1. All the virology on the WWW (http://www.virology.net/garryfavwebindex.html) - links to virology WWW servers by David M. Sander

2. ICTVdB (http://ictvonline.org/) - Universal virus taxonomy db

3. ViralZone (http://viralzone.expasy.org/) - Portal to viral UniProtKB/Swiss-Prot entries

4. Adenoviruses web site (http://www.vmri.hu/~harrach/)

5. HCVDB (http://euhcvdb.ibcp.fr/euHCVdb/) - Hepatitis C virus db

6. HIV (http://www.hiv.lanl.gov/content/index) - HIV and related species db

7. HPV (http://hpv-web.lanl.gov/) - Human papillomaviruses db

8. Picornavirus (http://www.picornaviridae.com/) - Picornavirus home page and access to db

9. VirOligo (http://viroligo.okstate.edu/) - virus-specific oligonucleotides database

10. PhageBase (http://phagebase.org/)

11. Phage Sequence Databank (http://phage.sdsu.edu/~rob/cgi-bin/phage.cgi/) at Sdsu Center for Universal Microbial Sequencing (currently not working)

12. The Bacteriophage Ecology Group (http://www.mansfield.ohio-state.edu/~sabedon?)

13. GOLD (https://gold.jgi-psf.org/) - Genomes On-line db

14. DOGS (http://www.cbs.dtu.dk/databases/DOGS/) - Database of genome sizes

Human mutation databases / resources

1. HGMD (http://www.hgmd.cf.ac.uk/ac/index.php) - Human Gene Mutation db

2. SVD (http://www.ebi.ac.uk/mutations/) - EBI Sequence variation db

3. HGVbase (http://www.hgvbaseg2p.org/index/)

4. HGVS (http://www.hgvs.org/) - The Human Genome Variation Society

5. LOVD (http://chromium.liacs.nl/LOVD2/home.php) - Leiden Open Variation database

6. The International HapMap Project (http://snp.cshl.org/)

7. dbSNP (http://www.ncbi.nlm.nih.gov/SNP/) - Human single nucleotide polymorphism (SNP) db

8. ALFRED (http://alfred.med.yale.edu/alfred/) - Allele Frequency Db

9. SeattleSNPs (http://pga.mbt.washington.edu/) - UW-FHCRC Variation Discovery Resource

10. PicSNP (http://plaza.umin.ac.jp/~hchang/picsnp/) - Catalog of non-synonymous SNP

11. List of mutation databases from OMIM (http://www.ncbi.nlm.nih.gov/Omim/allresources.html#LocusSpecific)

12. List of mutation databases from IMT (Finland) (http://bioinf.uta.fi/BTKbase/ database.html)

13. ADAbase (http://bioinf.uta.fi/ADAbase/) - Human adenosine deaminase (ADA) mutation db

14. Albinism Database (http://www.ifpcs.org/albinism/index.html)

15. Albumin Web site (http://albumin.org/)

16. AR mutations (http://androgendb.mcgill.ca/) - Human androgen receptor mutation db

17. Antithrombin mutation db (http://www.1.imperial.ac.uk/medicine/about/divisions/is/haemo/coag/antithrombin)

18. BIOMDB (http://www.bh4.org/BH4_Start.asp) - Db of mutations causing tetrahydrobiopterin deficiencies

19. BLMbase (http://bioinf.uta.fi/BLMbase/) - Human BLM mutation db (Bloom syndrome)

20. BTKbase (http://bioinf.uta.fi/BTKbase) - Human BTK mutation db (X-linked agammaglobulinemia)

21. CC_dbMD (http://www.wjc.ku.dk/~larsh/dbCC-MD//startdbCC_MD.htm) The Congenital Cataract Mutation Database

22. CD3Ebase (http://bioinf.uta.fi/CD3Ebase/) - Human CD3E mutation db

23. CD3Gbase (http://bioinf.uta.fi/CD3Gbase/) - Human CD3G mutation db

24. CD40Lbase (http://bioinf.uta.fi/CD40Lbase/index.php) - Human CD40 ligand mutation db

25. COL1/3 mutation (http://www.le.ac.uk/genetics/collagen/) - Human Type I and III collagen mutation db

26. Connexin-deafness (http://davinci.crg.es/deafness/) - Human connexins mutation db

27. CFTR mutation (http://www.genet.sickkids.on.ca/cftr/app) - Human cystic fibrosis mutation db (CFTR)

28. KMbloodDB (http://mutview.dmb.med.keio.ac.jp/ MutationView/jsp/ index.jsp) - Blood disease genes db

29. KMbrainDB (http://mutview.dmb.med.keio.ac.jp/ MutationView/jsp/ index.jsp) - Brain disease genes db

30. KMcancerDB - Cancer disease genes db

31. KMearDB - Ear disease genes db

32. KMeyeDB - Eye disease genes db

33. KMheartDB - Heart disease genes db

34. KMmuscleDB - Muscle disease genes db

35. KMsyndromeDB

36. MaiDB (autoimmune)

37. G6PD (http://rialto.com/g6pd/) - Human G6PD deficiency resource

38. G6PDdb (http://www.bioinf.org.uk/g6pd/) - Human G6PD mutation db

39. GNAS1 (http://www.le.ac.uk/genetics/maa7/GNAS1/) - Human GNAS1 mutation db

40. HAMSTeRS (http://europium.csc.mrc.ac.uk/) - The Haemophilia A Mutation db and Factor VII Resource site

41. Haemophilia B mutation db (http://www.kcl.ac.uk/ip/petergreen/haemBdatabase.html) - Factor IX

42. HbVar (http://globin.cse.psu.edu/globin/hbvar/) - Hemoglobin variants db

43. Hereditary hearing loss homepage (http://hereditaryhearingloss.org/)

44. LDLR mutation (http://www.ucl.ac.uk/ldlr/LOVDv.1.1.0/) - Human LDLR mutation db (Familial hypercholesterolemia)

45. NCF1base (http://bioinf.uta.fi/NCF1base/) - Human NCF1 mutation db

46. NCF2base (http://bioinf.uta.fi/NCF2base/) - Human NCF2 mutation db

47. Neuromuscular diseases web site (http://www.neuro.wustl.edu/ neuromuscular)

48. NCL (http://www.ucl.ac.uk/ncl/) - Neuronal Ceroid Lipofuscinoses mutation db

49. OCRL1 (http://research.nhgri.nih.gov/lowe/) - OCRL1 mutation db (Lowe Syndrome)

50. Cytochrome P450 alleles nomenclature (http://www.cypalleles.ki.se/)

51. IARC TP53 mutation db (http://p53.iarc.fr/) - International Agency for Research on Cancer

52. Germline p53 mutation db (http://stary.lf2.cuni.cz/projects/germline_mut_p53.htm) - University of Prague db of germline p53 mutations

53. PAHdb (http://www.pahdb.mcgill.ca/) - Human phenylalanine hydroxylase (PAH) mutation db

54. Prion (http://en.wikipedia.org/wiki/Prion) - Wikipedia Prion and prion disease

55. RAG1base (http://bioinf.uta.fi/RAG1base/) - Human RAG1 mutation db

56. RAG2base (http://bioinf.uta.fi/RAG2base/) - Human RAG2 mutation db

57. RB1base (http://rb1-lsdb.d-lohmann.de/home.php?select_db=RB1) - Human retinoblastoma-associated protein (RB) mutation db

58. RetNet (https://sph.uth.edu/Retnet/) - Retinal Information Network

59. Retina International Scientific Newsletter (http://www.retina-international.com/sci-news/) - Information on Retinal genes, proteins and diseases

60. Alsod.org (http://alsod.iop.kcl.ac.uk/) - ALS/SOD1 genetic mutations db

61. TGDB (http://alsod.iop.kcl.ac.uk/) - Tumor gene db

62. VMD2 mutation (http://www-huge.uni-regensburg.de/BEST1_database/home.php?select_db=BEST1) - Human VMD2 mutation db

63. vWF mutation (http://www.vwf.group.shef.ac.uk/) - Human von Willebrand factor (vWF) mutation db

64. WRN (http://www.pathology.washington.edu/research/werner/database/) - Human WRN mutation db (Warner disease)

65. X-ALD mutation (http://www.x-ald.nl/) - Human ABCD1 mutation db

Gene(s) / protein(s) specific databases / resources

1. Human ABC transporters (http://nutrigene.4t.com/humanabc.htm/)

2. ABCISSE (http://www1.pasteur.fr/recherche/unites/pmtg/abc/database.iphtml) - ABC systems : Information on Sequence Structure and Evolution

3. ADAMTS (http://www.lerner.ccf.org/bme/apte/adamts/) - Apte lab ADAMTS and ADAMTSL resource

4. Human albumin Web site (http://albumin.org/)

5. Nomenclature and entries of allergens in UniProtKB/Swiss-Prot (http://www.uniprot.org/docs/allergen)

6. Allergen sequence db (http://www.iit.edu/~sgendel/fa.htm)

7. Allergome (http://www.allergome.org/) - A platform for allergen knowledge

8. SDAP (http://fermi.utmb.edu/SDAP/) - Structural database of allergenic proteins

9. Alginate genes (http://www2.fiu.edu/~matheek/Alginate_Genes.htm) - Pseudomomonas alginate production genes

10. Entries of aminoacyl-tRNA synthetases in UniProtKB/Swiss-Prot (http://www.uniprot.org/docs/aatrnasy)

11. AARSDB (http://rose.man.poznan.pl/aars/) - Aminoacyl-tRNA synthetases db

12. Androgen Receptor Gene Mutations Database (http://androgendb.mcgill.ca/)

13. AMSDb (http://www.bbcm.univ.trieste.it/~tossi.pag1.htm) - Antimicrobial sequences db
14. Antibody resource page (http://www.antibodyresource.com/) - Links to antibody related Web resources
15. Linscott's Directory of Immunological & Biological Reagents (http://www.linscottsdirectory.com/)
16. AraC-XylS (http://www.eez.csic.es/arac-xyls/) - A db on a family of helix-turn-helix transcription factors from bacteria
17. Bcl-2 family database (http://bcl2db.ibcp.fr/)
18. Blood group antigens in UniProtKB/Swiss-Prot (http://www.uniprot.org/docs/bloodgrp)
19. BRENDA (http://www.brenda-enzymes.org/) - Db of enzyme functional data
20. EF-hand CaBP (http://structbio.vanderbilt.edu/cabp_database/) - EF-hand calcium-binding proteins data library
21. CAZy (http://structbio.vanderbilt.edu/cabp_database/) - Carbohydrate-Active enZYmes Web site
22. CBS domain (http://en.wikipedia.org/wiki/Cystathionine_beta_synthase) - Cystathionine Beta Synthase domain
23. CD antigens entries and nomenclature in UniProtKB/Swiss-Prot (http://www.uniprot.org/docs/cdlist)
24. cpnDB (http://cpndb.cbr.nrc.ca/) - A Chaperonin Database
25. CSDBase (http://www.chemie.uni-marburg.de/~csdbase/) - Cold shock domain db

26. COPE (http://www.copewithcytokines.de/) - Cytokines On-line Pathfinder Encyclopedia

27. dbCFC (http://cytokine.medic.kumamoto-u.ac.jp/) - Cytokine family db

28. DPInteract (http://arep.med.harvard.edu/dpinteract/) - DNA-Proteins interactions db

29. EMP (http://arep.med.harvard.edu/dpinteract/) - Enzymes and Metabolic Pathways db

30. ENZYME (http://enzyme.expasy.org/) - Enzymes nomenclature db

31. Worthington enzyme manual (http://www.worthington-biochem.com/index/ manual.html)

32. EpoDB (http://www.cbil.upenn.edu/EpoDB/) - Erythropoiesis gene expression db (Epo GED)

33. ESTHER (http://bioweb.ensam.inra.fr/ESTHER/definition/) - Esterases and alpha/beta hydrolase enzymes

34. Estrogen Receptor Resource (http://nrr.georgetown.edu/ EstrogenReceptor/ER-PAGE/Main.html)

35. Expansins web site (http://www.personal.psu.edu/ fsl/ExpCentral/)

36. Modules (http://www.bork.embl-heidelberg.de/Modules/) - Extracellular proteins modules (domains)

37. FADPNR (http://www.icgeb.org/~p450srv/GSHR_like.html) - FAD-dependent pyridine nucleotide oxidoreductases

38. Flavodoxins (http://www.icgeb.org/~p450srv/GSHR_like.html)

39. FYVE finger domain (http://www.uib.no/aasland/FYVE.html)
40. Globin (http://globin.cse.psu.edu/) - Globin gene server
41. Glucocorticoid Receptor Resource (http://nrr.georgetown.edu/GRR/grr1.html)
42. Nomenclature and entries of Glycosyl hydrolases in UniProtKB/Swiss-Prot (http://www.uniprot.org/docs/glycosid)
43. 7TM (http://www.uniprot.org/docs/7tmrlist) - Entries of 7-transmembrane G-linked receptors in UniProtKB/Swiss-Prot
44. GPCRDB (http://www.gpcr.org/7tm/) - G protein-coupled receptor db (7TM) at EMBL
45. GPCRs database (http://www.guidetopharmacology.org/GRAC/ReceptorFamiliesForward?type=GPCR)
46. GRR (http://www.guidetopharmacology.org/GRAC/ReceptorFamiliesForward?type=GPCR) - Glucocorticoid receptor resource
47. SSFA-GPHR (http://www.ssfa-gphr.de/) - Glycoprotein Hormone Receptors database
48. Arabidopsis Glycosyltransferases Family 1 (http://www.p450.kvl.dk/gst.shtml)
49. GnRH (http://www.tigr.org/~jeisen/GnRH/GnRH.html) - Gonadotropin-releasing hormones (GnRH) family
50. Histone (http://research.nhgri.nih.gov/histones/) - Histones db

51. HIVdb (http://xpdb.nist.gov/hivsdb/hivsdb.html) - HIV protease db

52. HORDE (http://genome.weizmann.ac.il/horde/) - Human Olfactory Receptor Data Exploratorium

53. Hox proteins (http://www.uniprot.org/docs/hoxlist) - Nomenclature and entries of vertebrate homeotic Hox proteins in UniProtKB/Swiss-Prot

54. IMGT (http://imgt.cines.fr/) - ImMunoGeneTics db [Mirror at EBI]

55. InBase (http://tools.neb.com/inbase/) - Inteins db from the New England Biolabs

56. Integrins (http://en.wikipedia.org/wiki/Integrin) - from Wikipedia

57. Initiation factors (http://www.uniprot.org/docs/initfact) - Entries of translation initiation factors in UniProtKB/Swiss-Prot

58. LGIC (http://lenoverelab.org/LGICdb/LGICdb.php) - Ligand Gated Ion Channel subunit db

59. Voltage-gated Ion Channels (http://lenoverelab.org/LGICdb/LGICdb.php)

60. KEGG (http://www.genome.jp/kegg/) - Kyoto Encyclopedia of Genes and Genomes

61. Klotho (http://www.biochem.info.org/klotho/) - Biochemical compounds declarative db

62. LED (http://www.led.uni-stuttgart.de/) - Lipase Engineering Database

63. MDB (http://metallo.scripps.edu/) - Metalloprotein Site Database and Browser
64. EPIMHC (http://imed.med.ucm.es/epimhc/) - A curated database of MHC ligands
65. Mitochondrial carriers pages from Nelson's lab (http://drnelson.utmem.edu/ mitocarriers.html)
66. NPD (http://npd.hgu.mrc.ac.uk/user/) - Nuclear Protein db
67. NucleaRDB (http://www.receptors.org/nucleardb/) - Federated db on nuclear receptors
68. P450 (http://www.icgeb.org/~p450srv/) - Directory of P450-containing systems
69. Arabidopsis P450 Web site (http://www.p450.kvl.dk/p450.shtml)
70. IARC p53 db (http://p53.iarc.fr/) - IARC db of somatic p53 mutations
71. PDE (http://depts.washington.edu/pde/) - Phosphodiesterases
72. Peroxibase (http://peroxibase.toulouse.inra.fr/) - the Peroxidase database
73. Classification and entries of peptidases in UniProtKB/ Swiss-Prot (http://www.uniprot.org/docs/peptidas)
74. MEROPS (http://merops.sanger.ac.uk/) - Peptidase db
75. PLACE (http://www.dna.affrc.go.jp/PLACE/) - Plant cis-acting regulatory DNA elements db
76. KinBase (http://www.kinase.com/kinbase/)

77. PKR (http://www0.nih.go.jp/mirror/Kinases/) - Protein Kinase Resource

78. PatBase (http://www.traplabs.dk/patbase/) - P-type ATPase db

79. PPAR (http://vbs.psu.edu/research/labs/vanden-heuvel) - Peroxisome Proliferator - Activated Receptor resource

80. Reactome (http://www.reactome.org/) - a curated knowledgebase of biological pathways

81. REBASE (http://rebase.neb.com/rebase/) - Restriction enzymes and methylases db

82. Classification and entries of restriction enzymes/methylases in UniProtKB/Swiss-Prot (http://www.uniprot.org/docs/restric)

83. Families and entries of ribosomal proteins in UniProtKB/Swiss-Prot (http://www.uniprot.org/docs/ribosomp)

84. RNA Helicase database (http://www.rnahelicase.org/)

85. RNase P (http://www.mbio.ncsu.edu/RNaseP/) - Ribonuclease P db

86. SABIO Reaction Kinetics Database (http://sabio.villa-bosch.de/)

87. SPAD (http://www.grt.kyushu-u.ac.jp/spad/) - Signalling pathway db

88. SRPDB (http://rnp.uthct.edu/mp/SRPDB/SRPDB.html) - Signal Recognition Particle db

89. SNF2 (http://www.snf2.net/) - SNF2 family protein resource

90. TTD (http://xin.cz3.nus.edu.sg/Group/ttd/ttd.asp) - Therapeutic Targets Database

91. TRANSFAC (http://www.gene-regulation.com/pub/databases.html#transfac) - Transcription factors db

92. TFII (http://tfiib.med.harvard.edu/transcription/basaltx.html) - Basal transcription factors

93. TRANSPATH (http://www.gene-regulation.com/pub/databases.html#transpath) - Signal Transduction Browser

94. TC-DB (http://www.biology.ucsd.edu/~msaier/transport/) - Transport Classification System from Milton Saier

95. VDR (http://vdr.bu.edu/) - Vitamin D Nuclear Receptor

96. WD-repeat (http://bmerc-www.bu.edu/projects/wdrepeat/) - WD-repeat proteins family

97. Wnt homepage (http://web.stanford.edu/~rnusse/wntwindow.html)

98. WormPep (http://www.sanger.ac.uk/research/projects/caenorhabditisgenomics/) - C.elegans proteins db

99. YTPdb (http://rsat.scmbb.ulb.ac.be/~sylvain/ytpdb/) - Yeast Transport Protein db

100. Tox-Prot (http://www.expasy.org/sprot/tox-prot/) - The UniProtKB/Swiss-Prot Toxin Annotation Program

101. ConoServer (http://research1t.imb.uq.edu.au/conoserver/)

102. The Venom Composition (http://grimwade.biochem.unimelb.edu.au/cone/vencomp.html) - Information on conotoxins from a Web site on cone shells

103. International venom and toxin db (http://www.kingsnake.com/toxinology/)

104. Snake database (http://ntrc.tamuk.edu/cgi-bin/serpentarium/snake.query) at Natural Toxins Research Center

Post-translational modifications databases and resources

1. DSDBASE (http://caps.ncbs.res.in/dsdbase/dsdbase.html) - Disulfide database (derived from 3D data)

2. GlycoSuiteDB (http://caps.ncbs.res.in/dsdbase/dsdbase.html) - Db of glycan structures

3. LIPID MAPS (http://www.lipidmaps.org/) - LIPID Metabolites And Pathways Strategy

4. GlycateBase (http://www.cbs.dtu.dk/databases/GlycateBase-1.0/) - Database of glycation data for epsilon amino groups of lysines

5. O-GlycBase (http://www.cbs.dtu.dk/databases/OGLYCBASE/) - O-glycosylated proteins db

6. Phospho.ELM (http://phospho.elm.eu.org/) - Phosphorylation sites db

7. PhosphoSite (http://www.phosphosite.org/messageAction.do;jsessionid=4F7ACE2983762F163F162D68FC95B825) - Db of phosphorylation sites in human and mouse proteomes

8. DOLOP (http://www.mrc-lmb.cam.ac.uk/genomes/dolop/) - Db of bacterial lipoproteins

9. UbiProt (http://ubiprot.org.ru/) - Db of ubiquitylated proteins

10. RESID (http://www.ebi.ac.uk/RESID) - Db of Amino Acid Modifications

11. Delta Mass (http://www.abrf.org/index.cfm/dm.home) - Db of mass of Post-Translational Modifications

Phylogenetics and taxonomy databases & resources

1. COG and KOG (http://www.ncbi.nlm.nih.gov/COG/) - Phylogenetic classification of proteins encoded in complete genomes

2. eggNog (http://eggnog.embl.de/version_4.0.beta/) - Automated construction and annotation of orthologous groups of genes

3. EGO (http://compbio.dfci.harvard.edu/tgi/ego/) - Eukaryotic Gene Orthologs

4. Ensembl Compara (http://www.ensembl.org/info/docs/api/compara/index.html) - Genome-wide species comparisons

5. HOGENOM (http://doua.prabi.fr/databases/hogenom/home.php?contents=query) - Homologous Sequences in Complete Genomes Database

6. HOVERGEN (http://pbil.univ-lyon1.fr/databases/hovergen.php) - Homologous Vertebrate Genes Database

7. InParanoid (http://inparanoid.sbc.su.se/cgi-bin/index.cgi) - Eukaryotic ortholog groups

8. KO (http://www.genome.jp/kegg-bin/get_htext?ko00001.keg) - KEGG Orthology

9. Metazome (http://www.metazome.net/IEsorry.php?refer=/) - Phylogenomic analysis of metazoan gene families

10. Optic (http://genserv.anat.ox.ac.uk/clades) - Orthologous and paralogous transcripts in clades

11. OMA (http://www.cbrg.ethz.ch/research/orthologous) - Orthologs Matrix Project (OMA)

12. OrthoDB (http://cegg.unige.ch/orthodb3) Hierarchical catalog of eukaryotic orthologs

13. OrthoMCL DB (http://www.orthomcl.org/orthomcl/) Ortholog grouping for protein sequences from multiple genomes

14. PhylomeDB (http://phylomedb.org/) - Database for phylomes (collections of phylogenetic trees for all proteins encoded in a given genome)

15. P-POD (http://ppod.princeton.edu/) - Princeton Protein Orthology Database with an emphasis on providing information about disease-related genes

16. Protein Clusters (http://www.ncbi.nlm.nih.gov/proteinclusters) - NCBI collection of related protein sequences (clusters)

17. PhyloFacts (http://phylogenomics.berkeley.edu/phylofacts/) - Pre-calculated structural and phylogenomic analyses of protein families and domains

18. TreeFam (http://www.treefam.org/) - Tree families database of phylogenetic trees of animal genes

19. CluSTr (http://www.ebi.ac.uk/clustr/) - Automatic classification of UniProtKB proteins into groups of related proteins

20. HomoloGene (http://www.ncbi.nlm.nih.gov/homologene) - Automated detection of homologs among the annotated genes of several completely sequenced eukaryotic genomes

21. ProtoNet (http://www.protonet.cs.huji.ac.il/) - Classification of the proteins into hierarchical clusters

22. NCBI Taxonomy Browser (http://www.ncbi.nlm.nih.gov/taxonomy)

23. Taxonomy (http://www.uniprot.org/taxonomy/) - UniProt Taxonomy Browser

24. The Tree of life (http://tolweb.org/tree/) - Collection of WWW pages on phylogeny and biodiversity of organisms

25. TreeBASE (http://www.treebase.org/treebase-web/home.html) - Relational db of phylogenetic information

Gene expression databases and resources

1. 4DXpress - a database for cross-species expression pattern comparisons

2. ArrayExpress (http://www.ebi.ac.uk/arrayexpress/) - MicroArray informatics at the EBI

3. Bgee (http://bgee.unil.ch/) - Retrieve and compare gene expression patterns across species

4. BioGPS (http://biogps.gnf.org/) - The Gene Portal Hub

5. CleanEx (http://cleanex.vital-it.ch/) - database of gene expression profiles

6. ExpressDB (http://twod.med.harvard.edu/ExpressDB/) - Yeast and E.coli RNA expression db

7. GeneX (http://genex.sourceforge.net/) - An open source Gene Expression database

8. GEO (http://www.ncbi.nlm.nih.gov/geo/) - Gene Expression Omnibus

9. GXD (http://www.informatics.jax.org/mgihome/GXD/about GXD.shtml) - MGI Gene Expression Database (mouse)

10. RAD (http://www.cbil.upenn.edu/RAD) - RNA abundance db

11. SMD (http://smd.princeton.edu/) - Stanford microarray db

12. MILANO (http://milano.md.huji.ac.il/) - Microarray Literature-based Annotation

13. Genevestigator (https://genevestigator.com/gv/) - a multi-organism, novel type of online meta-analysis tool for gene expression

14. GEMLeR (http://gemler.fzv.uni-mb.si/) - Gene Expression Machine Learning Repository

Biological software and databases catalog servers

1. CLC Free Workbench (http://www.clcbio.com/products/clc-sequence-viewer/) - A desktop program including a number of algorithms for DNA, RNA, and protein analyses. Available for Linux, MacOS X and Windows

2. CLC Protein Workbench (http://www.clcbio.com/products/clc-main-workbench/) - A desktop program including a number of advanced algorithms for protein sequence analysis. Available for Linux, MacOS X and Windows

3. CodonCode Aligner (http://www.codoncode.com/aligner/) - Sequence assembly and alignment

4. **LabLife** (http://www.labguru.com/features/lab-logistics/orders-and-inventory) - Lab tools for your lab research

5. BioCatalogue (https://www.biocatalogue.org/)

6. ChemSynthesis (http://www.chemsynthesis.com/) - Chemical Database

7. LIC Generator (http://noxtoolbox.ibs.fr/LICgenerator/) - A web-based software for Ligation Independent Cloning vector and primer design

8. Genamix Software Seek (http://www.genamics.com/software/)

Biocomputing server's homepages

Europe

1. EBI (http://www.ebi.ac.uk/) - European Bioinformatics Institute

2. EMBnet (http://www.embnet.org/) - European Molecular Biology Network

3. EMBL (http://www.embl.de/~biocomp/) - EMBL Biocomputing unit

4. SIB (http://www.isb-sib.ch/) - Swiss Institute of Bioinformatics

5. EMBnet CH (http://www.ch.embnet.org/) - Switzerland EMBnet node

6. ISREC (http://ccg.vital-it.ch/) - ISREC/SIB Computational Cancer Genomics group (Lausanne / Switzerland)

7. CBRG (http://www.cbrg.ethz.ch/) - Computational Biochemistry Research Group (Zurich / Switzerland)

8. ABIM (http://sites.univ-provence.fr/~wabim/) - Atelier BioInformatique (Marseille / FR)

9. B3E (http://www.b3e.jussieu.fr/) - Bioinformatique / Biostatistique / Biomathematique / Epidemiologie (Paris / FR)

10. Genethon (http://www.genethon.fr/) - Genethon (Evry / FR)

11. GeneStream (http://xylian.igh.cnrs.fr/) - Institut de Géné tique Humaine (Montpellier / FR)

12. GENOSCOPE (http://www.genoscope.cns.fr/spip/) - Centre National de Séquencage (Evry / FR)

13. GenoStar (http://www.genostar.org/) - Consortium for the development of a bioinformatic platform

14. IGS (http://igs-server.cnrs-mrs.fr/) - Information Génétique et Structurale (Structural and Genetic Information Laboratory) (Marseille / FR)

15. IMPBIO (http://impbio.lirmm.fr/) - Informatique, Mathématiques, Physique en Biologie moléculaire

16. Pasteur (http://www.pasteur.fr/fr) - Institut Pasteur (Paris / FR)

17. PBIL (http://doua.prabi.fr/) - Pole Bio-informatique Lyonnais (Lyon / FR)

18. Sanger (http://www.sanger.ac.uk/) - Sanger Centre (Hinxton / U.K.)

19. BMM (http://www.bmm.icnet.uk/) - Biomolecular Modelling laboratory at ICRF (London / U.K.)

20. BSM (http://www.biochem.ucl.ac.uk/bsm/) - Biomolecular Structure and modelling group at UCL (London / U.K.)

21. Manchester (http://bioinf.man.ac.uk/) - Manchester University Bioinformatics unit (U.K.)

22. HUSAR (http://genome.dkfz-heidelberg.de/husar/hs_home.html) - Biocomputing Service at DKFZ

23. AG BIODV (http://www.helmholtz-muenchen.de/en/ieg/group-ag-biodv/) - Software Development for Molecular Biology at Helmholtz Zentrum (Germany)

24. FLI (http://genome.imb-jena.de/) - Genome Analysis in Complex Diseases, Ageing and Model Organisms (Germany)

25. MDC:Bioinf (http://genome.imb-jena.de/) - Department of Bionformatic of the Max Delbruck Center for Molecular Medicine (Germany)

26. MIPS (http://www.helmholtz-muenchen.de/en/ibis) - Munich Information Centre for Protein Sequences (Germany)

27. PZR (http://tp12.pzr.uni-rostock.de/) - Bioinformatics at the Proteome Center Rostock (Germany)

28. BEN (http://www.be.embnet.org/) - Belgium EMBnet node

29. CBS (http://www.cbs.dtu.dk/) - Center for Biological Sequence Analysis (Technical University of Denmark)

30. CSC BioBox (http://www.csc.fi/english/research/sciences/biosciences) - Resources for Bioscientists

31. ABC (http://www.abc.hu/en/) - Agricultural Biotechnology Center (Budapest / Hungary)

32. Telethon Italy (https://www.telethon.it/)

33. CMBI (http://www2.cmbi.ru.nl/) - Center for Molecular and Biomolecular Bioinformatics; Netherland EMBnet node

34. BIO (http://www.biotek.uio.no/) - Biotechnology Centre of Oslo; Norway EMBnet node

35. IBB (http://www.ibb.waw.pl/) - Institute of Biochemistry and Biophysics (Warsaw); Poland EMBnet node

36. IGC (http://bioinformatics.igc.gulbenkian.pt/ubi/) - Bioinformatics and Computational Unit of the Instituto Gulbenkian de Ciencia; Portugal EMBnet Node

37. Belozersky Institute (http://www.genebee.msu.ru/) - GeneBee Molecular Biology server (Moscow); Russia EMBnet node

38. MGS (http://wwwmgs.bionet.nsc.ru/mgs/gnw/) - Molecular Biological Server (Novosibirsk / Russia)

39. CNB (http://www.cnb.csic.es/index.php/en/) - Centro Nacional de Biotecnologia; Spain EMBnet node

40. BMC (http://www.bmc.uu.se/) - BioMedical Centre at Uppsala; Sweden EMBnet node

41. KISAC (http://www.cgb.ki.se/cgb/groups/kisac/kisac.html) - Karolinska Institute (KI) Sequence Analysis Computer

42. LCB (http://www.bmc.uu.se/) - Linnaeus Centre for Bioinformatics

43. SBC (http://www.sbc.su.se/) - Stockholm Bioinformatics Center

USA and Canada

1. NCBI (http://www.ncbi.nlm.nih.gov/) - National Center for Biotechnology Information

2. ABCC (https://ncifrederick.cancer.gov/isp/abcc/) - Advanced Biomedical Computing Center at the NCI

3. ACGT (http://www.genome.ou.edu/) - Advanced Center for Genome Technology at the University of Oklahoma

4. BCM HGC (https://www.hgsc.bcm.edu/) - Baylor College of Medicine Human Genome Center

5. BDGP (http://www.fruitfly.org/) - Berkeley Drosophila Genome Project

6. BioTech (http://biotech.icmb.utexas.edu/) - Life Sciences Resources and Reference Tools

7. Biotechnology (http://www.nal.usda.gov/) - National Agricultural Library - Biotechnology

8. BMERC (http://www.bu.edu/bmerc/) - Biomolecular Engineering Research Center

9. BROAD Institute (http://www.broadinstitute.org/)

10. CBIL (http://www.cbil.upenn.edu/) - Computational Biology and Informatics Laboratory at the University of Pennsylvania

11. CCB (http://www.ibc.wustl.edu/) - Washington University Center for Computational Biology

12. CUBIC (http://cubic.bioc.columbia.edu/) - Columbia University Bioinformatics Center / RostLab

13. JCVI (http://www.jcvi.org/cms/home/) - J. Craig Venter Institute

14. JGI (http://jgi.doe.gov/) - Doe Joint Genome Institute

15. NCGR (http://www.ncgr.org/) - National Center for Genome Resources

16. NIH (http://molbio.info.nih.gov/) - Computational Molecular Biology at NIH

17. UCLA (http://www.bioinformatics.ucla.edu/) - UCLA Bioinformatics Institute

18. Bioinformatics & Research Computing at Whitehead Institute (http://jura.wi.mit.edu/bio/)

19. CCB (https://www.ccb.sickkids.ca/) - Centre for Computational Biology at the Hospital for sick children

Asia

1. APBioNet (http://www.apbionet.org/) - Asia-Pacific Bioinformatics network

2. BIDD (http://ang.cz3.nus.edu.sg/cgi-bin/prog/norm.pl) - Bioinformatics & Drug Design group (National University - Singapore)

3. DIC (http://bioinfo.ernet.in) - Bioinformatics Centre at the University of Pune

4. Japanese GenomeNet (http://www.genome.jp/)

5. NIG (http://www.nig.ac.jp/english/index.html) - National Institute of Genetics of Japan

6. KDRI (http://www.kazusa.or.jp/e/) - Kazusa DNA Research Institute

7. CBI (http://www.cbi.pku.edu.cn/) - Peking Center of Bioinformatics ; Chinese EMBnet node

8. MICRO-NET (http://www.cbi.pku.edu.cn/) - Microbial Information Network of China

9. HKBIC (http://www.hkbic.cuhk.edu.hk/) - Hong Kong Bioinformatics Center

10. BRIC (http://bric.postech.ac.kr/) - Biological Research Information Center (Korea)

11. MGRC (http://www.mgrc.com.my/) - Malaysian Genomics Resource Centre

12. BIC (http://www.bic.nus.edu.sg/) - BioInformatics Center of the National University of Singapore

Australia

1. APBioNet (http://www.apbionet.org/) - Asia-Pacific Bioinformatics network

2. ANGIS (http://www.angis.org.au/) - Australian National Genomic Information Service

3. ANU (http://biology.anu.edu.au/) - Australian National University Genomic Interactions group

4. APAF (http://www.proteome.org.au/) - Australian Proteome Analysis Facility

Others

1. HUJI (http://bioinfo.md.huji.ac.il/) - Hebrew University of Jerusalem genomic and bioinformatics server

2. Weizmann Bioinfo/BCU (http://bip.weizmann.ac.il/) - Weizmann Institute of Science Bioinformatics and Biological Computing

3. SANBI (http://www.sanbi.ac.za/) - South African BioInformatics Institute
4. ICGEB (http://www.icgeb.trieste.it/home.html) - International Center for Genetic Engineering and Biotechnology (Trieste / Italy)

International Nucleotide Sequence Database Collaboration (http://www.insdc.org/)

The International Nucleotide Sequence Database Collaboration (INSDC) is a long-standing foundational initiative that operates between DDBJ (http://www.ddbj.nig.ac.jp/), EMBL-EBI (https://www.ebi.ac.uk/) and NCBI (http://www.ncbi.nlm.nih.gov/). INSDC covers the spectrum of data raw reads, though alignments and assemblies to functional annotation, enriched with contextual information relating to samples and experimental configurations.

Data type	DDBJ	EMBL-EBI	NCBI
Next generation reads	Sequence Read Archive	European Nucleotide Archive (ENA)	Sequence Read Archive
Capillary reads	Trace Archive		Trace Archive
Annotated sequences	DDBJ		GenBank
Samples	BioSample		BioSample
Studies	BioProject		BioProject

The INSDC advisory board, the International Advisory Committee (http://www.insdc.org/advisors), is made up of members of each of the databases' advisory bodies. At their most recent meeting, members of this committee unanimously endorsed and reaffirmed the existing data-sharing policy of the three databases that make up the INSDC, which is stated below.

Individuals submitting data to the international sequence databases should be aware of INSDC policy (http://www.insdc.org/policy).

Primary nucleotide sequence databases [edit] (http://en.wikipedia.org/w/index.php?title=List_of_biological_databases&action=edit&section=1)**:**

International Nucleotide Sequence Database (INSD) (http://en.wikipedia.org/wiki/International_Nucleotide_Sequence_Database_Collaboration) consists of the following databases.

1. DNA Data Bank of Japan (http://en.wikipedia.org/wiki/DNA_Data_Bank_of_Japan (National Institute of Genetics) (http://en.wikipedia.org/wiki/National_Institute_of_Genetics)

2. EMBL (http://en.wikipedia.org/wiki/European_Molecular_Biology_Laboratory) (European Bioinformatics Institute) (http://en.wikipedia.org/wiki/European_Bioinformatics_Institute)

3. GenBank (http://en.wikipedia.org/wiki/GenBank) (National Center for Biotechnology Information) (http://en.wikipedia.org/wiki/National_Center_for_Biotechnology_Information)

The three databases, DDBJ (Japan), GenBank (USA) and European Nucleotide Archive (Europe), are repositories for nucleotide sequence (http://en.wikipedia.org/wiki/Biomolecular_structure#Primary_structure) data from all organisms (http://en.wikipedia.org/wiki/Organism). All three databases accept nucleotide sequence submissions, and then exchange new and updated data on a daily basis to achieve optimal synchronisation between them. These three databases are primary databases, as they house original sequence data.

Meta databases [edit] (http://en.wikipedia.org/w/index.php?title=List_of_biological_databases&action=edit&section=2):

These databases of databases collect data from different sources and make them available in new and more convenient form, or with an emphasis on a particular disease or organism.

1. BioGraph (http://biograph.be/) [University of Antwerp - (http://en.wikipedia.org/wiki/University_of_Antwerp), Vlaams Instituut voor Biotechnologie - (http://en.wikipedia.org/wiki/Vlaams_Instituut_voor_Biotechnologie)] - A knowledge discovery service based on the integration of more than 20 heterogeneous databases

2. Bioinformatic Harvester[1] (http://en.wikipedia.org/wiki/Bioinformatic_Harvester) (Karlsruhe Institute of Technology) (http://en.wikipedia.org/wiki/Karlsruhe_Institute_of_Technology) - Integrating 26 major protein/gene resources.

3. Neuroscience Information Framework[2] (http://en.wikipedia.org/wiki/Neuroscience_Information_Framework) [University of California San Diego) - (http://en.wikipedia.org/wiki/University_of_California,_San_Diego)] - Integrates hundreds of neuroscience relevant resources, many are listed below.

4. ConsensusPathDB (http://en.wikipedia.org/wiki/ConsensusPathDB) - A molecular functional interaction database, integrating information from 12 other databases.

5. Entrez[3] (http://en.wikipedia.org/wiki/Entrez) [National Center for Biotechnology Information (http://en.wikipedia.org/wiki/National_Center_for_Biotechnology_Information)]

6. Enzyme Portal (http://www.ebi.ac.uk/enzymeportal/) - Integrates enzyme information such as small-molecule chemistry, biochemical pathways and drug compounds. [European Bioinformatics Institute - (http://en.wikipedia.org/wiki/European_Bioinformatics_Institute)]

7. euGenes (http://eugenes.org/) [Indiana University - (http://en.wikipedia.org/wiki/Indiana_University_Bloomington)]

8. GeneCards (http://www.genecards.org/) [Weizmann Inst. - (http://en.wikipedia.org/wiki/Weizmann_Institute_of_Science)]

9. MetaBase[4] (http://en.wikipedia.org/wiki/MetaBase) [KOBIC - (http://en.wikipedia.org/wiki/KOBIC)] - A user contributed database of biological databases.

10. mGen (http://www.cyber-indian.com/bioperl/index.html) containing four of the world biggest databases GenBank, Refseq, EMBL and DDBJ - easy and simple program friendly gene extraction

11. MOPED (https://www.proteinspire.org/MOPED/mopedviews/proteinExpressionDatabase.jsf) [Seattle Children's Research Institute - (http://en.wikipedia.org/wiki/Seattle_Children%27s_Research_Institute)] - A multi-omics expression profiling database providing integrated proteomics and transcriptomics data from human, mouse, worm, and yeast.

12. PathogenPortal (http://pathogenportal.org/portal/portal/PathPort/Home) A repository linking to the Bioinformatics

Resource Centers (BRCs) (http://en.wikipedia.org/wiki/Bioinformatics_Resource_Centers) sponsored by the National Institute of Allergy and Infectious Diseases (NIAID)

13. SOURCE (http://smd.princeton.edu/cgi-bin/source/sourceSearch) [Stanford University - (http://en.wikipedia.org/wiki/Stanford_University)] encapsulates the genetics and molecular biology of genes from the genomes of *Homo sapiens*, *Mus musculus*, and *Rattus norvegicus* into easy to navigate GeneReports

14. iRefIndex (http://irefindex.org/wiki/index.php?title=iRefIndex) provides an index of protein interactions available in a number of primary interaction databases including BIND, BioGRID, CORUM, DIP, HPRD, InnateDB, IntAct, MatrixDB, MINT, MPact, MPIDB, MPPI and OPHID.

15. Pathway Commons (http://www.pathwaycommons.org/about/) [Memorial Sloan-Kettering Cancer Center (http://en.wikipedia.org/wiki/Memorial_Sloan_Kettering_Cancer_Center) and University of Toronto (http://en.wikipedia.org/wiki/University_of_Toronto)]

16. Nowomics (http://nowomics.com/) Tracks changes in several biological databases, users 'follow' genes and keywords to see news feed of new data and papers.

Genome databases (http://en.wikipedia.org/w/index.php?title=List_of_biological_databases&action=edit&section=3)

These databases collect genome (http://en.wikipedia.org/wiki/Genome) sequences, annotate and analyze them, and provide public access. Some add curation (http://en.wikipedia.org/wiki/Digital_curation) of experimental literature to improve computed annotations. These databases may hold many species genomes, or a single model organism (http://en.wikipedia. org/wiki/Model organism) genome.

1. Bioinformatic Harvester (http://en.wikipedia.org/wiki/ Bioinformatic_Harvester)

2. SNPedia (http://en.wikipedia.org/wiki/SNPedia)

3. CAMERA (http://camera.calit2.net/index.php/) Resource for microbial genomics and metagenomics

4. Corn (http://www.maizegdb.org/), the Maize Genetics and Genomics Database

5. EcoCyc (http://ecocyc.org/) a database that describes the genome and the biochemical machinery of the model organism (http://en.wikipedia.org/wiki/ Model organism) *E. coli K-12*

6. Ensembl (http://en.wikipedia.org/wiki/Ensembl) provides automatic annotation databases for human, mouse, other vertebrate (http://en.wikipedia.org/wiki/Vertebrate) and eukaryote (http://en.wikipedia. org/wiki/Eukaryote) genomes.

7. Ensembl Genomes (http://en.wikipedia.org/wiki/ Ensembl_Genomes) provides genome-scale data for bacteria, protists, fungi, plants and invertebrate metazoa, through a unified set of interactive and programmatic interfaces (using the Ensembl software platform).

8. PATRIC (http://patricbrc.vbi.vt.edu/portal/portal/patric/ Home), the PathoSystems Resource Integration Center

9. Flybase (http://en.wikipedia.org/wiki/FlyBase), genome of the model organism (http://en.wikipedia.org/wiki/

Model_organism) Drosophila melanogaster (http://en.wikipedia.org/wiki/Drosophila_melanogaster)

10. MGI Mouse Genome (http://www.informatics.jax.org/) (Jackson Lab. - (http://en. wikipedia.org/wiki/Jackson Laboratory)

11. JGI Genomes (http://genome.jgi.doe.gov/) of the DOE - Joint Genome Institute (http://en.wikipedia.org/wiki/Joint_Genome_Institute) provides databases of many eukaryote (http://en.wikipedia.org/wiki/Eukaryote) and microbial (http://en.wikipedia.org/wiki/Microbial) genomes.

12. National Microbial Pathogen Data Resource (http://www.nmpdr.org/FIG/ wiki/view.cgi). A manually curated database of annotated genome data for the pathogens Campylobacter (http://en.wikipedia.org/wiki/Campylobacter), Chlamydia (http://en.wikipedia.org/wiki/Chlamydia_%28genus%29), Chlamydophila (http://en. wikipedia.org/wiki/Chlamydophila), Haemophilus (http://en.wikipedia.org/wiki/Haemophilus), Listeria (http://en.wikipedia.org/wiki/Listeria), Mycoplasma (http://en.wikipedia.org/wiki/Mycoplasma), Neisseria (http://en.wikipedia.org/wiki/Neisseria), Staphylococcus (http://en.wikipedia.org/wiki/Staphylococcus), Streptococcus (http://en.wikipedia.org/wiki/Streptococcus), Treponema (http://en.wikipedia.org/wiki/Treponema), Ureaplasma (http://en.wikipedia.org/wiki/Mycoplasmataceae#Ureaplasma), and Vibrio (http://en.wikipedia.org/wiki/Vibrio).

13. RegulonDB (http://regulondb.ccg.unam.mx/) RegulonDB is a model of the complex regulation of transcription initiation or regulatory network of the cell E. coli K-12.

14. Saccharomyces Genome Database (http://en.wikipedia.org/wiki/Saccharomyces_Genome_Database), genome of the yeast (http://en.wikipedia.org/wiki/Yeast) model organism.

15. Viral Bioinformatics Resource Center (http://troy.bioc.uvic.ca/) Curated database containing annotated genome data for eleven virus families.

16. The SEED (http://seed-viewer.theseed.org/) platform for microbial genome analysis includes all complete microbial genomes, and most partial genomes. The platform is used to annotate microbial genomes using subsystems.

17. Xenbase (http://en.wikipedia.org/wiki/Xenbase), genome of the model organism (http://en.wikipedia.org/wiki/Model_organism) Xenopus tropicalis (http://en.wikipedia.org/wiki/Western_clawed_frog) and Xenopus laevis (http://en.wikipedia.org/wiki/African_clawed_frog)

18. Wormbase (http://en.wikipedia.org/wiki/WormBase), genome of the model organism Caenorhabditis elegans (http://en.wikipedia.org/wiki/Caenorhabditis_elegans).

19. Zebrafish Information Network (http://en.wikipedia.org/wiki/Zebrafish_Information_Network), genome of this fish (http://en.wikipedia.org/wiki/Fish) model organism.

20. TAIR (http://arabidopsis.org/), The Arabidopsis Information Resource.

21. UCSC Malaria Genome Browser (http://en.wikipedia.org/wiki/UCSC_Malaria_Genome_Browser), genome of malaria causing species (*Plasmodium falciparumata* and others)

22. RGD (http://rgd.mcw.edu/) Rat Genome Database (http://en.wikipedia.org/wiki/Rat_genome_database) : Genomic and phenotype data for Rattus norvegicus
23. [5] INTEGRALL: Database dedicated to integrons (http://en.wikipedia.org/ wiki/Integron), bacterial genetic elements involved in the antibiotic resistance
24. Fourmidable ant genome database (http://www.antgenomes.org/) provides ant genome blast (http://www.antgenomes.org/) search and sequence download (http://www.antgenomes.org/downloads/).
25. VectorBase The NIAID Bioinformatics Resource Center for Invertebrate Vectors of Human Pathogens
26. EzGenome, comprehensive information about manually curated genome projects of prokaryotes (archaea and bacteria) [2]

Protein sequence databases (http://en.wikipedia.org/wiki/Peptide_sequence) [edit] (http://en.wikipedia.org/w/index.php?title=List_of_biological_databases&action=edit&section=4):

UniProt (https://www.vectorbase.org/) Universal Resource [EBI (http://en.wikipedia.org/wiki/European_Bioinformatics_Institute), Swiss Institute of Bioinformatics (http://en.wikipedia.org/wiki/Swiss_Institute_of_Bioinformatics), PIR (http://en.wikipedia.org/wiki/Protein_Information_Resource)]

1. Protein Information Resource (http://en.wikipedia.org/wiki/Protein_Information_ Resource) (Georgetown University (http://en.wikipedia. org/wiki/Georgetown_ University) Medical Center (GUMC))

2. Swiss-Prot (http://en.wikipedia.org/wiki/UniProt#UniProtKB.2FSwiss-Prot) Protein Knowledgebase [Swiss Institute of Bioinformatics (http://en.wikipedia.org/wiki/Swiss_Institute_of_Bioinformatics)]

3. PEDANT (http://pedant.gsf.de/) Protein Extraction, Description and Analysis Tool (Forschungszentrum f. Umwelt & Gesundheit)

4. PROSITE (http://en.wikipedia.org/wiki/PROSITE) Database of Protein Families (http://en.wikipedia.org/wiki/Protein_family) and Domains (http://en.wikipedia.org/wiki/Protein_family)

5. Database of Interacting Proteins (http://en.wikipedia.org/wiki/Database_of_Interacting_Proteins) [Univ. of California (http://en.wikipedia.org/wiki/ University_of_California)]

6. Pfam (http://en.wikipedia.org/wiki/Pfam) Protein families database of alignments and HMMs [Sanger Institute (http://en.wikipedia.org/wiki/Wellcome_Trust_Sanger Institute)]

7. PRINTS (http://en.wikipedia.org/wiki/PRINTS) a compendium of protein fingerprints from [Manchester University (http://en.wikipedia.org/ wiki/PRINTS)]

8. ProDom (http://protein.foulouse.inra.fr/prodom/current/html/home.php) Comprehensive set of Protein Domain Families [INRA (http://en. wikipedia.org/wiki/Institut_national_de_la_recherche_agronomique) / CNRS (http://en.wikipedia.org/wiki/Centre_national_de_la_recherche_scientifique)]

9. SignalP 3.0 (http://www.cbs.dtu.dk/services/SignalP/) Server for signal peptide (http://en.wikipedia.org/wiki/Signal_

peptide) prediction (including cleavage site prediction), based on artificial neural networks (http://en.wikipedia.org/wiki/Artificial_neural_network) and HMMs

10. SUPERFAMILY (http://en.wikipedia.org/wiki/SUPERFAMILY) Library of HMMs representing super families and database of (super family and family) annotations for all completely sequenced organisms

11. Annotation Clearing House (http://clearinghouse.nmpdr.org/aclh.cgi) a project from the National Microbial Pathogen Data Resource (http://en.wikipedia.org/wiki/National_Microbial_Pathogen_Data_Resource)

12. InterPro (http://en.wikipedia.org/wiki/InterPro) Classifies proteins into families and predicts the presence of domains and sites.

Proteomics databases (http://en.wikipedia.org/wiki/Proteomics) [edit] (http://en.wikipedia.org/w/index.php?title=List_of_biological_databases&action=edit&section=5)

1. Proteomics Identifications Database (PRIDE) (http://www.ebi.ac.uk/pride/archive/) A public repository for proteomics data, containing protein and peptide identifications and their associated supporting evidence as well as details of post-translational modifications. [European Bioinformatics Institute (http://en.wikipedia.org/wiki/European_Bioinformatics_Institute)]

2. MitoMiner (http://mitominer.mrc-mbu.cam.ac.uk/release-3.1/begin.do) - A mitochondrial proteomics database integrating large-scale experimental datasets from mass spectrometry and GFP studies for 12 species. [MRC

Mitochondrial Biology Unit (http://en.wikipedia.org/wiki/ MRC_Mitochondrial_Biology_Unit)]

3. GelMap (https://gelmap.de/) - A public database of proteins identified on 2D gels [University of Hanover (http://en.wikipedia.org/wiki/University_of_Hanover) Proteomics Department]

Protein structure databases (http://en.wikipedia.org/wiki/ Protein_structure) [edit] (http://en.wikipedia.org/ w/index.php?title= List_of_biological_databases&action=edit&section=6)

Protein Data Bank (http://en.wikipedia.org/wiki/Protein_ Data_Bank) comprising:

1. Protein Data Bank in Europe (PDBe) (http://www.ebi.ac.uk/pdbe/)
2. Protein Data bank in Japan (PDBj) (http://www.pdbj.org/)
3. Research Collaboratory for Structural Bioinformatics (RCSB) (http://www.rcsb.org/pdb/home/home.do)

Secondary databases comprising:

1. SCOP (http://scop.mrc-lmb.cam.ac.uk/scop/) Structural Classification of Proteins (http://en.wikipedia.org/wiki/Structural_Classification_of_Pr oteins_ database)
2. CATH (http://www.cathdb.info/) Protein Structure Classification
3. PDBsum (http://www.ebi.ac.uk/pdbsum/)

For more protein structure databases, see also Protein structure database (http://en.wikipedia.org/wiki/Protein_structure_database)

Protein model databases (http://en.wikipedia.org/wiki/Protein_structure_prediction) [edit] (http://en.wikipedia.org/w/index.php?title=List_of_biological_databases&action=edit&section=7)

1. Swiss-model[6] (http://en.wikipedia.org/wiki/Swiss-model) Server and Repository for Protein Structure Models

2. ModBase[7] (http://en.wikipedia.org/wiki/ModBase) Database of Comparative Protein Structure Models [Sali (http://en.wikipedia.org/wiki/Andrej_%C5%A0ali) Lab, UCSF (http://en.wikipedia.org/wiki/University_of_California,_San_Francisco)]

3. Protein Model Portal[8] (http://en.wikipedia.org/w/index.php?title=Protein_Model_Portal&action=edit&redlink=1) (PMP) Meta database that combines several databases of protein structure models (Biozentrum, Basel, Switzerland)

RNA databases (http://en.wikipedia.org/wiki/RNA) [edit] (http://en.wikipedia.org/w/index.php?title=List_of_biological_databases&action=edit&section=8)

1. Rfam [9] (http://en.wikipedia.org/wiki/Rfam), a database of RNA families

2. miRBase [10] (http://en.wikipedia.org/wiki/MiRBase), the microRNA (http://en.wikipedia.org/wiki/MicroRNA) database

3. snoRNAdb (http://lowelab.ucsc.edu/snoRNAdb/), a database of snoRNAs (http://en.wikipedia.org/wiki/Small_nucleolar_RNA)

4. lncRNAdb (http://www.lncrnadb.org/), a database of lncRNAs

5. MONOCLdb (http://www.monocldb.org/) The MOuse NOnCode Lung database: Annotations and expression profiles of mouse long non-coding RNAs (lncRNAs) involved in Influenza and SARS-CoV infections.

6. piRNAbank (http://pirnabank.ibab.ac.in/) a database of piRNAs (http://pirnabank.ibab.ac.in/)

7. GtRNAdb (http://gtrnadb.ucsc.edu/), a database of genomic tRNAs (http://en.wikipedia.org/wiki/Transfer_RNA)

8. SILVA (http://www.arb-silva.de/), a database of ribosomal RNAs (http://en.wikipedia.org/wiki/Ribosomal_RNA)

9. RDP (http://rdp.cme.msu.edu/), the Ribosomal Database Project

10. tmRDB (http://www.ag.auburn.edu/mirror/tmRDB/), a database of tmRNAs (http://en.wikipedia.org/wiki/Transfer-messenger_RNA)

11. SRPDB (http://rth.dk/resources/rnp/SRPDB/), a database of signal recognition particle RNAs (http://en.wikipedia.org/wiki/Signal_recognition_particle_RNA)

12. yeast snoRNA database (http://people.biochem.umass.edu/fournierlab/ snornadb/main.php)

13. Sno/scaRNAbase (http://bioinfo.fudan.edu.cn/snoRNAbase.nsf) a database of snoRNA and scaRNAs

14. snoRNA-LBME-db (https://www-snorna.biotoul.fr//), a snoRNA database

Carbohydrate structure databases (http://en.wikipedia.org/wiki/Carbohydrate) [edit] (http://en.wikipedia.org/w/index.php?title=List_of_biological_databases&action=edit&section=9)

1. EuroCarbDB[11] (http://en.wikipedia.org/wiki/Eurocarbdb), A repository for both carbohydrate sequences/structures and experimental data.

Protein-protein and other molecular interactions (http://en.wikipedia.org/wiki/Protein%E2%80%93protein_interaction) [edit] (http://en.wikipedia.org/w/index.php?title=List_of_biological_databases&action=edit&section=10)

1. BIND Biomolecular Interaction Network Database (http://bond.unleashedinformatics.com/Action?)
2. BioGRID [12] (http://en.wikipedia.org/wiki/BioGRID) A General Repository for Interaction Datasets [Samuel Lunenfeld Research Institute (http://en.wikipedia.org/wiki/Lunenfeld-Tanenbaum_Research_Institute)]
3. CCSB Interactome (http://interactome.dfci.harvard.edu/)
4. DIP Database of Interacting Proteins (http://interactome.dfci.harvard.edu/)
5. IntAct molecular interaction database (http://ebi.ac.uk/intact/): a central, standards-compliant repository of molecular interactions, including protein–protein, protein–small molecule and protein–nucleic acid interactions.
6. NetPro (http://www.molecularconnections.com/home/en/home/resources/case-studies/alzheimer-disease-netpro/)

7. STRING: STRING is a database of known and predicted protein-protein interactions (http://string.embl.de/) [EMBL (http://en.wikipedia.org/wiki/ European_Molecular_Biology_ Laboratory)]

8. The Cell Collective (http://thecellcollective.org/cc.web/spring/user-login;jsessionid=A3957B0DB77EFE99C126 C4C0F161C95D? execution=e1s1)

9. MINT: Molecular INTeraction database (http://mint.bio.uniroma2.it/)

10. iRefIndex (http://irefindex.org/wiki/index.php?title= iRefIndex): provides an index of protein interactions available in a number of primary interaction databases including BIND, BioGRID, CORUM, DIP, HPRD, InnateDB, IntAct, MatrixDB, MINT, MPact, MPIDB, MPPI and OPHID.

11. RNA-binding protein database (http://en.wikipedia.org/wiki/ RNA-binding_ protein_database)

Signal transduction pathway databases (http://en.wikipedia.org/wiki/Signal_transduction) [edit] (http://en.wikipedia.org/w/index.php?title=List_of_biological_ databases&action=edit&section=11)

1. Cancer Cell Map (http://www.pathwaycommons.org/about/)

2. Netpath (http://en.wikipedia.org/wiki/Netpath) - A curated resource of signal transduction pathways in humans

3. NCI-Nature Pathway Interaction Database (http://en. wikipedia.org/wiki/NCI-Nature_Pathway_Interaction_ Database)

4. Reactome (http://en.wikipedia.org/wiki/Reactome) - Navigable map of human biological pathways, ranging from metabolic processes to hormonal signaling.

5. SignaLink Database (http://signalink.org/)

6. WikiPathways (http://en.wikipedia.org/wiki/WikiPathways)

7. The Cell Collective (http://thecellcollective.org/cc.web/spring/user-login;jsessionid=0C10589AADAC2CDD6319521DC7395FA4?execution=e1s1)

Metabolic pathway and Protein Function databases (http://en.wikipedia.org/wiki/Metabolic_pathway) [edit] (http://en.wikipedia.org/w/index.php?title=List_of_biological_databases&action=edit&section=12)

1. BioCyc Database Collection (http://en.wikipedia.org/wiki/BioCyc_database_collection) including EcoCyc (http://en.wikipedia.org/wiki/EcoCyc) and MetaCyc (http://en.wikipedia.org/wiki/MetaCyc)

2. BRENDA (http://en.wikipedia.org/wiki/BRENDA) The Comprehensive Enzyme Information System, including FRENDA, AMENDA, DRENDA, and KENDA, [13]

3. KEGG PATHWAY Database[14] (http://en.wikipedia.org/wiki/KEGG) [Univ. of Kyoto (http://en.wikipedia.org/wiki/Kyoto_University)]

4. MANET database [15] (http://en.wikipedia.org/wiki/MANET_database) [University of Illinois (http://en.wikipedia.org/wiki/University_of_Illinois_at_Urbana%E2%80%93Champaign)]

5. Metabolights (http://www.ebi.ac.uk/metabolights/): Metabolomics experiments and derived information: metabolite structures, reference spectra, biological roles, locations and concentrations. [European Bioinformatics Institute (http://en.wikipedia.org/wiki/European_Bioinformatics_Institute)]

6. MetaNetX (http://metanetx.org/) : Automated Model Construction and Genome Annotation for Large-Scale Metabolic Networks

7. Reactome[16] (http://en.wikipedia.org/wiki/Reactome) Navigable map of human biological pathways, ranging from metabolic processes to hormonal signaling. [Cold Spring Harbor Laboratory (http://en.wikipedia.org/wiki/Cold_Spring_Harbor_Laboratory), European Bioinformatics Institute (http://en.wikipedia.org/wiki/European_Bioinformatics_Institute), Gene Ontology Consortium]

8. Small Molecule Pathway Database (SMPDB) (http://smpdb.ca/)

Microarray databases [edit] (http://en.wikipedia.org/w/index.php?title=List_of_biological_databases&action=edit&section=13)

Main article: *Microarray databases* (http://en.wikipedia.org/wiki/Microarray_databases)

1. ArrayExpress (http://www.ebi.ac.uk/arrayexpress/) [European Bioinformatics Institute (http://en.wikipedia.org/wiki/European_Bioinformatics_Institute)]

2. Gene Expression Omnibus (http://www.ncbi.nlm.nih.gov/geo/) [National Center for Biotechnology Information

(http://en.wikipedia.org/wiki/National_Center_for_Biotechnology_Information)

3. GPX (http://www.gti.ed.ac.uk/GPX) (Scottish Centre for Genomic Technology and Informatics)
4. maxd (http://www.bioinf.man.ac.uk/microarray/maxd/index.html) [Univ. of Manchester (http://en.wikipedia.org/wiki/University_of_Manchester)]
5. Stanford Microarray Database (SMD) (http://smd.princeton.edu/) [Stanford University (http://en.wikipedia.org/wiki/Stanford_University)]
6. Genevestigator - Expression Search Engine (https://genevestigator.com/gv/) (Nebion AG)
7. Bgee (http://bgee.unil.ch/): Bgee is a database to retrieve and compare gene expression patterns between species. It contains wild-type and manually curated microarray experiments only.

Exosomal databases [edit] (http://en.wikipedia.org/w/index.php?title=List_of_biological_databases&action=edit&section=14)

1. ExoCarta (http://en.wikipedia.org/wiki/ExoCarta)

Mathematical model databases [edit] (http://en.wikipedia.org/w/index.php?title=List_of_biological_databases&action=edit&section=15)

1. Biomodels Database (http://en.wikipedia.org/wiki/BioModels_Database): published mathematical models describing biological processes.
2. CellML (http://models.cellml.org/cellml)

3. The Cell Collective (http://thecellcollective.org/cc.web/spring/user-login;jsessionid=C649F56AFEC41FB0FE220BC56A04EBBD?execution=e1s1): build and simulate large-scale models in real-time and in a highly collaborative fashion

PCR, Quantitative PCR and Primer databases

PCR - (http://en.wikipedia.org/wiki/Polymerase_chain_reaction) **Quantitave PCR** - (http://en.wikipedia.org/wiki/Real-time_polymerase_chain_reaction) **Primer databases** - (http://en.wikipedia.org/wiki/Primer_%28molecular_biology%29) [edit] (http://en.wikipedia.org/w/index.php?title=List_of_biological_databases&action=edit&section=16)

1. PathoOligoDB : A free QPCR oligo database for pathogens (http://www.pathooligodb.com/)
2. RTPrimerDB - a public primers and probes database for real-time PCR reactions (http://medgen.ugent.be/rtprimerdb/index.php/)

Specialized databases [edit] (http://en.wikipedia.org/w/index.php?title=List_of_biological_databases&action=edit&section=17)

1. Antibody Central (http://antibody-central.com/) Antibody information database and search resource.
2. AntibodyRegistry.org (http://antibodyregistry.org/) assigns unique identifiers used to track antibody reagents in published literature.
3. Bgee (http://bgee.unil.ch/) Bgee is a database to retrieve and compare gene expression patterns between species.

4. BIOMOVIE (http://biomovie.ethz.ch/) (ETH Zurich) (http://en.wikipedia.org/wiki/ETH_Zurich) movies related to biology and biotechnology

5. BioNumbers (http://bionumbers.hms.harvard.edu/) a database of useful biological numbers

6. Barcode of Life Data Systems (http://en.wikipedia.org/wiki/Barcode_of_Life_Data_Systems), a database of DNA barcodes (http://en.wikipedia.org/wiki/DNA_barcoding)

7. CGAP Cancer Genes (http://cgap.nci.nih.gov/Genes/GeneFinder) [National Cancer Institute (http://en.wikipedia.org/wiki/National_Cancer_Institute)]

8. Clone Registry Clone Collections (http://www.ncbi.nlm.nih.gov/clone) [National Center for Biotechnology Information (http://en.wikipedia.org/wiki/National_Center_for_Biotechnology_Information)

9. Connectivity map (http://www.broadinstitute.org/cmap/) Transcriptional expression data and correlation tools for drugs

10. CTD (http://ctdbase.org/) The Comparative Toxicogenomics Database (http://en.wikipedia.org/wiki/Comparative_Toxicogenomics_Database) describes chemical-gene-disease interactions

11. DBGET H.sapiens (http://www.genome.jp/dbget-bin/www_bfind?h.sapiens) [Univ. of Kyoto (http://en.wikipedia.org/wiki/Kyoto_University)]

12. DiProDB (http://en.wikipedia.org/wiki/DiProDB): A database to collect and analyze thermodynamic, structural and other dinucleotide properties.

13. Drug2Gene (http://www.drug2gene.com/) : Provides integrated information for identified and reported relations between genes/proteins and drugs / compounds

14. Dryad (http://en.wikipedia.org/wiki/Dryad_%28repository%29): A repository of data underlying scientific publications in the basic and applied biosciences.

15. Edinburgh Mouse Atlas (http://en.wikipedia.org/wiki/EMAGE)

16. FunSecKB (http://proteomics.ysu.edu/secretomes/fungi.php): The fungal secretome knowledgebase.

17. FunSecKB2 (http://proteomics.ysu.edu/secretomes/fungi2/index.php) The fungal secretome and subcellular proteome knowledgebase (version 2)

18. GreenPhylDB (http://www.greenphyl.org/v2/cgi-bin/index.cgi) (A phylogenomic database for plant comparative genomics)

19. GDB Hum. Genome Db (http://www.gdb.org/gdb) [Human Genome Organisation (http://en.wikipedia.org/wiki/Human_Genome_Organisation)]

20. HGMD disease-causing mutations (http://www.hgmd.cf.ac.uk/ac/index.php) (HGMD Human Gene Mutation Database)

21. HUGO (http://www.gene.ucl.ac.uk/nomenclature) (Official Human Genome Database : HUGO Gene Nomenclature Committee)

22. HvrBase++ (http://www.hvrbase.org/) Human and primate mitochondrial DNA

23. INTERFEROME (http://interferome.its.monash.edu.au/interferome/home.jspx) The Database of Interferon Regulated Genes

24. List with SNP-Databases (http://hgvbase.cgb.ki.se/databases.htm)

25. MetazSecKB (http://proteomics.ysu.edu/secretomes/animal/index.php) The metazoa [human/animal] secretome and subcellular proteome knowledgebase

26. Minimotif Miner (http://en.wikipedia.org/wiki/Minimotif_Miner) - Database of short contiguous functional peptide motifs

27. NCBI-UniGene (http://www.ncbi.nlm.nih.gov/unigene) (National Center for Biotechnology Information)

28. Oncogenomic databases (http://en.wikipedia.org/wiki/List_of_databases_for_oncogenomic_research). A compilation of databases that serve for cancer research.

29. OMIM Inherited Diseases (http://www.ncbi.nlm.nih.gov/omim) (Online Mendelian Inheritance in Man)

30. OrthoMaM (http://www.orthomam.univ-montp2.fr/orthomam/html/) (A database of Orthologous Mammalian Markers)

31. OrthoMCL (http://orthomcl.org/orthomcl/) Ortholog Groups of Protein Sequences from Multiple Genomes including Archaea, Bacteria and Eukaryotes.

32. p53 (http://p53.bii.a-star.edu.sg/) The p53 Knowledgebase

33. PASD (http://proteomics.ysu.edu/altsplice/) The plant alternative splicing database

34. PhenCode (http://globin.bx.psu.edu/phencode/) linking human mutations with phenotype

35. PhenomicDB (http://www.phenomicdb.de/) multi-organism database linking genotype to phenotype

36. PHI-base (http://en.wikipedia.org/wiki/PHI-base) Pathogen-host interaction database. It links gene information to phenotypic information from microbial pathogens on their hosts. Information is manually curated from peer reviewed literature.

37. PlantSecKB (http://proteomics.ysu.edu/secretomes/plant/index.php) The plant secretome and subcullular proteome knowledgebase

38. Plasma Proteome Database (http://www.plasmaproteomedatabase.org/) Human plasma proteins along with their isoforms

39. SABIO-RK (http://sabiork.h-its.org/): SABIO-RK is a curated database that contains information about biochemical reactions, their kinetic rate equations with parameters and experimental conditions.

40. SciClyc (http://www.sciclyc.com/): An Open-access database to shared antibodies, cell cultures, and documents for biomedical research.

41. Selectome (http://selectome.unil.ch/): Selectome is a database of positive selection based on a rigorous branch-site specific likelihood test. Positive selection is detected using CODEML on all branches of animal gene trees.

42. SHMPD (http://shmpd.bii.a-star.edu.sg/) : The Singapore Human Mutation and Polymorphism Database

43. SNPSTR database (http://www.sbg.bio.ic.ac.uk/~ino/cgi-bin/SNPSTRdatabase.html): A database of SNPSTRs - compound genetic markers consisting of a microsatellite (STR) and one tightly linked SNP - in human, mouse, rat, dog and chicken.

44. TDR Targets (http://en.wikipedia.org/wiki/TDR_Targets): A chemogenomics database focused on drug discovery in tropical diseases.

45. TRANSFAC (http://en.wikipedia.org/wiki/TRANSFAC): A database about eukaryotic transcription factors, their genomic binding sites and DNA-binding profiles.

46. TreeBASE (http://treebase.org/) : An open-access database of phylogenetic trees and the data behind them

47. Treefam (http://www.treefam.org/) : TreeFam (Tree families database) is a database of phylogenetic trees of animal genes

48. XTractor (http://www.beby.in/) Discovering Newer Scientific Relations Across PubMed Abstracts. A tool to obtain manually annotated relationships for Proteins, Diseases, Drugs and Biological Processes as they get published in PubMed.

Taxonomic databases [edit] (http://en.wikipedia.org/w/index.php?title=List_of_biological_databases&action=edit&section=18)

1. Catalogue of Life source databases (http://www.catalogueoflife.org/info/databases)
2. Encyclopedia of Life (http://eol.org/)

3. Integrated Taxonomic Information System (http://www.itis.gov/)
4. EzTaxon-e (http://en.wikipedia.org/wiki/EzTaxon_Database), database for the identification of prokaryotes based on 16S ribosomal RNA gene sequences

Wiki-style databases [edit] (http://en.wikipedia.org/w/index.php?title=List_of_biological_databases&action=edit&section=19)

1. CHDwiki (http://homes.esat.kuleuven.be/~bioiuser/chdwiki/index.php/Main_Page)
2. EcoliWiki (http://ecoliwiki.net/colipedia/index.php/Welcome_to_EcoliWiki)
3. Gene Wiki (http://en.wikipedia.org/wiki/Gene_Wiki)
4. GyDB (http://gydb.uv.es/index.php/Main_Page)
5. NeuroLex (http://neurolex.org/)
6. OpenWetWare (http://openwetware.org/wiki/Main_Page)
7. PDBWiki (http://pdbwiki.org/)
8. Proteopedia (http://www.proteopedia.org/wiki/index.php/Main_Page)
9. RiceWiki (http://ricewiki.big.ac.cn/index.php/Main_Page)
10. Topsan (http://www.topsan.org/)
11. WikiGenes (http://www.wikigenes.org/)
12. WikiPathways (http://www.wikipathways.org/index.php/WikiPathways)
13. WikiProfessional (http://en.wikipedia.org/wiki/WikiProfessional)

14. YTPdb (http://ytpdb.biopark-it.be/ytpdb/index.php/Main_Page)

Metabolomic Databases [edit] (http://en.wikipedia.org/w/index.php?title=List_of_biological_databases&action=edit&section=20)

1. MetaboLights (http://www.ebi.ac.uk/metabolights/)
2. Human Metabolome Database (HMDB) (http://www.hmdb.ca/)
3. Yeast Metabolome Database (YMDB) (http://www.ymdb.ca/)
4. E. coli Metabolome Database (ECMDB) (http://www.ecmdb.ca/)
5. DrugBank (http://www.drugbank.ca/)
6. ChEBI (https://www.ebi.ac.uk/chebi/)
7. BioMagResBank (http://www.bmrb.wisc.edu/)
8. Golm Metabolome Database (http://gmd.mpimp-golm.mpg.de/)
9. MassBank (http://massbank.ufz.de/MassBank/)

List of biological databases

1. Sequencing (http://en.wikipedia.org/wiki/Sequencing)
2. Sequence database (http://en.wikipedia.org/wiki/Sequence_database)
3. Sequence alignment (http://en.wikipedia.org/wiki/Sequence_alignment)
4. Molecular phylogenetics (http://en.wikipedia.org/wiki/Molecular_phylogenetics)

Metabolomic Databases (http://en.wikipedia.org/w/index.php?title=List_of_biological_databases&action=edit&section=20)

1. MetaboLights (http://www.ebi.ac.uk/metabolights/)
2. Human Metabolome Database (HMDB) (http://www.hmdb.ca/)
3. Yeast Metabolome Database (YMDB) (http://www.ymdb.ca/)
4. E. coli Metabolome Database (ECMDB) (http://www.ecmdb.ca/)
5. DrugBank (http://www.drugbank.ca/)
6. ChEBI (https://www.ebi.ac.uk/chebi/)
7. BioMagResBank (http://www.bmrb.wisc.edu/)
8. Golm Metabolome Database (http://gmd.mpimp-golm.mpg.de/)
9. MassBank (http://massbank.ufz.de/MassBank/)

Chapter 10: APPLICATION OF BIOINFORMATICS TOOLS AND SOFTWARE

Phenotyper (http://trost.mpimp-golm.mpg.de/en/supple.html) - Data management pipeline for plant phenotyping in a multisite project. The website provides standardized data storage for meaningful data evaluation and statistical analysis.

GMD (http://gmd.mpimp-golm.mpg.de/) - The Golm Metabolome Database (GMD) provides access to GC/MS mass spectral libraries, metabolite compound information, and annotation tools and services.

Phos3D (http://phos3d.mpimp-golm.mpg.de/) - Phos3D is a web server for the prediction of phosphorylation sites (P-sites) in proteins. The approach is based on Support Vector Machines trained on sequence profiles enhanced by information from the spatial context of experimentally identified P-sites.

ChlamyCyc (http://chlamycyc.mpimp-golm.mpg.de/) - ChlamyCyc is an integrative systems biology database and web-portal for Chlamydomonas reinhardtii. It provides extensive metabolic pathway information including comparative analysis, a genome browser, gene and protein-related sequence data, a Blast server for sequence search and alignments against various databases, annotation of proteins to MapMan BINs, domain information, peptide covering, ESTs, RNAs and their mapping onto genomic sequence, orthology relationships, and links to external Chlamydomonas-related resources.

GraPPLE (http://grapple.mpimp-golm.mpg.de/) - GraPPLE is a computational method for predicting functional non-coding RNA and classifying them to RNA families. The method relies on describing RNA structures as graphs, and introduces the use of associated graph properties as features in Support Vector Machines for prediction purposes.

GabiPD (http://www.gabipd.org/) - GabiPD (The GABI Primary Database) is a web-accessible database established in the frame of the German initiative GABI (Genome Analysis of the Plant Biological System) to integrate, analyze and visualize primary data generated in GABI projects. Plant data from different 'omics' fronts representing more than 10 different model or crop species are integrated in GabiPD.

Satlotyper (http://www.gabipd.org/projects/satlotyper/) - SATlotyper is a software tool designed for inferring haplotypes from polyploid and polyallelic unphased SNP data.

BioNet Reasoning (http://bioinformatics.mpimp-golm.mpg.de/research-projects-publications/tools-services/bionet-reasoning) - Command line application for modeling biological systems. It allows reasoning, i.e. predicting, explaining, and planning, about biological systems that are described in the action language C_TAID.

Capiu (http://bioinformatics.mpimp-golm.mpg.de/projects/own/capiu/) - Clustering using a priori information via unsupervised decision trees is a method for extracting groups of samples in a microarray experiment. The result is directly interpretable as the method uses pre-defined classes of genes (such as those from Gene ontology or MapMan) to build a clustering tree with informative gene classes as its nodes and groups of samples as its leaves.

MapCave (http://mapman.gabipd.org/web/guest/mapcave) - Unified classification structure for genes from different organisms for use in the MapMan tool.

MetaGeneAlyse (http://metagenealyse.mpimp-golm.mpg.de/) - Web-based tool for the visualization and analysis of large-scale transcript and metabolite profile datasets. Standard methods (PCA, clustering) are provided as well as state-of-the-art methods such as independent component analysis (ICA).

PaVESy (http://gmd.mpimp-golm.mpg.de/projects/own/pavesy/) - Pathway Visualization and Editing System. Allows user-driven, interactive creation and visualization of pathway maps.

Robin (http://mapman.gabipd.org/web/guest/robin) - Robin (the helper of MapMan) is a user friendly graphical interface for powerful microarray data processing.

D2CMA ((http://gmd.mpimp-golm.mpg.de/projects/own/d2cma/) - Design 2 Color MicroArrays contains a few R-scripts, mainly the function optimize.MA.design which builds upon the daMA package.

PROMI (http://promi.mpimp-golm.mpg.de/home.shtml) - The tool PROfile analysis based on Mutual Information (PROMI) enables comparative protein sequence analysis in terms of group-specific conservation. Positions in user-defined protein sequence motifs are identified that exhibit group-specific (e.g. species-specific) conservation and, thus, allows the elucidation of evolutionary characteristics.

CERMT - CERMT (**C**ovariance-based **E**xtraction of **R**egulatory targets using **M**ultiple **T**ime series) is a method for predicting transcription factor targets given a particular transcription factor of interest. Targets are defined as the genes that respond similarly, but possibly time shifted, to the transcription factor under two or more treatments.

OGDraw (http://ogdraw.mpimp-golm.mpg.de/) - OGDraw (**OrganelleGenomeDraw**) is a tool that enables the user to quickly generate high-quality graphical maps of circular DNA sequences. Though especially designed and optimized for the display of small organelle genomes like the chloroplast or mitochondrial genome, it is applicable to all circular DNA sequences. The input data can be provided as GenBank files or GenBank accession numbers.

List of Bioinformatics Tools at International Bioinformatics Centers

There are many bioinformatics tools over the Internet. Thanks to the contributions of the scientific community of bioinformatics research and development. They make the bioinformatics programs and packages freely available to the end user biologists. We use both web-based plantforms such as WebLab (http://weblab.cbi.pku.edu.cn/) and desktop packages such as Jemboss (http://emboss.sourceforge.net/Jemboss/). Please see the following list for the tools we may use for self learning.

i. ExPASy tools (http://www.expasy.org/) - A comprehensive list of online web-based bioinformatics tools provided by ExPASy and worldwide.

ii. EBI tools (http://www.ebi.ac.uk/services) - The entry page for the EBI bioinformatics tools.

iii. NCBI tools (http://www.ncbi.nlm.nih.gov/guide/all/#tools_) - The entry page for the NCBI bioinformatics tools.

iv. CBS tools (http://www.cbs.dtu.dk/services/) - The entry page for the bioinformatics tools at the Center for Biological Sequence Analysis, Technical University of Denmark.

v. EMBL tools (http://www.embl.de/services/bioinformatics/) - The entry page for the EMBL bioinformatics tools and databases.

Free Online Bioinformatics Tools

(http://www.progenitorcells.org/content/bioinformatics-and-genomics-tools)

Software & Online Tools

(http://bitesizebio.com/category/soft-skills-tools/software-online-tools/): A handful of websites that will help you locate established as well as fresh new and (mostly) free online molecular biology and bioinformatics databases and tools.

There are already thousands of online bioinformatics resources available, with undoubtedly many more to come. One of the limiting factors of the field is the difficulty in navigating the vast array of resources to identify the most appropriate tool(s) for what you need to do, whether that's finding information on SNPs, locating pathway analysis software, or designing PCR primers. Here are four websites that will help you with your search.

BioMed Central Databases

(http://databases.biomedcentral.com/) - The BioMed Central Databases maintains a catalog of Web-based databases as well as a **Biology Image Library** (http://images.biologyimagelibrary.com/). The collection can be browsed by subject area or searched by name, description, contents, and/or subject area. The scientific community is welcome to create a database or simply house it on the BioMed Central Databases site.

The "G6G Directory of Omics and Intelligent Software" (www.g6g-softwaredirectory.com) published by G6G Consulting Group. This directory lists data mining and additional software that is from two exciting and increasingly integrated technology fields, those of biotechnology and artificial intelligence. Currently contains over 280 different advanced Software product abstracts (Not just links)… and it is searchable via Google…

In the Software Products by Application, products are listed in two sections.

(1) Omics and Intelligent Software for Biological Scientists, Biostatisticians, Bio-IT students & Professionals, Life Science Researchers, Students and Mathematical Biologists.

Each product is categorized by a major biotechnology group followed by subgroups:

Genomics

a) Gene Expression Analysis / Profiling / Tools

b) Gene Expression Database / Tools

c) Genetic Data Analysis / Tools Research Project Design / Tools

Cross-omics

a) Biomarker Discovery / Analysis / Tools

b) Data/Text Mining Systems / Tools

c) Knowledge Bases/Databases / Tools

d) Next Generation Sequence Analysis / Tools

e) Pathway Analysis / Tools

f) Pathway Knowledge Bases/Databases / Tools

g) Sequence Analysis / Tools

Proteomics

a) Mass Spectrometry Analysis / Tools

(2) Intelligent Software for Software Developers, Bio-IT Students & Professionals, and IT Students & Professionals

Each product is categorized by a major "Intelligent" technology group:

Intelligent Software

a) Bayesian Network Systems / Tools

b) Data Mining Systems / Tools

c) Expert (Knowledge Based) Systems / Tools

d) Fuzzy Logic Systems / Tools

e) Gene Expression Programming Systems / Tools

f) Genetic Algorithm Systems / Tools

g) Genetic Programming Systems / Tools

h) Neural Network Systems / Tools

A nice collection of basic tools that I have often used and recommended to for students can be found at (http://www.bioinformatics.org). This group is based out of the University of Massachusetts at Lowell.

(http://www.bioinfoman.com) requires registration, but is free for individual users.

They have multiple programs that I find useful for my lab– BxItems is the best–I don't think we'll ever lose a sample or reagent again! We also use BxSeqTools for all of our sequencing work. The system is fully integrated with BLAST and works great for creating foolproof constructs.

When you need simple basic tools for DNA manipulation, or to create random DNA and proteins, use the online bioinformatics tools at (http://www.bioinfx.co.cc) ; Tool Insurance (http://www.toolinsurance.net)

If anyone is interested on biomedical text mining and extracting normalized concepts from text give BioLabeler a try: http://www.biolabeler.com

Source: (http://bitesizebio.com/1046/free-online-bioinformatics-tools/)

List of software developed by BGI

SOAPdenovo – SOAPdenovo, a short read de novo assembly tool, is a package for assembling short oligonucleotide into contigs and scaffolds. SOAP family software can be found here (http://soap.genomics.org.cn/).

RePS (repeat-masked Phrap with scaffolding) – RePS is a WGS sequence assembler. It identifies repeated kmer sequences and deletes WGS sequence prior to assembly. The established software Phrap is used to compute meaningful error probabilities for each base. Clone-end-pairing information is used to construct scaffolds that order and orient the contigs. The updated version of RePS incorporates some of the ideas introduced by Phusion on clustering.

Exon_Capture_Pipeline – Whole-genome exon trapping analysis software.

Maq (Mapping and Assembly with Quality) – Maq builds assemblies by mapping short reads to reference sequences. Maq was previously known as mapass2.

ReAS – Software to recover ancestral sequences for transposable elements using unassembled reads from whole genome shotgun sequencing.

SOAPaligner/soap2 – SOAPaligner/soap2 is a program for faster and more efficient alignment for short oligonucleotide onto reference sequences. SOAPaligner/soap2 is compatible with numerous applications, including single-read or pair-end resequencing.

SOAPsnp – SOAPsnp is an accurate consensus sequence builder based on Soap1 and SOAPaligner/soap2's alignment output. It calculates a quality score for each consensus base, which can be used for any latter process to call SNPs.

SOAPindel - SOAPindel is developed to find the insertion and deletion especially for re-sequence technology.

SOAPsv – SOAPsv is a program for detecting the structural variation.

SOAP3/GPU – SOAP3 is GPU-based software for aligning short reads with a reference sequence. It can find all alignments with k mismatches, where k is chosen from 0 to 3. When compared with its previous version SOAP2, SOAP3 can be up to tens of times faster.

MIEREAP – This is used to identify both known and novel microRNAs from small RNA libraries that were deeply sequenced using Illumina-Solexa/454/Solid technology.

FGF - (Fishing Gene Family) (http://fgf.genomics.org.cn/) – This finds gene families, plots phylogenetic trees, and provides evolutionary information to gene duplication.

SVBP – This provides reliability tests and results visualization for sequence assembly.

WEGO - (Web Gene Ontology Annotation Plot, (http://wego.genomics.org.cn/cgi-bin/wego/index.pl) – Web Gene Ontology Annotation Plot is a useful tool for plotting GO annotation results especially for comparative genomics.

HIBAIS – Ancestor deduction software based on HapMap.

SOLEXA-MRNATAG_PIPELINE – Digital gene expression software based on Illumina-Solexa sequencing data

CAT (Cross-species Alignment Tool) – Allows mRNA sequence and mammalian genome alignment across species

KaKs_Calculator - This calculates nonsynonymous (Ka) and synonymous (Ks) substitution rates. More information is available here (http://evolution.genomics.org.cn/ software.htm).

(Source: http://bgiamericas.com/data-analysis/bioinformatics-software/)

Links of University of Michigan Medical School

Department of Computational Medicine and Bioinformatics - University of Michigan Medical School (http://www.ccmb.med.umich.edu/)

Bioinformatics Core (http://www.ccmb.med.umich.edu/bioinf-core)

- About Us (http://www.ccmb.med.umich.edu/bioinf-core/about)
- Services/Cost (http://www.ccmb.med.umich.edu/bioinf-core/services)
- Current Projects (http://www.ccmb.med.umich.edu/bioinf-core/projects)
- People (http://www.ccmb.med.umich.edu/biocore/people)
- Bioinformatics Tools (http://www.ccmb.med.umich.edu/bioinf-core/tools)

LGTC - Next-generation Sequencing Analysis

(http://www.lgtc.nl/services/next_generation_sequencing/ngs_bioinformatics.php)

The group primarily works on analysis of next-generation sequencing (NGS) data, as well as providing advice to NGS users. This includes knowledge of how to handle different platforms and applications, as well as keeping up to date with current NGS analysis tools. We also develop our own in-house analysis pipelines and tools. An additional project of this group includes support of CORE_TF (http://grenada.lumc.nl/HumaneGenetica/CORE_TF/), a web site for identification of conserved and over-represented transcription factor binding sites in ChIP and expression data.

1) Michiel van Galen : data analysis support and tool developer (mailto:M.van_Galen@lumc.nl)

2) Jaap van der Heijden : genome variation data analysis and tool developer (mailto:j.w.f.van_der_heijden@lumc.nl)

3) Yuching Lai : genome variation data analysis and tool developer (mailto:y.lai@lumc.nl)

4) Henk Buermans : micro-RNA data analysis and tool developer (mailto:h.p.j.buermans@lumc.nl)

5) Matthew Hestand : coordinator, data analysis support, and tool developer (mailto:M.S.Hestand@lumc.nl)

Microarray Analysis (http://www.humgen.nl/MicroarrayAnalysisGroup.html):

The group works on different aspects of microarray data analysis, including platform comparison, sample size determination, and study design. In addition to expression profiling, we work on the analysis of different types of microarray data, e.g. array-CGH, SNP arrays, and methylation arrays. We develop new statistical tools for optimizing study design and for the analysis and integration of microarray experiments and apply them to genomics projects carried out within our institute.

1) Peter-Bram 't Hoen : developer and superuser of microarray analysis tools (mailto:p.a.c.hoen@lumc.nl)

2) Maarten van Iterson : statistical methods and tools for design, analysis, and integration of genomic experiments (mailto:M.van_Iterson.HG@lumc.nl)

3) Judith Boer : coordinator, developer, and superuser of microarray analysis tools (mailto:j.m.boer@lumc.nl)

Databases and Annotation (http://www.humgen.nl/BioinfSupGroup.html):

The group works on the development and maintenance of the web-based locus-specific database LOVD (http://www.lovd.nl/3.0/home) (Leiden Open source sequence Variation Database) and on proper nomenclature of sequence variations. This latter aspect, in the Mutalyzer (https://mutalyzer.nl/) package, also aims to determine the functional effects of sequence variations (under development).

1) Ivo Fokkema: LOVD and HCG database developer (mailto:i.f.a.c.fokkema@lumc.nl)

2) Jacopo Celli : LOVD database set-up and curator support (mailto:j.celli@lumc.nl)

3) Gerard Schaafsma : LOVD tool developer (mailto:G.C.P.Schaafsma@lumc.nl)

4) Jeroen Laros : Development of algorithms and tools for sequence (variant) analysis and annotation (mailto:j.f.j.laros@lumc.nl)

5) Peter Taschner : coordinator (mailto:p.taschner@lumc.nl)

BioSemantics (http://www.biosemantics.org/):

The BioSemantics group investigates and develops new ways to analyse biological data and information through computational means. A prime focus is methodology for discovering hidden biological relations from text, biological databases, and knowledge held by experts; resources that go beyond a single researcher or a single group. In Leiden we focus on applying this research ('meta-analysis') to help build better hypotheses for a number of cases within the Human Genetics department. Thereby we establish a feedback loop between computer scientists, software developers and biologists. The group is a collaboration between the Center for Human and Clinical Genetics (http://www.humgen.nl/) at the Leiden University Medical Center (https://www.lumc.nl/) and the Medical Informatics department (http://www.erasmusmc.nl/med_informatica/?lang=en) of the ErasmusMC University Medical Center of Rotterdam (http://www.erasmusmc.nl/)

LUMC members:

1) Herman van Haagen : research and tool developer (mailto:h.h.h.b.m.van_haagen@lumc.nl)

2) Bharat Singh : software development (mailto:b.singh@lumc.nl)

3) Peter-Bram 't Hoen : 'user expert' of BioSemantic methods (mailto:P.A.C._t_Hoen@lumc.nl)

4) Marco Roos : project coordination and bioinformatics research, e-science liaison (mailto:M.Roos1@UVA.nl)

5) Barend Mons : founder and senior advisor (mailto:barend.mons@nbic.nl), founder of the Concept Web Alliance (http://www.nbic.nl/research/CWA/)

Bioinformatics Courses and Tutorials

1) DNA chip and array technology : "Analysis of microarray gene expression data" (http://www.medgencentre.nl/) - Lectures & Practicals

2) Next-gen sequencing technology : "Next generation sequencing (NGS) data analysis" (http://www.medgencentre.nl/)

3) Getting started in R : (http://www.humgen.nl/microarray_analysis_getting_started_with_R.html) information for first time R users including several practicals for microarray data analysis

Tools originating from the department

1) Anni 2.1 (http://www.biosemantics.org/index.php?page=anni-2-0) : a multipurpose text-mining tool for the life sciences

2) CORE_TF (http://grenada.lumc.nl/HumaneGenetica/CORE_TF/): Conserved and Over-REpresented Transcription Factor binding sites (http://grenada.lumc.nl/HumaneGenetica/CORE_TF/)

3) LOVD (http://www.lovd.nl/) : Leiden Open source sequence Variation Database

4) MaRe (http://grenada.lumc.nl/HumaneGenetica/MaRe/) : Microarray Retriever

5) Mutalyzer (https://www.mutalyzer.nl/) : Sequence variant nomenclature check

6) SIM (http://bioconductor.org/packages/2.5/bioc/html/SIM.html) : Integrated Analysis on two human genomic datasets

7) SSPA (http://bioconductor.org/packages/2.5/bioc/html/SSPA.html) : Sample Size and Power Analysis for Microarray Data

Online Bioinformatics Tutorials

There are many bioinformatics tutorials available on the web. Below are some suggestions from reputable organisations.

Train online (http://www.ebi.ac.uk/training/online/train-online)

These online bioinformatics tutorials demonstrate how to use tools and databases supplied by EMBL-EBI to carry out a range of bioinformatics tasks.

Free Open Helix Resources (http://www.openhelix.com/cgi/freeTutorials.cgi)

Open Helix provides a small number of free tutorials covering topics such as searching the RCSB Protein Data Bank.

Exploring Genomes : Bioinformatics Tutorials (http://bcs.whfreeman.com/iga9e/pages/bcs-main.asp?s=00010&n=99000&i=99010.01&v=category&o=|00510|00520|00530|00540|00550|00560|00570|00580|00010|00020|00030|00040|00050|01000|02000|03000|04000|05000|06000|07000|08000|09000|10000|11000|12000|13000|14000|15000|16000|17000|18000|19000|20000|99000|&ns=0&uid=0&rau=0)

Bioinformatics Tutorials

How to use all this stuff:

2can (http://www.ebi.ac.uk/2can) - Bioinformatics Educational Resource at the **European Bioinformatics Institute** (http://www.ebi.ac.uk/index.html).

Online Lectures on Bioinformatics (http://lectures.molgen.mpg.de/ online_lectures.html) -The Max Planck Institute for Molecular Genetics provides an excellent course on bioinformatics.

BioActivity (http://www.bioinf.man.ac.uk/dbbrowser/bioactivity/)

Bio Tools Info

Biotools.info (http://www.biotools.info/)

Education home (http://www.biotool.info/education/edu.html)

a) Teaching science (http://www.biotools.info/education/tedu.html)
b) Science for kids (http://www.biotools.info/education/kedu.html)
c) Science literature & dictionaries (http://www.biotools.info/education/ literature.html)
d) Resources for the molecular biologist (http://www.biotools.info/tools.html)

Molecular Biology - Gateways & Tools

Gateways (http://www.biotools.info/tools.html#a)

Tools & Protocols (http://www.biotools.info/tools.html#b) (Genome Analysis, Sequence Analysis, Primer Design, Phylogeny, RNA Analysis)

NCBI Resources for Genes & Genomes (http://www.biotools.info/links/A1bioinfo.pdf)

From the Publishers (http://www.biotools.info/tools.html#c)

Science literature & dictionaries (http://www.biotools.info/education/literature.html)

Bioinformatics Support Service of the Max-Planck-Society (http://www.biochem.mpg.de/en/facilities/ivs/SupportTraining/Workshop/BioInfoSup/index.html) with the Workshops on Bioinformatics Tools & Techniques / Hand-out file:///I:\(Workshops on Bioinformatics Tools & Techniques \ Hand-out) (http://www.biochem.mpg.de/en/facilities/ivs/SupportTraining/Workshop/BioInfo_WS/index.html)

Gateways

1) BioinfoWiki (http://www.bioinfowiki.mpg.de/index.php/Main_Page) - A Wiki on BioTools developed in the Max Planck Society.

2) European Bioinformatics Institute (EBI) (http://www.ebi.ac.uk/) - Center for research and services in bioinformatics. The Institute manages databases of biological data including nucleic acid, protein sequences and macromolecular structures.

3) ExPASy Life Science Directory (http://www.expasy.org/) - A well organized collection of < 1000 web links from the Expert Protein Analysis System, a Proteomics and

Molecular Biology Server for the analysis of protein sequences and structures as well as 2-D PAGE.

4) National Center for Biotechnology Information (NCBI) (http://www.ncbi.nlm.nih.gov/) - Creates public databases, conducts research in computational biology, develops software tools for analyzing genome data, and disseminates biomedical information.

5) OBRC: Online Bioinformatics Resources Collection (http://www.hsls.pitt.edu/obrc/) - The website of the UPMC (University of Pittsburgh Medical Center) contains annotations and links for more than 1600 open source bioinformatics databases and software tools.

6) WWW Virtual Library (http://vlib.org/)

Tools & Protocols

Genome Analysis

a) ENSEMBL Genome Server (http://www.ensembl.org/index.html)

b) NCBI MapViewer (http://www.ncbi.nlm.nih.gov/mapview/)

c) UCSC Genome Bioinformatics (http://genome.ucsc.edu/)

Sequence Analysis

a) CLUSTAL W (http://www.ebi.ac.uk/Tools/msa/) - Multiple Sequence Alignments (EBI).

b) Genedoc (http://www.psc.edu/biomed/genedoc/)

c) Sequence Manipulation Suite (http://bioinformatics.org/sms2/)

Restriktionsanalyse in WWW

a) NEB Cutter (http://rebase.neb.com/rebase/rebtools.html)

b) Restrictionmapper (http://www.restrictionmapper.org/)

c) REBASE (http://rebase.neb.com/rebase/rebase.html) - The database of restriction enzymes.

d) Silent (http://mobyle.pasteur.fr/cgi-bin/portal.py?#forms::silent)

e) Mapper (http://arbl.cvmbs.colostate.edu/molkit/mapper/index.html)

Primer Design

a) PCR Links (http://www.pcrlinks.com/)

b) Design PCR Primers (http://molbiol-tools.ca/ PCR.htm)

c) OligoAnalyzer (SciTools) (http://sg.idtdna.com/calc/analyzer)

d) Primer3 (http://primer3.ut.ee/)

e) Primer BLAST (NCBI) (http://www.ncbi.nlm.nih.gov/tools/primer-blast/index.cgi?LINK_LOC= BlastHome)

f) Quantitative RT-PCR & PCR Array (http://www.sabiosciences.com/RTPCR.php? adwords=PCR)

g) Phylogeny
Treeview (http://taxonomy.zoology.gla.ac.uk/rod/treeview.html)

h) Phylodendron (http://iubio.bio.indiana.edu/treeapp/)

i) MEGA (http://www.megasoftware.net/)

j) Phylogeny and Reconstructing Phylogenetic Trees (http://aleph0.clarku.edu/~djoyce/java/Phyltree/cover.html) - These few pages describe the problem of reconstructing phylogenetic trees.

k) Software products for phylogenetic analysis (http://taxonomy.zoology.gla.ac.uk/software/ software.html)

RNA Analysis

a) Comparative RNA Web Site (http://www.rna.icmb.utexas.edu/)

b) RNA Modification Database (http://rna-mdb.cas.albany.edu/RNAmods/) - From the Departments of Medicinal Chemistry and Biochemistry, Univ. of Utah.

c) RNA World (http://www.rna.uni-jena.de/rna.php) - From the Institute of molecular biotechnology (Jena, Germany).

d) RNAi Technical Resources (http://www.lifetechnologies.com/in/en/home/brands/ambion.html) - from Ambion - The RNA Company

Primer Design

Rules to design primers (http://bioinformatics.igc.gulbenkian.pt/resources/tools/primer_rules/)

1) Primer3 (http://bioinfo.ut.ee/primer3-0.4.0/primer3/) - Primer3 is a **widely used** program for designing PCR primers.

2) Primaclade (http://www.umsl.edu/services/kellogg/primaclade.html) - Application that accepts a multiple species nucleotide alignment file as input and identifies a set of PCR primers that will bind across the alignment. The

program iteratively runs the Primer3 application for each alignment sequence and collates the results.

3) ProbeFinder   (http://qpcr2.probefinder.com/input.jsp) - Design intron-spanning assays for your target gene. You can select the organism of interest and enter the target-gene name, gene ID or nucleotide sequence.

4) RT-Primer Design (https://www.genscript.com/ssl-bin/app/primer) - Real Time PCR primer design.

5) CODEHOP (http://blocks.fhcrc.org/codehop.html) - The Consensus-degenerate hybrid oligonucleotide primers program designs PCR primers from protein multiple-sequence alignments and is intended for cases where the protein sequences are distant from each other and **degenerate primers** are needed Help (http://blocks.fhcrc.org/blocks/help/CODEHOP/ CODEHOP_help.html).

6) MEME for primer design (http://bioinf-mac.uniandes.edu.co/design/) - Method for designing degenerate primers based on multiple local alignments employing the MEME algorithm supported with electronic PCR.

Finding Genes

1) GENSCAN (http://genes.mit.edu/GENSCAN.html) - Gene identification program which analyzes genomic DNA sequences from a variety of organisms including human, other vertebrates, invertebrates and plants.

2) GeneMark (http://exon.gatech.edu/GeneMark/) - Package of programs for gene prediction in Bacteria, Archaea and

Metagenomes; Eukaryotes; Viruses, Phages and Plasmids and EST.

3) Softberry (http://www.softberry.com/all.htm) - Gene finding in Eukaryote, Bacteria and Virus.

4) GrailEXP (http://compbio.ornl.gov/grailexp/) - Software that predicts exons, genes, promoters, polyAs, CpG islands, EST similarities, and repetitive elements within DNA sequence.

5) Generation (http://compbio.ornl.gov/generation/) - Software that performs gene predictions on microbial and model organisms and produces a set of data which can be used by GrailEXP v3.0 to recognize genes in these organisms.

6) DragonGSF (http://sdmc.lit.org.sg/promoter/dragonGSF1_0/genestart.htm) - Prediction of gene start location in mammalian genomes, by combining information about CpG islands, transcription start sites (TSSs), and signals downstream of the predicted TSSs.

7) GeneWise (http://www.ebi.ac.uk/Tools/psa/genewise/) - Software thar compares a protein sequence to a genomic DNA sequence, allowing for introns and frame shifting errors.

8) Link (http://bioinformatics.ca/links_directory/?subcategory_id=39) - A list of gene prediction programs for both eukaryotic and prokaryotic organisms.

Finding Promoters and Regulatory Elements

1) TFSEARCH (http://www.cbrc.jp/research/db/TFSEARCH.html) - Searching DNA for eukaryotic transcription Factor Binding Sites and DNA-binding profiles (searches TransFAC).

2) ConSite (http://asp.ii.uib.no:8090/cgi-bin/CONSITE/consite) - Tool for finding cis-regulatory elements in genomic sequences. Predictions are based on the integration of binding site prediction generated with high-quality transcription factor models and cross-species comparison filtering (phylogenetic footprinting).

3) TESS (http://www.cbil.upenn.edu/tess) - Web tool for predicting transcription factor binding sites in DNA sequences. It can identify binding sites using site or consensus strings and positional weight matrices from the TRANSFAC, JASPAR, IMD, CBIL-GibbsMat database. You can use TESS to search a few of your own sequences or for user-defined CRMs genome-wide near genes throughout genomes of interest.

4) Softberry (http://www.softberry.com/berry.phtml) - Gene finding in Eukaryote, Bacteria and Virus. Go to **Test on Line** on the left side, and search on **search Motifs** menu.

5) NNPP (http://www.fruitfly.org/seq_tools/promoter.html) - Neural Network Promoter Prediction - Promoter Prediction by Neural Network for prokaryotes or eukaryotes.

6) PromoterScan (http://www-bimas.cit.nih.gov/molbio/proscan/) - Predicts Promoter regions based on scoring homologies with putative eukaryotic Pol II promoter sequences.

7) Promoter (http://www.cbs.dtu.dk/services/Promoter/) - Predicts transcription start sites of vertebrate PolII promoters in DNA sequences.

Align Two Sequences

1) bl2seq (http://blast.ncbi.nlm.nih.gov/Blast.cgi?PAGE_TYPE=BlastSearch&PROG_DEF=blastn&BLAST_PROG_DEF=megaBlast&BLAST_SPEC=blast2seq) - This tool produces the alignment of two given sequences using the NCBI BLAST engine for local alignment. The output shows the similar region.

2) Needle (http://www.ebi.ac.uk/Tools/emboss/) - EMBOSS Pair wise Alignment Algorithms tool used to compare 2 sequences when you want an alignment that covers the whole length of both sequences.

3) Water (http://www.ebi.ac.uk/Tools/emboss/) - EMBOSS Pair wise Alignment Algorithms tool used when you are trying to find the best region of similarity between two sequences.

Multiple Sequence Alignment

1) Multalin (http://multalin.toulouse.inra.fr/multalin/multalin.html) - Multiple sequence alignment for DNA or proteins with hierarchical clustering.

2) Clustal Omega (http://www.ebi.ac.uk/Tools/msa/clustalo/) - Multiple sequence alignment program for DNA or proteins sequences. Clustal Omega is a new multiple sequence alignment program that uses seeded guide trees and HMM profile-profile techniques to generate alignments.

3) Tcoffee (http://igs-server.cnrs-mrs.fr/Tcoffee/tcoffee_cgi/index.cgi) - Computes a multiple sequence alignment and the associated phylogenetic tree for a set of sequences (Proteins or DNA). T-Coffee allows the combination of a collection of multiple/pairwise, global or local alignments into a single

model. It also allows estimating the level of consistency of each position within the new alignment with the rest of the alignments.

BLAST

1) BLAST (http://blast.ncbi.nlm.nih.gov/Blast.cgi) - The Basic Local Alignment Search Tool (NCBI) finds regions of local similarity between sequences. The program compares nucleotide or protein sequences to sequence databases and calculates the statistical significance of matches Tutorial (http://www.ncbi.nlm.nih.gov/Education/BLASTinfo/tutl.html).

2) Blast@EBI (http://www.ebi.ac.uk/ebisearch/search.ebi?query=Blast%40EBI& db=allebi&requestFrom=searchBox) - Here you can find a list of all the Blast's available at the EBI including the Ensembl Multi BlastView to the annotated genomes.

Source: (http://www.egosumdaniel.se/bioinfo/)

(http://bioinformatics.igc.gulbenkian.pt/resources/tools/sequenceanalysis/)

Access to computing servers for high-throughput bioinformatics

Computing servers of the bioinformatics platform are using the linux/unix operating system (OS). Connection to the servers can be carried out using a ssh (secure shell) program. The connection gives access to a personal zone which is secured by a login and password. Using the servers requires mastering the linux/unix OS, to know how to run command line programs and how to submit jobs to queues (qsub). The platform maintains bioinformatics databases (Swissprot,

Trembl, PDB, transcripts, ...) that can be accessed by SRS (Sequence Retrieval System) using the getz program. Further command-line programs (read mappers, blast tools, R, ...) are also installed on the servers and shared between users. Server resources are limited (disk space, CPU and RAM) and good usage rules apply, such as deleting old files, monitoring RAM and submitting jobs to queues n order to dispatch CPU load on different machines. Every user is responsible for his information processing and should not do anything that could be a prejudice against the informatics network and the server integrity.

If you wish to have an access and a work environment on the servers, please make a request to us.

(http://bioinformaticsonline.com/phylogeny.php)

(http://website-tools.net/google-keyword/site/stattrek.com)

PHYLIP (http://evolution.genetics.washington.edu/phylip.html)

PAUP (http://paup.csit.fsu.edu/)

MEGA 2.1 (www.megasoftware.net/)

TREEVIEW
(http://taxonomy.zoology.gla.ac.uk/rod/treeview.html)

Extensive list of software
(http://evolution.genetics.washington.edu/phylip/software.html)
(http://karchinlab.org/fcbb2_spr10)   (http://www.drugbank.ca)

Indiana Genomics Initiative: (http://www.ingen.iu.edu/)

Inproteo (Indiana Proteomics Consortium):
(http://www.inproteomics.com/index.html)

Bio Crossroads (Central Indiana Life Science Network):
(http://www.biocrossroads.com/default.htm)

Websites related to motif search

PCPMer: (http://landau.utmb.edu:8080/WebPCPMer/HomePage/index.html) used in this course

BLOCKS: (http://blocks.fhcrc.org/) relies on conserved stretches of protein families

MEME: (http://meme.sdsc.edu/meme/website/intro.html) combine HMM search with profile methods

PROSITE: (http://us.expasy.org/prosite/) catalogue of biological important sequence patterns

HMMER: (http://hmmer.wustl.edu/) Profile Hidden Markov Models

SAM: (http://www.soe.ucsc.edu/research/compbio/sam.html) several software packages implementing HMM

PFAM: (http://www.sanger.ac.uk/Software/Pfam/) collection of MSA and hidden Markov models of many common protein domains

i. PROSITE : (http://www.expasy.ch/prosite/)

ii. PRINTS : (http://www.bioinf.man.ac.uk/dbbrowser/PRINTS/)

iii. BLOCKS : (http://blocks.fhcrc.org/blocks/)

iv. PFAM : (http://www.sanger.ac.uk/Software/Pfam/)

v. eMOTIFS : (http://dna.stanford.edu/identify)

InterPro: (http://www.ebi.ac.uk/interpro/scan.html)

Major Pathway databases

i. Boehringer Pathways : (http://www.expasy.ch/cgi-bin/search-biochem-index)

ii. KEGG : (http://www.genome.ad.jp/kegg/)

iii. BioCyc / EcoCyc : (http://www.biocyc.org/)

iv. Reactome : (http://www.reactome.org/)

v. STKE : (http://stke.sciencemag.org/)

vi. Brenda : (http://www.brenda.uni-koeln.de/aMaze)

Source: (http://www.amaze.ulb.ac.be/)

i. Center for Computational Biology and Bioinformatics at Indianapolis (http://www.compbio.iupui.edu/)

ii. Center for Genomics and Bioinformatics (http://cgb.indiana.edu/)

iii. Biocomplexity Institute (http://biocomplexity.indiana.edu/)

iv. Proteomics Research and Development Facility (http://www.chem.indiana.edu/facilities/proteomics/PRDFhomepage.htm)

v. Flybase Drosophila Genome Database (http://flybase.bio.indiana.edu/)

vi. (http://www.ncbi.nlm.nih.gov/Class/MLACourse/index.html)

Genetic Databases

i. BLAST - Basic Local Alignment Search Tool (http://www.ncbi.nlm.nih.gov/BLAST/)

ii. Cancer Genome Anatomy Project (http://cgap.nci.nih.gov/)

iii. DNA Data Bank of Japan (DDBJ) (http://www.ddbj.nig.ac.jp)

iv. Entrez, The Life Sciences Search Engine (Entrez) (http://www.ncbi.nlm.nih.gov/Entrez/)

v. Entrez Genome (http://www.ncbi.nlm.nih.gov/sites/entrez?db=genome)

vi. ExPASy Molecular Biology Server (Expert Protein Analysis System) (http://au.expasy.org)

vii. Nucleic Acid Database (US Department of Energy) (http://ndbserver.rutgers.edu)

viii. Nucleotide (GenBank) (http://www.ncbi.nlm.nih.gov/sites/entrez?db=nucleotide)

ix. Nucleotide Sequence Database (EMBL) (http://www.ebi.ac.uk/embl/)

Genome Projects

i. Human Genome Resources (NCBI) : (http://www.ncbi.nlm.nih.gov/genome/guide/human/)

ii. National Human Genome Research Institute (NIH) : (http://www.nhgri.nih.gov)

iii. Stanford Genome Resource : (http://genome-www.stanford.edu/)

iv. The Genome Projects (TIGER) : (http://www.tigr.org/tdb/)

v. The Human Genome Project (DOE) (http://www.ornl.gov/sci/techresources/Human_Genome/publicat/primer/index.shtm)

Chapter 11: BIOINFORMATICS LINKS DIRECTORY

The Bioinformatics Links Directory features curated links to molecular resources, tools and databases. The links listed in this directory are selected on the basis of recommendations from bioinformatics experts in the field. We also rely on input from our community of bioinformatics users for suggestions. Starting in 2003, we have also started listing all links contained in the NAR Webserver issue.

🗗 Hide Resources (174) (http://bioinformatics.ca/links_directory/?filter=databases%2Ctools) ≡ Hide Databases (623) (http://bioinformatics.ca/links_directory/?filter=resources%2Ctools) ⚙ Hide Tools (1549) (http://bioinformatics.ca/links_directory/?filter=resources%2Cdatabases)

☐ Computer Related (83) (http://bioinformatics.ca/links_directory/category/computer-related) - This category contains links to resources relating to programming languages often used in bioinformatics. Other tools of the trade, such as web development and database resources, are also included here.

☐ DNA (604) (http://bioinformatics.ca/links_directory/category/dna) - This category contains links to useful resources for DNA sequence analyses such as tools for comparative sequence analysis and sequence assembly. Links to programs for sequence manipulation, primer design, and sequence retrieval and submission are also listed here.

☐ Expression (395) (http://bioinformatics.ca/links_directory/category/expression) -Links to tools for predicting the expression, alternative splicing, and regulation of a gene sequence are found here. This section also contains links to databases, methods, and analysis tools for protein expression, SAGE, EST, and microarray data.

☐ Human Genome (238) (http://bioinformatics.ca/links_directory/category/human-genome) - This section contains links to draft annotations of the human genome in addition to resources for sequence polymorphisms and genomics. Also included are links related to ethical discussions surrounding the study of the human genome.

☐ Model Organisms (378) (http://bioinformatics.ca/links_directory/category/ model-organisms) - Included in this category are links to resources for various model organisms ranging from mammals to microbes. These include databases and tools for genome scale analyses.

☐ Other Molecules (117) (http://bioinformatics.ca/links_directory/category/other-molecules) - Bioinformatics tools related to molecules other than DNA, RNA, and protein. This category will include resources for the bioinformatics of small molecules as well as for other biopolymers including carbohydrates and metabolites.

☐ Protein (1009) (http://bioinformatics.ca/links_directory/category/protein) - This category contains links to useful resources for protein sequence and structure analyses. Resources for phylogenetic analyses, prediction of protein features, and analyses of interactions are also found here.

☐ RNA (203) (http://bioinformatics.ca/links_directory/category/rna) - Resources include links to sequence retrieval programs, structure prediction and visualization tools, motif search programs, and information on various functional RNAs.

☐ Sequence Comparison (271) (http://bioinformatics.ca/links_directory/category/sequence-comparison) - Tools and resources for the comparison of sequences (nucleic acid or protein) including sequence similarity searching, alignment tools, classification and general comparative genomics resources.

☐ Education (75) (http://bioinformatics.ca/links_directory/category/education) - Links to information about the techniques, materials, people, places, and events of the greater bioinformatics community. Included are current news headlines, literature sources, educational material and links to bioinformatics courses and workshops.

☐ Literature (86) (http://bioinformatics.ca/links_directory/category/literature) - Links to resources related to published literature, including tools to search for articles and through literature abstracts. Additional text mining resources, open access resources, and literature goldmines are also listed.

⌀ Hide Resources (174) (http://bioinformatics.ca/links_directory/?filter= databases%2Ctools) ≡ Hide Databases (623) (http://bioinformatics.ca/links_directory/ ?filter=resources%2Ctools)

Computer Related: This category contains links to resources relating to programming languages often used in bioinformatics. Other tools of the trade, such as web development and database resources, are also included here.

🔊 RSS Feed (http://bioinformatics.ca/links_directory/category/computer-related/feed)

⇆ Compact View (http://bioinformatics.ca/links_directory/category/computer-related?mode=compact)

⇆ Sort by Links Directory Index (http://bioinformatics.ca/links_directory/category/computer-related?sort=citation count)

DOWNLOAD ⬇ List as XML (http://bioinformatics.ca/links_directory/xml/category/89782?download=true) ⬇ List as JSON (http://bioinformatics.ca/links_directory/json/category/89782?download=true) ⬇ List as TSV (http://bioinformatics.ca/links_directory/xml/category/89782?download=true) ⬇ List as CSV (http://bioinformatics.ca/links_directory/csv/category/89782?download=true)

⊘ Hide Resources (34) (http://bioinformatics.ca/links_directory/category/computer-related?filter=databases%2Ctools) ≡ Hide Databases (2) (http://bioinformatics.ca/links_directory/category/computer-related?filter=resources%2Ctools) ⚙ Hide Tools (62) (http://bioinformatics.ca/links_directory/category/computer-related?filter=resources%2C databases)

☐ Bio-* Programming Tools (20) (http://bioinformatics.ca/links_directory/category/computer-related/bio-programming-tools) - This section contains links that include information on software development tools, such as BioJava and BioPerl. Other application programming interfaces (API) which are specifically designed for processing biological data are also listed here.

☐ C/C++ (3) (http://bioinformatics.ca/links_directory/category/computer-related/cc) - These resources contain information about the C/C++ programming languages.

☐ Databases (7) - (http://bioinformatics.ca/links_directory/category/computer-related/databases). This section contains links that describe several different flavors of the open source SQL (structured query language) used in many bioinformatics databases.

☐ Java (4) (http://bioinformatics.ca/links_directory/category/computer-related/java) - These sites contain information and tutorials relating to the programming language, Java.

☐ Linux/Unix (10) (http://bioinformatics.ca/links_directory/category/computer-related/linuxunix) - This section contains introductory material to the Linux/Unix environment.

☐ Math and Statistics (11) (http://bioinformatics.ca/links_directory/category/computer-related/math-and-statistics) - Links to resources for the statistical analysis of bioinformatics data including protein sequences and expression analysis. Also contains mathematical models and other math related resources.

☐ PERL (5) (http://bioinformatics.ca/links_directory/category/computer-related/perl) - Links to programming in Perl are included in this section. Information on the use of BioPerl is also included here.

☐ PHP (1) (http://bioinformatics.ca/links_directory/category/computer-related/php) - This section contains links that include PHP (pre-hypertext processor) development sites.

☐ Web Development (3) (http://bioinformatics.ca/links_directory/category/computer-related/web-development) - This section contains development sites for the World Wide Web. These include open source developer forums and informative tutorials on web specific technologies.

☐ Web Services (25) (http://bioinformatics.ca/links_directory/category/computer-related/web-services) - This section has links to applications which have released Web Service API's.

☐ Workflows (http://bioinformatics.ca/links_directory/category/computer-related/workflows)

🔊 RSS Feed (http://bioinformatics.ca/links_directory/category/education/feed)

⇄ Compact View (http://bioinformatics.ca/links_directory/category/education?mode=compact)

⇄ Sort by Links Directory Index (http://bioinformatics.ca/links_directory/category/education?sort=citation_count)

DOWNLOAD ⬇ List as XML (http://bioinformatics.ca/links_directory/xml/category/89786?download=true) ⬇ List as JSON (http://bioinformatics.ca/links_directory/json/category/89786?download=true) ⬇ List as TSV (http://bioinformatics.ca/links_directory/tsv/category/89786?download=true) ⬇ List as CSV (http://bioinformatics.ca/links_directory/csv/category/89786?download=true)

🍃 Hide Resources (73) (http://bioinformatics.ca/links_directory/category/education?filter=databases%2Ctools) ≡ Hide Databases (8) (http://bioinformatics.ca/links_directory/category/education?filter=resources%2Ctools) ✱ Hide Tools (10) (http://bioinformatics.ca/links_directory/category/education?filter=resources%2Cdatabases)

☐ Bioinformatics Related News Sources (11) (http://bioinformatics.ca/links_directory/category/education/bioinformatics-related-news-sources) - Contains up to date information and the latest news on what's happening in the world of bioinformatics today.

☐ Community (21) (http://bioinformatics.ca/links_directory/category/education/_community) - Resources include links to people and places in the bioinformatics community, mainly within Canada.

☐ Courses, Programs and Workshops (5) (http://bioinformatics.ca/links_directory/category/education/courses-programs-and-workshops) - This section contains links to various bioinformatics related courses and workshops around the world and in Canada.

☐ Directories and Portals (25) (http://bioinformatics.ca/links_directory/category/education/directories-and-portals) - Links in this section include web directories and other link-sites for biology and bioinformatics related material.

☐ General (17) (http://bioinformatics.ca/links_directory/category/education/general) - Links to reference and educational materials for DNA, genomes, bioinformatics, evolution and beyond. Includes glossaries, articles, educational websites and more.

☐ Tutorials and Directed Learning Resources (11) [Source: (http://bioinformatics.ca/links_directory/category/education/tutorials-and-directed-learning-resources)]

Links to on-line tutorials and other educational reference material, such as bioinformatics-related course materials, available on the web.

Canadian Neuroinformatics and Computational Neuroscience community (http://bioinformatics.ca/links_directory/resource/14018/canadian-neuroinformatics-and-computational-neuroscience-community)

http://www.neuroinfocomp.ca/ [open in a new window]

Education (http://bioinformatics.ca/links_directory/category/education)

Education > Bioinformatics Related News Sources (http://bioinformatics.ca/links_directory/category/education/bioinformatics-related-news-sources)

Education > Community (http://bioinformatics.ca/links_directory/category/education/ community)

Education > Courses, Programs and Workshops (http://bioinformatics.ca/links_directory/category/education/courses-programs-and-workshops)

Education > Directories and Portals (http://bioinformatics.ca/links_directory/category/education/directories-and-portals)

This web site is a portal for communication with the community. Our goal is to enhance the visibility and impact of Neuroinformatics and Computational Neuroscience in Canada. We share our knowledge and encourage knowledge transfer through commonly organized events, mailing lists and open-access teaching and research resources. We hope to promote new collaborations and encourage scientific coordination leading to more efficient knowledge advancement and transfer.

Human Genome Source (http://bioinformatics.ca/links_directory/category/human-genome)

This section contains links to draft annotations of the human genome in addition to resources for sequence polymorphisms and genomics. Also included are links related to ethical discussions surrounding the study of the human genome?

🔊 RSS Feed (http://bioinformatics.ca/links_directory/category/human-genome/feed)

⇄ Compact View (http://bioinformatics.ca/links_directory/category/human-genome?mode=compact)

⇄ Sort by Links Directory Index (http://bioinformatics.ca/links_directory/category/human-genome?Sort=citation count)

DOWNLOAD ⬇ List as XML (http://bioinformatics.ca/links_directory/xml/category/89783?download=true) ⬇ List as JSON (http://bioinformatics.ca/links_directory/json/category/89783?download=true) ⬇ List as TSV (http://bioinformatics.ca/links_directory/tsv/category/89783?download=true) ⬇ List as CSV (http://bioinformatics.ca/links_directory/csv/category/89783?download=true)

🌐 Hide Resources (29) (http://bioinformatics.ca/links_directory/category/human-genome?filter=databases%2Ctools) ≡ Hide Databases (104) (http://bioinformatics.ca/links_directory/category/human-genome?filter=resources%2Ctools) ⚙ Hide Tools (167) (http://bioinformatics.ca/links_directory/category/human-genome?filter=resources%2Cdatabases)

☐ Annotations (45) (http://bioinformatics.ca/links_directory/category/human-genome/annotations) - This section contains links related to annotations of the human genome. Different sites provide automated and curated annotations. See also DNA: Sequence Features and DNA: Gene Prediction.

☐ Databases (58) (http://bioinformatics.ca/links_directory/category/human-genome/databases) - This section contains human genome and ORFs, genetics, polymorphism, gene-/system-/disease-specific information.

☐ Ethics (6) (http://bioinformatics.ca/links_directory/category/human-genome/ethics) - Links in this section deal with research and discussion related to the ethical and moral questions of human genome research.

☐ Genomics (33) (http://bioinformatics.ca/links_directory/category/human-genome/genomics) - These links provide up-to-date and relevant information for genomic researchers.

☐ Health and Disease (65) (http://bioinformatics.ca/links_directory/category/human-genome/health-and-disease) - Resources in this section encompass genomic research related to human health and disease.

☐ Other Resources (30) (http://bioinformatics.ca/links_directory/category/human-genome/other-resources) - Resources include databases, gene-collections, portals, and various tools related to the human genome.

☐ Sequence Polymorphisms (63) (http://bioinformatics.ca/links_directory/category/human-genome/sequence-polymorphisms) - Links to various sequence polymorphism databases and resources concerning SNPs, short deletion, insertion polymorphisms and other unique genomic features.

Model Organisms (http://bioinformatics.ca/links_directory/category/model organism)

Included in this category are links to resources for various model organisms ranging from mammals to microbes. These include databases and tools for genome scale analyses.

🔊 RSS Feed (http://bioinformatics.ca/links_directory/category/model-organisms/feed) ⇄ Compact View (http://bioinformatics.ca/links_directory/category/model-organisms?mode=

compact) ⇌ Sort by Links Directory Index (http://bioinformatics.ca/links_directory/category/ model-organisms?sort=citation count)

DOWNLOAD ⬇ List as XML (http://bioinformatics.ca/links_directory/xml/category/89781?download=true) ⬇ List as JSON (http://bioinformatics.ca/links_directory/json/category/89781?download=true) ⬇ List as TSV (http://bioinformatics.ca/links_directory/tsvl/category/89781?download=true) ⬇ List as CSV (http://bioinformatics.ca/links_directory/csv/category/89781?download=true)

⌀ Hide Resources (30) (http://bioinformatics.ca/links_directory/category/model-organisms?filter=databases%2Ctools) ≡ Hide Databases (240) (http://bioinformatics.ca/links_directory/category/model-organisms?filter=resources%2Ctools) ✱ Hide Tools (198) (http://bioinformatics.ca/links_directory/category/model-organisms?filter=resources%2C databases)

☐ Databases (125) (http://bioinformatics.ca/links_directory/category/model-organisms/databases) - This section contains databases of model organism genomes, vertebrate / non-vertebrate / plant / organelle genomes, and taxonomy/identification.

☐ Fish (10) (http://bioinformatics.ca/links_directory/category/model-organisms/fish) - Resources include sequences, annotations, and comparative vertebrate genomics for various species of fish.

☐ Fly (28) (http://bioinformatics.ca/links_directory/category/model-organisms/fly) - This section contains links to genome resources, tools, and databases for flies including Drosophila and the mosquito.

☐ General Resources (34) (http://bioinformatics.ca/links_directory/category/model-organisms/general-resources) - The resources listed here include tools and databases for general information on a variety of model organisms.

☐ Microbes (87) (http://bioinformatics.ca/links_directory/ category/model-organisms/microbes) - This section contains links to microbial genome resources including: genome sequences, annotations and comparative analyses. Includes bacteria, virus and fungi species.

☐ Mouse and Rat (48) (http://bioinformatics.ca/links_ directory/category/model-organisms/mouse-and-rat) - Resources include sequences, annotations, and comparative vertebrate genomics for mice and rats.

☐ Other Organisms (24) (http://bioinformatics.ca/links_ directory/category/model-organisms/other-organisms) - This section includes links to genome databases, resource centers, and consortiums for various other model organisms.

☐ Other Vertebrates (15) (http://bioinformatics.ca/links_ directory/category/model-organisms/other-vertebrates) - Links in this section include genomic databases and resources specific to other vertebrates.

☐ Plants (48) (http://bioinformatics.ca/links_directory/ category/model-organisms/plants) - In this section are links specific to plant resources including those for Maize and Arabidopsis.

☐ Worm (17) (http://bioinformatics.ca/links_directory/ category/model-organisms/worm) - This section contains links to genome resources and databases for worms including the nematode, C. elegans.

☐ Yeast (31) (http://bioinformatics.ca/links_directory/category/ model-organisms/ yeast) - These links include resources specific to yeast such as gene indices and genome databases.

Protein Source (http://bioinformatics.ca/links_directory/category/protein)

This category contains links to useful resources for protein sequence and structure analyses. Resources for phylogenetic analyses, prediction of protein features, and analyses of interactions are also found here.

RSS Feed (http://bioinformatics.ca/links_directory/category/protein/feed)

Compact View (http://bioinformatics.ca/links_directory/category/ protein?mode= compact)

Sort by Links Directory Index (http://bioinformatics.ca/links_directory/category/ protein? sort=citation count)

DOWNLOAD List as XML (http://bioinformatics.ca/links_directory/xml/category/89785?download=true) List as JSON (http://bioinformatics.ca/links_directory/json/category/89785?download=true) List as TSV (http://bioinformatics.ca/links_directory/tsv/ category/89785?download=true) List as CSV (http://bioinformatics.ca/links_directory/csv/category/89785?download=true)

Hide Resources (44) (http://bioinformatics.ca/links_directory/category/protein?filter=databases%2Ctools) Hide Databases (305) (http://bioinformatics.ca/links_directory/category/protein?filter=resources%2Ctools) Hide Tools (1146) (http://bioinformatics.ca/linksdirectory/category/protein?Filter=resources%2Cdatabases)

☐ 2-D Structure Prediction (77) (http://bioinformatics.ca/links_directory/category/ protein/2-d-structure-prediction) - This sections contains links to several programs which predict protein secondary structure. A link to resources for the evaluation of protein structure prediction is also found here.

☐ 3-D Structural Features (125) (http://bioinformatics.ca/links_directory/category/protein/3-d-structural-features) - This section includes tools for searching for structural motifs, biochemical features found in protein structures, and functional sub-structures such as binding sites.

☐ 3-D Structure Comparison (83) (http://bioinformatics.ca/links_directory/category/protein/3-d-structure-comparison) - Resources for the comparison of sequences at the level of tertiary structure are also found here. This includes tools for superimposing structures and for creating structural alignments.

☐ 3-D Structure Prediction (111) (http://bioinformatics.ca/links_directory/category/protein/3-d-structure-prediction) - This section contains links to resources to aid in protein 3D structure prediction.

☐ 3-D Structure Retrieval/Viewing(67) (http://bioinformatics.ca/links_directory/ category/protein/3-d-structure-retrievalviewing) - Links to tools for visualization of 3D structures are found here. This section also contains links to many 3D structure databases.

☐ Annotation and Function (82) (http://bioinformatics.ca/links_directory/category/protein/annotation-and-function) - This section contains links to tools for annotating proteins and predicting protein function, localization, and other classifications.

☐ Biochemical Features (64) (http://bioinformatics.ca/links_directory/category/ protein/biochemical-features) - The resources in this section include protein identification tools as well as tools which can give you information on the chemical structures and amino acid properties of peptide sequences.

☐ Databases (168) (http://bioinformatics.ca/links_directory/category/protein/ databases) - This section contains databases of protein sequences, properties, targeting, motifs, domains, structures, and protein families.

☐ Do-it-all Tools for Protein (20) (http://bioinformatics.ca/links_directory/category/protein/do-it-all-tools-protein) - These resources are free, publicly available, multi-purpose tools for protein sequence analysis. This is a good place to start if you're looking for a general sequence analysis package.

☐ Domains and Motifs (154) (http://bioinformatics.ca/links_directory/category/protein/domains-and-motifs) - This section includes links to tools which can give information about protein domains and/or predict motifs, domains, and patterns in peptide sequences.

☐ Identification, Presentation and Format (15) (http://bioinformatics.ca/links_directory/category/protein/identification-presentation-and-format) - You can find links to several good tools for manipulating the appearance and format of protein sequences, collections of protein sequences, and alignments in this section. Protein identification mapping tools are also located here.

☐ Localization and Targeting (48) (http://bioinformatics.ca/links_directory/category/protein/localization-and-targeting) - This section contains links to tools related to predicting sub cellular localization, the presence of transmembrane regions, and/or targeting including the prediction of signal peptides.

☐ Molecular Dynamics and Docking (61) (http://bioinformatics.ca/links_directory/category/protein/molecular-dynamics-and-docking) - This section includes resources for molecular dynamics including tools that can predict the movements of structures and/or conformational changes. Molecular docking servers are also included here.

☐ Networks & Interactions, Pathways and Enzymes (183) (http://bioinformatics.ca/links_directory/category/protein/networks-interactions-pathways-and-enzymes) - These links include tools and resources for enzyme, metabolic and proteomic pathways and networks. Many of these resources contain dynamic pathway diagrams. Protein-protein interactions are also represented here.

☐ Phylogeny Reconstruction (60) (http://bioinformatics.ca/ links_directory/category/protein/phylogeny-reconstruction) - This section contains links to tools and databases for phylogeny reconstruction, including taxonomy resources

☐ Protein Expression (12) (http://bioinformatics.ca/links_ directory/category/ protein/protein-expression) - This section contains links to protein expression data and resources for analysis of data including 2D gels.

☐ Proteomics (45) (http://bioinformatics.ca/links_directory/ category/protein/proteomics) - This section contains links to general proteomics resources, methods, software, and databases includes mass spectrometry tools.

☐ Sequence Comparison (21) (http://bioinformatics.ca/links_ directory/category/ protein/sequence-comparison) - The links from this subcategory have been moved. They are now located in Top: Sequence Comparison.

☐ Sequence Data (9) (http://bioinformatics.ca/links_ directory/category/protein/sequence-data) - These are the sites to visit to find the sequence and/or structure records for your protein of interest.

☐ Sequence Features (61) (http://bioinformatics.ca/links_directory/category/ protein/sequence-features) - This section includes links to tools which can predict primary sequence features for the residues of a protein.

☐ Sequence Retrieval (29) (http://bioinformatics.ca/links_directory/category/protein/sequence-retrieval) - These resources include links to protein sequence retrieval tools including BLAST, EMBOSS, Entrez, and SRS.

Sequence Comparison [Source: (http://bioinformatics.ca/links_directory/category/sequence comparison)]

Tools and resources for the comparison of sequences (nucleic acid or protein) including sequence similarity searching, alignment tools, classification and general comparative genomics resources.

RSS Feed (bioinformatics.ca/links_directory/category/sequence-comparison/feed)

Compact View (http://bioinformatics.ca/links_directory/category/sequence-comparison? Mode=compact)

Sort by Links Directory Index (http://bioinformatics.ca/links directory/category/sequence-comparison? sort=citation count)

DOWNLOAD List as XML (http://bioinformatics.ca/links_directory/xml/category/89788?download=true) List as JSON (http://bioinformatics.ca/links_directory/json/category/89788?download=true) List as TSV (http://bioinformatics.ca/links_directory/tsv/category/89788?download=true) List as CSV (http://bioinformatics.ca/links_directory/csv/category/89788?download=true)

⚙ Hide Resources (9) (http://bioinformatics.ca/links_directory/category/sequence-comparison?filter=databases%2Ctools)
☰ Hide Databases (20) (http://bioinformatics.ca/links_directory/category/sequence-comparison?filter=resources%2Ctools) ⚙ Hide Tools (330) (http://bioinformatics.ca/links_directory/category/sequence-comparison?filter=resources%2Cdatabases)

☐ Alignment Editing and Visualization (33) (http://bioinformatics.ca/links_directory/category/sequence-comparison/alignment-editing-and-visualization) - Tools for viewing, colouring, and editing sequence alignments.

☐ Analysis of Aligned Sequences(73) (http://bioinformatics.ca/links_directory/category/sequence-comparison/analysis-aligned-sequences) - Resources for the interpretation of the results of comparing sets of sequences includes tools for functional inference from multispecies comparisons.

☐ Comparative Genomics (50) (http://bioinformatics.ca/links_directory/category/sequence-comparison/comparative-genomics) - General resources for comparison of sequences and genomes.

☐ Multiple Sequence Alignments(84) (http://bioinformatics.ca/links_directory/category/sequence-comparison/multiple-sequence-alignments) - Resources for generating multiple sequence alignments from sets of sequences.

☐ Other Alignment Tools (19) (http://bioinformatics.ca/links_directory/category/sequence-comparison/other-alignment-tools) - Tools for aligning sets of sequences to a reference sequence (for example, cDNA to genomic).

☐ Pairwise Sequence Alignments(44) (http://bioinformatics.ca/links_directory/category/sequence-comparison/pair wise-sequence-alignments) - Methods and tools for aligning pairs of sequences.

☐ Similarity Searching and Classification (56) (http://bioinformatics.ca/links_directory/category/sequence-comparison/similarity-searching-and-classification) - Resources for retrieving sequences similar to your query. Also includes tools for searching for similar sequence profiles and classifying sequences.

DNA [Source: (http://bioinformatics.ca/links_directory/category/DNA)]

This category contains links to useful resources for DNA sequence analyses such as tools for comparative sequence analysis and sequence assembly. Links to programs for sequence manipulation, primer design, and sequence retrieval and submission are also listed here.

RSS Feed (http://bioinformatics.ca/links_directory/category/dna/feed)

Compact View (http://bioinformatics.ca/links_directory/category/dna?mode=compact)

Sort by Links Directory Index (http://bioinformatics.ca/links_directory/category/ dna?sort=citation count)

DOWNLOAD List as XML (http://bioinformatics.ca/links_directory/xml/category/89780?download=true) List as JSON (http://bioinformatics.ca/links_directory/json/category/89780?download=true) List as TSV (http://bioinformatics.ca/links_directory/tsv/category/89780?download=true) List as CSV (http://bioinformatics.ca/links_directory/csv/ category/89780?download=true)

Hide Resources (34) (http://bioinformatics.ca/links_directory/category/dna?filter=databases%2Ctools) Hide Databases (128) (http://bioinformatics.ca/links_directory/category/

dna?filter=resources%2Ctools) ✱ Hide Tools (545) (http://bioinformatics.ca/links_directory/category/dna?filter=resources%2Cdatabases)

☐ Annotations (81) (http://bioinformatics.ca/links_directory/category/dna/_annotations) - This section contains tools and links related to genome annotation. Different sites provide automated and curated annotations. See also DNA: Gene Prediction, DNA: Sequence Features.

☐ Databases (77) (http://bioinformatics.ca/links_directory/category/dna/databases) - This section contains databases of coding/non-coding DNA, nucleic acid and gene structure, transcriptional regulator sites, transcription factors, molecular probes, and primers.

☐ DNA and Genomic Analysis (70) (http://bioinformatics.ca/links_directory/category/dna/dna-and-genomic-analysis) - These resources are free, publicly available, multi-purpose tools for genomic and DNA sequence analysis. Links to resources for sequence presentation, manipulation tasks, and format conversion are found here. As well, tools for genomic data analysis are included.

☐ Gene Prediction (43) (http://bioinformatics.ca/links_directory/category/dna/gene-prediction) - This section includes links to gene prediction programs for both eukaryotic and prokaryotic organisms. Resources that evaluate the available gene predicting programs are also included.

☐ Mapping and Assembly (33) (http://bioinformatics.ca/links_directory/category/dna/mapping-and-assembly) - This section contains links to mapping data, contig assembly, and genome resources used by many genome sequencing projects.

☐ Methylation Analysis (1) (http://bioinformatics.ca/links_directory/category/dna/methylation-analysis) - This section features tools and databases for DNA methylation analysis.

☐ Phylogeny Reconstruction (59) (http://bioinformatics.ca/links_directory/category/dna/phylogeny-reconstruction) - This section contains links to tools and databases for phylogeny reconstruction, including taxonomy resources.

☐ Sequence Polymorphisms (66) (http://bioinformatics.ca/links_directory/category/dna/sequence-polymorphisms) - Links to various sequence polymorphism databases and resources concerning SNPs, short deletion, insertion polymorphisms and other unique genomic features.

☐ Sequence Retrieval and Submission (31) (http://bioinformatics.ca/links_directory/category/dna/sequence-retrieval-and-submission) - This section contains links for sequence retrieval and submission. The resources include alignment, sequence analysis as well as visualization tools.

☐ Structure and Sequence Feature Detection (166) (http://bioinformatics.ca/links_directory/category/dna/structure-and-sequence-feature-detection) - This section contains links to tools for DNA structure prediction and finding regulatory sequences, the base composition, binding sites and motifs in your sequence of interest.

☐ Tools For the Bench (80) (http://bioinformatics.ca/links_directory/category/dna/tools-bench) - These links contain programs which can create restriction enzyme maps for your sequence of interest. Also included are tools for the design of oligonucleotide probes and PCR primers.

RNA [Source: (http://bioinformatics.ca/links_directory/category/RNA)]

Resources include links to sequence retrieval programs, structure prediction and visualization tools, motif search programs, and information on various functional RNAs.

🔊 RSS Feed (http://bioinformatics.ca/links_directory/category/rna/feed)

⇌ Compact View (http://bioinformatics.ca/links_directory/category/rna?mode=compact)

⇌ Sort by Links Directory Index (http://bioinformatics.ca/links_directory/category/rna?sort=citation count)

DOWNLOAD ⬇ List as XML (http://bioinformatics.ca/links_directory/xml/category/89784?download=true) ⬇ List as JSON (http://bioinformatics.ca/links_directory/json/category/89784?download=true) ⬇ List as TSV (http://bioinformatics.ca/links_directory/tsv/category/89784?download=true) ⬇ List as CSV (http://bioinformatics.ca/links_directory/csv/category/89784?download=true)

⌀ Hide Resources (6) (http://bioinformatics.ca/links_directory/category/rna?filter=databases%2Ctools) ≡ Hide Databases (54) (http://bioinformatics.ca/links_directory/category/rna?filter=resources%2Ctools) ✱ Hide Tools (178) (http://bioinformatics.ca/links_directory/category/rna?filter=resources%2Cdatabases)

☐ Databases (35) (http://bioinformatics.ca/links_directory/category/rna/databases) - This section contains databases of RNA sequences.

☐ Functional RNAs (58) (http://bioinformatics.ca/links_directory/category/rna/functional-rnas) - This section contains information on various functional RNAs. Included are tRNAs, non-coding RNAs, rRNAs and snoRNAs.

☐ General Resources (16) (http://bioinformatics.ca/links_directory/category/rna/general-resources) - A collection of links to various RNA resource hubs in addition to RNA-related technical resources and databases.

☐ Motifs (31) (http://bioinformatics.ca/links_directory/category/rna/motifs) - Included are RNA motif search programs to help analyze recurrent subsets of nucleotide arrangements in secondary or tertiary structure.

☐ Sequence Retrieval (13) (http://bioinformatics.ca/links_directory/category/rna/sequence-retrieval) - Resources in this section include sequence retrieval programs such as BLAST, EMBOSS, and Entrez.

☐ Structure Prediction, Visualization, and Annotation (85) (http://bioinformatics.ca/links_directory/category/rna/structure-prediction-visualization-and-annotation) - Contains links to applications for the visualization, prediction, and design of RNA molecules including siRNAs, secondary structure, and folding kinetics.

Other Molecules [Source: (http://bioinformatics.ca/links_directory/category/ other molecules)]

Bioinformatics tools related to molecules other than DNA, RNA, and protein. This category will include resources for the bioinformatics of small molecules as well as for other biopolymers including carbohydrates and metabolites.

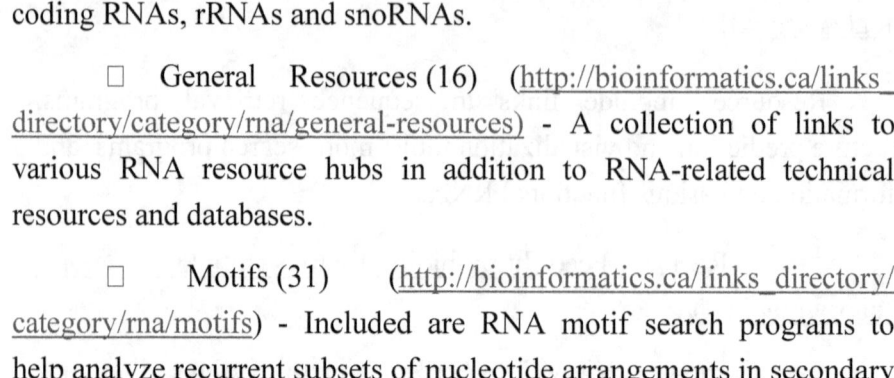 RSS Feed (http://bioinformatics.ca/links_directory/category/other-molecules/feed)

⇄ Compact View (http://bioinformatics.ca/links_directory/category/other-molecules?mode=compact)

⇄ Sort by Links Directory Index (http://bioinformatics.ca/links_directory/category/other-molecules?sort=citation count)

DOWNLOAD ⬇ List as XML (http://bioinformatics.ca/links_directory/xml/category/89789?download=true) ⬇ List as JSON (http://bioinformatics.ca/links_directory/json/category/89789?download=true) ⬇ List as TSV (http://bioinformatics.ca/links_directory/tsv/category/89789?download=true) ⬇ List as CSV (http://bioinformatics.ca/links_directory/csv/category/89789?download=true)

⌀ Hide Resources (7) (http://bioinformatics.ca/links_directory/category/other-molecules?filter=databases%2Ctools) ≡ Hide Databases (48) (http://bioinformatics.ca/links_directory/category/other-molecules?filter=resources%2Ctools) ✱ Hide Tools (78) (http://bioinformatics.ca/links_directory/category/other-molecules?filter=resources%2Cdatabases)

☐ Carbohydrates (13) (http://bioinformatics.ca/links_directory/category/other-molecules/carbohydrates) - Tools for dealing with the bioinformatics of carbohydrate structures

☐ Compounds (21) (http://bioinformatics.ca/links_directory/category/other-molecules/compounds) - Tools and resources for the analysis of compounds

☐ Databases (37) (http://bioinformatics.ca/links_directory/category/other-molecules/databases) - This section contains databases of biologically relevant enzymes, molecules and drugs.

☐ Enzymes (2) (http://bioinformatics.ca/links_directory/category/other-molecules/enzymes) - Tools and resources for the analysis of biologically important classes of enzymes.

☐ Metabolites (21) (http://bioinformatics.ca/links_directory/category/other-molecules/metabolites) - Tools and resources for the analysis of metabolites

☐ Peptides (9) (http://bioinformatics.ca/links_directory/category/other-molecules/peptides) - Tools and resources for the prediction and analysis of peptides.

☐ Small Molecules, Immunoglobulins (30) (http://bioinformatics.ca/links_directory/category/other-molecules/small-molecules-immunoglobulin's) - Tools for dealing with the bioinformatics of small molecules and immunoglobulin's.

Expression [Source: (http://bioinformatics.ca/links_directory/category/expression)]

Links to tools for predicting the expression, alternative splicing, and regulation of a gene sequence are found here. This section also contains links to databases, methods, and analysis tools for protein expression, SAGE, EST, and microarray data.

🔊 RSS Feed (http://bioinformatics.ca/links_directory/category/expression/feed)

⇄ Compact View (http://bioinformatics.ca/links_directory/category/expression? mode=compact)

⇄ Sort by Links Directory Index (http://bioinformatics.ca/links_directory/category/ expression? sort=citation count)

DOWNLOAD ⬇ List as XML (http://bioinformatics.ca/links_directory/xml/category/89787?download=true) ⬇ List as JSON (http://bioinformatics.ca/links_directory/json/category/89787?download=true) ⬇ List as TSV (http://bioinformatics.ca/links_directory/tsv/category/89787?download=true) ⬇ List as CSV (http://bioinformatics.ca/links_directory/csv/category/89787?download=true)

⊘ Hide Resources (13) (http://bioinformatics.ca/links_directory/category/expression?filter=databases%2Ctools) ☰ Hide Databases (83) (http://bioinformatics.ca/links_directory/category/expression?filter=resources%2Ctools) ✿ Hide Tools (400) (http://bioinformatics.ca/links_directory/category/expression?filter=resources%2Cdatabases)

☐ cDNA, EST, SAGE (43) (http://bioinformatics.ca/links_directory/category/expression/cdna-est-sage) - Links to clone repositories, expression data, methods, and tools for expressed sequence tags (EST) and serial analysis of gene expression (SAGE) are found here.

☐ Databases (34) (http://bioinformatics.ca/links_directory/category/expression/databases) - This section contains databases of microarray data and other gene expression data.

☐ Gene Regulation (156) (http://bioinformatics.ca/links_directory/category/expression/gene-regulation0 - This section contains links to tools and resources for predicting gene regulation, such as promoter analysis and analysis of ChIP-Seq data. It also contains tools and resources for evaluation of the regulatory role of miRNA and other functional RNA molecules.

☐ Gene Set Analysis (46) (http://bioinformatics.ca/links_directory/category/expression/gene-set-analysis) - Tools for evaluation of gene sets generated through any number of expression technologies.

☐ Networks (28) (http://bioinformatics.ca/links_directory/category/expression/networks) - This section contains links for integrating and analyzing a variety of biological data sets.

☐ Protein Expression (23) (http://bioinformatics.ca/links_directory/category/expression/protein-expression) - This section contains links to protein expression data and resources for analysis of data including 2D gels.

☐ Splicing (26) (http://bioinformatics.ca/links_directory/category/expression/splicing) - There are links that deal with the splicing of gene sequences in this section.

☐ Transcript Expression Analysis(140) (http://bioinformatics.ca/links_directory/ category/expression/transcript-expression-analysis) - This section contains links to microarray methods, standards for microarray data, and analysis tools for expression data from other high-throughput technologies. Also contains tools for transcript expression in general.

Literature [Source: (http://bioinformatics.ca/links_directory/category/literature)]

Links to resources related to published literature, including tools to search for articles and through literature abstracts. Additional text mining resources, open access resources, and literature goldmines are also listed.

🔊 RSS Feed (http://bioinformatics.ca/links_directory/category/literature/feed)

⇌ Compact View (http://bioinformatics.ca/links_directory/category/literature?mode= compact)

⇌ Sort by Links Directory Index (http://bioinformatics.ca/links_directory/category/ literature? sort=citation count)

DOWNLOAD ⬇ List as XML (http://bioinformatics.ca/links_directory/xml/category/89790?download=true) ⬇ List as JSON (http://bioinformatics.ca/links_directory/json/category/89790?download=true) ⬇ List as TSV (http://bioinformatics.ca/links_directory/tsv/category/89790?download=true) ⬇ List as CSV (http://bioinformatics.ca/links_directory/csv/category/ 89790?download=true)

⊘ Hide Resources (6) (http://bioinformatics.ca/links_directory/category/literature? filter=databases%2Ctools) ☰ Hide Databases (28) (http://bioinformatics.ca/links_directory/category/literature?filter=resources%2Ctools) ✲ Hide Tools (59) (http://bioinformatics.ca/links_directory/category/literature?filter=resources%2Cdatabases)

☐ Databases (13) (http://bioinformatics.ca/links_directory/category/literature/databases) - This section contains databases of literature texts or data mined from literature sources.

☐ Goldmines (5) (http://bioinformatics.ca/links_directory/category/literature/goldmines) - Links to literature or lists of literature that provide a wealth of bioinformatics-related information or a good overview of components of the field.

☐ Open Access Resources (5) (http://bioinformatics.ca/links_directory/category/literature/open-access-resources) - Links to literature resources that are freely available to all.

☐ Search Tools (12) (http://bioinformatics.ca/links_directory/category/literature/search-tools) - Links to resources facilitating searching for articles of interest.

☐ Text Mining and Semantics (58) (http://bioinformatics.ca/links_directory/category/literature/text-mining-and-semantics) -

Links to tools for more complex searching and for making connections between text and other scientific information. This section focuses specifically on text such as scientific publications, article abstracts, or NCBI GenBank records. It also covers the role of growing field of semantic web content in biological data integration.

Chapter 12: INVALUABLE ACCESS TO TIME SAVING WEB TUTORIALS, TOOLS AND RESOURCES

Web Tutorials

There are thousands of bioinformatics and genomics resources that are free and publicly accessible. However, trying to find the right resource for your need, and learn how to use the often complex features and functions can be difficult. The book explores ways that you can quickly find and effectively learn how to use resources. It will include a tour of example resources, organized by categories such as Algorithms and Analysis tools, expression resources, genome browsers (General, Eukaryotic and Prokaryotic/Microbial), Literature and text mining resources, and resources focused on nucleotides, proteins, pathways, disease and variation. At the end of the chapter, you'll learn how to find resources with the Open Helix **free search interface** (http://www.openhelix.com/index.shtml), learning to use resources with Open Helix **tutorials** (http://www.openhelix.com/cgi/tutorials.cgi) and a discussion of additional methods of learning about resources.

You'll learn:

i. about several bioscience resources in various subject categories
ii. to find the right resource using the Open Helix search interface
iii. how to quickly learn to use resources through Open Helix tutorials,

iv. site documentation, mailing lists, etc.
v. about additional resources for discovering resources to meet your research needs

Find, Learn and Deliver

Find **the most relevant resource quickly and easily:** Open Helix searches hundreds of genomics resources, tutorial suites, and other material to deliver the most relevant resources in seconds. Search at Open Helix saves time and effort--avoid massive generalized searches or hunting and pecking through lists of databases. With a subscription, you'll be able to access all the Open Helix training materials delivered in search results.

Learn **how to use the resource:** Save time and money with a subscription to nearly 100 Open Helix online tutorial suites:

i. You can independently, effectively and efficiently learn to use a resource.
ii. You and your staff can save time for your critical needs by relying on Open Helix tutorials to provide the introductory training on resources.
iii. You and your institution save time and money when teaching others by using the provided PowerPoint slides, suggested script, slide handouts, and exercises.

Deliver **breakthrough research:** More efficient use of the most relevant resources means quicker and more effective research. With a subscription, you and your institution can further enable breakthrough research. You can deliver Open Helix tutorial suites within your already existing information portal or through the Open Helix site.

The most effective and efficient way to leverage genomics resources

   i.   Quickly learn how to use a resource when you need it
   ii. Have a reference and teaching resource at your fingertips
   iii. Know you'll be using the most proven-effective training available
   iv. Have the confidence you have the best, most updated information
   v.   Have peace of mind you are using materials created by experts

Quickly learn how to use a resource when you need it - The 30-60 minute online narrated tutorials, which run in just about any browser, highlight and explain all the features and functionality needed to start using the resource effectively. The tutorials also include a "movie," which walks the user through a sample exercise while the narrator explains and completes each step. Use the tutorial to introduce yourself to a new resource, to view new features and functionality, or simply as a reference tool to refresh your memory of the resource.

Have a reference and teaching resource at your fingertips - In addition to the tutorials, you also receive useful training materials (http://openhelix.com/cgi/subscriptions.cgi?tab=3) which can save time and effort to create classroom content.

Know you'll be using the most proven-effective training available - You will get the most effective and efficient way to learn how to use genomic resources. Online learning has proven to be as effective as on-site training for genomics resources, with the added benefit of lower cost and convenient any-time access.

Have the confidences you have the best, most updated information - Open Helix updates its tutorial suites as the resources change, and add new tutorials suites all the time.

Have peaces of mind you are using materials created by experts - OpenHelix has been providing training on genomics resources for over six years. OpenHelix trainers all have PhDs in biological sciences, intimate knowledge of the resources, and have years of experience with on-site and online training. You can trust OpenHelix expertise since many of the top resource provider's contract with OpenHelix to provide their outreach and training.

Invaluable access to time saving content

An OpenHelix subscription gives you complete access to a catalog of 100 tutorial suites (http://www.openhelix.com/cgi/tutorials.cgi) in a wide range of categories (http://www.openhelix.com/cgi/tutorialCategory.cgi). The breadth and depth of the resources covered assures you'll have the tutorial suite on the resources you need to learn Each Tutorial Suite includes (see an example with one of our sponsored tutorial suites - http://www.openhelix.com/cgi/freeTutorials.cgi):

i. An **online narrated tutorial**, which runs in just about any browser, can be viewed from beginning to end or navigated using chapters and forward and backward sliders. The 30-60 minute tutorials highlight and explain all the features and functionality needed to start using the resource effectively. The tutorials also include a "movie," which walks the user through a sample exercise while the narrator explains and completes each step.

ii. Complete **PowerPoint slide set** with animations and suggested script.

iii. **Step-by-step exercises** for hands-on experience.

iv. PDF of slides for **handouts**

v. Access to all **new and updated tutorial suites**.

In addition to the subscription, all Open Helix users have the advantage of:

a) Using the OpenHelix **Search** function to quickly find and access the training materials you need.

b) Access to hundreds of brief video tips on features and functions of bioinformatics tools with the OpenHelix blog (http://blog.openhelix.com/) "tip-of-the-week" feature.

c) The OpenHelix Newsletter (http://www.openhelix.com/cgi/seminars.cgi?tab=5) giving you information on bioinformatics tools and resources, resource news, and updates on new and updated tutorials.

Washington University, USA - List of all Open Helix Tutorials (http://www.openhelix.com/cgi/createAccount.cgi)

This is the full list of tutorials offered by OpenHelix. Clicking on a tutorial name will display detailed information, together with a list of all available training materials. To get a list of all tutorials in a particular category, click on the category name or display all tutorials grouped by category (http://www.openhelix.com/cgi/tutorialCategory.cgi).

Table: List of all Open Helix Tutorials

Name	Description	Category	Resources
Allen Mouse Brain Atlas	Mapped gene expression data in mouse brain	Expression	Allen Mouse Brain Atlas
Alternative Splicing and Transcript Diversity (ASTD) database	A bioinformatics resource for alternative splice events and transcripts for human, mouse, and rat	Expression, Nucleotides, EBI	ASTD
ArrayExpress	A public repository for microarray gene expression data at the EBI	Expression, EBI	ArrayExpress
BiologicalNetworks	Analyze and visualize molecular interaction networks	Ye Olde Tutorials	BiologicalNetworks
BioMart	Management and querying of many types of biological data	Genome Databases (eu), Algorithms and Analysis, EBI	BioMart

Name	Description	Category	Resources
BioSystems	Database of Biological Systems	Pathways, NCBI	NCBI BioSystems
BLAST	Basic Local Alignment and Search Tool	Algorithms and Analysis, NCBI	NCBI BLAST
CGAP	Characterize the molecular genetic changes that cause a normal cell to become a cancer cell	Variation & Medical	CGAP
CleanEx	A Database of Heterogeneous Gene Expression Data Based on A Consistent Gene Nomenclature	Expression	CleanEx
ClustalW2	Performs multiple sequence alignments	Algorithms and Analysis, EBI	Clustal W
CMR	Comprehensive Microbial Resource	Genome Databases (pro), Nucleotides	TIGR Comprehensive Microbial Resource

Name	Description	Category	Resources
Complete Microbial Genomes	An extensive collection of data, resources and tools for prokaryotic genomic analysis	Genome Databases (pro), NCBI	Complete Microbial Genomes
Complete Microbial Genomes	An extensive collection of data, resources and tools for prokaryotic genomic analysis	Genome Databases (pro), NCBI	Complete Microbial Genomes
Consensus	A pattern and motif recognition program	Nucleotides, Proteins, Algorithms and Analysis	Consensus
Controlled Vocabularies	Standardized term lists that can enhance interactions with biological databases	Literature and Text Mining	Controlled Vocabularies (including Open Biomedical Ontologies)
Cytoscape	An open-source software platform used for visualization and analysis of molecular	Pathways	Cytoscape

Name	Description	Category	Resources
	interaction and network data		
DAVID	A tool that analyzes large lists of genes to provide biological meaning	Expression, Pathways	DAVID
dbGaP	A database of genotypes and phenotypes with extensive variation data and clinical details	Variation & Medical, NCBI	dbGaP
dbSNP	NCBI's SNP database	Variation & Medical, NCBI	NCBI dbSNP
DBTSS	Database of Transcrip-tional Start Sites	Expression, Nucleotides	DBTSS
DCODE	DCODE.org Comparative Genomics Deve-lopments, collec-tion of powerful comparative genomics tools	Algorithms and Analysis, NCBI	Dcode.org anthology of comparative genomic tools

Name	Description	Category	Resources
DGV: Database of Genomic Variants	Database of Genomic Variants, DGV, catalogs and displays structural variation in the human genome	Variation & Medical	DGV: Database of Genomic Variants
DrugBank	A chemoinformatics and bioinformatics resource	Genome Databases (eu)	DrugBank
ENCODE Data at UCSC	ENCODE Data at UCSC	Genome Databases (eu)	ENCODE Data Coordination Center at UCSC
ENCODE Foundations	ENCyclopedia of DNA Elements	Genome Databases (eu)	ENCODE Data Coordination Center at UCSC
Ensembl	Ensembl Genome Browser	Genome Databases (eu), EBI	Ensembl
Ensembl Legacy	Older version of Ensembl	Genome Databases	Ensembl

Name	Description	Category	Resources
	Genome Browser	(eu), Genome Databases (pro), EBI	
Entrez Gene	NCBI's Entrez tool for gene-centric information	Nucleotides, NCBI	NCBI Entrez Gene
Entrez Overview	Overview of NCBI's Entrez Search Resource	Miscellaneous, NCBI	NCBI Entrez
Entrez Protein	NCBI's Entrez Protein for amino acid-centric information	Proteins, NCBI	NCBI Protein database
FASTA	FASTA sequence algorithm	Algorithms and Analysis, EBI	FASTA
FlyBase	A resource for the genes, genome and molecular biology of Drosophila melanogaster and related species.	Genome Databases (eu)	FlyBase

Name	Description	Category	Resources
Functional Glycomics Gateway	The home for Functional Glycomics research	Expression, Proteins	Consortium for Functional Glycomics
GAD: Genetic Association Database	An archived database associating human genes and polymorphisms with diseases	Variation & Medical	GAD: Genetic Association Database
Galaxy	Analysis tools for researchers	Algorithms and Analysis	Galaxy
GBrowse	GBrowse User Introductory Tutorial	Genome Databases (eu), Genome Databases (pro)	GBrowse
Gene Expression Omnibus (GEO)	A gene expression / molecular abundance repository and a curated, online resource for gene expression data	Expression, Algorithms and Analysis, NCBI	Gene Expression Omnibus (GEO)
GeneMANIA	GeneMANIA:	Proteins,	GeneMANI

Name	Description	Category	Resources
	Fast Gene Function Predictions	Pathways	A
Gene Ontology	Gene Ontology controlled vocabularies in biology	Literature and Text Mining	Gene Ontology (GO)
GeneSNPs	An integrated view of gene structure and SNP variations	Ye Olde Tutorials	GeneSNPs
GeneTests	GeneTests, a current, comprehensive genetic testing resource	Ye Olde Tutorials	GeneTests
Genetics Home Reference	A collection of data describing the effects of genetic variability on human health and disease	Variation & Medical	Genetics Home Reference
GenMAPP	A freely available open source software application for visualizing microarray data	Pathways	GenMAPP- -Gene Microarray Pathway Profiler

Name	Description	Category	Resources
	in the context of biological pathways.		
GenoCAD	Computer-Assisted Design software for synthetic biology	Nucleotides	GenoCAD
GenoCAD Advanced Topics	Computer-Assisted Design software for synthetic biology	Nucleotides	GenoCAD
Genome Variation Server (GVS)	A database providing rapid access to human genotype data and analysis tools.	Variation & Medical	GVS
GENSAT	Provides an extensive amount of high quality images of gene expression in the central nervous system of the mouse.	Expression, NCBI	GENSAT
Gibbs Motif Sampler	A motif finder and analysis tool	Nucleotides, Proteins, Algorithms and	Gibbs

Name	Description	Category	Resources
		Analysis	
GoMiner	Ascribe biological significance to large lists of genes by annotating them with their corresponding GO categories	Algorithms and Analysis	GoMiner
Gramene	A resource on rice and other grass genomes	Genome Databases (eu)	Gramene
HapMap	HapMap, a database and analysis resource of human variation	Variation & Medical	HapMap
iHOP	Information Hyperlinked Over Proteins text mining resource	Literature and Text Mining	iHOP
IntAct protein interaction database	IntAct is an open source database and analysis resource of protein interaction data	Proteins, Pathways, EBI	IntAct

Name	Description	Category	Resources
Integrated Microbial Genomes (IMG)	IMG is a powerful community resource for the comparative analysis and annotation of microbial genome data.	Genome Databases (pro)	IMG
Integrated Microbial Genomes with Microbiome samples (IMG/M)	IMG/M provides tools for analyzing the functional capability of microbial communities based on their metagenome sequence	Genome Databases (pro)	IMG/M
InterPro	A comprehensive protein signature resource	Proteins, Algorithms and Analysis, EBI	The InterPro Database
KEGG	KEGG, The Kyoto Encyclopedia of Genes and Genomes	Pathways	KEGG

Name	Description	Category	Resources
Madeline 2.0	Human pedigree diagram tools	Variation & Medical	Madeline 2.0
Map Viewer	Map Viewer Genome Browser from NCBI	Genome Databases (eu), NCBI	NCBI Map Viewer
MDscan	Motif Discovery scan for nucleotide and protein motifs	Nucleotides, Proteins, Algorithms and Analysis	MDscan
Melina II	A Web-Based Tool for Promoter Analysis	Nucleotides, Algorithms and Analysis	Melina II
MEME Algorithm	Multiple Expectation Maximum for Motif Elicitation	Nucleotides, Proteins, Algorithms and Analysis	MEME
MEME Suite GLAM2 Algorithm	Part of a motif discovery tool that can detect conserved motifs in a set of DNA or protein sequences.	Algorithms and Analysis	GLAM2

Name	Description	Category	Resources
MEME Suite Overview	Motif-based sequence analysis tools	Algorithms and Analysis	MEME
MEME Suite Sequence Annotation Tools	MEME suite motif finding and annotating tools	Algorithms and Analysis	MEME
MEME Suite TOMTOM and GOMO algorithms	Motif discovery tool that can detect conserved motifs in a set of DNA or protein sequences that you provide	Algorithms and Analysis	MEME
MINT	Molecular Interaction Database	Proteins, Pathways	MINT
miRBase	microRNA sequences, targets and gene nomenclature	Nucleotides	miRBase
MMDB	Molecular Modeling Database at NCBI	Proteins, NCBI	MMDB
Mouse Genome Informatics	The Mouse Genome Informatics	Genome Databases (eu)	Mouse Genome Informatics

Name	Description	Category	Resources
(MGI)	resource provides data, tools, and analyses for the mouse model organism.		(MGI)
NCBI Overview	Home to many commonly used publicly available databases and tools in molecular biology.	Miscellaneous, NCBI	Database resources of the National Center for Biotechnology Information
NIEHS SNPs	National Institute for Environmental Health Sciences Environ-mental Genome Project (EGP) SNPs	Variation & Medical	NIEHS SNPs Program
OMIM	Online Mendelian Inheritance in Man (OMIM): A database of human genes, genetic diseases and disorders	Variation & Medical	OMIM

Name	Description	Category	Resources
Overview of Genome Browsers	Various Genome Browsers examined	Genome Databases (eu), Genome Databases (pro)	GBrowse IMG Ensembl NCBI Map Viewer
Pathway Interaction Database	A resource of pathway and network data and displays	Proteins, Pathways	NCI / Nature Pathway Interaction Database
Pfam	Protein Domain families	Proteins	Pfam
PhenomicDB	Phenotypes database	Expression, Variation & Medical	PhenomicDB
PlantGDB	Plant Genome Database	Genome Databases (eu)	PlantGDB
Primer3	Pick primers from a DNA sequence.	Nucleotides, Algorithms and Analysis	Primer3
PROSITE	Database of protein domains, families and functional sites	Proteins	PROSITE

Name	Description	Category	Resources
PubMatrix	PubMatrix, an on-line tool for multiplex literature mining of the PubMed database.	Literature and Text Mining	PubMatrix
PubMed	PubMed access to biomedical research literature	Literature and Text Mining, Variation & Medical, NCBI	NCBI PubMed
Rat Genome Database (RGD)	Rat Genome Database	Genome Databases (eu)	Rat Genome Database (RGD)
RCSB PDB	RCSB Protein Data Bank	Proteins	RCSB PDB
Reactome	Knowledgebase of biological processes	Pathways	Reactome
Reactome Legacy	Older version of the current Reactome knowledgebase of biological processes.	Pathways	Reactome
RefSeq	Provides molecular	Nucleotides, NCBI	RefSeq

Name	Description	Category	Resources
	sequence records to help locate gene and protein data.		
Saccharomyces Genome Database (SGD)	Saccharomyces Genome Database	Genome Databases (eu)	SGD
SeattleSNPs	Human SNPs in genes	Variation & Medical	SeattleSNPs
SMART	Protein domain annotation and analysis of domain architectures	Proteins	SMART
STRING	known and predicted protein-protein interactions	Literature and Text Mining, Proteins, Pathways	STRING
Structural Biology Knowledgebase	The Protein Structure Initiative Structural Biology Knowledgebase	Proteins	The Protein Structure Initiative Structural Biology Knowledgebase

Name	Description	Category	Resources
TAIR	The Arabidopsis Information Resource	Genome Databases (eu)	The Arabidopsis Information Resource (TAIR)
Textpresso	Text-mining the biological literature	Literature and Text Mining	Textpresso
UCSC Archaeal Genome Browser	Provides you with many research and analysis tools that can be used to examine the genomes of more than 50 microbial species from the domain archaea.	Genome Databases (pro)	The UCSC Archaeal Genome Browser
UCSC Genome Browser: An Introduction	The UCSC Genome Browser Introduction	Genome Databases (eu), Algorithms and Analysis	UCSC Genome Browser
UCSC Genome Browser: Custom Tracks and	UCSC Genome Browser advanced topics	Genome Databases (eu), Algorithms and Analysis	UCSC Genome Browser

Name	Description	Category	Resources
Table Browser			
UCSC Genome Browser: The Additional Tools	Additional tools at the UCSC Genome Browser	Algorithms and Analysis, Expression, Genome Databases (eu), Nucleotides, Proteins	UCSC Genome Browser
UniProt	UniProt, Universal Protein Resource	Proteins, Algorithms and Analysis	UniProt
VBRC	The Viral Bioinformatics Resource Center	Genome Databases (pro), Algorithms and Analysis	VBRC
Viral Genomes at NCBI	Viral genome resources including single-stranded or double-stranded RNA or DNA viruses	Genome Databases (pro), NCBI	NCBI Viral Resources

Name	Description	Category	Resources
VisANT	A web-based or downloadable software platform used for visualization and analysis of networks and interaction pathways	Pathways	VisANT
VISTA	Tools for Comparative Genomics	Algorithms and Analysis, Expression, Nucleotides, Variation & Medical	VISTA
World Tour of Genomics Resources	A World Tour of Genome Resources for finding and learning the right resource for your needs.	Algorithms and Analysis, Expression, Genome Databases (eu), Genome Databases (pro), Literature and Text Mining, Miscellaneo	UCSC Genome Browser

Name	Description	Category	Resources
		us, Nucleotides, Pathways, Proteins, Variation & Medical	
WormBase	molecular and genetic information on Caenorhabditis elegans and related species	Genome Databases (eu)	WormBase
WormBase	molecular and genetic information on Caenorhabditis elegans and related species	Genome Databases (eu)	WormBase
XplorMed	eXploring Medline abstracts	Literature and Text Mining	XplorMed
ZFIN	The Zebra fish Information Network	Genome Databases (eu)	ZFIN

Chapter 13: TUTORIALS AND VIDEOS

Tutorials

A great place to start, whether you come from a biological, physical or computational background is at Martin Vingron's superb online bioinformatics tutorial (http://lectures.molgen.mpg.de/). (Begin by choosing a section from the left-hand-side menu bar.)

Tom Smith and Don Emmeluth have produced a nice little exploration (http://www.angelfire.com/ga2/nestsite2/bioinform.html) of bioinformatics using NCBI resources and tools.

I recently stumbled upon a promising set of online lecture notes (http://www.genzentrum.lmu.de/) currently under construction by B. Steipe at the Genzentrum (Gene Center) (http://www.genzentrum.lmu.de/) at the Ludwig-Maximilians-Universität München (http://www.uni-muenchen.de/index.html) (University of Munich).

Chemistry for all: A defiantly frames-free chemistry tutorial site (http://dbhs.wvusd.k12.ca.us/Chem_Team_Index.html).

Mathematics for biologists: First of all, an almost completely painless introduction (https://gitso-outage.oracle.com/thinkquest) to the horrors of the quadratic equation by Peter Whalen, James Walker, and Drew Marticorena.

C. J. Schwarz (http://people.stat.sfu.ca/~cschwarz/) of the Department of Statistics and Acturial Science (http://www.stat.sfu.ca/), Simon Fraser University (http://www.sfu.ca/) has produced a course in statistics which is accompanied by set of sound, online PDF handouts (http://people.stat.sfu.ca/~cschwarz/Stat-650/).

Here is a great guide (http://www.helsinkifi/~jpuranen/links.html) to a whole array of statistical learning/teaching resources prepared by Juha Puranen (http://www.helsinkifi/~jpuranen/) of the University of Helsinki (http://www.helsinki.fi/) [English (http://www.helsinki.fi/english/)].

Computers for biologists : Programming for biologists : General introduction to biology for computer scientists : Estrella Mountain Community College (http://www. emc.maricopa.edu/) in the States offers this excellent short introduction (http://www2.estrellamountain.edu/faculty/farabee/BIOBK/BioBookintro.html) to biology (actually "The Nature of Science and Biology"). It's a great place for keyboard jockeys to start their journey to enlightenment. Thanks to Alex O'Neill for pointing out the broken link.

Genetics: The Dolan DNA Learning Center at Cold Spring Harbor has an outstanding interactive tutorial (http://www.dnaftb.org/1/) introducing genetics. To take full advantage of the multimedia elements you should download the Flash (http://www.adobe.com/products/flashruntimes.html) and Real (http://www.real.com/) players.

Molecular biology for computer scientists: The Institute of Arable Crop Research Beginner's Guide to Molecular Biology (http://www.rothamsted.bbsrc.ac.uk/ notebook/courses/guide/).

Protein chemistry for computer scientists: Unilever Education Advanced Series tutorial on proteins (http://www.schoolscience.co.uk/content/5/chemistry/proteins/index.html).

Cell biology for computer scientists: The University of Arizona (http://www.arizona.edu/) has made available a high-quality tutorial in cell biology (http://www.biology.arizona.edu/cell_bio/cell_bio.html). Not only does it cover the facts, but it also attempts to introduce some of the philosophy of the field---recommended. Even better, it's also available *en Español* (http://www.biologia.arizona.edu/cell/cell.html) and *in Italiano* (http://www.biologia-it.arizona.edu/cell_bio/cell_bio.html).

Once you've worked your way through that you might like to see some scanning electron microscope images (http://www.heuserlab.wustl.edu/v2.0/images/galleries/index.shtml) of some of the structures you've read about taken by members of John Heuser's lab (http://www.heuserlab.wustl.edu/v2.0/heuser-cv.shtml).

Evolution for computer scientists: Bob Patterson maintains his "Darwiniana" (http://hometown.aol.com/darwinpage/) with amazing diligence.

Bioinformatics Tutorials

Introduction to Bioinformatics

1) Bioinformatics (Genomics) (http://post.queensu.ca/~forsdyke/bioinfor.htm)

2) Biocomputing in a Nutshell. (http://www.techfak.uni-bielefeld.de/bcd/ForAll/Basics)

3) Biologist's Guide to Internet Resources

4) Computational Molecular Biology Course (http://cmb.washington.edu/)

5) Course on Bioinformatics (http://www.cbi.pku.edu.cn/Doc/)

6) EMBNet Biocomputing Tutorials (http://www.hgmp.mrc.ac.uk/Embnetut/Universi/embnettu.html)

7) Finding the genes in the genomic sequences (http://helpdesk.ugent.be/webhosting/rugac.php)

8) The Genetic Programming Tutorial (http://geneticprogramming.com/)

9) Jose R. Valverde's training course documents (http://www.es.embnet.org/Doc/)

10) Principles of Computational Biology, Steven Salzberg. (http://www.cs.jhu.edu/~salzberg/cs439.html)

11) Principles of Protein Structure Using the Internet (http://www.cryst.bbk.ac.uk/PPS2/course/)

12) Practical Course "Bioinformatics: Computer Methods in Molecular Biology" (http://www.icgeb.trieste.it/net/courses/bioinfo98.html)

13) Sequence analysis course (José R, Valverde, EMBNet/CNB) (http://www.es.embnet.org/Doc/ECJ/ECJ-1999-01/course/cnb/)

14) Bioinformatics (http://post.queensu.ca/~forsdyke/bioinfor.htm) - An excellent review on genetic code and information processing

15) Molecular Sequence Analysis (http://www.sequenceanalysis.com/) - Introductory sequence analysis by Andrew S Louka

16) Homology Modelling (http://swift.embl-heidelberg.de/course/) - Protein and homology modelling for beginners

17) Biocompanion (http://www.doelz.com/) - Tutorial for sequence analysis

18) Bioinformatics and Genomic Analysis (http://www.blc.arizona.edu/courses/bioinformatics/) - Link to graduate student course at the university of Arizona

19) EMBnet Biocomputing Tutorials - Introduction (http://www.hgmp.mrc.ac.uk/Embnetut/universl/index.html)

20) Integrative Bioinformatics: Practical Kinetic Modeling of Biological Systems (http://www.bioinformaticsservices.com/bis/resources/cybertext/IBcont.html)

21) Biocomputing For Everyone ! (http://www.techfak.uni-bielefeld.de/bcd/ForAll/welcome.html)

22) The Biocomputing Glossary (http://www.cryst.bbk.ac.uk/BCD/bcdgloss.html)

23) Computational Biology Course, Martin Tompa (http://courses.cs.washington.edu/courses/cse527/00wi/)

24) Course Distance Learning in Bioinformatics (http://130.88.90.2:8900/)

25) Functional genomics glossaries (http://ihome.cuhk.edu.hk/~b400559/glossaries.html)

26) How to become a bioinformatics expert (http://www.techfak.uni-bielefeld.de/bcd/ForAll/Econom/study.html)

27) Internet for biologists (http://biobase.dk/Embnetut/Ifb/ifb_intr.html)

28) Jose R. Valverde's 'dirty' training course documents (http://www.es.embnet.org/Doc/Training/)

29) Algorithms in Molecular Biology (University of Washington) (http://www.cs.washington.edu/education/cources/590bi/98w/)

30) Protein Sequence Analysis in the Genomic Era (http://lipid.biocomp.unibo.it/school/)

31) Protein sequence and structure analysis : A practical guide. (http://www.biochem.ucl.ac.uk/bsm/dbbrowser/jj/)

32) Topics of Evolutionary Computation (http://www.evalife.dk/index.php?lefturl=/eacourse2000/topicsofEC2000.php)

33) VSNS BioComputing Division (http://www.techfak.uni-bielefeld.de/bcd/welcome.html)

34) Bioinformatics (http://twod.med.harvard.edu/seqanal/index.html) - Primer on biosequence comparisons

35) Algorithms in Molecular Biolgy (http://www.math.tac.ac.il/~rshamir/algmb/algmb98.html) - Excellent for learning bascis about many bioinfo tools

36) Biocomputing (http://www.hgmp.mrc.ac.uk/Embnetut/Universi/embnettu.html) - Biocomputing tutorial at EBI

37) Bioinforamtics Training Resources (http://www.med.nyu.edu/customerror/ 404) - Links to an excellent selection of bioinformatics tools training at NYU

38) DNA composition and Exon prediction (http://www.pdg.cnb.uam.es/cursos/FVi2001/GenomAna/GeneIdentification/SearchContent/main.html) - Sequence based measures indicative of protein-coding function in genomic DNA

39) BCD BioComputing Tutorial (http://www.techfak.uni-bielefeld.de/bcd/ Curric/welcome.html)

Virtual Online Tutorials

1) Virtual Institute of Bioinformatics (http://www.bioinf.org/vibe/index.html) - **National University of Ireland, Ireland**

2) UNIX, GCG, SEQLAB and STADEN Tutorials (http://www.molbiol.ox.ac.uk/tutorials.shtml) - Oxford Univ., UK

3) BIOTOOLS96 (http://www.vsms.nottingham.ac.uk/vsms/biotools/index.html) - (Univ of) Nottingham, UK, Virtual school of molecular sciences

4) the principles of protein structure, using the internet (http://www.cryst.bbk.ac.uk/PPS2/top.html) - Birkback College (Univ of London), UK

5) Free online bioinformatics courses! s-star.org (http://s-star.org/main.htm)

6) Science and technology directory (http://www.technolgy-resource.co.uk/)

7) Weizmann Institute of Science Genome and Bioinformatics (http://www.bioinfo.wizmann.ac.il/bioinfo.html)

8) Algorithms for Molecular Biology (http://www.cs.tau.ac.il/~rshamir/algmb.html) - Bioinformatics course notes, Tel Aviv University (TAU, Israel)

9) Certificate Program in Bioinformatics (http://scpd.stanford.edu/home) - Standford

10) Courses Offered by BU Bioinformatics Program (http://engpub1.bu.edu/bioinfo/course.html)

11) ISCB Training information (http://www.iscb.org/training.html)

12) Penn Database Research Group- Classes (http://www.db.cis.upenn.edu/Classes/)

13) VSNS Biocomputing Division (http://www.techfak.uni-bielefeld.de/bcd/welcome.html)

14) Yale Bioinformatics -- Courses and Lectures (http://bioinfo.mbb.yale.edu/lectures/)

15) Bioinformtics Online lecture (I) (http://lectures.molgen.mpg.de/)

16) Bioinformtics Online lecture (II) (http://www.genzentrum.lmu.de/) or (http://www.Imb.uni-muenchen.de/groups/bioinformatics/bioifo.html)

17) MRes Biomolecular Sciences Lecture Notes: 1. The Gene and Bioinformatics (http://www.hgmp.mrc.ac.uk/~dcouncel/MRes/MRes.html)

18) MRes Biomolecular Sciences Lecture Notes: 2. The Gene and Bioinformatics

19) biocomputing, on internet (http://www.techfak.uni-bielefeld.de/bcd/ welcome.html) (Univ of) Bielefeld, Germany Virtual School of Natural Sciences

20) Sequence comparison (http://www.dir.univ-rouen.fr/~charras/seqcomp/) Universite de Rouen, France

21) A Guide to Molecular Sequence Analysis (http://www.sequenceanalysis.com/) National Hospital Univ of Oslo, Norway

22) Distant homologies: motifs, patterns, profiles (http://www.icgeb.trieste.it/net/courseware/Tiotle.htm) International Centre for Genetic Engineering and Biotechnology, Trieste, Italy

23) Virtual School of Natural Sciences BioComputing Division (http://merlin.mbcr.bcn.tme.edu:8001/bcdusa/welcome.html) - Virtual biocomputing course

24) Algorithms for Computational Biology (Advanced Topics #6, 236606) (http://bioinfo.cs.technion.ac.il/) - Israel Institute of Technology

25) CSE 590BI (http://www.cs.washington.edu/education/cources/590bi/) - Computational Biology, University of Washington

26) MBB 447b3 (747b3) Classes (http://bioinfo.mbb.yale.edu/course/classes/) - Yale

27) UCSC School of Engineering- Class Home Pages (https://courses.soe.ucsc.edu/classes/) - University of California at Santa Cruz

28) Virtual Bioinformatics Distance Learning (http://protein.uta.fi/bioinfo_courses) - Bioinformatics and Functional genomics courses offered by IMC Bioinformatics, University of Tampere

29) Tutorials using NCBI Bioinformtics Tools (http://www.angelfire.com/ga2/nestsite2/bioinform.html)

Practical Bioinformatics: Other lists of Bioinformatics Tutorials: More Tutorials Websites:

a) (http://spdbv.vital-it.ch/TheMolecularLevel/Matics/)

b) (http://www.mrc-lmb.cam.ac.uk/rlw/text/bioinfo_tuto/introduction.html)

c) (https://genome.ucsc.edu/training.html)

d) (http://mendel.informatics.indiana.edu/~yye/lab/teaching/fall 2011-I519.php)

e) (https://www.bits.vib.be/index.php/training/122-basic-bioinformatics)

f) (http://spdbv.vital-it.ch/TheMolecularLevel/Matics/)

g) (http://www.mrc-lmb.cam.ac.uk/rlw/text/bioinfo_tuto/introduction.html)

h) (https://genome.ucsc.edu/training.html)

i) (http://mendel.informatics.indiana.edu/yye/lab/teaching/fall2011-I519.php)

j) (https://www.bits.vib.be/index.php/training/122-basic-bioinformatics)

Imp basic concept: (https://www.bits.vib.be/index.php/training/122-basic-bioinformatics)

Imp-Bioinfo-Solutions: (http://www.thebioinformatica.com/onlinetutorial.htm)

Dummies: (http://spdbv.vital-it.ch/TheMolecularLevel/Matics/)

BioMedNet Research Tools : (http://research.bmn.com/)

CMS Molecular Biology Resource: (http://mbcf.dfci.harvard.edu/cmsmbr/)

Genetics Tutorials: (http://science.nhmccd.edu/biol/genetics.html)

Health Web/Genetics: (http://healthweb.org/browse.cfm?subjectid=42)

Morgan--GeneticTutorial : (http://morgan.rutgers.edu/morganWebFrames/ How_to_use/HTU_Frameset.html)

Online Mendelian Inheritance in Men (NCBI): (http://www.ncbi.nlm.nih.gov/sites/entrez?db=nucleotide)

Protein Information Resource : (http://pir.georgetown.edu/)

Talking Glossary of Genetic Terms: (http://www.genome.gov/glossary.cfm)

WWW Virtual Library-Genetics: (http://www.ornl.gov/sci/techresources/Human_Genome/genetics.shtml)

VIDEOS

Bioinformatics Tutorials & Articles are here. Tutorials classified laying foundation course for both science and computer students for those aspiring bioinformatics. List also includes Bioinformatics Tutorials & Articles related to various tools.

Foundation Tutorials for Bioinformatics Aspirants: Computer Tutorials for Science Stream Students

Introduction to computer Concepts:

a) (www.compume.com)

b) (www.grassrootsdesign.com)

c) (www.fayette.k12.il.us)

d) (www.glencoe.com)

e) (www.comedition.com)

f) (www.hitmill.com)

g) (www.pstcc.cc.tn.us)

Introduction to Internet:

a) (http://oac3.hsc.uth.tmc.edu/staff/snewton/tcp-tutorial/)

b) (http://www.cisco.com/)

c) (http://www.ch.embnet.org/bio-www/archive/florianW3_1.html) or (http://www.ch.embnet.org/error.html)

HTML Tutorials:

a) (www.htmlgoodies.com/)

b) (www.bfree.on.ca)

c) (www.pagetutor.com)

d) (www.davesite.com)

e) (www.webreference.com)

f) (www.pageresource.com)

g) (http://www.devry-phx.edu)

h) (http://www.ncsa.uiuc.edu)

i) (http://www.w3.org/)

j) (http://archive.ncsa.uiuc.edu)

Java Tutorials:

a) (java.sun.com/docs/books/tutorial/) (http://docs.oracle.com/javase/tutorial/)

b) (http://www.oracle.com/technetwork/java/index.html)

c) (javaboutique.internet.com/tutorials/)

d) (www.freewarejava.com/tutorials/index.shtml)

e) (www.javacoffeebreak.com/tutorials/)

f) (www.apl.jhu.edu/~hall/java/FAQs-and-Tutorials.html)

g) (http://www.javaworld.com/)

Perl Tutorials:

a) (www.devdaily.com/perl/)

b) (www.pageresource.com/cgirec/index2.htm)

c) (www.perl.com/pub/q/resources)

d) (www.perlmonks.org)

e) Perl for Biologists (Weizmann Institute) (http://www.uni-hohenheim.de/~rebhan/ perl/)

f) (www.webknowhow.net/dir/Perl/Tutorials/)

g) Perl for Biologists (http://www.mrc-lmb.cam.ac.uk/genomes/jong/perl_bio_book.html)

h) (savage.net.au/Perl-tutorials.html)

i) Welcome to the Bioperl Project ! (http://www.techfak.uni-bielefeld.de/bcd/Perl/Bio/welcome.html)

XML Tutorials:

a) (www.w3schools.com)

b) (www.zvon.org)

c) (www.xmlfiles.com)

d) (http://wdvl.internet.com/)

e) (www.finetuning.com)

SQL Tutorials:

a) (www.sqlcourse.com/)

b) (www.w3schools.com/sql/default.asp)

c) (www.sqlcourse2.com/)

d) (php.weblogs.com/sql_tutorial)

e) (perl.about.com/cs/beginningsql/)

f) (www.db.cs.ucdavis.edu/teaching/sqltutorial/)

Oracle Tutorials:

a) (www.hot-oracle.com/)

b) (www.oraclepower.com/)

c) (www.oraclepower.com)

d) (www.orafaq.org/suptutor.htm)

e) (www.vb-bookmark.com/OracleTutorial.html)

C & C++ Tutorials:

a) (www.cyberdiem.com/vin/learn.html)

b) (www.webwareindex.com/tutorials/C.html)

c) (www.cprogramming.com/tutorial.html)

d) (www.gustavo.net/programming/c__tutorials.shtml)

e) (http://www.dmoz.org/Computers/Programming/Languages/C/FAQs%2C_Help%2C_and_Tutorials/)

CGI Tutorials:

a) (www.htmlgoodies.com/beyond/cgi.html)

b) (www.cgi-resources.com/Documentation/CGI_Tutorials/)

c) (www.gustavo.net/programming/cgi.shtml)

d) (www.cgidir.com/Tutorials/)

e) (webdesign.about.com/cs/cgi/)

f) (http://www.cgi101.com/class/)

Visual Basic Tutorials:

a) (www.imt.net/~joe/matt/program/vb/Tutorials/)

b) (visualbasic.about.com/)

c) (visualbasic.ittoolbox.com/)

d) (members.tripod.com/~vkliew/vb.html)

e) (www.developerfusion.com/)

UNIX / Linux Tutorials:

a) (www.ee.surrey.ac.uk/Teaching/Unix/)

b) (webreference.com/programming/unix/)

c) (www.uwsg.iu.edu/uhelp/tutorials/toc.html)

d) (www.unixtools.com/tutorials.html)

e) (www.networkcomputing.com/unixworld/archives/tutorials.html)

f) (www.unix-manuals.com/)

g) (http://www.isu.edu/departments/comcom/unix/workshop/unixindex.html)

h) (http://www.ee.surrey.ac.uk/Teaching/Unix/)

i) (http://www.linuxnewbie.org/)

Science Tutorials for Computer Stream Students

Introduction to Biology:

a) (scidiv.bcc.ctc.edu)

b) (library.thinkquest.org/12413/)

c) (www.biology-online.org/tutorials/home.htm)

d) (www.lsic.ucla.edu/ls3/tutorials/)

e) (biology-online.org/)

f) **Cartoon Guide to Genetics** (http://www.amazon.com/exec/obidos/ASIN/0062730991/o/qid=957735943/sr=2-1/103-6986286-3259052)

g) (genomebiology.com/tutorials/)

h) (http://biomed.nus.sg/HIS/txt/menu/tacmenu.html)

i) **Tutorials in Molecular Biology** (http://locutus.lsic.ucla.edu/ls3/tutorials/)

j) (http://www.iacr.bbsrc.ac.uk)

k) (http://gened.emc.maricopa.edu/Bio/BIO181/BIOBK/BioBookgloss.html) - **BioBook Glossary**

l) (http://highveld.com) - Internet Directory of Biology and Biotechnology

m) (http://esg-www.mit.edu:8001/esgbio/7001main.html) - **ESG Biology Hyper-textbook Home Page**)

n) (http://web.ornl.gov/sci/techresources/Human_Genome/redirect.shtml) - **DOE Primer on Molecular Genetics**)

Introduction to Chemistry:

a) (www.chemistrycoach.com/tutorial.htm)

b) (http://users.rcn.com/bobsalsa/tutorial.htm)

c) (lrc-srvr.chemistry.ohio-state.edu/under/chemed/chemed.htm)

d) (http://www.unm.edu/~dmclaugh)

e) (http://www.chem.umr.edu)

f) (http://www.chem.umr.edu/Organic/index.html?organic+chemistry)

g) (http://turner.lamf.uwindsor.ca)

h) (http://www.chem.vt.edu)

i) Periodic table of the elements - (http://pearl1.lanl.gov/periodic/)

j) Interactive periodic table of the elements - (http://www.chemicalelements.com/)

Introduction to Biochemistry:

a) (www.biology.arizona.edu/biochemistry/biochemistry.html)

b) (www.umanitoba.ca/faculties/medicine/biochem/tutorials/)

c) (www.ahpcc.unm.edu/~aroberts/main/biochemistry_tutorials.htm)

d) (www.massey.ac.nz/~wwbioch/Prot/tutehome/tutepage.htm)

e) (http://xray.bmc.uu.se/Courses/Bke1/Tutorials/Tutorialindex.html)

f) (http://www.jonmaber.demon.co.uk/)

About DNA:

a) (http://biog-101-104.bio.cornell.edu/BioG101_104/tutorials/recomb_DNA.html)

b) (http://avery.rutgers.edu/WSSP/Tutorials/) (chime plug-in required)

c) (www.umass.edu/molvis/freichsman/)

d) (www.tutorgig.com/showurls.jsp?group=6732&index=0)

e) (www.scientific.org/tutorials/articles/riley/riley.html)

f) (www.tulane.edu/~biochem/nolan/lectures/rna/intro.htm)

g) (http://lenti.med.umn.edu/recombinant_dna/recombinant_flowchart.html)

h) DNA tutorial (http://www.101science.com/dna.html)

i) DNA from the beginning (http://www.dnaftb.org/)

j) Central Dogma Glossary (http://homepage.smc.edu/hodson_kent/Dictionary/ Glossary.htm)

About RNA:

a) (www.imsb.au.dk/~raybrown/)

b) (http://zombie.imsb.au.dk/~raybrown/)

c) (ndbserver.rutgers.edu/NDB/structure-finder/tutorials/full_ndb.dna.rna.res.html)

About Genome:

a) (http://genomebiology.com/tutorials/)

b) (http://www.genomeweb.com/)

c) (http://anatomy.med.unsw.edu.au/cbl/GENOME/tutorials.htm)

d) (http://rsat.ulb.ac.be/rsat/tutorials/tut_genome-scale-patser.html)

e) (home.uchicago.edu/~ebetran/guides.html)

f) Basic Genome Glossary - (http://www.nytimes.com/library/national/science/062600sci-genome-glossary.html)

g) Limited Genome Glossary - (http://homepage.smc.edu//hodson_kent/Dictionary/Glossary.htm)

h) Genome Glossary - (https://gitso-outage.oracle.com/thinkquest)

i) The Gene-School Glossary (https://gitso-outage.oracle.com/thinkquest)

j) Glossary of Genetic Terms (http://www.nhgri.nih.gov/DIR/VIP/Glossary/)

Video Tutorials

1) Imp: (http://digitalworldbiology.com/dwb/bioinformatics-tutorials)

2) (http://www.youtube.com/watch?v=UohaqFb8_ME)

3) (http://nihlibrary.nih.gov/Services/Bioinformatics/Pages/Biotutorials.aspx)

4) (https://www.countway.harvard.edu/menuNavigation/libraryServices/classes/videoTutorials.html)

5) (http://www.youtube.com/user/bimaticsblog)

6) (http://bioinformaticsonline.com/bookmarks/view/3868/next-generation-sequencing-ngs-tutorials

7) (http://mybio.wikia.com/wiki/Tutorials_in_bioinformatics)

8) (http://lectures.molgen.mpg.de/online_lectures.html)

9) (http://www.bioperl.org/wiki/HOWTO:Beginners#Abstract)

10) (http://www.ccg.unam.mx/~vinuesa/Bioinformatics_resources_web.html)

Important Tutorial Videos

(http://digitalworldbiology.com/dwb/bioinformatics-tutorials)

(http://www.youtube.com/watch?v=UohaqFb8_ME)

(http://nihlibrary.nih.gov/Services/Bioinformatics/Pages/Biotutorials.aspx)

(https://www.countway.harvard.edu/menuNavigation/librarySe rvices/classes/ videoTutorials.html)

(http://www.youtube.com/user/bimaticsblog)

(http://bioinformaticsonline.com/bookmarks/view/3868/next-generation-sequencing-ngs-tutorials)

(http://mybio.wikia.com/wiki/Tutorials_in_bioinformatics)

(http://lectures.molgen.mpg.de/online_lectures.html)

(http://www.bioperl.org/wiki/HOWTO:Beginners#Abstract)

(http://www.ccg.unam.mx/~vinuesa/Bioinformatics_resources_web.html)

Tutorial videos of bioinformatics

In recent years, biological web resources such as databases and tools have become more complex because of the enormous amounts of data generated in the field of life sciences. Traditional methods of distributing tutorials include publishing textbooks and posting web documents, but these static contents cannot adequately describe recent dynamic web services. Due to improvements in computer technology, it is now possible to create dynamic content such as video with minimal effort and low cost on most modern computers. The ease of creating and distributing video tutorials instead of static content improves accessibility for researchers, annotators and curators. This section focuses on online video repositories for educational and tutorial videos provided by resource developers and users. It also describes a project in Japan named Togo TV (http://togotv.dbcls.jp/en/) and discusses the production and distribution of high-quality tutorial videos, which would be useful to viewer, with examples. This article intends to stimulate and encourage researchers who develop and use databases and tools to distribute how-to videos as a tool to enhance product usability.

Recent advances in life sciences technology have dramatically changed the research style from hypothesis-driven research (bottom-up style) to data-driven research (top-down style). Current 'omics' projects have produced vast amounts of data that have been stored in various online databases. Simultaneously, many types of web tools have been developed to analyze the stored data. Traditional methods for distributing educational content include publishing textbooks and web documents. Although the contents of a textbook are sustainable, they quickly become obsolete because of frequent updates of web interfaces and improvement in web service functions.

Video Repositories

Several web services are already available for video distribution. YouTube is the most popular online video sharing service, and it contains many tutorial videos and lectures in many fields. Similarly, there are repository services such as Dailymotion and Vimeo (for more examples, see the Wikipedia article entitled 'List of video hosting services'). Most services are free to use, and any registered user can upload video. Live streaming services such as Ustream, Justin.tv and Stickam also exist. As the term 'live streaming' suggests, these services provide live streaming services for lectures, workshops, seminars and meetings that are recorded and may be played back at a later time.

In the scientific field, the *Journal of Visualized Experiments* has been published since 2006. It is a peer-reviewed, PubMed-indexed journal devoted to the publication of biological research in a video format. SciVee offers a comprehensive set of rich media solutions to enhance the discovery and collaboration of knowledge. It provides **Video and Podcasts** (standard videos and podcasts), **PubCast** (synchronized video abstracts of peer-reviewed articles), **PaperCast** (synchronized video abstracts of non-peer-reviewed articles), **SlideCast** (synchronized videos of slide presentations) and PosterCast (synchronized videos of posters or other conference presentations) in collaboration with scientists and researchers, as well as journals and publishers, societies, conference organizers, universities and research institutions. Dnatube is a community-based repository of scientific videos including educational materials, seminars and lectures. This site has over 5000 videos and 30 000 community members. Individual videos can be found using keyword search, category tags and topics.

Some universities and organizations also administer a video repository server, especially for providing lecture videos that are part of OpenCourseWare (OCW). The Massachusetts Institute of Technology (MIT) hosts MIT OCW and MIT World, and the University of Tokyo provides UT OCW. Academic Earth provides online courses of the world's top scholars from Harvard University and Stanford University among other top academic institutions. YouTube also has a special channel for education from colleges and universities named YouTube EDU, and another channel, Technology, Entertainment, Design (TED), delivers interesting lectures by respected individuals. A complete list of OCW websites is found at the OCW Consortium Website, and other useful services are listed in the Wikipedia article entitled 'List of educational video websites'.

In addition to repository-type services, delivery-type services named vodcasts (video podcasts) are available via Really Simple Syndication (RSS) technology. If a user subscribes to a vodcast program in a vodcast player such as iTunes, the contents of the program are automatically updated when new content arrives. Since the vodcast programs can be transferred to portable devices such as the iPod, iPhone or iPad, the user can watch them anytime, anywhere. Although vodcast programs are mainly focused on news, entertainment and fashion, educational programs are also provided. Indeed, some institutes have already used the podcast/vodcast for education. Apple collects and webcasts educational contents via the iTunes store called iTunes U.

Video Tutorials Provided by Resource Developers and Users: As noted earlier, the publishing of tutorial videos by some providers has increased as the creation and distribution costs of videos have decreased. For example, National Center for Biotechnology Information provides tutorial videos of some services both on the YouTube channel and on their server such as dbGaP, the database of Genotypes and Phenotypes, that archives and distributes the results of studies that have investigated the interaction of genotype and phenotype and PubMed that is a database of citations and abstracts for biomedical literature from MEDLINE and additional life sciences journals. Some projects in the European Bioinformatics Institute also distributed how-to videos for tools such as Ensembl that is genome databases for vertebrates and other eukaryotic species, QuickGO that is a fast web-based browser for Gene Ontology (GO) terms and annotations, and GOA, Gene Ontology Annotation, that provides high-quality GO annotations to proteins in the UniProt Knowledgebase and International Protein Index.

Not only service providers in national institutes but also individual service providers including relatively small communities distributed tutorial videos. Galaxy, a collaboration system for genomic research, is a highly functional and complex system, but the procedure is easily understandable because the developers provide tutorial videos on their website. Taverna, which is an open source and domain-independent workflow management system (a suite of tools used to design and execute scientific workflows and aid *in silico* experimentation), is also described in the tutorials in a video format. ATTED-II, which provides co-regulated gene relationships to estimate gene function, has YouTube channel for tutorials. There are many video tutorials provided by the database and tool developers.

In addition, educators and users of web resources who do not develop any databases or tools also contribute to the scientific community by providing tutorial videos. BITS, Bioinformatics Tutorials Series, are a collaboration work of the MIT Engineering and Science Libraries and Harvard's Countway Library. BIREC, Bioinformatics Information Resource and eLearning Center, also provides tutorial videos. **OpenHelix** provides over 100 well-organized tutorial suites including videos on web-based bioinformatics and genomic resources. It also has many tutorial videos in 'Tip of this week' tagging articles in the blog section. In addition to videos provided by organizations, a YouTube search by database or tool name will provide many tutorial videos produced by volunteers.

(http://bib.oxfordjournals.org/content/ 13/2/258.full#sec-3)

(http://bib.oxfordjournals.org/content/13/2/258. full#sec-13)

Togo TV: Online Tutorial Video Distribution Trial in Japan

To bridge the gap between service providers and users, we created and distributed tutorial videos of databases and web tools. We describe in this article, a methodology for making and distributing videos and elaborate on this methodology with examples. Togo TV ('Togo' means 'integration' in Japanese; pronunciation symbol is [toɯgoɯ]) that is one of the services in the Integrated Database Project in Japan (Figure 1) is a portal site of tutorial and lecture videos about bioinformatics resources. Although the original Togo TV site is mostly written in Japanese, there is the English interface for international users. The site contains our original videos and third-party videos from publicly available website such as YouTube. All contents provided by us are distributed under the Creative Commons Attribution 2.1 Japan license and also provided as vodcasts that can be viewed using a portable device and on YouTube. Although most of the contents are described in Japanese, there are 19 original programs in English, most of which explain a service developed in the Integrated Database Project such as TogoWS, which provides an integrated SOAP and REST APIs for interoperable bioinformatics Web services and OReFiL, which is an online resource finder for life science. We plan to expand our own English contents so as to enable our service to be used all over the world.

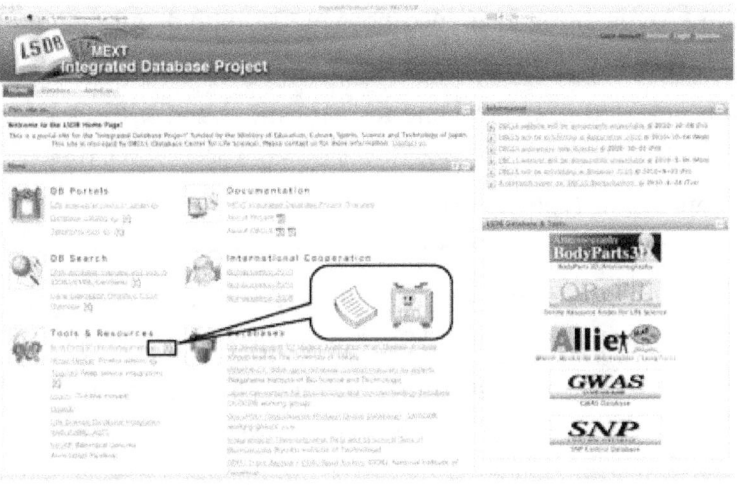

Figure 1: (http://bib.oxfordjournals.org/content/13/2/258.full#F1)

Screenshot of the MEXT Integrated Database Project portal (http://lifesciencedb.jp/en/). Paper icons and TV icons zoomed in the call-out following service names are linked to PDF documents and tutorial videos, respectively. MEXT, Ministry of Education, Culture, Sports, Science and Technology of Japan.

Currently, two types of video are provided: (i) tutorial videos of databases and tools (screencasts) and (ii) lecture videos of symposiums and workshops (live action). For screencast videos, a screen where the database or tools were operated was captured and edited using screencast software equipped with a caption-adding function, such as Camtasia Studio (TechSmith Corporation, Okemos, MI, USA) for Windows and DesktopToMovie (Pencil Software, Okinawa, Japan; only a Japanese-language version is available) for Mac. Recently, Camtasia: Mac (TechSmith Corporation) has been released, and we recommend its use rather than DesktopToMovie. For live-action videos, a lecture was recorded using a digital video camera or voice recorder, and then the source media was edited or embedded with presentation slides using tools such as Final Cut Pro (Apple Inc.) or iMovie (Apple Inc.). It is also possible to output presentations in Keynote (Apple Inc.) to videos. After capturing and editing, the source media was encoded in QuickTime format (.mov) and MPEG-4 format (.m4v) for distribution via websites and vodcast, respectively. The video compression type was set to H.264, and the sound format was specified to AAC if an audio track was included. For encoding in the QuickTime format, the 'Prepare for Internet Streaming' option was set to 'Fast Start' rather than 'Fast Start—Compressed Header' because the compressed header file format is impossible to play on Flash players. Other useful software packages for screencasting are listed in the article of Wikipedia entitled 'Comparison of screencasting software'.

To create user-friendly and high-quality tutorials, we suggest the following points: plan the tutorial; do a run-through before recording; edit adequately; pause at essential points; make the duration as short as possible and keep effects to a minimum. To capture a video smoothly, it is important to create a plan and run through it before recording. Editing costs may increase considerably if these preparatory steps are skipped. Here, editing involves deleting unnecessary frames and loading animation frames, thus ultimately reducing video downloading time, user viewing time and also file size. At key operating points, it is necessary to pause the animation; viewers need time to understand and absorb the information. In TogoTV videos, we insert a pause of about 5–10 s, depending on the situation. We also recommend that the video duration be made as short as possible and that animation effects be suppressed to a minimum. Most Togo TV contents fit in a 5-min video, except for lectures. Excessive production not only increases the production cost but also conceals the essence of the video. In general, since a dynamic video tends to increase file size, suppression of excessive animation will reduce the file size. Most video repositories have upload limitations based on video length and file size.

The most important thing when creating a video is to create a high-quality video that would be useful to viewers. When one creates video easily without any consideration of the quality of the product, it would be a waste of viewer's time and content creator's time and would add to the already overwhelming 'noise' of available training materials. Because both creating and viewing video are time consuming, one needs to create a video carefully. In a case of Togo TV, we have adopted an internal review in order to ensure quality. From planning to drafting, reviewing and publishing takes about a week in our case.

In May 2011, we have 310 tutorial videos in Togo TV (excluding lecture videos), and a total of 54 videos are updated ones.

Examples of tutorial videos in Togo TV

How to use BodyParts3D/anatomography

Anatomography is a 3D rendering tool for human anatomy and has been developed as part of the Integrated Database Project. A user can generate anatomical images by selecting body parts stored in the BodyParts3D database and setting their opacities, colors and viewpoint. The image is useful for communication between physicians and patients, and it can be generated as a heat map of the human body based on an organ name and a numeric value such as organ-specific gene expression data and cancer mortality. Figure 3A shows a screenshot of the BodyParts3D/anatomography tutorial video. This video describes how to build a 3D image, how to manipulate viewpoint and size, how to set opacities and colors and how to output to an image file. Videos of other services provided by the Integrated Database Project are also available at the project page. A TV icon after the service name provides a link to a tutorial video.

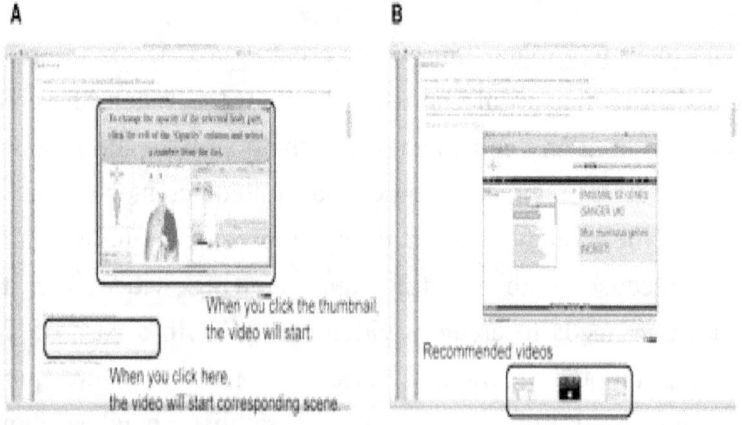

Figure 2: (http://bib.oxfordjournals.org/content/13/2/258.full#F3)

Screenshot of TogoTV's tutorial programs. Clicking the thumbnail in the center of the page will start the video. When the summary text of a video is clicked, the video will start the scene corresponding to the summary. There are links to recommended videos that are related playing video at the bottom of the page. *(A)* This video is entitled 'How to use BodyParts3D/Anatomography 2010'. *(B)* This video is entitled 'How to make probeID list for microarray using BioMart'.

How to use BioMart

We provide how-to videos of not only our own services but also useful tools all over the world. BioMart, a query-oriented data management system, is one of the most important tools in genome science. Users can submit various queries to retrieve lists of interest from BioMart. A screenshot of the tutorial video entitled 'How to make probeID list for microarray using BioMart' is shown in Figure 2B. In this video, the process for creating an ID conversion list for microarray analysis on the BioMart central portal website is introduced. From all genes in the mouse genome, genes that have corresponding entries in the Affymetrix mouse430 2 GeneChip are considered for further analysis. Genes with the Affymetrix GeneChip ID mentioned above are associated with the Agilent ProbeID and RefSeq ID via the Ensembl Gene ID. The results are downloadable in the tab separated value format with GNU-zip (.gzip) compression.

Lectures

Lectures are also distributed from Togo TV. Currently, we broadcast eight lectures in English. One is a video of a lecture about this service (Togo TV) held at the 2007 Annual Conference of the Japanese Society for Bioinformatics (JSBi2007, Figure 3A). The second lecture is about Gendoo, a functional profiling tool for gene and disease features using the Mesh vocabulary, held at JSBi2008. The third is about copyright and data sharing in science entitled 'Copyright in the Digital Age and Its Impact on Scientific Data Sharing' by

Professor Lawrence Lessig from Harvard Law School from the 'Balancing Intellectual Property Protection and Data Sharing in Science' symposium (Figure 3B). The others are about processing of large genomic data from 'Workshop on Parallel and Distributed Processing of Large Genome Data'.

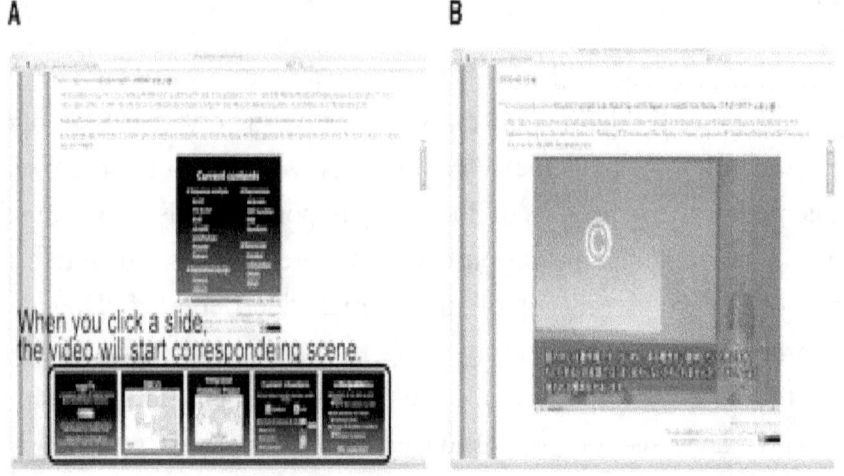

Figure 3: (http://bib.oxfordjournals.org/content/13/2/258.full#F4)

*Screenshot of Togo TV's lecture programs. There are the slides appeared in the presentation at the bottom of the page. When you click a slide, the video will start corresponding scene. **(A)** Video of voice-over on slides. **(B)** Live-action video.*

Chapter 14: BIOINFORMATICS RESOURCES FOR REVOLUTIONARY GENOMICS

The primers4clades web server

(http://maya.ccg.unam.mx/primers4clades/) : Tree-guided design of degenerate PCR oligonucleotide primers from multiple sequence alignments for metagenomic and molecular systematic studies - (http://floresta.eead.csic.es/primers4clades/) Contreras-Moreira, B., Sachman-Ruiz, B., Figueroa-Palacios, I., and Vinuesa, P. (2009). primers4clades: a web server that uses phylogenetic trees to design lineage-specific PCR primers for metagenomic and diversity studies. Nucl. Acids Res. (*Advance Access published on May 21, 2009;* doi: 10.1093/nar/gkp377.) http://nar.oxfordjournals.org/content/early/2009/05/26/nar.gkp377.full)

Bernardo Sachman-Ruíz, Bruno Contreras-Moreira, Enrique Zozaya, Cristina Martínez-Garza and **Vinuesa P*,** 2011 - Primers4clades, a web server to design lineage-specific PCR primers for gene-targeted metagenomics. Chapter 51 *in* Frans J. de Bruijn (ed.), Handbook of Molecular Microbial Ecology vol.I: Metagenomics and Complementary Approaches. Wiley/Blackwell. ISBN: 978-0-470-64479-9.

The primers4clades (http://maya.ccg.unam.mx/primers4clades/) is an easy-to-use web server developed for researchers interested in designing PCR primers for cross-species amplification of novel sequences from metagenomic DNA or from uncharacterized organisms belonging to user-specified phylogenetic clades or taxonomic groups. It implements an extended CODEHOP primer design strategy (http://maya.ccg.unam.mx/~marfil/tutorial.html#extended_codehop) based on both DNA and protein multiple sequence alignments of coding sequences. It evaluates a comprehensive set of thermodynamic properties of the oligonucleotide pairs, as well as the phylogenetic information content of the theoretical amplicons, which is computed from the branch support values of maximum likelihood phylogenies estimated for each molecular marker. Phylogenetic trees displayed on screen make it easy to target the primer design for particular species groups or sequence clusters selected by the user. The server is useful to design taxon-specific PCR primers for molecular ecology and systematic studies of bacteria and eukaryotes.

Primers4clades is developed by Bruno Contreras-Moreira (Laboratorio de Biología Computacional, Estación Experimental Aula Dei, CSIC, Spain) (http://www.eead.csic.es/compbio/staff/bruno_contreras_moreira.html) and Pablo Vinuesa (Center for Genomic Sciences, UNAM, Mexico) (http://www.ccg.unam.mx/~vinuesa/) and is mirrored at two sites : primers4clades - Mexico (http://www.ccg.unam.mx/~vinuesa/) and primers4clades - Spain (http://floresta.eead.csic.es/primers4clades/) . If you use it, we would greatly appreciate your feedback in order to improve the documentation and extend the FAQs list!

Other useful PCR-related sites and WebPages

1) GenomeWeb, Hamburg University - PCR (http://www.biologie.uni-hamburg.de/b-online/library/genomeweb/GenomeWeb/nuc-primer.html)

2) Molecular Biology protocols and resources, Canada. - Design PCR primers (http://molbiol-tools.ca/PCR.htm)

3) Peter Taschner's page on PCR-related web resources (http://www.humgen.nl/ primer_design.html)

4) The Bioinformatics Links Directory - DNA tools for the bench (http://bioinformatics.ca/links directory/index.php?subcategory_id=63)

Home (http://www.ccg.unam.mx/~vinuesa/index.html) back to table of contents (http://www.ccg.unam.mx/~vinuesa/Bioinformatics_resources_web.html#table_of_contents)

Unix, Linux, databases, the WWW and scripting for bioinformatics

Figure 4: Apache software foundation (http://www.apache.org/)

1) Bash programming - introductory HOWTO (http://tldp.org/HOWTO/Bash-Prog-Intro-HOWTO.html)

2) Bash programming - advanced guide (http://tldp.org/LDP/abs/html/)

3) BioInformatics.org software (http://bioinformatics.org/wiki/Software)

4) BioPerl (http://www.bioperl.org/wiki/Main_Page)

5) BioPython (http://biopython.org/wiki/Main_Page)

6) CPAN (http://www.cpan.org/)

7) CRAN(http://www.cran.r-project.org/)

8) Free software foundation (http://www.fsf.org/)

9) GNU's Not Unix (http://www.gnu.org/)

10) HTML goodies tutorial site (http://www.htmlgoodies.com/)

11) Linux.com(http://www.linux.com/)

12) Linux.org (http://www.linux.org)

13) linuxtopia.org - technical library (http://www.linuxtopia.org/)

14) MySQL open source database (http://www.mysql.com/)

15) O'Reilly's CD bookshelf (http://docstore.mik.ua/orelly/bookshelf.html)

16) R - The R project for statistical computing (http://www.r-project.org/)

17) Perl.com (http://www.perl.com/)

18) Perl.org (http://www.perl.org/)

19) Perl pocket reference - Rex Swain's HTMLized version of Johan Vromans' text (http://www.rexswain.com/perl5.html)

20) PHP (http://www.php.net/)

21) Python (https://www.python.org/)
22) The Bash-Hackers Wiki (http://wiki.bash-hackers.org/doku.php)
23) The Linux Journal (http://www.linuxjournal.com/)
24) The Linux Tutorial (http://www.linux-tutorial.info/)
25) The Comprehensive Perl Archive Network (CPAN) (http://www.cpan.org/)
26) Unix tutorial for beginners (http://www.ee.surrey.ac.uk/Teaching/Unix/)
27) Unix-Linux tutorials and courses at Ohio State University
28) w3c - The World Wide Web Consortium (http://www.w3.org/)
29) W3Schools - online web tutorials (http://www.w3schools.com/)
30) wikibook - guide to unix (http://www.w3schools.com/)
31) WWW Security FAQ from the w3c (http://www.w3.org/Security/Faq/)

Home (http://www.ccg.unam.mx/~vinuesa/index.html) back to table of contents (http://www.ccg.unam.mx/~vinuesa/Bioinformatics_resources_web.html#table_of_contents)

Navigating and Mining Genome Sequences

1) Genomes Online (GOLD) (http://www.genomesonline.org/)
2) JGI Integrated Microbial Genomes (IMG) (http://img.jgi.doe.gov/cgi-bin/w/main.cgi)
3) Kyoto Encyclopedia of Genes and Genomes (KEGG) (http://www.genome.jp/kegg/kegg2.html)

4) Microbial Genome Database for Comparative Analysis (MGGD) (http://mbgd.genome.ad.jp/)

5) Regulatory Sequence Analysis Tools (RSAT) (http://rsat.ulb.ac.be/rsat/)

Home (http://www.ccg.unam.mx/~vinuesa/index.html) Back to table of contents (http://www.ccg.unam.mx/~vinuesa/ Bioinformatics resources_web.html#table_of_contents)

Molecular Evolution and Phylogenetics: Resources and Programs

1) Filogenetica.org (http://www.flogenetica.org/) - servicio de información y contacto de la comunida filogenética hispanoparlante

2) HyPhy datamonkey (http://www.datamonkey.org/) - fast positive and negative selection detection

3) Interactive tree of life (iTOL) (http://itol.embl.de/itol.cgi)

4) List of phylogeny programs (http://evolution.genetics. washington.edu/phylip/software.html) maintained by Joe Felsenstein (http://evolution. genetics.washington.edu/phylip/ felsenstein.html)

5) Phylemon - a suite of web-tools for molecular evolution, phylogenetics and phylogenomics (http://phylemon.bioinfo. cipf.es/)

6) Phylogeny.fr - Robust phylogenetic analysis for the non-specialist (http://www.phylogeny.fr/)

7) Phylogenetic Analysis by Maximum Likelihood (the PAML package) (http://abacus.gene.ucl.ac.uk/software/paml.html) by Ziheng Yang (http://abacus.gene.ucl.ac.uk/)

8) The Evolution Directory (EvolDir) (http://evol.mcmaster.ca/brian/evoldir.html)

9) University of Oxford (U.K.) Evolutionary Biology Group (http://evolve.zoo.ox.ac.uk/Evolve/Welcome.html)

10) Workshop on Molecular Evolution at Woodshole (http://www.molecularevolution.org/)

11) Cursos y tutoriales sobre bioinformática y filogenética en español http://www.ccg.unam.mx/~vinuesa/Tutoriales_y_cursos_bioinfo_filogen%C3%A9tica_espa%C3%B1ol_PV.html

Horizontal Gene Transfer and Mobile Elements in Prokaryotes

1) The Horizontal Gene Transfer Database (HGT-DB) (http://usuaris.tinet.cat/debb/HGT/)

2) The Insertion Sequences Database (IS-DB) (https://www-is.biotoul.fr//)

Tools for getting started

NCBI (http://www.ncbi.nlm.nih.gov/) houses sets of databases of sequences for everything under the sun

Searching with BLAST (http://serc.carleton.edu/exploring_genomics/chamaecrista/searching_blast.html) **BLAST** known sequences against the Chamaecrista transcriptome

The *Chamaecrista* genome has not been sequenced. You can explore the transcriptome in a genomics context by taking advantage of the soybean genome since soy is one of *Chamaecrista's* closer relatives. (http://serc.carleton.edu/exploring_genomics/chamaecrista/soybean_genome_.html)

The Next Generation Biology Workbench offers a suite of bioinformatics tools. It is convenient "one stop shopping, (http://www.ngbw.org).

JMP Genomics Tools

JMP Genomics is a statistical software package that lets you look for gene expression patterns. The two links that follow provide the directions and data needed to visualize patterns in gene expression among the different *Chamaecrista* tissue types. Work through this exercise before you go on to plan your own strategy for working with the expression data.

JMP Genomics Gene Expression Exercise (http://serc.carleton.edu/files/exploring_genomics/chamaecrista/jmp_exercise.v6.docx), Microsoft Word 2007 (.docx) 38Kb.

Data File for JMP Genomics Gene Expression Exercise (http://serc.carleton.edu/files/exploring_genomics/chamaecrista/jmp_exercise_data.v2.txt) (Text File 5.5MB)

Paper on Analyzing Gene Expression (http://serc.carleton.edu/files/exploring_genomics/chamaecrista/jmp_expression_white_paper.pdf) (Acrobat (PDF) 4.7MB) the figures may be helpful as you reflect on the results of your JMP analysis.

Links that will help you relate genes to the biology of organisms

(http://plantontology.org). Plant Ontology is run out of Oregon State University. We have an invitation to help develop Chamaecrista ontology. If you're interested

in thinking about ontology, you might want to incorporate what you learnt.

Gene Ontology (GO) is focused on what happens at the cell level and below, while Plant Ontology focuses on the level of the cell and above.

Annotation tools

Pfam (http://www.pfam.org/). **Pfam** is a database of evolutionarily conserved protein families, and annotations about the functions of those families.

KAAS (http://www.genome.jp/kass-bin/kass_main). (KEGG Automatic Annotation Server) provides functional annotation of genes by BLAST comparisons against the manually curated KEGG GENES database and mapping them onto known biochemical/metabolic pathways.

Alignment, Phylogeny and Evolutionary Analysis Tools

Clustal (http://www.ebi.ac.uk/Tools/msa/clustalw2/): **Clustal** will align multiple DNA or protein sequences. It is available over many different sites; in this case we are providing a link to EMBL's Clustalw server.

(http:/www.phylo.org/sub_section/portal) CIPRES is a portal for the inference of large phylogenetic trees.

(http://www.megasoftware.net) **MEGA** is a program for constructing alignments and constructing phylogenetic trees. **Important:** this software does NOT run from the web. You must download it onto a PC and run it locally.

Primer Design Tools

Primer 3 (http://bioinfo.ut.ee/primer3-0.4.0/primer3/) is an excellent tool for designing primers. You will find this helpful in your functional analysis.

Sequence Analysis Tools

There are a number of tools available to analyze sequence data, including 4Peaks, Student Interface to Biology Workbench, and Laser Gene. Click here (http://.www.serc.karleton.edu/files//exploring_genomicschamaecrista/analysing_your_pcr_sequence.docx).

Searching with BLAST

Basic Local Alignment Search Tool, or BLAST, is a tool that enables a researcher to search through large databases of sequences to find all sequences that are similar to a sequence-of-interest. Blast works by taking the researcher's sequence of interest (called the **query** sequence), and comparing it to every sequence in a large database of sequences. BLAST evaluates the degree of similarity and then pulls out all sequences that share at least a small region of similarity to the query. The researcher must evaluate the list of sequences to make a determination as to whether blast hits really represent true homologs. The BLAST algorithm was developed and implemented by Stephen Altschul at the U.S. National Center for Biotechnology Information

You can now easily find Genome-specific BLAST pages using the search box on the BLAST homepage under the "BLAST Assembled Genomes" section. This new feature allows you to quickly access and search BLAST databases for the genome of an organism of interest. Simply start typing your organism name into the box and suggestions will appear. The auto complete accepts species or strain-level eukaryotic and microbial names as well as metagenomic taxa (community and organism associated metagenomes). Once you select a suggestion, you will be taken to a BLAST page with the best (most complete, reference) genomic database preselected. In cases where there is no assembled genome sequence, the page will load with whole genome shotgun databases for the organism. Or, if there is no specific genome-sequencing project, the page will load with default nucleotide database (nr/nt) limited to the organism of interest.

- NCBI BLAST : (http://blast.ncbi.nlm.nih.gov/Blast.cgi)

Performing a BLAST Search

Questions you must be able to answer in order to perform a blast search:

1. What sequence(s) is the subject of my research ? These are called *query* sequences. Example: I am examining the potential roles of the 10 most abundant sequences in the Chamaecrista sequence dataset. I will use these as the query sequences in a blast search.

2. What subject database is the most appropriate to search, given my research question?

   a) If the goal is to identify potential homologs in soybean, it would be appropriate to search against the soybean genome using Phytozome (http://www.phytozome.net/ soybean.php).

   b) If the goal is to determine whether these genes have been sequenced in any other species, it would be appropriate to search against GenBank (http://blast.ncbi.nlm.nih.gov/Blast.cgi) at NCBI.

   c) If the goal is to determine whether or not a sequence exists in the *Chamaecrista* transcriptome, it would be appropriate to search against the Chamaecrista transcriptome (http://.www.serc.karleton.edu/blast/blast. html). For this search the username is Carleton and password is blastnow.

If the goal is to determine whether these genes contain any functional protein domains that are known to confer particular functions, it would be appropriate to search against Pfam (http://pfam.xfam.org/).

BLAST	Query sequence is	Database to search against is....
blastp	Protein	Protein
blastn	DNA	DNA
blastx	DNA (translated)	Protein
tblastn	Protein	DNA (translated)
tblastx	DNA (translated)	DNA (translated)

(http://serc.carleton.edu/details/images/15295.html)

How to perform a blast search

Step 1: Retrieve a **query sequence** you want to use and make sure it is in FASTA format

Step 2: Navigate to the **database** you want to search against

Step 3: Select the **BLAST program** that will use the query sequence to search the database that you selected.

Step 4: Adjust any parameters, as appropriate

Once you have your sequence(s) you're ready to use BLAST

1. BLAST (http://blast.ncbi.nlm.nih.gov/Blast.cgi?CMD= Web& PAGE_TYPE=BlastDocs&DOC_TYPE=ProgSelectionGuide) (Basic Local Alignment Search Tool) is a tool that allows you to compare sequences to find the similar sequences. You

can BLAST a single sequence or multiple sequences against a database at one time.

2. Link this site (http://serc.carleton.edu/exploring_genomics/ chamaecrista/ searching_blast.html) for a Blast tutorial.

Program	Description
blastp	Compares an amino acid query sequence against a protein sequence database.
blastn	Compares a nucleotide query sequence against a nucleotide sequence database.
blastx	Compares a nucleotide query sequence translated in all reading frames against a protein sequence database. You could use this option to find potential translation products of an unknown nucleotide sequence.
tblastn	Compares a protein query sequence against a nucleotide sequence database dynamically translated in all reading frames.
tblastx	Compares the six-frame translations of a nucleotide query sequence against the six-frame translations of a nucleotide sequence database. Please note that the tblastx program cannot be used with the nr database on the BLAST Web page because it is computationally intensive.

(http://serc.carleton.edu/details/images/14301.html)

a. You BLAST "against" known data sets to find similar sequences.

b. NCBI has a huge repository of sequences from many organisms that can be searched using BLAST (http://blast.ncbi.nlm.nih.gov/Blast.cgi) on their website.

c. LIS (http://www.comparative-legumes.org/) and Phytozome (http://www.phytozome.net/soybean) are focused on legumes and are searchable with BLAST.

You can BLAST known sequences against the *Chamaecrista* transcriptome locally at the Blast *Chamaecrista* (http://serc.carleton.edu/blast/blast.html) site. The dropdown menu will allow you to choose the database you want to BLAST. You will want to read the description of the different assemblies before selecting one in the local BLAST (http://serc.carleton.edu/files/exploring_genomics/chamaecrista/description_transcriptome_asse.v2.txt) (Text File 5kB)

Figure 5

Basic Blasting in 3 easy steps

Gene expression: Illumina / Solexa whole transcriptome sequencing provides information about gene expression, as well as nucleotide sequence. The more copies of a specific transcript in an RNA isolation, the more times that transcript will be sequenced. Transcript abundance correlates directly with gene expression levels.

Tissues used in expression analysis: Transcriptome libraries from shoots, roots, and nodules of *Chamaecrista fasciculata* plants at different stages of development were used for Illumina/Solexa sequencing. Before sequencing, mRNA was purified from the total RNA. You can get more information about the stages by downloading the linked PowerPoint slides. Shoot, root, and nodule libraries (http://serc.carleton.edu/files/exploring_genomics/chamaecrista/ tissue_libraries.pptx) (PowerPoint 2007 (.pptx) 14MB Jan19 09)

JMP Genomics exercise to get you thinking about gene expression: JMP Genomics is a statistical software package that lets you look for gene expression patterns. The two links that follow provide the directions and data needed to visualize patterns in gene expression among the different *Chamaecrista* tissue types. Work through this exercise before you go on to plan your own strategy for working with the expression data. The software is available for all faculty and students in the Biology Department. It is currently on the machines in CMC 109 and the Biology Computer Lab. As a student in the class, you can download your own copy from the COLLAB server folder (Departments/Biology) onto a Windows machine.

JMP Genomics Gene Expression Exercise (http://serc.carleton. edu/files/exploring_genomics/chamaecrista/jmp_exercise.v6.docx) (Microsoft Word 2007 (.docx) 38kB)

Data File for JMP Genomics Gene Expression Exercise (http://serc.carleton.edu/files/exploring_genomics/chamaecrista/ jmp_exercise_data.v2.txt) (Text File 5.5MB)

Paper on Analyzing Gene Expression (http://serc.carleton.edu/files/exploring_genomics/chamaecrista/jmp_expression_white_paper.pdf) (Acrobat (PDF) 4.7MB) the figures may be helpful as you reflect on the results of your JMP analysis.

Expression Data

The expression data is available in a number of formats. Reads per million calibrates the data across samples.

Expression Data - Unique reads per million (http://serc.carleton.edu/files/exploring_genomics/chamaecrista/expression_data_unique_reads.txt) (Text File 5.5MB Jan11 10) - **Only the latest version of Excel will show you all the data.**

Expression Data - Total unique reads (http://serc.carleton.edu/files/exploring_genomics/chamaecrista/expression_data_total_unique.txt) (Text File 1.2MB Jan11 10) - **Only the latest version of Excel will show you all the data.**

Expression Data - Reads per million (http://serc.carleton.edu/files/exploring_genomics/chamaecrista/expression_data_reads_per.txt) (Text File 5.5MB Jan11 10 - **Only the latest version of Excel will show you all the data**).

Expression Data - Reads (http://serc.carleton.edu/files/exploring_genomics/chamaecrista/expression_data_reads.txt) (Text File 1.2MB Jan11 10 - **Only the latest version of Excel will show you all the data**).

Asking questions with expression data

a) What is the overall pattern of gene expression for the shoot transcriptome?

b) Using the youngest shoot library, can you rank the genes based on expression and plot your results?

c) What happens if you then plot the data for the other shoot libraries? How do they compare to each other?

d) Can you compare expression patterns in roots, shoots, and nodules? How might you organize and present the data?

e) If you worked on candidate genes, can you use that information to look at expression patterns of specific genes as a function of tissue type and developmental stage?

Protein predictions

Nonsynonomous SNPs will have a greater or lesser effect on protein structure depending on the change in the R group of the predicted amino acid. If you would like to try your hand at protein modelling, check out the information on the SERC Protein Structure (http://serc.carleton.edu/genomics/tool_workspace/index.html) page. An alternative is to try the protein structure predictor available on Biology Workbench (http://workbench.sdsc.edu/). You will need to set up a Biology Workbench account which will allow you to use a range of tools at that site. Click here (http://medsocnet.ncsa.illinois.edu/MSSW/tutorials_current/How3.2/) to access a tutorial that will show you how you can use Biology Workbench for protein prediction and visualization.

To work on protein structure prediction, you need to know where the SNP is in a sequence (you have this in the SNP dataset, but you also need the sequence).

Functional genomics

Strategies for testing and extending genomics data are at the bench. Functional genomics refers to the use of molecular biology tools to understand the function of genes identified in sequencing projects. While sequencing projects yield static results, functional genomics focuses on dynamic aspects including regulation of gene expression. Functional genomics is a way to test and extend hypotheses that emerge from the analysis of sequence data.

What are functional genomics questions? Here are some examples based on the Chamaecrista transcriptome:

Is the number of Illumina reads of a contig a good proxy for the level of gene expression?

My 'favorite gene' appears to increase in expression as Chamaecrista shoots age when I look at my Solexa sequence data. Can I verify this by quantifying the transcript levels in young and old plants using standard molecular approaches?

Will flowering genes that I have identified be expressed later in the late flowering accessions ofChamaecrista that have not yet been fully characterized?

I've found some putative leaf homologs in the Chamaecrista transcriptome. Will they be expressed only in leaves of the plants?

I'm interested in a few SNP alleles that vary between MN and OK ecotypes. Will the more southerly accessions in the USDA collection have the SNP allele more commonly found in the OK ecotype?

What tools can help me answer functional genomics questions? PCR (polymerase chain reaction) can amplify a specific gene of interest.

Show Using PCR (javascript: swapDiv (327241, true)

Quantitative PCR allows you to compare the relative amounts of a specific transcript in two or more RNA isolations. For example, you are curious about the relative amounts of a gene you believe is present in both roots and shoots. You start with equal amounts of total RNA, convert the RNA to cDNA with reverse transcriptase, and then amplify your gene of interest by using gene specific primers and PCR. Equal volumes of PCR product are loaded on an agarose gel that is run and stained for the DNA. You can then use an imager to compare the intensity of the PCR bands on the gel and estimate relative levels of expression.

Real time PCR is PCR with an additional twist. In addition to the primers a fluorescent probe is added. During each amplification cycle, the probe lands on the DNA and fluoresces. The real time PCR machine detects the amount of fluorescence each cycle and that information corresponds to the amount of DNA present. Some probes are designed to be specific to a gene sequence. Others are more general and the primers alone determine specificity. This real time PCR animation (http://www.scanelis.com/spip.php?page=_article&id_article=39) should help.

SNP analysis can be done with sequencing of PCR amplified products. There are also very specific primer/probe sets for real time PCR that can distinguish between two SNP alleles. These two approaches are expensive and time consuming. A good first step would be to identify a restriction enzyme that cuts one of the SNP alleles and not the other. Biology Workbench (http://workbench.

sdsc.edu/) can do this for you. If you're not sure how to start, go to the 'Variation among ecotypes' strategy page for some suggestions.

In situ hybridization allows you to see where genes are expressed within a tissue. Tissues are cut into very thin sections and placed on a microscope slide that is probed with a labelled sequence complementary to your gene of interest. You can then see both the cells and the labelled probe under the correct microscope (e.g. fluorescence scope if you have a fluorescent probe). click here for a more detailed explanation (http://en.wikipedia.org/wiki/ In_situ_ hybridization)

Primer Design

These resources will help you design primers for your functional genomics experiment.

Resources for designing primers - Oligo Calc (Oligonucleotide Properties Calculator) Click here for Oligo Calc (http://www.basic.northwestern.edu/biotools/oligocalc.html)

Primer3 **Click here for Primer3** (http://bioinfo.ut.ee/primer3-0.4.0/primer3/)

Chapter 15: BIOINFORMATICS WEB PRACTICAL AT UMBER

University of Manchester Bioinformatics Education and Research – (http://bioinf.man.ac.uk/)

These step-by-step tutorials by Paul G. Young of Queens University, Australia are provided by W.H. Freeman as accompanying material to the popular undergraduate textbook 'Introduction to Genetic Analysis' by Griffiths et al.

- Henry Stewart Talks (http://hstalks.com/main/browse_talks.php?father_id=40&c=252)

- Population Genetics Studies in Africa : Curiosity and Challenges (42 mins) (http://hstalks.com/main)

Prof. Himla Soodyall – University of the Witwatersrand and National Health Laboratory Service, South Africa

Ms. Elaine Gunter – Specimen Solutions, LLC, USA

- Diagnosis of Early Relapse in Ovarian Cancer Using Serum Proteomic Profiling (40 mins) (http://hstalks.com/main)

    Dr. Jean Gao – Department of Computer Science and Engineering, University of Texas at Arlington, USA

    MOBILE

    Bioinformatics and Genome Analysis (http://hstalks.com/main/browse_talks.php?father_id=40&c=252)

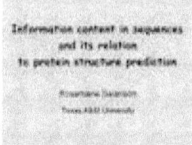

- Information Content in Sequences and its Relation to Protein Structure Prediction (47 mins) (http://hstalks.com/main)

    Dr. Rosemarie Swanson – Department of Biochemistry and Biophysics, Texas A&M University, USA   MOBILE

- Unity and Diversity in Microbial Genomes (29 mins) (http://hstalks.com/main)

    Dr. Kishore Sakharkar – National University Medical Institutes, National University of Singapore, Singapore.

    MOBILE

- Pattern Discovery in Bioinformatics (40 mins) (http://hstalks.com/main)

  Prof. Giri Narasimhan – Bioinformatics Research Group, Florida International University, USA

- Analysis of Protein-Protein Interaction, Transcriptional Regulation and Metabolic Networks (38 mins) (http://hstalks.com/main)

  Dr. Andreas Wagner – Department of Biology, University of New Mexico, USA

  Human Disease (http://hstalks.com/main/browse_talks.php?father_id=40&c=252)

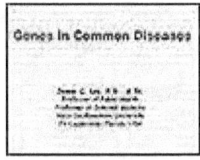 

- Genes in Common Diseases (38 mins) (http://hstalks.com/main)

  Prof. Jennie Lou – College of Medicine, Nova South-eastern University, USA

- Impact of Genomic Architecture and Diversity on Human and Infectious Diseases (41 mins) (http://hstalks.com/main)

  Dr. Vincent Chow – School of Medicine, National University of Singapore, and Dr. Meena Sakharkar - Nanyang Center for Supercomputing and Visualization, Nanyang Technological University, Singapore

  Dr. Meena Sakharkar – Nanyang Center for Supercomputing and Visualization, Nanyang Technological University, Singapore

- Exploring and Predicting Phenotype and Function in Cancer Biology: Working in High Dimensional Data Spaces (39 mins) (http://hstalks.com/main)

  Prof. Robert Clarke – Lombardi Comprehensive Cancer Center, Georgetown University, USA

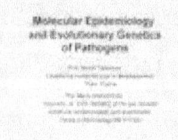

- Molecular Epidemiology and Evolutionary Genetics of Pathogens (32 mins) (http://hstalks.com/main)

Prof. Michel Tibayrenc – Institut de Recherche pour le Developpement, Bangkok, Thailand MOBILE

Genomic Variation
(http://hstalks.com/main/browse_talks.php?father_id= 40&c=252)

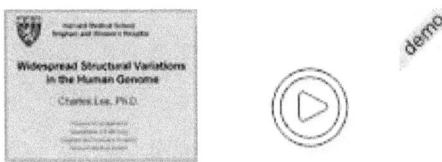

- Widespread Structural Variations in the Human Genome (59 mins) (http://hstalks.com/main)

Dr. Charles Lee – Brigham and Women's Hospital, Harvard Medical School, USA   MOBILE

- Human Genome Variation (39 mins) (http://hstalks.com/main)

Dr. Kelly Frazer – Genomics, Perlegen Sciences, Inc., USA
MOBILE

- Human Genetic Variation and Therapeutic Development (36 mins) (http://hstalks.com/main)

Dr. Sally John – Division of Epidemiology and Health Sciences, University of Manchester, and Dr. Nick Davies - Pfizer, UK (Dr. Nick Davies – Pfizer, UK)

- Evolving Genomic Approaches to the Study of Complex Cardiovascular Diseases in Human Populations: Genetic and Genomic Epidemiology (62 mins) (http://hstalks.com/main)

Dr. Christopher O'Donnell – National Heart, Lung and Blood Institute, USA

The Henry Stewart Talks provide recorded presentations from experts in many areas of biology. This series of talks on 'Using Bioinformatics in the Exploration of Genetic Diversity' provides practical examples of the applications of bioinformatics.

Chapter 16: PATH CASE SYSTEMS BIOLOGY

As computational models of complete pathways, cellular metabolism of specific tissues, and organs are developed and interconnected, new enhanced functionalities and database-enabled software tools are required to (i) link the ever expanding body of molecular information to an understanding of how intact organisms function via multiscale mechanistic models of the system and (ii) facilitate interactive model development and dynamic analysis of responses in an effective and efficient manner. We propose to build a new set of integrated database-enabled tools for regulatory metabolic networks, called PathCase-SB, with interfaces for model-based querying, visualization, simulation, and model building. The aim of PathCase-SB is to build a database-enabled framework and tools towards effective and efficient systems biology model development for multiscale mechanistic models of biological systems. Our approach is to integrate the model database with an existing metabolic network database, PathCase, (as well as other metabolic network data from other sources) in order to enable us to build 'one-shop' querying, visualization, simulation, and modeling capabilities.

People: Ali Cakmak, Xinjian Qi, Sarp Coskun, En Cheng, A. Ercument Cicek, Lei Yang, Rishiraj Jadeja, Nicola Lai, Ranjan Dash, Gultekin Ozsoyoglu, Z. Meral Ozsoyoglu (http://www.aec.edu)

Project Web Site (http://nashua.cwru.edu/Pathwaysweb/)

Information Theory and Metabolic Network Based Metabolic Profile Analysis

Recent improvements in analytical methodology and large sample throughput allow for creation of large datasets of metabolites that reflect changes in metabolic dynamics due to disease or a perturbation in the metabolic network. However, current methods of comprehensive analyses of large metabolic datasets (metabolomics) are limited, unlike other "omics" approaches where complex techniques for analyzing co expression/co regulation of multiple variables are applied. We address shortcomings of current metabolomics data analysis techniques, and research on new information theory based and metabolic network aided techniques

People: *A. Ercument Cicek*, Gultekin Ozsoyoglu (http://www.aec.edu)

Steady - State Metabolic Network Dynamics Analysis

As an endeavor of automated analysis of metabolomics data in terms of the dynamic behavior of the metabolic network, we propose, analyze, and empirically evaluate a framework, called Steady-state Metabolic network Dynamics Analysis (SMDA), to reason about the dynamic behavior of the metabolic network at steady-state, and locate possible alternatives for active/inactive metabolic sub networks. Under a user designated metabolic network, given that a set of bio-fluid (e.g., blood) metabolite concentration values and, perhaps, a number of tissue-based metabolite concentration values are measured at steady-state, we apply biochemistry-based rules to generate and output possible alternative steady-state metabolic network dynamic behavior scenarios with reasons to reach the results.

People: Ali Cakmak, Xinjian Qi, *A. Ercument Cicek*, Gultekin Ozsoyoglu (http://www.aec.edu)

Project Web Site (http://nashua.cwru.edu/PathwaysSMDA/)

Pedigree Data Management

A Pedigree is a "record of ancestry or purity of breed". Pedigrees are hierarchical hereditary structures and are typically represented as directed acyclic graphs. Stud books (listings of pedigrees for horses, dogs, etc.) and herdbooks (records for cattle, swine, sheep, etc.) are maintained by governmental or private record associations or breed organizations in many countries. In human genetics, pedigree diagrams are utilized to trace the inheritance of a specific trait, abnormality, or disease, calculate disease risk factors, identify individuals at risk, and facilitate genetic counseling. In addition to medical genetics, pedigrees are also commonly used in animal breeding (e.g., Horse racing & pet breeding), plant studies (self-pollinated plant breeding), and genealogical studies. As the volume of this structured pedigree data expands, there is a pressing need for better ways to manage, store, and efficiently query this data.

People: En Cheng, Brendan Elliott, S. Fatih Akgul, Meral Ozsoyoglu (http://www.aec.edu)

Chapter 17: IMPORTANT WEBINAR AND BLOGS ON BIOINFORMATICS

What is Web-Based Seminar (Webinar)?

A web-based seminar (webinar) is a conference that is hosted in near real-time over the Internet. Webinars allow groups in remote geographic locations to listen and participate in the same conference regardless of the geographic distance between them. Webinars also have interactive elements such as two-way audio (VoIP) and video that allows the presenters and participants to discuss the information as it is presented. Some common uses for webinars include meetings, remote training and workshops. Webinars can also be recorded for later viewing or distribution, but this removes the interactive elements for later viewers. In this sense, a recorded webinar becomes a webcast - a presentation that includes one-way audio and video without any interaction between speakers and listeners.

Techopedia explains Web-Based Seminar (Webinar): Webinars use Internet technologies, particularly TCP/IP connections. Generally, some software must be downloaded by people who want to join a webinar. Before a webinar, participants are usually provided with a means of interfacing via email, common calendars or other collaboration mechanisms in preparation for the event. Some webinars also provide for anonymous participation, while others identify the current speaker by a user ID or code name. Both methods protect the identity of the audience participant. Webinars may include extra features, such as:

a) Screen sharing, where anything on the presenter's computer display is also displayed on all audience computer displays

b) Shared control, where the participants can control the presenter's display screen

c) Polling survey capability, which allows presenters to query the audience with multiple choice questions

Vendors that host webinar services may charge by the minute, by a flat monthly fee, or by the number of audience participants. Significant vendors of Web-based seminars include BigBlueButton, Fuze Meeting, Microsoft Office Live Meeting, Open meetings, Skype and WebTrain, among many others. Web-based seminars may be provided as hosting service, as web-based software or as an appliance, which requires hardware and may also be called in-house or on-premise Web conferencing.

Bioinformatics Webinar / Seminar available at the web link (https://www.biostars.org/u/313/) and (https://www.biostars.org/p/6572/).

Bioinformatics Explained [Biostars : (https://www.biostars.org/)] - If interested in finding latest Bioinformatics related tools, applications & course *Webinar* visit BioStar that list the *University, Company, Blog* which organizes above listed **Webinar** in free?

a) tool (https://www.biostars.org/t/tool/?sort=answers&limit=all%20time&q=)

b) Asian Bioinformatics Research Network (ABREN) (http://gibk21.bio.kyutech.ac.jp/ABREN/index.php) conducts free virtual workshop for bioinformatics training every year. This blogpost (http://www.scilogs.com/saras/2010/11/16/the-

4th-abren-2010-virtual-training-workshop-on-bioinformatics/) refers to the 4th one that was conducted in 2010.

c) NHGRI's youtube channel GenomeTV (https://www.youtube.com/user/GenomeTV#p/p) has excellent talks. I would suggest exploring the videos in Current Topics in Genome Analysis 2010 (https://www.youtube.com/user/GenomeTV#p/c/1EAD845FB35BD74F) playlist. NHGRI also seems to have a webinar series (http://www.genome.gov/27527023).

d) Canadian Bioinformatics Workshops (CBW) series (http://bioinformatics.ca/) the most useful. It contains series of downloadable lectures (http://bioinformatics.ca/workshops/open_access/) from basics of Bioinformatics to the current issues for advance learner. And above all CBW promotes open access.

e) One can access EMBL-EBI on-line courses (all for free), (http://www.ebi.ac.uk/training/online/).

f) This one is video based on Analysis of High-Throughput Sequencing data: (http://www.ebi.ac.uk/training/online/course/embo-practical-course-analysis-high-throughput-seq).

Source: (https://www.youtube.com/playlist?list=PLRosqf3DDcTGP7wL9x0E_cvuPd7iq-uNJ).

Biology & Bioinformatics Recorded Webinars by DNA Learning Center (https://www.youtube.com/user/DNALearningCenter)

This playlist includes recorded webinars on a variety of topics in biology and bioinformatics. Many webinars include helpful step-by-step demonstrations of laboratory and bioinformatics techniques.

a) DNA Subway Blue Line Refresher (Recorded Webinar) (https://www.youtube.com/watch?v=LNkv_UBGIZw&index=1&list=PLRosqf3DDcTGP_7wL9x0E_cvuPd7iq-uNJ)

b) Introduction to iPlant - Overview and New Release Updates (Recorded Webinar) (https://www.youtube.com/watch?v=cLwVALTswQQ&index=2&list=PLRosqf3DDcTGP7wL9x0E_cvuPd7iq-uNJ)

c) DNA Barcoding Techniques Refresher (Recorded Webinr) (https://www.youtube.com/watch?v=bMgkMroXD5U&index=3&list=PLRosqf3DDcTGP7wL9x0E_cvuPd7iq-uNJ)

Source: (https://www.youtube.com/user/DNALearning Center/videos)

Cytoscape Webinar (http://jeansong.wordpress.com/2011/09/09/cytoscape-webinar/): The Taubman Health Sciences Library (http://www.lib.umich.edu/_taubman-health-sciences-library) and the National Center for Integrative Biomedical Informatics (NCIBI) (http://www.ncibi.org/) are offering a remote Cytoscape training class via Adobe Connect. Cytoscape (http://www.cytoscape.org/) is an open source molecular interactions visualization tool. For more information about this class and to register, please go to (http://portal.ncibi.org/gateway/cytotraining.html).

BLAST Webinar (http://jeansong.wordpress.com/2010/03/17/blast-webinar/):

Dr. Peter Cooper from NCBI is offering yet another webinar. This webinar's topic will be on BLAST (Basic Local Alignment Search Tool) (http://blast.ncbi.nlm.nih.gov/Blast.cgi) and all of its recent updates. Dr. Cooper will also touch on Primer BLAST (http://www.ncbi.nlm.nih.gov/tools/primer-blast/) and COBALT (http://www.ncbi.nlm.nih.gov/tools/cobalt/cobalt.cgi?link_loc= BlastHomeAd) so be prepared to be impressed.

Benchtop Sequencing Data Analysis - Webinar Series (http://seqanswers.com/forums/showthread.php?t=192): Hosting an online seminar series (http://blog.avadis-ngs.com/2012/02/webinar-series-benchtop-sequencing-data-analysis/) on the alignment and analysis of genomics data from "benchtop" sequencers, i.e. MiSeq and Ion Torrent. Webinar panellists will give a tour of various bioinformatics functions in **Avadis NGS** that will enable researchers and clinicians to derive biological insights from their benchtop sequencing data. Seminar #1: MiSeq Data Analysis (http://blog.avadis-ngs.com/2012/02/webinar-series-benchtop-sequencing-data-analysis/) Avadis NGS 1.3 provides special support for analyzing data generated by MiSeq™ sequencers. In this webinar, we will describe how the data in a MiSeq generated "run folder" is automatically loaded into the Avadis NGS software during small RNA alignment and DNA variant analysis. This is especially helpful in processing the large number of files generated when the TruSeq™ Amplicon Kits are used. We will describe how to use the Quality Control steps in Avadis NGS to check if the amplicons have sufficient coverage in all the samples. Regions with unexpected coverages can easily be identified using the new region list clustering feature. Webinar attendees will learn how to use the "Find Significant SNPs" feature to quickly identify high-confidence SNPs present in a majority of the samples, rare variants, etc. Seminar #2: Ion Torrent Data Analysis (http://blog.avadis-ngs.com/2012/02/webinar-series-benchtop-sequencing-data-analysis/) Avadis NGS 1.3 includes a new aligner – COBWeb – that is fully capable of aligning the long, variable-length reads generated by Ion Torrent sequencers. In this webinar, we will show the pre-alignment QC plots and illustrate how they can be used to set appropriate alignment parameters for aligning

Ion Torrent reads. For users who choose to import the BAM format files generated by the Ion Torrent Server, we will describe the steps needed for importing amplicon sequencing data into Avadis NGS. Users of the Ion AmpliSeq™ Cancer Panel will learn how to easily import the targeted mutation list and verify the genotype call at the mutation sites. We will also show the new "Find Significant SNPs" feature which helps quickly identify high-confidence SNPs present in a majority of the samples, rare variants, etc. Free registration - (http://www.avadis-ngs.com/webinar) or (http://www.bemgi.be/events/bemgi-bioinformatics-wg-webinar/).

Source: (http://www.cloudera.com/content/cloudera/en/resources/library/recordedwebinar/the-data-deluge-of-next-generation-bioinformatics.html).

The volume of data generated by next generation sequencing machines, bioinformatics analytics, biomedical imaging, clinical trials, and other patient care data is overwhelming clinicians and researchers. The Hadoop platform can help with this problem.

Cloudera and A-TRAC discuss the future of Hadoop in bioinformatics. Learn how Hadoop is providing dramatic improvements in bioinformatics processing time at significantly lower costs.

(https://www.google.co.in/webhp?sourceid=chrome-instant&ion=1&cspv=2&ie=UTF-8#q=bioinformatics+seminar&revid=1838572739)

(https://twitter.com/rstudio/status/529670099301830656)

(http://bioinformatics.ca/resources/other-activities)

(http://blog.avadis-ngs.com/2012/02/webinar-series-benchtop-sequencing-data-analysis/)

Recorded Webinars

Title: PCBC Introductory Genomics Webinar on "Choosing the technology, designing the experiment, and preparing the samples to get the best data."

A recording is available for your review. Please click on the link below to play it: (https://epiumd.webex.com/epiumd/lsr.php?RCID=47c321c8fb8904305379ed63b5bd89d8).

Title: Data Mining from the New Progenitor Cell Biology Consortium (PCBC) Genomics Expression Atlas

Topics for discussion: Cell, RNA, and DNA samples in the PCBC Cell Characterization Core.

Cell phenotype and genomics analyses have been performed (e.g., cell samples analyzed by RNAseq, miRseq, DNA methylation)

Finding what a gene of interest is doing in the different samples - Pathways and interactions that are active in different cells or involve genes of interest - Gene lists for similarity to signatures in the PCBC database - Splice forms of the RNAseq data from PCBC samples.

Please click on the link (https://epiumd.webex.com/epiumd/lsr.php?RCID=330b9ad6a5986c13734b6a277970fb47).

Title: Bioinformatics Core - Synapse Webinar

Click on the link to play this webinar recording: (https://epiumd.webex.com/epiumd/lsr.php?RCID=3c06c71fae59d471433f7540bbeece4a).

Title: Accessing PCBC Generated Data in Synapse. The topics covered are -

a) how to access, download, query PCBC generated data as stored in Synapse,

b) how to use the PCBC web portal in Synapse to perform hierarchal clustering of user specified genes and link out to enrichment analysis,

c) how to get started in accessing the data from within R and Python, and

d) how to store your own analysis results in Synapse.

As the series progresses, more advanced topics in genomics and bioinformatics from visualization to batch correction to differential expression analysis will be covered.

Click on the link to view the recording of this webinar: (https://www.youtube.com/playlist?List=PL0QrRbpf8KbSO8eTNFs IPUZJ85u6gtNkQ).

Title / Date: Normalization, artefact detection and correction in Synapse. **Presenter:** Larsson Omberg. The second webinar covered the following topics:

a) Principal component analysis and visualization

b) Correlation analysis with covariates

c) Corrections using linear models

d) Given enough time we will cover Surrogate Variable Analysis

Click on the link to play this webinar recording: (http://youtu.be/ZcnSencVkEY).

Webinar Series: What about Privacy and Progress in Whole Genome Sequencing? (http://beckerinfo.net/bioinformatics/webinar-series-what-about-privacy-and-progress-in-whole-genome-sequencing/)

From the great folks at Genetic Alliance: What about Privacy and Progress in Whole Genome Sequencing? A Year-Long Webinar Series Registration is free: (http://www.geneticalliance.org/webinars). The Presidential Commission for the Study of Bioethical Issues recently released a report entitled Privacy and Progress in Whole Genome Sequencing.

The Importance of Bioinformatics in NGS

(http://webinar.sciencemag.org/webinar/archive/importance-bioinformatics-ngs)

Breaking the Bottleneck in Data Interpretation

VIDEO: This event occurred on Wednesday, May 14, 2014

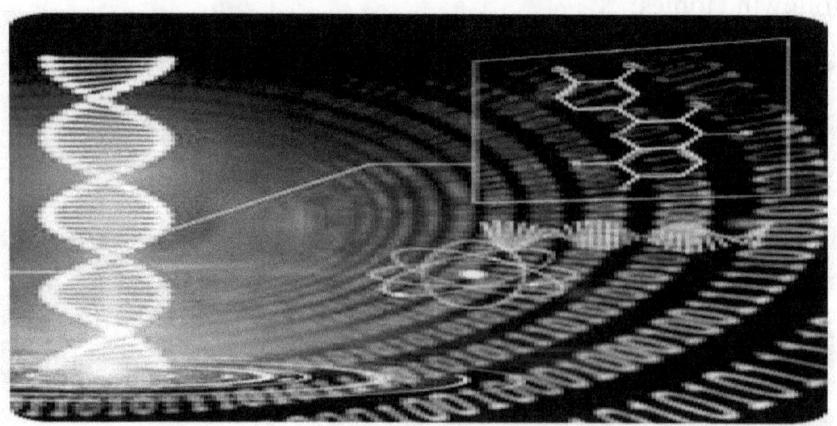

Unprecedented advances have been made in the speed and throughput of next generation sequencing (NGS) platforms over the last decade. This progress has imposed increasingly high demands on the bioinformatics tools necessary for analysis of the data generated, which has grown exponentially. Although hundreds of thousands of samples have been sequenced, our ability to find, associate, and implicate genetic variants and candidate disease genes far outstrip our ability to understand them. Many researchers are comfortable with NGS technology, but encounter difficulties with the bioinformatics portion of their workflow, rendering NGS a less attractive option as their primary sequencing platform. However, once clear bioinformatics procedures are established and optimized this bottleneck can be removed, resulting in smooth and routine data interpretation processes and expedited research discoveries. During this webinar, our expert speakers will discuss their bioinformatics strategies and applications in range of fields of clinical research.

During the webinar, viewers

a) Be introduced to the bioinformatics workflow and the importance of accurate NGS data analysis and interpretation
b) Learn how bioinformatics concepts are applied to detect and characterize disease-related mutations
c) Hear about the use of bioinformatics workflows in a translational setting for tumour mutation detection
d) Have their questions answered live by our expert panel!

Webinar: World Tour of Genomics Resources (http://www.openhelix.com/cgi/webinarInfo.cgi?id=33):

There are thousands of bioinformatics and genomics resources that are free and publicly accessible. However, trying to find the right resource for your need, and learn how to use the often complex features and functions can be difficult.

Wiki Pathways

The PCBC Bioinformatics Core is posting a series of tutorials that will walk researchers through the process of creating reference digital pathways for analysis with their own omics data and those produced by the Cincinnati Cell Characterization Core (C4). It is recommended that people view these tutorials and follow along prior to group pathway creation or editing sessions. All videos are open-access.

Tutorial

A basic introduction for creating a WikiPathway from an existing progenitor differentiation pathway figure is shown in the below video. This video walks the user through downloading PathVisio, finding the pathway, entering the gene IDs into PathVisio, making a nicely curated pathway and uploading it to WikiPathways. Creating a Lineage Specification Pathway in Pathvisio (TBA) (http://youtu.be/GRtaLihkTGM).

Translational Medicine & Human Health (http://beckerinfo.net/bioinformatics/translational-medicine-human-health/): The AAAS Center for Public Engagement with Science and Technology just released a great set of lectures on translational medicine. The lectures are part of the Abelson Advancing Science Seminar Series.

NIH Video casts

Have you had an opportunity to check out the videocasts from NIH? The Center for Information Technology (CIT) makes special NIH events, seminars, and lectures available to viewers on the NIH network and the Internet from the VideoCast web site. There are a wide variety of topics offered and this is a great opportunity to [...] (http://beckerinfo.net/bioinformatics/nih-videocasts/).

Bioinformatics Tutorials (http://beckerinfo.net/bioinformatics/bioinformatics-tutorials-2/)

There are a number of great tutorials on the web for bioinformatics-related applications and topics. BioInformatics Tutorials Series (BITS) from Countway Library of Medicine at Harvard are on the following topics.

Bioinformatics (http://beckerinfo.net/bioinformatics/category/bioinformatics/)

BLAST (http://beckerinfo.net/bioinformatics/category/blast/)

database (http://beckerinfo.net/bioinformatics/category/database/)

EBI (http://beckerinfo.net/bioinformatics/category/ebi/)

education (http://beckerinfo.net/bioinformatics/category/education/)

Ensembl (http://beckerinfo.net/bioinformatics/category/ensembl/)

genome (http://beckerinfo.net/bioinformatics/category/genome/)

genome browser (http://beckerinfo.net/bioinformatics/category/genome-browser/)

helpful (http://beckerinfo.net/bioinformatics/category/helpful/)

informatics (http://beckerinfo.net/bioinformatics/category/informatics/)

Information (http://beckerinfo.net/bioinformatics/category/information/)

NCBI (http://beckerinfo.net/bioinformatics/category/ncbi/)

resources (http://beckerinfo.net/bioinformatics/category/resources/)

sequence (http://beckerinfo.net/bioinformatics/category/sequence/)

tool (http://beckerinfo.net/bioinformatics/category/tool/)

tutorial (http://beckerinfo.net/bioinformatics/category/tutorial/)

webinar (http://beckerinfo.net/bioinformatics/category/webinar/)

Free online training from GeneGo (http://beckerinfo.net/bioinformatics/free-online-training-from-genego-july-dates/):

I received the information below in an email from GeneGo yesterday: July 6th : Knowledge mining GeneGo content, EZ Search and MetaSearch Tired of spending hours searching the public domain building your research objectives ? GeneGo now provides a new Google-like interface to search your favorite gene, protein, disease or compound with just one click. In this you will find details about **expression** (http://beckerinfo.net/bioinformatics/category/expression/), **genomics** (http://beckerinfo.net/bioinformatics/category/genomics/), **Information** (http://beckerinfo.net/bioinformatics/category/information/), **tutorial** (http://beckerinfo.net/bioinformatics/category/tutorial/), **webinar** (http://beckerinfo.net/bioinformatics/category/webinar/).

National Library of Medicine update (http://beckerinfo.net/bioinformatics/nlmnews/):

I went to the Medical Library Association (MLA) annual meeting this week (in Honolulu!) and heard some interesting news during the National Library of Medicine (NLM) update. Dr. Lindberg discussed the increasing need for libraries to play a role in supporting clinical trials and he also discussed disaster preparedness efforts at NLM. Coverage on bioinformatics (http://beckerinfo.net/bioinformatics/category/bioinformatics/) database (http://beckerinfo.net/bioinformatics/category/database/), event (http://beckerinfo.net/bioinformatics/category/event/), Information (http://beckerinfo.net/

bioinformatics/category/information/), NCBI (http://beckerinfo.net/bioinformatics/category/ncbi/), NLM (http://beckerinfo.net/bioinformatics/category/nlm/), resources (http://beckerinfo.net/bioinformatics/category/resources/), science (http://beckerinfo.net/bioinformatics/category/science/), tutorial (http://beckerinfo.net/bioinformatics/category/tutorial/), webinar (http://beckerinfo.net/bioinformatics/category/ webinar/).

Genetic Alliance webinars and resources (http://beckerinfo.net/bioinformatics/genetic-alliance/): Genetic Alliance "transforms health through genetics." They offer a large number of good resources for patients, caregivers, and clinicians on a host of genetic conditions. More about what they do: Leveraging the expertise of the genetics community builds capacity in our members through collaborative engagement. Genetic Alliance is at the crossroads of the genetics community.

Source: (http://beckerinfo.net/bioinformatics/category/webinar/)

New Release of CDART (http://jeansong.wordpress.com/): NCBI has announced its new release of CDART, Conserved Domain Architecture Retrieval Tool with enhanced features such as:

a) improved performance for long query proteins

b) expanded input options: protein sequence, set of conserved domains

c) display of similarity scores

d) filtering of results

You'll find CDART at: (http://www.ncbi.nlm.nih.gov/Structure/lexington/lexington.cgi)

EBI Bioinformatics Roadshow (http://jeansong.wordpress.com/2011/07/14/ebi-bioinformatics-roadshow/)

We are looking to have the European Bioinformatics Institute (EBI) (http://www.ebi.ac.uk/training/about/html) do a Bioinformatics Roadshow (http://www.ebi.ac.uk/training/roadshow/) at the University of Michigan (http://umich.edu/).

dbVar (https://jeansong.wordpress.com/2010/03/17/dbvar/): NCBI has a new database for structural variation called dbVar, the Database of Genomic Structural Variation. dbVar contains data from studies on large-scale genomic variation. You can read more in the NCBI News (http://www.ncbi.nlm.nih.gov/books/NBK26469/).

NCIBI Researcher Profiles (https://jeansong.wordpress.com/2010/02/19/ncibi-researcher-profiles/): I am interested in interviewing people who have been using any of the National Center for Integrative Biomedical Informatics' tools to profile you on the center's homepage. If you have used any of the center's tools including but not limited to: Gene2MeSH (http://gene2mesh.ncibi.org/), MiMI Web (http://gene2mesh.ncibi.org/), MiMI Cytoscape plug-in (http://mimi.ncbi.org/cytoscape/launcher), Metscape (metscape.ncbi.org), Cytoscape plug-in, ConceptGen (http://conceptgen.ncibi.org/core/conceptGen/index.jsp), MiSearch (http://misearch.ncibi.org/), or have been using any of its web services (http://portal.ncbi.org/gateway/tryourtools.html) please contact me so I can make you famous !

NCIBI on Facebook: National Center for Integrative Biomedical Informatics on Facebook (http://jeansong.wordpress.com/2010/01/14/ncibi-on-facebook/).

PubMed User Search Behavior (https://jeansong.wordpress.com/2009/12/10/pubmed-user-search-behavior/): A recently

published article in the journal, Database: the Journal of Biological Databases and Curation, investigates the needs and behavior of PubMed users through the analysis of log data. The authors analyzed 23 million user sessions with more than 58 million user queries. It's difficult to find large analyses such as these specific to health information seeking behaviour, so it's worth having a look. The full text of the article is available here: (http://database.oxfordjournals.org/cgi/content/full/2009/0/bap018).

PMCID Converter for NIHMSIDs (https://jeansong.wordpress.com/2009/12/02/pmcid-converter-for-nihmsids/)

The PMCID Converter will now list NIHMSIDs along with PMCIDs, so we're all in luck. Here's the link: (http://www.ncbi.nlm.nih.gov/sites/pmctopmid).

In the past, you couldn't get the NIHMSID unless you were the one to submit the manuscript, so this should make everyone's life a little bit easier.

Here are some brief tips:

a) Enter PMIDs into the box – on separate lines OR with spaces OR with commas in between
b) Only 2000 PMIDs can be entered in one box
c) Check the "Write result to file" box to output the results into a CSV file.

NCBI Short Read Archive of NexGen Sequencing Data (http://jeansong.wordpress.com/2009/08/19/ncbi-short-read-archive-of-nexgen-sequencing-data/):

They are now maintaining the Short Read Archive (SRA) (http://www.ncbi.nlm.nih.gov/Traces/sra/) for parallel sequencing technologies. SRA allows you to:

a) Search and display SRA project data through their homepage

b) Search and display SRA project data through Entrez (http://www.ncbi.nlm. nih.gov/sra?term=all%5Bsb%5D)

c) Download data through Aspera Connect (http://www.aspera.com/en/software-license-management/)

d) BLAST service (http://blast.ncbi.nlm.nih.gov/Blast.cgi?PROGRAM=blastn&BLAST_PROGRAMS=megaBlast&PAGE_TYPE=BlastSearch&BLAST_SPEC=SRA) for sequence similarity searching of 454 sequencing reads for transcriptome studies

NCBI 3D Structure Help (https://jeansong.wordpress.com/2009/08/05/ncbi-3d-structure-help/)

So the folks at NCBI have posted a whole bunch of useful help files on the web for their 3D structure resources, 3D Macromolecular Structure (http://www.ncbi.nlm.nih.gov/Structure/MMDB/docs/mmdb_how_to.html) and Conserved Domains (http://www.ncbi.nlm.nih.gov/Structure/cdd/docs/cdd_how_to.html). There are also other helpful how-to files which the fabulous Kristi Holmes over at Becker Library at Wash U has already blogged about here (http://beckerinfo.net/bioinformatics/2009/07/29-3d-structure-help-from-ncbi/). Oh, there's a link to that blog, Bioinformatics@Becker (http://beckerinfo.net/bioinformatics/), in my blogroll in case you haven't already checked it out.

Data Manipulation with R (http://jeansong.wordpress.com/2009/07/14/data-manipulation-with-r/): So for you bioinformaticists using R, I thought you might be interested in knowing that the book, Data Manipulation with R, by Phil Spector is available as an e-book in

Mirlyn. Get the full Mirlyn record here (http://mirlyn.lib.umich.edu/Record/005700682) with the link to the book. You'll have to login if you aren't already, using your Kerberos password. I don't know anything about R, but the book has decent reviews (http://www.amazon.com/Data-Manipulation-R-Use/dp/0387747303/ref=pd_sim_b_3) on Amazon. Have fun!

BioSystems Database (https://jeansong.wordpress.com/2009/07/07/biosystems-database/)

The NCBI folks have created another database, NCBI BioSystems, which is the aggregation of several public databases. This database connects biosystem records with literature, molecular and chemical data from the Entrez system. Biological pathways from KEGG nd BioCyc are currently included. Links to this database are included in records from NCBI Gene, HomoloGene, OMIM and the Protein Clusers databases. Get the full details on NCBI BioSystems here (http://www.ncbi.nlm.nih.gov/Structure/biosystems/docs/biosystems_about.html).

Protein Interaction Networks (http://jeansong.wordpress.com/2009/06/23/protein-interaction-networks/) - In case you don't know what a Cited by search is, these are searches where you determine how many times and by whom your work has been cited.

Raditional Cited By searches are conducted using database tools such as Web of Science (https://weblogin.umich.edu/?cosign-www.lib&https://www.lib.umich.edu/cgi/l/login/proxy-session-init-qurl?qurl=http%3a%2f%2fisiknowledge.com%2f) (Thomson Reuters) or Scopus (Elsevier). However, as we all know, these resources are only available to those institutions that can afford these extremely expensive products.

Google Scholar (http://scholar.google.co.in/) (U of M proxy here) (https://weblogin.umich.edu/?cosign-www.lib& https://www.lib.umich.edu/cgi/l/login/proxy-session-init-qurl?qurl=http%3a%2f%2fscholar.google.com%2f) is an excellent alternative. It's available to the general public for free. As well all know, this makes me very happy. More importantly, if you are publishing in non-traditional methods like Open Access journals or to blogs, wikis, online only publications, then Google Scholar may be the only resource that is able to track who is citing you. Google considers Google Scholar to be Beta, but hey, we know that Google's beta is often better than anyone else's production products.

UM Extends Partnership with Google (http://jeansong.wordpress.com/2009/05/21/um-extends-partnership-with-google/) - University of Michigan is extending its partnership with Google in regards to the digitization of books.

PubChem's 3D Conformers (http://jeansong.wordpress.com/2009/04/15/pubchems-3d-conformers/) So PubChem (http://pubchem.ncbi.nlm.nih.gov/) is featuring calculated three dimensional conformers for about 88% of the records in its compound database. It also is clustering similar conformers and is providing a standalone small molecule conformer viewer called Pc3D. Pc3D is the small molecule equivalent of Cn3D.

Libraries and Translational Research (http://jeansong.wordpress.com/2009/04/07/libraries-and-translational-research/)

Consortium for Stem Cell Therapies (https://jeansong.wordpress.com/2009/03/11/consortium-for-stem-cell-therapies/) - The University of Michigan announced (http://ns.umich.edu/new/releases/

7030) the creation of the A. Alfred Taubman Medical Research Institute Consortium for Stem Cell Therapieas to create embryonic stem cell lines.

This is the first major embryonic stem cell research program launched in Michigan since the November 4th passage of a state constitutional amendment allowing scientists to create new stem cell lines using surplus embryos from fertility clinics.

IEEE Xplore Adds MeSH Indexing (http://jeansong.wordpress.com/2008/12/17/ieee-xplore-adds-mesh-indexing/): So, wanna be able to search those IEEE publications using MeSH? Well, now you can (for some). Use the U of M proxy for IEEE Xplore (https://weblogin.umich.edu/?cosign-www.lib&https://www.lib.umich.edu/cgi/l/login/proxy-session-init-qurl?qurl=http%3a%2f%2fwww.ieee.org%2fieeexplore) and the following publications have MeSH indexing back to 2006 :

1. IEEE Engineering in Medicine and Biology Magazine
2. IEEE Trans on Bio-medical Engineering
3. IEEE Trans on Image Processing
4. IEEE trans on IT in biomedicine
5. IEEE Trans on Medical Imaging
6. IEEE Trans on Nanobioscience
7. IEEE Trans on Neural Networks
8. IEEE Trans on Neural Systems and Rehabilitation Engineering
9. IEEE Trans on Systems, Man, and Cybernetics: Part B – Cybernetics

10. IEEE Trans on Ultrasonics, Ferroelectrics, and Frequency Control
11. IEEE/ACM Trans on Computational Biology and Bioinformatics
12. IEEE Computer Graphics and Applications
13. IEEE Trans on Pattern Analysis and Machine Intelligence
14. IEEE Trans on Visualization and Computer Graphics
15. The Annual International Conference of the IEEE EMBS

NIH's SHARe-Asthma Resource Project (https://jeansong.wordpress.com/2008/12/17/nihs-share-asthma-resource-project/) -NIH

has created the largest public access collection of clinical asthma and genetic data by expanding their SHARe (SNP Health Association Resource) project to the newly expanded SHARP (SHARe Asthma Resource Project) which includes data on 2,332 with asthma and 805 families whose DNA was tested for 1 million genetic variations. Clinical data was also included in the database. SHARP can be accessed through dbGaP. Additional information can be found in the NIH news release (http://www.nih.gov/news/health/dec2008/nhlbi-15.htm).

Increased Embryonic Stem Cell Research (https://jeansong.wordpress.com/2008/12/16/increased-embryonic-stem-cell-research/) - Science this week talks about the possibility of increasing the number of embryonic stem cell research lines with the incoming Obama administration. Read the full story here (http://www.sciencemag.org/content/322/ 5908/1619.full?rss=1).

PubMed Adds Additional 70,000 Old Citations (https://jeansong.wordpress.com/2008/12/01/pubmed-adds-additional-70000-old-citations/): 70,000 citations from the 1948 Current List of Medical Literature from the National Library of Medicine were added to the OLDMEDLINE citation subset in PubMed. To search just the OLDMEDLINE subset in Medline, you will need to use jsubsetom. That NLM does good work, eh?

Facebook and Pubmed (https://jeansong.wordpress.com/2008/08/26/facebook-and-pubmed/) So, if you're on Facebook (https://www.facebook.com/), do you use it only socially? If NCIBI created an application that linked Face book with Pubmed (http://www.ncbi.nlm.nih.gov/pubmed/) say through MiSearch (http://misearch.ncibi.org/), would you use it? This is a fundamental question of how Face book is used. My personal behaviour is that I don't necessarily like to use my social networking sites to do work, but then again, the only blog I have is this one, and it is work related. So frankly, some people would ask the question: Do you poop where you sleep? On the other hand, for some people work is social. Heaven knows that I went back to work after being a full-time mom because I needed work to get a break from the kids. Huh, it's a good question.

Social Networking (https://jeansong.wordpress.com/2008/08/13/social-networking/) - A recent Information Week article describes social networking sites as growing so hopefully all of this blogging, twittering, flickering...is not in vain. Read the full article at (http://www.informationweek.com/news/internet/social_network/showArticle.jhtml?articleID= 210003458).

flickr (https://jeansong.wordpress.com/2008/07/23/flickr/) : In case you are looking for images to use for your presentations and worry about copyright implications, flickr (https://www.flickr.com/) is a great resource for finding images that have a Creative Commons (http://creativecommons.org/) license so that you may use the image according to the CC licensing terms.

Blogroll

a) American Medical Informatics Association (http://www.amia.org/)

b) Bioinformatics@Becker (http://beckerinfo.net/bioinformatics/)

c) Center for Computational Biology and Medicine (http://www.ccmb.med.umich.edu/)

d) Kristiology (http://kristiology.blogspot.com/)

e) National Center for Integrative Biomedical Informatics (http://www.ncibi.org/)

f) Open Access News (http://legacy.earlham.edu/~peters/fos/fosblog.html)

g) PolITiGenomics (http://www.politigenomics.com/)

The following blog sites offer a wide range of news and views on a diversity of biosciences-related topics from individuals ranging from graduate students to established principal investigators and science writers. The rankings provided reflect a composite of the quality and quantity of content on the blog site as well as how directly related they are to the focus of Kinetica Online.

The front page of Bioinformatics.Org (http://www.bioinformatics.org/) itself is a bioinformatics 'Blog.

The Bio-Web (http://cellbiol.com/) links to resources online for molecular and cell biologists and covers current news in various biological/computational fields.

Genehack (http://genehack.org/) is the first bioinformatics 'Blog I ever encountered.

List of Other Bioinformatics Blogs

Site	Rating	Description
123 bioinformatics (http://forum.123bioinformatics.com/)	*	A blog site with over 1167 biotechnology help topics but these often relate to non-scientific issues.
All-wow videos- Mass Spectrometry (http://www.wowtube.ru/index.php?key=Spectrometry)	**	Over 50 short videos related to mass spectrometry. The Wow sites also provide instructional videos on a wide range of other topics.
American Biotechnologist (http://www.americanbiotechnologist.com/blog/)	**	This blog from Bio-Rad (Hercules, CA) has been created as a place where PIs, Graduate Students, Technicians and Science Educators can network, post and view articles, videos, seminars, techniques etc of interest and generally find subject matter relevant to them.
Aetiology (http://scienceblogs.com/aetiology/)	**	A personal blog site from Dr. Tara Smith, who is an assistant professor of Epidemiology in Iowa, which focuses on the causes, origins, evolution and implication of disease and other phenomena.

Site	Rating	Description
Bad Science (http://www.badscience.net/)	**	A personal blog site from Dr. Ben Goldacre, who is a medical doctor, writer and broadcaster. Bad Science covers a wide range of health and science topics.
Becker (http://beaker.sanfordburnham.org/)	**	A blog site produced by Sanford-Burnham Medical Research Institute (La Jolla, CA) that covers recent medical research with commentaries from diverse individuals.
Bench Marks (http://www.chhblogs.org/cshprotocols/category/proteins-and-proteomics/)	***	The focus of this blog is the discussion of methods used in biology laboratories. This blog is kept by David Crotty, the Executive Editor of Cold Spring Harbor Protocols (Woodbury, NY).
Beyond The Human Eye (http://beyondthehumaneye.blogspot.in/)	***	A personal blog site from Phil Gates, a botanist at Durham University, on botanist at Durham University, with commentaries and outstanding microphoto images on microbiology topics.
BioBOOM -The Biotech Blog (http://bioboom.blogspot.in/)	***	A blog site produced by Yali Friedman and focuses on the business of biotechnology with news of medical breakthroughs and the biopharma industry.

Site	Rating	Description
Biochemistry and Bioinformatics (http://biosiva.blogspot.in/2010_01_01_archive.html)	**	This website features diverse articles on biochemistry and bioinformatics and is produced by the Sri Sankara Arts and Science College (Enathur, Kanchipuram).
Biocrowd (http://www.biocrowd.com/)	**	BioCrowd is an on-line social network started by Drs. Clifford S. Mintz and Vincent Racaniello and designed for interactions between individuals involved and interested in the biosciences. Professionals. It features only very recent blogs.
Biohacker (https://biohacker.wordpress.com/)	**	This website is produced by a physicist identified as Dimitri that is learning biochemistry.
Biohealth Investor (http://biohealthinvestor.com/)	*	A commercial blog site from Biohealth Investor (New Rochelle, NY) that provides daily updates on companies and trends in the biotech industry.
BioImplement (http://bioimplement.blogspot.in/)	*	A personal blog site from Christopher Hogue (Singapore) that has not been updated since Feb. 2009.
Bioinfoblog (http://bioinfoblog.it/)	*	Not too many blogs on this website from Italy with infrequent updates.

Site	Rating	Description
Bioinformatics Organization (http://www.bioinformatics.org/)	*	The website for the Bioinformatics Organization with news and commentaries.
Bioinformatics SnowDeal (http://bioinformatics.snowdeal.org/)	*	A personal blog site from Eric C. Snowdeal III devoted to bioinformatics. However, it has not been updated since June 2006.
Bioinformatics: biology by other means (http://blogs.scientifik.info/ bioinformatics/?cat=3)	*	A personal blog site from Alberto Labarga (Granada, Spain) that has not been since Oct. 2009.
Bioinformatics@Becker (http://beckerinfo.net/ bioinformatics/)	**	A blog site with updates and Musings from the Bioinformatics team at Becker Medical Library.
Biology in Science Fiction (http://blog.sciencefictionbiology.com/)	**	A personal blog site produced by Peggy discusses cloning, genetic engineering, mutant monsters, longevity treatments and all the other biology behind science fiction.
BioMed Central Blog (http://blogs.biomedcentral.com/bmcblog/)	***	This website produced by BioMEd Central features articles on diverse topics in biology.
Biopharmconsortium	**	A commercial blog site from Allan

Site	Rating	Description
Blog (http://www.biopharmconsortium.com/blog/)		B. Haberman (Wayland, MA) on various biotechnology advances.
Bioscience Technology (http://www.biosciencetechnology.com/blogs)	*	A blog site from Bioscience Technology with commentaries related to biological sciences and biotechnology.
Biosearch Tech Blog (http://blog.biosearchtech.com/)	**	This website from the company Biosearch Technologies and covers diagnostics methodologies.
Bio-Synthesis (http://bio-synthesis.blogspot.in/)	*	A commercial blog site from Bio-Synthesis, Inc. that appears to mainly profile their products.
Biotech Blog (http://www.biotechblog.com/)	**	A blog site produced by Yali Friedman (Washington, DC) has commentaries on commercial, legal, political and scientific trends in biotechnology.
BIOtechNOW (http://www.biotech-now.org/)	**	BIOtechNOW (Mississauga, Ontario) seeks to contribute to public conversation about the impact of biotechnology on our lives and our world. It explores how biotechnology helps heal, fuel, and feed our global community through sound, video, and the

Site	Rating	Description
		printed word. It is produced by the Biotechnology Industry Organization (BIO).
BioTuesdays (http://biotuesday.ca/)	**	A blog site produced by Leonard Zehr and Stephen Kilmer tracks developments in healthcare companies, particularly in Canada.
Biowizard (http://biotuesday.ca/)	**	This website features a wide range of articles and is sponsored by Chemblog and Sigma (Wayne, PA).
BioWorld (http://www.bioworld.com/)	***	BioWorld Today is a daily source of news about developments in companies in the biotechnology industry. Subscription required.
Bitesize bio (http://bitesizebio.com/303/kinase-structures-and-autoinhibition/)	**	Bitesize Bio is an online magazine and community for molecular and cell biology researchers.
Blind.Scientist (http://blindscientist.genedrift.org/)	*	A personal blog site from a bioinformaticist with very brief musings on bioinformatics and other science topics.
Blog.Bioethics.Net (http://www.bioethics.	***	This website from the editors of the American Journal of Bioethics is

Site	Rating	Description
net/)		dedicated to the study and teaching of ethical dimensions of health care and health policy.
Blogged (http://blogged.com/)	**	An expansive website that covers diverse topics. The website's search engine provides for the retrieval of news and blogs on more specific subjects including cell biology and biochemistry.
Blogging the Business of Biotech (http://insidebioia.com/)	***	This website produced by the Biotechnology Industry Organization features updates on biotech companies and the biotechnology industry.
Blogtoplist (http://www.blogtoplist.com/ rss/)	**	An expansive website that covers diverse topics. The website's directory provides for the retrieval of blogs based on catogories that are located in alphabetical order.
Boston Blog (http://blogs.nature.com/ boston/2007/07/26/ combining-cell-biology-with-cinema)	**	This website features news and commentary on the Boston science scene.
Business, bytes, genes, molecules (http://blog.deepaksingh.	***	A personal blog site from Deepak Singh with commentaries on

Site	Rating	Description
net/)		science, data and computing.
Canadian BioTechnologist2.0 (https://cbt20.wordpress.com/)	***	A commercial website from Bio-Rad that features contributions from undergraduate and post-graduate students, bench scientists, and technologists that includes posters, tools, research, presentations, articles, white papers, multimedia, music downloads and entertainment, conference announcements, and videos.
Cell Biology (http://cellbiology.newsheet.com/category/Cell_Biology_Blogs)	**	Cell Biology Newsbeet is social news, blog and bookmarking site where people can discuss all about blogs, news and information of Cell Biology.
Chemblogs (http://www.chemblogs.com/?f)	**	A commercial blog site from Sigma-Aldrich as a feedback panel for the global chemical community, with posts written by Sigma-Aldrich personnel and invited posts from leaders in academia and industry.
ChEMBL-og (http://chembl.blogspot.in/)	**	A blog site from the Computational Chemical Biology Group (ChEMBL) based at the EMBL-EBI Outstation at Hinxton, U.K. It

Site	Rating	Description
		covers news and progress related to drug discovery and provides access to databases.
Chemical blog space (http://cb.openmolecules.net/ blogs.php?category= Biochemistry)	*	A blog site with relatively few comments actually linked to chemistry.
Clinical Cases and Images: Caseblog (http://casesblog.blogspot.in/)	**	A website with health news updated by an assistant professor at the University of Chicago.
Comprendia (http://comprendia.com/category/blog/)	*	A commercial blog site produced by Mary Canady with suggestions for marketing to life science companies.
Comprendia Blog (http://comprendia.com/category/blog/)	**	This website produced by the Comprendia Biosciences Consulting Group and contains commentary on effective marketing.
Confessions of a (former) Lab Rat (http://occamstypewriter.org/rpg/)	**	A personal blog site from Richard P. Grant of the Nature Publishing Group, which focuses on diverse science
Corante - In the Pipeline	**	A personal blog site from Dr.

Site	Rating	Description
(http://pipeline.corante.com/archives/2006/02/12/kinase_inhibitors_doomed_from_the_start.php)		Derek Lowe, who is an organic chemist that has worked a several major pharmaceutical companies. Corante presents through the eyes of leading observers, analysts, thinkers, and doers, critical themes and memes in technology, business, law, science, and culture.
Culture Dish (http://scienceblogs.com/culturedish/)	**	A personal blog site from science writer Rebecca Skloot about diverse topics in science and medicine.
Daily Tech (http://www.dailytech.com/New+DNA+Microarray+Technique+Based+on+Electrostatics/article12233.htm)	*	A website with daily broad technology news and commentary. Biomedical related topics appear every two to three weeks.
Developing Intelligence (http://scienceblogs.com/developingintelligence/)	**	A personal blog site from Chris Chatham, a graduate student at the University of Colorado (Boulder, CO) with a focus on developmental and computational cognitive neuroscience, comparative psychology, psychometrics and artificial intelligence.
DNA bloggers (https://twitter.com/DNA	*	A blog site with commentaries on genomics-related topics, but not

Site	Rating	Description
bloggers)		very recent (San Francisco, CA).
DNA exchange (http://thednaexchange.com/)	**	A blog site with commentaries from a group of genetic counsellors with an interest in public discussion of genetics-related issues.
Ensembl Weblog (http://ensembl.blogspot.in/)	*	The Ensemble Weblog contains information on updates to databases in Ensembl (UK).
Experimental Man Project (http://www.technologyreview.com/contributor/david-ewing-duncan/)	**	A blog site with genomics and disease commentaries from David Ewing Duncan, who is a journalist and author, and the Director of the Center for Life Science Policy at UC Berkeley.
Eye on DNA (http://www.eyeondna.com/)	**	A blog site with commentary from Dr. Hsien-Hsien Lei and videos related to DNA.
FuturePundit (http://www.futurepundit.com/)	**	A blog site with commentary from Randall Parker and news about future technological trends and their likely effects on human society, politics and evolution.
GEN (http://www.genengnews.com/	***	The blog site for Genetic Engineering and Biotech News.

Site	Rating	Description
500.aspx?aspxerrorpath=/public/ blog/default.aspx)		
Gene Dog Blog (http://genedog.com/blog/2009/06/jmcb/)	**	A personal blog site from Gerry Gao (a biological science student of Shanghai Jiao Tong University, China) with a focus on Developmental Biology.
Gene Expression (http://scienceblogs.com/gnxp/)	***	A personal blog site from Razib Khan that features a wide variety of comments related to the biological sciences including book reviews.
Gene Forum (http://www.geneforum.org/blog)	***	Geneforum is a nonprofit affiliate of the Portland State University Foundation created in 1998 to "promote dialogue at the intersection of genetics, ethics, and public values."
Gene Sherpas (http://www.thegenesherpa.blogspot.in/)	***	A blog site produced by Dr. Steve Murphy (New York, NY) with commentary on medical genetics and personalized medicine.
Genetic Future (http://scienceblogs.com/geneticfuture/)	***	A blog site with commentary from Dr. Daniel MacArthur (New York, NY) on human genetics and personal genomics.

Site	Rating	Description
Genetic Interference (http://www.genetic-inference.co.uk/)	**	A blog site with commentary on disease genetics, genomics, statistics and public health, as well as communication of science by Luke Jostins, a Graduate Student at King's College, Cambridge and the Sanger Institute.
Genetic Engineering & Biotechnology News (http://www.genengnews.com/)	**	A website that includes web-exclusive news and features, Webinars, videos, podcasts, and newsletters related to the biomedical advances and the biotechnology industry.
GeneticsBlogs (http://geneticsblogs.com/)	**	This blog is dedicated to the subject of Genetics and DNA Testing and includes commentaries and videos.
Genome Alberta Blogs (http://genomealberta.ca/blogs/)	***	This website is a source of information related to genomics, proteomics, bioinformatics and bioethics research in Alberta. It is based on the main website of Genome Alberta (Calgary, Alberta).
Genomes Unzipped (http://genomesunzipped.org/)	**	Genomes Unzipped is a group blog providing expert, independent commentary on the personal genomics industry.

Site	Rating	Description
Genomeweb (https://www.genomeweb.com/)	****	This website provides a daily listing of news from the biotechnology industry and advances in biomedical research (New York, USA).
Genomeweb - The Daily Scan (https://www.genomeweb.com/scan)	****	This website provides a daily listing of interesting blogs from a wide range of other blog sites (New York, USA).
Genomicron (http://www.genomicron.evolverzone.com/)	**	A personal blog site with commentary from T. Ryan Gregory, an evolutionary biologist specializing in genome size evolution at the University of Guelph in Canada.
Genomics Law Report (http://www.genomicslawreport.com/)	**	Genomics Law Report is a publication of the law firm Robinson, Bradshaw & Hinson focusing on the legal implications of important developments in the fields of genomics and personalized medicine.
Health Blog (http://blogs.wsj.com/health/2008/06/17/mixed-results-for-experimental-alzheimers-antibody/)	***	Health Blog offers news and analysis on health and the business of health. The blog is written by Katherine Hobson and includes contributions from staffers at The Wall Street Journal, WSJ.com and

Site	Rating	Description
		Dow Jones Newswire.
Here Be Answers (http://www.herebeanswers.com/ p/links-to-all-posts-on-here-be-answers.html)	**	A website that contains answers to a wide range of interesting questions in science, technology and business.
HPC info (http://hpcinfo.com/)	**	A website produced by Gary Stiehr with information and discussion about High Performance Computing as largely applied to genomics.
IamBiotech (http://www.biotech-now.org/)	***	A blog site produced by produced by the Biotechnology Industry Organization (BIO) that is dedicated to helping the biotech community address those challenges and support the industry's work to Heal, Fuel and Feed the world.
iBiome (http://ibiome.typepad.com/)	*	A personal blog site from Brain Yates with commentary on general biology topics.
IguanaBio (http://www.iguanabio.com/)	**	This website is a daily pharma and biotech tabloid that takes a colorful and unique perspective on the industry's breaking news, developments, events and

Site	Rating	Description
		personalities.
IVDTinsight (http://www.ivdtechnology.com/blog)	**	IVD Technology is a trade journal designed for manufacturers of in vitro diagnostic products with peer-reviewed articles covering a wide range of technical and regulatory topics. The publications primary focus is on diagnostics technologies--including research, development, and manufacturing.
JCVI Weblog (http://blogs.jcvi.org/)	***	A blog site produced by the J. Craig Venter Institute (Rockville, MD) that has news and articles related to genomics studies.
Jim's Corner (http://www.biotech-now.org/jims-corner)	**	A personal blog site that features the thoughts and perspectives from the Biotechnology Industry Organization's president and CEO Jim Greenwood.
Kosmix (http://health.kosmix.com/)	**	An expansive website with news and views on diverse subjects, including health care and science.
Lab Manager Editor's Buzz (http://www.labmanager.com/blogs/Editor)	**	A blog site edited by Pam Ahlberg (Midland, ON) with commentary about laboratory technology, research news and trends, and

Site	Rating	Description
		events.
LC Sciences Blog (http://www.lcsciences.com/blog/)	**	A commercial blog site from LC Sciences website (Houston, TX).
Lymphoma Info (http://www.lymphomainfo.net/blog)	**	A blog site that covers lymphoma-related issues by providing concise, up-to-date information and a meeting place for lymphoma patients and those who care about them.
Mass Genomics (http://massgenomics.org/)	**	A personal blog site that features comments about genomics from Dan Koboldt, who works in the Medical Genomics group of the Genome Sequencing Center at Washington University in St. Louis.
Mass Spectrometry Blog (http://mass-spec.lsu.edu/blog/)	**	A Web log of mass spectrometry websites, discussion groups, mailing lists and other links and items of interest to the mass spectrometry community. This blog is run by Kermit Murray, professor of chemistry at Louisiana State University.
Mayo Clinic (http://www.mayoclinic.o	***	This website contains a wealth of information, including questions

Site	Rating	Description
rg/ diseases-conditions)		and answers about many different diseases (Rochester, MN).
Medchem Blog (http://medchemblog.blogspot.in/)	**	This blog site provides information on drug discovery related topics such as medicinal chemistry and pharmacological aspects of drugs as well as simple lab techniques.
Medical Blogs (http://blogs.jwatch.org/)	**	This website includes medical-related blogs that are tracked by Journal Watch.
Medical News, Articles and Blogs (http://www.medinews.co.uk/forum)	**	This website features medical news, articles and blogs with several medical-focused forums.
MedWorm-Bioinformatics Blog (http://www.medworm.com/ rss/blogs.php)	**	This blog site features a wide range of medical focused forums with blogs from other blog sites.
Microarray BiochipTechnology (http://arrayit.blogspot.in/)	*	A commercial blog site from Arrayit Corporation and Todd Martinsky covering microarray technology advancements.
Microarray Blog (https://microarray.wordpress.com/ feed/)	**	A blog site with commentary and news from Albin Paul on microaray technology and other

Site	Rating	Description
		biotechnology.
Microbial Art (http://www.microbialart.com/)	***	A website that features a collection of unique artworks created using living bacteria, fungi, and protists.
Microbiology Blog (http://www.horizonpress.com/ blogger/)	**	A blog site with microbiology news and views that focuses on journal articles and book reviews (UK).
MicrobiologyBytes (https://microbiologybytes.wordpress.com/)	**	A blog site produced by Dr. Alan Cann with news and comments related to microbiology topics.
miRNA blog (http://mirnablog.com/)	**	A blog site dedicated to tracking advances in the microRNA field with news, commentaries and blogs.
Molecular Biology Blog (http://www.horizonpress.com/ blogger/)	**	A blog site with commentary on current research, forthcoming conferences, hot research topics, high impact publications (UK).
My Biotech Life (http://my.biotechlife.net/)	**	A blog site with commentary by Ricardo Vidal about life sciences and biotechnology topics.
Nascent (http://blogs.nature.com/nascent/)	**	A commercial blog site from the Nature Publishing Grioup on web technology and science.

Site	Rating	Description
Nature.com ZBlogs (http://blogs.nature.com/)	***	A websire with blogs written by the editors and journalists and members of Nature Network and also includes posts from hundreds of third party science blogs.
Neurologica Blog (http://theness.com/neurologicablog/)	***	A personal blog site from Dr.Steven Novella, who is an academic clinical neurologist at Yale University School of Medicine. His blog covers news and issues in neuroscience, but also general science, scientific skepticism, philosophy of science, critical thinking, and the intersection of science with the media and society.
Neurophilosophy (http://scienceblogs.com/neurophilosophy/)	***	A personal blog site produced by a molecular and developmental neurobiologist turned science writer.
Nex-Gen Sequencing (http://nextgenseq.blogspot.in/)	***	A blog site from Stuart Brown, an associate professor in the Dept. of Cell Biology at NYU School of Medicine, which focuses on the rapidly developing world of Next-Generation DNA sequencing, with an emphasis on bioinformatics.
NSGC President's Blog	**	A personal blog site from Liz

Site	Rating	Description
(http://nsgcpresident.blogspot.in/)		Kearney, who is the President of National Society of Genetic Counsellors (NSGC). The blog covers topics related to the interests of NSGC.
Omics! Omics! (http://omicsomics.blogspot.in/)	**	A personal blog site from Dr. Keith Robinson, a computational biologist, on new technologies, genomics and proteomics.
PCR blog (http://www.highveld.com/pcr/)	*	A blog site with information on PCR reviews, PCR technology, tips and advice, and troubleshooting (UK).
PepCyber (http://www.pepcyber.org/PPEP/)	****	PepCyber: P~Pep is the largest public database of human protein-protein interactions mediated by phosphoprotein binding domains (PPBDs). The database is hand curated from peer-reviewed literature and is a rich information source emphasizing the reported, experimentally validated data for specific PPBD-PPEP interactions. The current release of the PepCyber: P~Pep database V1.2 (May 2010) includes 11,269 records of interactions between 387 PPBD proteins and 1,471 substrate proteins, curated from 4,852 publi

Site	Rating	Description
Pharma Strategy Blog (http://www.pharmastrategyblog.com/)	**	A commercial blog site from Dr. Sally Church of Icarus Consultants, Inc., with a focus on developments in oncology, haematology, immunology, respiratory and HIV.
PIMM - Partial Immortalization (https://pimm.wordpress.com/2008/04/23/human-proteome-project-21000-genes1-protein-10-years-1-billion/)	*	A personal blog site from Attila Chordash, who is a molecular biologist and biotechnologist. His blog site covers personal genetics, stem cells and mitochondria, regenerative medicine, biotechnology, indefinite life extension, science hacks and bioDIY amongst others.
Plant Biotech Blog (http://www.plantbiotechblog.com/)	**	A personal blog site from Dr. Chavali Kameswara Rao, who is a professor in the Department of Sericulture at the Bangalore University in Bangalore, India. Plant Biotech Blog features analyses and views on various issues of modern agricultural biotechnology.
PMC Blog (https://ageofpersonalizedmedicine.wordpress.com/)	***	A blog site with commentaries from the Personalized Medicine Coalition.
PolITiGenomics	**	PolITiGenomics is a blog by David

Site	Rating	Description
(http://www.politigenomics.com/)		Dooling about the confluence (and sometimes incongruence) of several of the most important topics surrounding the future of human health: genomics, information technology, and politics.
PolitiGenomics (http://www.politigenomics.com/)	**	A personal blog site from David Dooling, who runs the Analysis Developers, Laboratory Information Management Systems (LIMS), and the Information Systems groups at The Genome Center at Washington University in St. Louis School of Medicine. PolitiGenomics is devoted to commentary about the confluence (and sometimes incongruence) of several of the most important topics surrounding the future of human health: genomics, information technology, and politics.
Proteomics 2.0 (http://www.proteomics2.com/)	**	A blog and discussion forum from the compant SageN Research, Inc. for tools, insights and approaches for the next generation of proteomics analysis.
Public Rambling (http://www.evocellnet.com/p/ research.html)	**	A personal blog site from Dr. Pedro Beltrao with comments on bioinformatics science and

Site	Rating	Description
		technology.
Red Orbit (http://www.redorbit.com/news/health/)	**	A website with news on a wide diversity of science and technology-related subjects as well as education, entertainment, business, politics and sports (Texas).
Regina's Biology Blog (http://biology.about.com/)	**	A personal blog site from Regina Lynn Bailey, who is a science educator, with news and comments related to scientific insights in biology and health.
Research Blog (http://researchblogging.org/)	**	A website that links to blog sites on diverse subjects in science and the humanities.
RNA bioinformatics (http://www.rnabioinformatics.org/)	**	A personal blog site from Yi Xing, an Assistant Professor in the Department of Internal Medicine and Department of Biomedical Engineering, University of Iowa. It focuses on genomics and bioinformatics but has not been updated since 2007.
Sandwalk (http://sandwalk.blogspot.in/)	**	A personal blog site from Dr. Laurence Moran, who is a biochemistry professor at the

Site	Rating	Description
		University of Toronto.
Sci Blogs (http://sciblogs.co.nz/code-for-life/2010/03/21/bioinformatics-blog-carnival/)	**	A personal blog site from a computational biologist that covers a wide range of science-related topics (New Zealand).
Science 2.0 (http://www.science20.com/all_blogs)	**	This website features news and commentaries on a wide range of life and physical science-, medicine- and social sciences-related topics.
Science Base Blog (http://www.sciencebase.com/science-blog/)	***	This general science website produced by David Bradley features science news, interviews and commentaries.
Science Blog (http://scienceblog.com/)	***	A large blogsite with news and commentaries on general science.
Science Blogs (http://scienceblogs.com/channel/life-science/?utm_source=globalChannel&utm_medium=link)	***	A website with news and commentary on a wide range of topics in the life sciences.
Science Careers Blog (http://sciencecareers.scie	**	This blog site from Science Magazine provides updates from

Site	Rating	Description
ncemag.org/career_magazine)		the science-career trenches including advice, opinion, news, funding opportunities, and links to other career-related resources.
Science Life (http://sciencelife.uchospitals.edu/ tag/cell/)	**	This blog site is produced by Jeremy Manier and Rob Mitchum at the University of Chicago Medical Center and provides news and commentary about clinical and theoretical advances �from new kinds of cancer treatments to new ideas about how life evolved. Contributors to the blog include some of the world�s leading authorities on complex surgery, cancer, evolution, genetics, heart disease, organ transplants, and many other fields.
Science Roll (http://scienceroll.com/)	**	A website produced by Dr. Bertalan Mesko (Hungary) with commentaries and other features related to genomics and medicine.
Science-based Medicine (http://www.sciencebasedmedicine. org/)	**	This blog site explores issues and controversies in the relationship between science and medicine. The editorial staffs of Science-Based Medicine is composed of physicians who, alarmed at the manner in which unscientific and

Site	Rating	Description
		pseudoscientific health care ideas have increasingly infiltrated academic medicine and medicine at large, have decided to do their part to examine these claims in the light of science and scepticism.
Scienceforums (http://www.scienceforums.net/)	**	This website features a large variety of forms with thousands of blogs on different subjects including science and medicine.
Scientist Solutions (http://www.scientistsolutions.com/ science-forum.aspx)	***	This website features a large variety of forms with news and commentaries on different techniques and equipment used in biomedical research.
Sigma Bioblogs (http://www.sigmabioblogs.com/)	*	This commercial blog site from Sigma Life Science with comments primarily about products and services for biomedical research.
Spoonful of Medicine (http://blogs.nature.com/spoonful/)	**	This blog site produced by the Nature Group contains commentaries on science, medicine and politics.
Stem Cell Daily (http://stemcelldaily.com/)	**	This website is collection of news articles about stem cells and research.

Site	Rating	Description
Steve's Systems Biology Blog (http://www.stevecheckley.co.uk/blog/)	*	A personal blog site from Steve Checkley, who is a Ph.D. graduate student in systems biology at the University of Manchester (UK).
Target Health Global (http://blog.targethealth.com/?p=11815)	**	A commercial website produced by Target Health Inc. with news and videos about biomedical advances (New York, NY).
The Bioinformatics Blog (http://bioinformatics.whatheblog.com/)	**	A blog site with commentaries from volunteer writers and Bioinformaticists from around the world.
The Biotech Ethics Blog (http://biotechethicsblog.com/)	**	This blog site produced by Dr. Chris MacDonald is focused on ethical issues in the biotechnology industry, including health biotech, food biotech, and industrial biotech.
The Cross-border Biotech Blog (http://crossborderbiotech.ca/)	*	This blog site edited by Dr. Jeremy Grushcow covers developments in the biotech industry in Canada, the U.S. and abroad.
The Evilutionary Biologist (http://evilutionarybiologist.blogspot.in/)	**	A personal blog site from John Dennehy, an evolutionary biologist affiliated with Queens College and the CUNY Graduate Center.

Site	Rating	Description
The Genetic Genealogist (http://www.thegeneticgenealogist.com/)	**	A blog site produced by Blaine Bettinger that seeks to examine the intersection of traditional genealogical techniques and modern genetic research. The blog also explores the latest news and developments in the related field of personal genomics.
The Genetic Link (http://blog.dnagenotek.com/blogdnagenotekcom)	*	This is commercial blog site from DNA Genotek that is focused on providing new insights about DNA and RNA sample collection.
The Great Beyond (http://blogs.nature.com/news/category/biology-biotechnology)	**	A Nature Group blog site that focuses on biology and biotechnology.
The Haystack (http://cenblog.org/the-haystack)	**	A blog site from Central Science that features news and commentary on chemistry and life sciences advances.
The Health Care Blog (http://thehealthcareblog.com/)	***	This website features news about health care advances and includes interviews and videos. It prints original material from many contributors and syndicates posts from other bloggers.

Site	Rating	Description
The In Vivo Blog (http://invivoblog.blogspot.in/)	***	This website, produced by Elsevier Business Intelligence. features daily news about medical advances and is
The Loom (http://blogs.discovermagazine.com/loom/)	**	A blog site from science writer Carl Zimmer provides news and commentary on diverse science-related subjects.
The Microarray Blog (http://microarray.scienceboard.net/)	*	A blog site produced in collaboration between the Science Advisory Board and Albin Paul, who is a pharmacologist, is a focus on who enjoys the fields of drug discovery & development and bioinformatics; and in particular, microarray technology. The site does not seem to be recently updated.
The Open Helix Blog (http://blog.openhelix.com/)	**	A blog site with commentary and news from Jennifer and other staff at Open Helix.
The Personal Genome (http://thepersonalgenome.com/)	**	This website features commentaries and short video interviews on genomics and personalized medicine. It is produced by Jason Bobe, who is the Director of Community for the Personal Genome Project based out of George Church's lab at Harvard Medical School.

Site	Rating	Description
The Science Advisory Board (http://www.scienceboard.org/community/blogs.asp)	*	A website that links to a series of blog sites produced in collaboration with The Science Advisory Board. It aims to improve communications between medical and life science professionals and the companies who provide this community with products and services.
The Weblog Biotech (http://www.biotech-weblog.com/)	***	A blog site produced by Creative Weblogging that covers advances in medicine and biotechnology.
Think Gene (http://www.thinkgene.com/)	**	A bio blog produced by Josh Hill and Kevin Fischer about genetics, genomics, and biotechnology.
Thoughtomics (http://www.lucasbrouwers.nl/blog/2010/04/phosphorylation-without-a-cause/)	**	A personal blog site from Lucas Brouwers, who is a M.Sc. student in Molecular Mechanisms of Disease in Nijmegen (Netherlands). The blog provides commentary on evolution, bioinformatics, music and assorted random thoughts.
Transcription and Translation (http://scienceblogs.com/transcript/)	**	A personal blog site from Dr. Alex Palazzo, an assistant professor in Biochemistry at the University of Toronto, which focuses on mRNA, cell biology and related topics.

Site	Rating	Description
Tree of Life (http://feeds.feedburner.com/ phylogenomics)	**	A personal blog site produced by Jonathan Eisen, an evolutionary biologist at the University of California, Davis.
UTNE Blogs (http://www.utne.com/blogs/blog-landing.aspx)	**	A broad website that covers everything from the science and technology to the environment to the economy, politics to pop culture.
Virology Blog (http://www.virology.ws/)	**	A personal blog site from Dr. Vincent Racaniello, a Professor of Microbiology at Columbia University Medical Center, that provides educational insights into viruses and viral diseases.
What You're Doing Is Rather Desperate (https://nsaunders.wordpress.com/)	**	A personal blog site from Neil Saunders, a statistical bioinformatician with CSIRO Mathematics, Information and Statistics, with a focus on genome-scale analysis and the computational tools.
Wikio-Biochemistry (http://www.wikio.co.uk/)	*	Wikio is a personalisable news page featuring a news search engine that searches media sites, blogs and the contributions of Wikio members.

Site	Rating	Description
Wired Science (http://www.wired.com/category/ wiredscience)	***	This website produced by Wired Magazine contains general science articles.
Yokofakun (http://plindenbaum.blogspot.in/)	**	A personal blog site from bioinformaticist Dr. Pierre Lindenbaum (Paris, France) about bioinformatics, semantic web, comics and social networks.

Chapter 18: BIOINFORMATICS IN SOCIAL MEDIA

(http://www.webicina.com/bioinformatics/news-and-information-on-bioinformatics/#package_container)

Curated Social Media Resources in Medicine & Healthcare!
Over 140 medical topics, 5000 resources, 20 languages.

Social Media

The number of communities and repositories dedicated to Bioinformatics is rapidly growing so finding relevant resources takes more and more time and efforts. Webicina selected only relevant social media resources for you.

news

(http://www.webicina.com/bioinformatics/news-and-information-on-bioinformatics#package_container)

blog
(http://www.webicina.com/bioinformatics/bioinformatics-in-the-blogosphere#package_container)

podcast

(http://www.webicina.com/bioinformatics/bioinfomatics-podcasts-and-interviews#package_container)

community
http://www.webicina.com/bioinformatics/bioinformatics-community-sites-facebook-groups-and-forums#package_container)

twitter
(http://www.webicina.com/bioinformatics/microblogging-twitter-and-friendfeed#package_container)

wiki
(http://www.webicina.com/bioinformatics/bioinformatics-wikis#package_container)

video
(http://www.webicina.com/bioinformatics/bioinformatics-videos-animations-and-videocasts#package_container)

mobile phone
(http://www.webicina.com/bioinformatics/mobile-applications#package_container)

search engine
(http://www.webicina.com/bioinformatics/medical-search-engines#package_container)

 other resources (http://www.webicina.com/bioinformatics/ bioinformatics-resources#package_container)

slideshow (http://www.webicina.com/bioinformatics/ slideshows-about-bioinformatics#package_ container)

News and Information on Bioinformatics

There are more and more resource collections and networks focusing on Bioinformatics. Here are the best repositories of Bioinformatics-related information.

Bioinformatics-related medical blogs

In the huge cloud of Bioinformatics blogs, you will find hundreds of blogs containing spams and uncontrolled advertisements. Here we collected only the best blogs that have been providing quality information for a long time.

Bioinformatics Podcasts and Interviews

Patients like listening to quality interviews about Bioinformatics rather than reading such articles. We collected both the active and inactive podcasts.

Bioinformatics Community Sites, Face Book Groups and Forums

If you do a search for "Bioinformatics community" or forum in Google, you will find thousands of sites and also similar Face book groups, but the majorities of them have no relevance. On Webicina, we feature only the best Facebook groups, applications, community sites and networks.

Micro-blogging: Twitter and Friend-feed in Bioinformatics

Sometimes it is easier to share messages and interesting links dedicated to Bioinformatics than writing blog entries or longer articles. Through microblogging, you can access relevant content in just seconds but only if you follow Twitter accounts of medical professional and empowered patients, patient communities, and book authors who write about Bioinformatics.

Bioinformatics Wikis

Wikipedia and medical wikis where only medical professionals can edit entries provide great content devoted to Bioinformatics.

Bioinformatics videos, animations and video casts

There are numerous useful video channels in Bioinformatics, but finding the best resources is really challenging. We have not only collected the most informative video channels but also interviews and animations.

Bioinformatics on Mobile

In Bioinformatics, mobile applications can have an important role such as facilitating collaboration, making new contacts or sharing pieces of advice.

Social Bookmarking in Bioinformatics

If you are looking for quality Bioinformatics links and resources, you can spend a lot of time and effort dealing with common search engines, but we only feature the most relevant collections.

Medical Search Engines in Bioinformatics

Google, Bing or Yahoo searches show you any kind of content from spams to advertisements. If you need only medically relevant information on Bioinformatics, here are medical search engines that search in selected content.

Slideshows about Bioinformatics

Many professionals upload interesting slideshows focusing on Bioinformatics and practical pieces of advice. We collected the most informative presentations for you.

Source: (http://www.webicina.com/bioinformatics/)

Chapter 19: BIOINFORMATICS FREQUENTLY ASKED QUESTIONS

(http://bioinformatics.org/wiki/Bioinformatics.FAQ)

Mirrored from (http://bioinformatics.org/faq/) thanks to the open publication licence adopted by **Damian Counsell** (http://counsell.com/) **for this document.**

Bioinformatics FAQ

1. Bioinformatics (http://bioinformatics.org/wiki/Bioinformatics_FAQ#Bioinformatics)

2. Fields related to bioinformatics (http://bioinformatics.org/wiki/Bioinformatics_FAQ#Fields_related_to_bioinformatics)

3. Books : Can you recommend any bioinformatics books ? (http://bioinformatics.org/wiki/Bioinformatics_FAQ#Books:_Can_you_recommend_any_bioinformatics_books.3F)

4. Centers of bioinformatics activity : Where is bioinformatics done ? (http://bioinformatics.org/wiki/Bioinformatics_FAQ#Centers_of_bioinformatics_activity:_Where_is_bioinformatics_done.3F)

5. Online resources : What bioinformatics websites are there ? (http://bioinformatics.org/wiki/Bioinformatics_FAQ#Online_resources:_What_bioinformatics_websites_are_there.3F)

6. Education : Where can I study bioinformatics ? (http://bioinformatics.org/wiki/Bioinformatics_FAQ#Education:_Where_can_I_study_bioinformatics.3F)
7. Careers : How can I become a bioinformatics practitioner ? (http://bioinformatics.org/wiki/Bioinformatics_FAQ#Careers:_How_can_I_become_a_bioinformatics_practitioner.3F)
8. Practical tips (http://bioinformatics.org/wiki/Bioinformatics_FAQ#Practical_tips)
9. Glossary of bioinformatics terms (http://bioinformatics.org/wiki/Bioinformatics_FAQ#Glossary_of_bioinformatics_terms)

Bioinformatics:

What is bioinformatics ? (http://bioinformatics.org/wiki/Bioinformatics)

What are the origins of bioinformatics ? (http://bioinformatics.org/wiki/Origins_of_bioinformatics)

What are the most common bioinformatics programs ? (http://bioinformatics.org/wiki/Common_programs)

What are the most common bioinformatics technologies ? (http://bioinformatics.org/wiki/Common_technologies)

How are data analyzed in bioinformatics ? (http://bioinformatics.org/wiki/Data_analysis)

Fields related to Bioinformatics

What is biophysics? (http://bioinformatics.org/wiki/Biophysics)

What is computational biology? (http://bioinformatics.org/wiki/Computational_biology)

What is medical informatics ? (http://bioinformatics.org/wiki/Medical_informatics)

What is cheminformatics? (http://bioinformatics.org/wiki/Cheminformatics)

What is genomics? (http://bioinformatics.org/wiki/Genomics)

What is mathematical biology? (http://bioinformatics.org/wiki/Mathematical_biology)

What is proteomics? (http://bioinformatics.org/wiki/Proteomics)

What is pharmacogenomics? (http://bioinformatics.org/wiki/Pharmacogenomics)

What is pharmacogenetics? (http://bioinformatics.org/wiki/Pharmacogenetics)

Centers of bioinformatics activity: Where is bioinformatics done?

Genome Web (http://www.rfcgr.mrc.ac.uk/GenomeWeb/) at the Rosalind Franklin Centre for Genomics Research (http://www.rfcgr.mrc.ac.uk/) at the Genome Campus (http://www.hinxton.org/) near Cambridge (https://www.cambridge.gov.uk/), UK, provides some of the links below.

Research centers (http://bioinformatics.org/wiki/Research_centers)

Sequencing centers (http://bioinformatics.org/wiki/Sequencing_centers)

Standard centers (http://bioinformatics.org/wiki/Standard_centers)

Virtual centers for bioinformatics activity (http://bioinformatics.org/wiki/Virtual_centers_for_bioinformatics_activity)

Online resources: What bioinformatics websites are there?

Blogs (http://bioinformatics.org/wiki/Blogs)

General information websites (http://bioinformatics.org/wiki/General_information_websites)

Directories (http://bioinformatics.org/wiki/Directories)

Societies (http://bioinformatics.org/wiki/Societies)

Collections of tools (http://bioinformatics.org/wiki/Collections_of_tools)

Portals (http://bioinformatics.org/wiki/Portals)

Tutorials (http://bioinformatics.org/wiki/Tutorials)

Education: Where can I study bioinformatics?

Below are complete, full-time degree programmes. You can go to other places, however, if you are looking for short courses. Rockefeller has a list (http://lab.rockefeller.edu/ott/) that is mirrored at various other sites. ICSB also maintains a list (http://www.iscb.org/univ.shtml)

Africa (http://bioinformatics.org/wiki/Africa)

The Americas (http://bioinformatics.org/wiki/The_Americas)

Asia (http://bioinformatics.org/wiki/Asia)

Australia (http://bioinformatics.org/wiki/Australia)

Europe (http://bioinformatics.org/wiki/Europe)

Distance or correspondence courses (http://bioinformatics.org/wiki/Distance_or_correspondence_courses)

Careers: How can I become a bioinformatics practitioner?

Careers (http://bioinformatics.org/wiki/Careers)

Getting involved (http://bioinformatics.org/wiki/Getting_involved)

Practical tips

This section includes some simple rules-of-thumb to apply when performing common bioinformatics tasks.

Finding a sequence (http://bioinformatics.org/wiki/Finding_a_sequence)

Aligning two sequences (http://bioinformatics.org/wiki/Sequence_alignment)

Predicting the functions of a gene (http://bioinformatics.org/wiki/Gene_function_prediction)

Predicting the structure of a sequence (http://bioinformatics.org/wiki/Sequence_structure_prediction)

Simulating a biomolecule (http://bioinformatics.org/wiki/Simulating_a_biomolecule)

Publishing (http://bioinformatics.org/wiki/Publishing)

Glossary of bioinformatics terms

Here are some common terms in bioinformatics:

Sequence alignment (http://bioinformatics.org/wiki/Sequence_alignment)

DNA array (http://bioinformatics.org/wiki/DNA_array)

Homologue (http://bioinformatics.org/wiki/Homologue)

Ontology (http://bioinformatics.org/wiki/Ontology)

Scoring matrix (http://bioinformatics.org/wiki/Scoring_matrix)

Log in (http://bioinformatics.org/w/index.php?title=Special:UserLogin&returnto= Bioinformatics_FAQ)

Login with OpenID (http://bioinformatics.org/w/index.php?title=Special: OpenIDLogin&returnto=Bioinformatics_FAQ)

Page (http://bioinformatics.org/wiki/Bioinformatics_FAQ)

Discussion (http://bioinformatics.org/wiki/Talk:Bioinformatics_FAQ)

Read (http://bioinformatics.org/wiki/Bioinformatics_FAQ)

View source (http://bioinformatics.org/w/index.php?title=Bioinformatics_FAQ&action=edit)

View history (http://bioinformatics.org/w/index.php?title=Bioinformatics_FAQ&action=history)

Toolbox

1) What links here (http://bioinformatics.org/wiki/Special:WhatLinksHere/ Bioinformatics_FAQ)

2) Related changes (http://bioinformatics.org/wiki/Special:RecentChanges Linked/Bioinformatics_FAQ)

3) Special pages (http://bioinformatics.org/wiki/Special:SpecialPages)

4) Printable version (http://bioinformatics.org/w/index.php?title=Bioinformatics_FAQ&sh=&sc=&sb=&ph=&drone=&ahbl=&dbl=&tvo=&efn=&tor=&dach=&sach=&hach=&zach=&blde=&printable=yes)

5) Permanent link (http://bioinformatics.org/w/index.php?title=Bioinformatics_ FAQ&oldid=7646)

6) Browse properties (http://bioinformatics.org/wiki/Special:Browse/Bioinformatics_FAQ)

7) This page was last modified on 24 November 2010, at 03:00.

8) This page has been accessed 238,321 times.

9) Content is available under GNU Free Documentation License 1.3 (http://www.gnu.org/copyleft/fdl.html).

Answers to Frequently Asked Questions

This chapter will give answers to many questions frequently encountered by researchers in the field of biotechnology/Bioinformatics.

Overview (http://www.cellbiol.com/bioinformatics_faq.php)

1) Latest changes (http://www.cellbiol.com/bioinformatics_faq.php#latestChanges)

2) Introduction (http://www.cellbiol.com/bioinformatics_faq.php#introduction)

3) Overview (http://www.cellbiol.com/bioinformatics_faq.php#overview)

4) Contents (http://www.cellbiol.com/bioinformatics_faq.php#contents)

5) Definitions (http://www.cellbiol.com/bioinformatics_faq.php#definitions)

6) Books (http://www.cellbiol.com/bioinformatics_faq.php#books)

7) Bioinformatics Centres (http://www.cellbiol.com/bioinformatics_faq.php#centres)

8) Online Resources (http://www.cellbiol.com/bioinformatics_faq.php#online)

9) Education (http://www.cellbiol.com/bioinformatics_faq.php#study)

10) Careers (http://www.cellbiol.com/bioinformatics_faq.php#careers)

11) Practical Tips (http://www.cellbiol.com/bioinformatics_faq.php#practical)

12) Acknowledgments (http://www.cellbiol.com/bioinformatics_faq.php# acknowledgements)

13) Glossary (http://www.cellbiol.com/bioinformatics_faq.php#glossary)

14) Small Print (http://www.cellbiol.com/bioinformatics_faq.php#smallprint)

Are there any standards in bioinformatics?

a) "Virtual" centres (for example consortia and communities) (http://www.cellbiol.com/bioinformatics_faq.php#centresVirtual)

   i. Online Resources: What bioinformatics Websites are there? (http://www.cellbiol.com/bioinformatics_faq.php#online)

   ii. 'Blogs (http://www.cellbiol.com/bioinformatics_faq.php#onlineBlogs)

   iii. Information (http://www.cellbiol.com/bioinformatics_faq.php#onlineInformation)

   iv. Directories (http://www.cellbiol.com/bioinformatics_faq.php#onlineDirectories)

- - v. Portals (http://www.cellbiol.com/bioinformatics_faq.php#onlinePortals)
  - vi. Societies (http://www.cellbiol.com/bioinformatics_faq.php#onlineSocieties)
  - vii. Collections of Tools (http://www.cellbiol.com/bioinformatics_faq.php# onlineTools)
  - viii. Tutorials (http://www.cellbiol.com/bioinformatics_faq.php#onlineTutorials)
 - b. Education : Where can I study bioinformatics (http://www.cellbiol.com/bioinformatics_faq.php#study)
   - i. ...in Africa ? (http://www.cellbiol.com/bioinformatics_faq.php#studyAfrica)
   - ii. ...in the Americas ? (http://www.cellbiol.com/bioinformatics_faq.php#studyAmerica)
   - iii. ...in Asia ? (http://www.cellbiol.com/bioinformatics_faq.php#studyAsia)
   - iv. ...in Australasia ? (http://www.cellbiol.com/bioinformatics_faq.php#studyAustralasia)
   - v. ...in Europe (http://www.cellbiol.com/bioinformatics_faq.php#studyEurope)
   - vi. ...in the UK (http://www.cellbiol.com/bioinformatics_faq.php#studyEuropeUK)
   - vii. ...Remotely (Distance/Correspondence Courses) (http://www.cellbiol.com/bioinformatics_faq.php#studyDistance)
 - c. Careers: How can I become a bioinformatician? (http://www.cellbiol.com/ bioinformatics_faq.php#careers)

- i. I am a newbie and I want to do bioinformatics. (http://www.cellbiol.com/bioinformatics_faq.php#involvedNewbie)
- ii. I am a biologist and I want to do bioinformatics. (http://www.cellbiol.com/bioinformatics_faq.php#involvedBiologist)
- iii. I am a computer scientist and I want to do bioinformatics. (http://www.cellbiol.com/bioinformatics_faq.php#involvedComputerScientist)
- iv. More general advice (http://www.cellbiol.com/bioinformatics_faq.php# involvedMoreGeneral)
- v. Where can I find bioinformatics jobs ? (http://www.cellbiol.com/ bioinformatics_ faq.php#jobs)

d. Practical Tips: How can I tackle specific, common bioinformatics tasks? (http://www.cellbiol.com/bioinformatics_faq.php#practical)

- i. How can I find a sequence ? (http://www.cellbiol.com/bioinformatics_faq.php#sequence)
- ii. ...I have a description. (http://www.cellbiol.com/bioinformatics_faq. php#sequenceDescription)
- iii. ...I have an accession number. (http://www.cellbiol.com/bioinformatics_faq.php# sequenceAccession)
- iv. ...I have another sequence. (http://www.cellbiol.com/bioinformatics_faq.php#sequenceSequence)
- v. ...I'm not sure whether to use the defaults. (http://www.cellbiol.com/bioinformatics_faq.php#sequenceDefaults)

- vi. How can I align two sequences? (http://www.cellbiol.com/bioinformatics_faq.php#alignment)
- vii. How can I predict the function of a gene (product) ? (http://www.cellbiol.com/bioinformatics_faq.php#functionPrediction)
- viii. How can I predict the structure of a sequence ?(http://www.cellbiol.com/bioinformatics_faq.php#structurePrediction)
- ix. How can I write up ? (http://www.cellbiol.com/bioinformatics_faq.php#writeup)
- e. Glossary of bioinformatics terms (http://www.cellbiol.com/bioinformatics_faq.php#glossary)
  - i. What is an alignment ? (http://www.cellbiol.com/bioinformatics_faq.php#glossary Alignment)
  - ii. What is a DNA array ? (http://www.cellbiol.com/bioinformatics_faq.php#glossary DNAarray)
  - iii. What is a homologue ? (http://www.cellbiol.com/bioinformatics_faq.php#glossary Homologue)
  - iv. What is an ontology ? (http://www.cellbiol.com/bioinformatics_faq. php#glossary Ontology)
  - v. What is a scoring matrix ? (http://www.cellbiol.com/bioinformatics_faq.php#glossaryScoringMatrix)
- f. Acknowledgments (http://www.cellbiol.com/bioinformatics_faq.php#acknowledgements)
  - i. Questions (http://www.cellbiol.com/bioinformatics_faq.php#acknowledgementsQuestions)

- ii. Links (http://www.cellbiol.com/bioinformatics_faq.php#acknowledgementsLinks)
- iii. Answers (http://www.cellbiol.com/bioinformatics_faq.php#acknowledgementsAnswers)
- g. Small Print (http://www.cellbiol.com/bioinformatics_faq.php#smallprint)
  - i. Author and licensing (http://www.cellbiol.com/bioinformatics_faq.php# smallprintAuthor)
  - ii. Version control information (http://www.cellbiol.com/bioinformatics_faq.php#smallprint VersionControl)

Definition of Bioinformatics: What is Bioinformatics?

Roughly, bioinformatics describes *any use of computers to handle biological information.*

In practice, the definition used by most people is narrower; bioinformatics to them is a synonym for "computational molecular biology"---*the use of computers to characterize the molecular components of living things.*

Definitions of Fields Related to Bioinformatics

What is Biophysics? Molecular biology itself grew out of biophysics (http://en.wikipedia.org/wiki/Biophysics). The British Biophysical Society (http://www.britishbiophysics.org.uk//) defines biophysics as:

"An interdisciplinary field which applies techniques from the physical sciences to understanding biological structure and function"

Mike Goodrich wrote to ask what the status of biophysics was given the definition of computational biology submitted by Paul Schulte (below). A recent article in *The Scientist* dealt with this question---thanks to Jo Wixon (Managing Editor of Comparative and Functional Genomics) (http://www.hindawi.com/journals/ijg/) for the reference.

What is Computational Biology? Computational biologists might object, but, I find that people use "computational biology" when discussing that subset of bioinformatics (in the broadest sense) closest to the field of classical general biology.

Computational biologists interest themselves more with evolutionary, population and theoretical biology rather than cell and molecular biomedicine. It is inevitable that molecular biology is profoundly important in computational biology, but it is certainly *not* what computational biology is all about (see next paragraph). In these areas of computational biology it seems that computational biologists have tended to prefer statistical models for biological phenomena over physico-chemical ones. This is often wise...

One computational biologist (Paul J Schulte) did object to the above and makes the entirely valid point that this definition derives from a popular use of the term, rather than a correct one. Paul works on water flow in plant cells. He points out that biological fluid dynamics is a field of computational biology in itself. He argues that this, and any application of computing to biology, can be described as "computational biology" (see also the "loose" definition of bioinformatics (http://www.cellbiol.com/bioinformatics_faq.php#definitionOfBioinformaticsLoose) below). Where we disagree, perhaps, is in the conclusion he draws from this---which I reproduce in full:

"Computational biology is not a "field", but an "approach" involving the use of computers to study biological processes and hence it is an area as diverse as biology itself."

Richard Durbin, Head of Informatics at the Wellcome Trust Sanger Institute (http://www.sanger.ac.uk/), expressed an interesting opinion on this distinction in an interview:

"I do not think all biological computing is bioinformatics, *e.g.* mathematical modelling is not bioinformatics, even when connected with biology-related problems. In my opinion, bioinformatics has to do with management and the subsequent use of biological information, particular genetic information."

What is Medical Informatics? The Medical Informatics FAQ (http://www.faqs.org/faqs/medical-informatics-faq/) (no relation) provides the following definition:

"Biomedical Informatics is an emerging discipline that has been defined as the study, invention, and implementation of structures and algorithms to improve communication, understanding and management of medical information."

That FAQ also points here (http://www.mc.vanderbilt.edu/dbmi/informatics.html).

Aamir Zakaria, the author of the FAQ, emphasises that medical informatics is more concerned with structures and algorithms for the manipulation of medical data, rather than with the data itself.

This suggests that one difference between bioinformatics and medical informatics as disciplines lies with their approaches to the data; there are bioinformaticians interested in the theory behind the manipulation of that data *and* there are bioinformatics scientists concerned with the data itself and its biological implications. (I believe that a good bioinformatics researcher should be interested in both of these aspects of the field.)

Medical informatics, for practical reasons, is more likely to deal with data obtained at "grosser" biological levels---that is information from super-cellular systems, right up to the population level---while most bioinformatics is concerned with information about cellular and biomolecular structures and systems.

On both of these points I'd be happy for any medical informatics specialists to correct me.

What is Cheminformatics? The Web advertisement for Cambridge Healthtech Institute's Sixth Annual Cheminformatics conference describes the field thus:

"The combination of chemical synthesis, biological screening, and data-mining approaches used to guide drug discovery and development"

But this, again, sounds more like a field being identified by some of its most popular (and lucrative) activities, rather than by including all the diverse studies that come under its general heading.

The story (http://webpub.allegheny.edu/employee/r/rmumme/FS101/ResearchPapers/SusanStreble.html) of one of the most successful drugs of all time, penicillin (http://en.wikipedia.org/wiki/Penicillin), seems bizarre, but the way we discover and develop drugs even now has similarities, being the result of chance, observation and a lot of slow, intensive chemistry. Until recently, drug design always seemed doomed to continue to be a labour-intensive, trial-and-error process. The possibility of using information technology, to plan intelligently and to automate processes related to the chemical synthesis of possible therapeutic compounds is very exciting for chemists and biochemists. The rewards for bringing a drug to market more rapidly are huge, so naturally this is what a lot of cheminformatics works is about.

Here is a page (http://www.molinspiration.com/chemoinformatics.html) with a commercial slant which links to some interesting discussions of the term "cheminformatics", what it means, whether or not it exists as a distinct discipline, and even whether it should be replaced by "chemoinformatics".

The span of academic cheminformatics is wide and is exemplified by the interests of the cheminiformatics groups at the Centre for Molecular and Biomolecular Informatics (http://www.cmbi.kun.nl/) at the University of Nijmegen (http://www.kun.nl/) in the Netherlands. These interests include -

Synthesis Planning

Reaction and Structure Retrieval

3-D Structure Retrieval

Modelling

Computational Chemistry

Visualisation Tools and Utilities

Trinity University's (http://www.trinity.edu/) Cheminformatics Web page (http://hackberry.chem.trinity.edu/), for another example, concerns itself with cheminformatics as the use of the Internet in chemistry.

What is Genomics? Genomics is a field which existed before the completion of the sequences of genomes, but in the crudest of forms, for example the oft-re-referenced estimate of 100 000 genes in the human genome derived from a(n) (in)famous piece of "back of an envelope" genomics, guessing the weight of chromosomes and the density of the genes they bear. Genomics is any attempt to analyze or compare the entire genetic complement of a species or species (plural). It is, of course possible to compare genomes by comparing more-or-less representative subsets of genes within genomes.

What is Mathematical Biology? Mathematical biology is easier to distinguish from bioinformatics than computational biology. Mathematical biology also tackles biological problems, but the methods it uses to tackle them need not be numerical and need not be implemented in software or hardware. Indeed, such methods need not "solve" anything; in mathematical biology it would be considered reasonable to publish a result which merely establishes that a biological problem belongs to a particular general class.

The distinction between bioinformatics and mathematical biology was illuminated by an email I received from Alex Kasman (http://kasmana.people.cofc.edu/) at the College of Charleston (http://www.cofc.edu/). According to his working definition, he distinguished *bioinformatics* which [under the tight definition (http://www.cellbiol.com/bioinformatics_faq.php#definition OfBioinformaticsTight) at least]...

"...seems to focus almost exclusively on specific algorithms that can be applied to large molecular biological data sets..."

...from *mathematical biology* which...

"...includes things of theoretical interest which are not necessarily algorithmic, not necessarily molecular in nature, and are not necessarily useful in analyzing collected data."

What is Proteomics? A recent review on proteomics (http://www.ncbi.nlm.nih.gov/pubmed/12634792?dopt=Abstract) in the journal Nature defined the field this way:

"The term proteome was first coined (http://www.ncbi.nlm.nih.gov/pubmed/9636313?dopt=Abstract&holding=npg) to describe the set of proteins encoded by the genome. The study of the proteome, called proteomics, now evokes not only all the proteins in any given cell, but also the set of all protein isoforms and modifications, the interactions between them, the structural description of proteins and their higher-order complexes, and for that matter almost everything 'post-genomic'."

Michael J.Dunn, the Editor-in-Chief of Proteomics (http://onlinelibrary.wiley.com/journal/10.1002/%28ISSN%291615-9861) defines the "proteome" as : "the PROTEin complement of the genOME" and proteomics to be concerned with : "qualitative and quantitative studies of gene expression at the level of the functional proteins themselves" that is : "an interface between protein biochemistry and molecular biology".

Characterizing the many tens of thousands of proteins expressed in a given cell type at a given time---whether measuring their molecular weights or isoelectric points, identifying their ligands or determining their structures---involves the storage and comparison of vast numbers of data. Inevitably this requires bioinformatics. Here is a constructively skeptical review (http://www.ncbi.nlm.nih.gov/pubmed/12511871?dopt=Abstract) by Lukas Huber (https://www.i-med.ac.at/cellbio/labore/sigtranslab/index.html.de).

What is Pharmacogenomics? Pharmacogenomics is the application of genomic approaches and technologies to the identification of drug targets. Examples include trawling entire genomes for potential receptors by bioinformatics means, or by investigating patterns of gene expression in both pathogens and hosts during infection, or by examining the characteristic expression patterns found in tumours or patients samples for diagnostic purposes (possibly in the pursuit of potential cancer therapy targets).

The term "pharmacogenomics" is used for the more "trivial"---but arguably more useful---application of bioinformatics approaches to the cataloguing and processing of information relating to pharmacology and genetics, for example the accumulation of information in databases like this one (http://xin.cz3.nus.edu.sg/group/ttd/ttd_ns.asp) (Thanks to Ivanovi.)

What is Pharmacokinetics? All individuals respond differently to drug treatments; some positively, others with little obvious change in their conditions and yet others with side effects or allergic reactions. Much of this variation is known to have a genetic basis. Pharmacogenetics is a subset of pharmacogenomics which uses genomic/bioinformatic methods to identify genomic correlates, for example SNPs (*S*ingle *N*ucleotide *P*olymorphisms), characteristic of particular patient response profiles and use those markers to inform the administration and development of therapies. Strikingly, such approaches have been used to "resurrect" drugs thought previously to be ineffective, but subsequently found to work with in subset of patients. They can also be used for optimizing the doses of chemotherapy for particular patients.

Overview of most common bioinformatics programs

Everyday bioinformatics is done with sequence search programs like BLAST, (http://blast.ncbi.nlm.nih.gov/Blast.cgi) sequence analysis programs, like the EMBOSS (http://emboss.sourceforge.net/) and Staden (http://staden.sourceforge.net/) packages, structure prediction programs like THREADER (http://bioinf.cs.ucl.ac.uk/psipred/?program=genthreader) or PHD (https://www.predictprotein.org/) or molecular imaging / modeling programs like RasMol (http://rasmol.org/) and WHATIF (http://swift.cmbi.ru.nl/whatif/).

533

Applying bioinformatics to biological research

One outstanding general text for the biologist is David W. Mount's "*Bioinformatics*" (http://www.amazon.co.uk/Bioinformatics-Sequence-Analysis-David-Mount/dp/ 0879697121/) [Cold Spring Harbor Press; ISBN 0879696087]. It's not cheap, but it's the best I've seen if you are studying bioinformatics *itself*.

Bioinformatics has been dismissed by some as "the science of BLAST searches". The best collection of advice so far on doing BLAST searches is O'Reilly's (http://www.oreilly.com/) *BLAST* (http://www.amazon.co.uk/BLAST-Ian-Korf/dp/ 0596002998/) book by Ian Korf, Mark Yandell and Joseph Bedell [O'Reilly ISBN 0-596-00299-8]. I reviewed it enthusiastically, but not uncritically, for the UK UNIX Users' Group (http://www.ukuug.org/) magazine. I'd go as far as to say that all biologists thinking of using BLAST in their research should read the relevant sections before they even go near a computer.

If you wish to use general bioinformatics *tools*, especially if you are a little wary of computers, my new "best" book is "*Bioinformatics for Dummies*" (http://www.amazon.com/Bioinformatics-Dummies-Jean-Michel-Claverie-Ph/dp/0470089857/). It is (obviously) aimed at people who are beginners, who are happier using the Web rather than typing commands, and who are more interested in learning than in impressing people---the writing is friendly clear and unpretentious. However, like several of my other tips (below) it concentrates on Web-based resources so it will, inevitably, date. This is partially compensated for by there being a companion Website (http://www.dummies.com/DummiesTitle/productCd-0764516965.html).

Also, if you're coming to the subject as a computer user with a biological background, looking to exploit the many tools available, you might want to try Terry Attwood and David Parry-Smith's *"Introduction to Bioinformatics"* (http://books.bioinformatics.org/bioinfo.php#0582327881) [Longman Higher Education; ISBN 0582327881], or Des Higgins and Willie Taylor's *"Bioinformatics : Sequence Structure and Databanks"* (http://books.bioinformatics.org/bioinfo.php#0199637903) [Oxford University Press; ISBN 0199637903]. Another excellent practical introduction is Andreas Baxevanis and Francis Oulette's *"Bioinformatics : A Practical Guide to the Analysis of Genes and Proteins"* (http://onlinelibrary.wiley.com/book/10.1002/0471223921) [Wiley-Interscience; ISBN 9780471383901], now in its new and improved second edition. Bax teaches bioinformatics all over Canada and the experience shows. Arthur Lesk has also produced an excellent teaching book particularly for protein bioinformatics in his *Introduction to Bioinformatics* (http://www.amazon.co.uk/Introduction-Bioinformatics-Arthur-Lesk/dp/0199208042/).

Bioinformatics.Org also recommends Cynthia Gibas and Per Jambeck's *"Developing Bioinformatics Skills"* (http://www.amazon.co.uk/Developing-Bioinformatics-Computer-Skills-Cynthia/dp/1565926641/) [O'Reilly, 2001 ISBN 1-56592-664-1].

Stuart Brown recommends his own book *"Bioinformatics: A Biologist's Guide to Biocomputing and the Internet"* (http://www.amazon.co.uk/Bioinformatics-Biologists-Guide-Biocomputing-Internet/dp/188129918X/) [Eaton Pub Co; ISBN: 188129918X]. If he sends me a review copy I might recommend it too.

Chapter 20: CENTERS OF BIOINFORMATICS ACTIVITY

The biggest and best source of bioinformatics links encountered is the Genome Web (http://www.rfcgr.mrc.ac.uk/GenomeWeb/) at the Rosalind Franklin Centre for Genomics Research (http://www.rfcgr.mrc.ac.uk/) at the Genome Campus (http://www.hinxton.org/) near Cambridge (https://www.cambridge.gov.uk/), UK. Most of the links below come from that resource. My list is necessarily limited by comparison.

a) Research centres (http://www.cellbiol.com/bioinformatics_faq.php#centresResearch)

b) Sequencing centres (http://www.cellbiol.com/bioinformatics_faq.php#centresSequencing)

c) Standards centres (http://www.cellbiol.com/bioinformatics_faq.php#centresStandards)

Are there any standards in bioinformatics?

a) "Virtual" centres (for example consortia and communities) (http://www.cellbiol.com/bioinformatics_faq.php#centresVirtual)

Research centers

a) Centro Nacional de Biotecnologia (CNB) (http://www.cnb.csic.es/index.php/en/)

b) Computational Biology and Informatics Laboratory at the University of Pennysylvania (http://www.cbil.upenn.edu/)

c) CIRB: Centro Interdipartimentale di Ricerche Biotecnologiche (http://www.biocomp.unibo.it/)

d) Cold Spring Harbor Labs (http://www.cshl.org/)

e) European Molecular Biology Laboratory (EMBL) (http://www.embl.de/)

f) Généthon (http://www.genethon.fr/)

g) GIRI: Genetic Information Research Institute (http://www.girinst.org/)

h) MRC Human Genetics Unit (http://www.hgu.mrc.ac.uk/)

i) MRC Rosalind Franklin Centre for Genomics Research (RFCGR) (http://www.rfcgr.mrc.ac.uk/)

Sequencing centers

a) The Department of Genome Analysis at the Institute of Molecular Biotechnology, Jena, Germany (http://genome.imb-jena.de/)

b) The Australian Genome Resesarch Facility (http://www.agrf.org.au/about.html)

c) Baylor College of Medicine (https://www.hgsc.bcm.edu/)

d) Michael Smith Genome Sciences Centre, Canada (http://www.bcgsc.ca/)

Standard centers

a) International Center for Cooperation in Bioinformatics network (ICCBnet) (http://www.iccbnet.org/)

b) Belgian EMBnet node (http://ben.vub.ac.be/)

GLOSSARY

3-D or 3D: Three-dimensional.

Accession number: An Accession number is a unique identifier given to a sequence when it is submitted to one of the DNA repositories (GenBank, EMBL, DDBJ). The initial deposition of a sequence record is referred to as version 1. If the sequence is updated, the version number is incremented, but the Accession number will remain constant.

***Alu*:** The *Alu* repeat family comprises short interspersed elements (SINES) present in multiple copies in the genomes of humans and other primates. The *Alu* sequence is approximately 300 bp in length and is found commonly in introns, 3' untranslated regions of genes, and intergenic genomic regions. They are mobile elements and are present in the human genome in extremely high copy number. Almost 1 million copies of the *Alu* sequence are estimated to be present, making it the most abundant mobile element. The *Alu* sequence is so named because of the presence of a recognition site for the *Alu*I endonuclease in the middle of the *Alu* sequence. Because of the widespread occurrence of the *Alu* repeat in the genome, the *Alu* sequence is used as a universal primer for PCR in animal cell lines; it binds in both forward and reverse directions. The *Alu* universal primer sequence is as follows: 5'-GTG GAT CAC CTG AGG TCA GGA GTT TC-3' (26-mer).

Allele: One of the variant forms of a gene at a particular locus on a chromosome. Different alleles produce variation in inherited characteristics such as hair colour or blood type. In an individual, one form of the allele (the dominant one) may be expressed more than another form (the recessive one). When "genes" are considered simply as segments of a nucleotide sequence, allele refers to each of the possible alternative nucleotides at a specific position in the sequence. For example, a CT polymorphism such as CCT[C/T]CCAT would have two alleles: C and T.

API: Application Programming Interface. An API is a set of routines that an application uses to request and carry out lower-level services performed by a computer's operating system. For computers running a graphical user interface, an API manages an application's windows, icons, menus, and dialog boxes.

ASN1: Abstract Syntax Notation 1 is an international standard data-representation format used to achieve interoperability between computer platforms. It allows for the reliable exchange of data in terms of structure and content by computer and software systems of all types.

BAC: Bacterial Artificial Chromosome. A BAC is a large segment of DNA (100,000–200,000 bp) from another species cloned into bacteria. Once the foreign DNA has been cloned into the host bacteria, many copies of it can be made.

BankIt: BankIt is a tool for the online submission of one or a few sequences into GenBank and is designed to make the submission process quick and easy. (BankIt also automatically uses VecScreen to identify segments of nucleic acid sequence that may be of vector, adapter, or linker origin to combat the problem of vector contamination in GenBank.)

bit score: The value S' is derived from the raw alignment score S in which the statistical properties of the scoring system used have been taken into account. By normalizing a raw score using the formula:

$$S' = \frac{\lambda S - \ln K}{\ln 2}$$

A "bit score" S' is attained, which has a standard set of units, and where K and *lambda* are the statistical parameters of the scoring system. Because bit scores have been normalized with respect to the scoring system, they can be used to compare alignment scores from different searches.

BLAST: Basic Local Alignment Search Tool (Altschul et al., J Mol Biol 215:403-410; 1990). A sequence comparison algorithm that is optimized for speed is used to search sequence databases for optimal local alignments to a query. See the BLAST chapter (Chapter 15) or the tutorial or the narrative guide to BLAST.

Blastn: nucleotide–nucleotide BLAST. blastn takes nucleotide sequences in FASTA format, GenBank Accession numbers, or GInumbers and compares them against the NCBI Nucleotide databases.

Blastp: protein–protein BLAST. blastp takes protein sequences in FASTA format, GenBank Accession numbers, or GI numbers and compares them against the NCBI Protein databases.

BLAT: A DNA/Protein sequence analysis program to quickly find sequences of 95% and greater similarity of length 40 bases or more. It may miss more divergent or shorter sequence alignments. BLAT on proteins finds sequences of 80% and greater similarity of length 20 amino acids or more. BLAT is not BLAST. (See the BLAT web page.)

Blink: BLAST Link. BLink displays the results of BLAST searches that have been done for every protein sequence in the Entrez Protein data domain. It can be accessed by following the

BLink link displayed beside any hit in the results of an Entrez Protein search. In contrast to Entrez's **Related Sequences** feature, which lists the titles of similar sequences, BLink displays the graphical output of precomputed blastp results against the non-redundant (nr) protein database. The output includes the positions of up to 200 BLAST hits on the query sequence, scores, and alignments. BLink offers a variety of display options, including the distribution of hits by taxonomic grouping, the best hit to each organism, the protein domains in the query sequence, similar sequences that have known 3D structures, and more. Additional options allow you to specify from which taxa you would like to exclude, increase, or decrease the BLAST cut-off score or filter the BLAST hits to show only those from a specific source database, such as RefSeq or SWISS-PROT. See the BLink help document for additional information.

BLOB: Binary Large Object (or binary data object). BLOB refers to a large piece of data, such as a bitmap. A BLOB is characterized by large field values, an unpredictable table size, and data that are formless from the perspective of a program. It is also a keyword designating the BLOB structure, which contains information about a block of data.

BLOSUM 62: Blocks Substitution Matrix. It is a substitution matrix in which scores for each position are derived from observations of the frequencies of substitutions in blocks of local alignments in related proteins. Each matrix is tailored to a particular evolutionary distance. In the BLOSUM 62 matrix, for example, the alignment from which scores were derived was created using sequences sharing no more than 62% identity. Sequences more identical than 62% are represented by a single sequence in the alignment to avoid overweighting closely related family members (Henikoff and Henikoff, Proc Natl Acad Sci U S A 89:10915-10919; 1992).

Boolean: This term refers to binary algebra that uses the logical operators AND, OR, XOR, and NOT; the outcomes consist of logical values (either TRUE or FALSE). The keyword Boolean indicates that the expression or constant expression associated with the identifier takes the value TRUE or FALSE. The logical-AND (&&) operator produces the value 1 if both operands have nonzero values; otherwise, it produces the value 0. The logical-OR (||) operator produces the value 1 if either of its operands has a nonzero value. The logical-NOT (!) operator produces the value 0 if its operand is true (nonzero) and the value 1 if its operand is FALSE (0). The exclusive OR (XOR) operator yields TRUE only if one of its operands are TRUE and the other is FALSE. If both operands are the same (either TRUE or FALSE), the operation yields FALSE.

Build: A run of the genome assembly and annotation process of the set of products generated by that run.

CCAP: Cancer Chromosome Aberration Project. CCAP was designed to expedite the definition and detailed characterization of the distinct chromosomal alterations that are associated with malignant transformation. The project is a collaboration among the NCI, the NCBI, and numerous research labs.

CD: Conserved Domain. CD refers to a domain (a distinct functional and/or structural unit of a protein) that has been conserved during evolution. During evolution, changes at specific positions of an amino acid sequence in the protein have occurred in a way that preserve the physico-chemical properties of the original residues, and hence the structural and/or functional properties of that region of the protein.

CDART: Conserved Domain Architecture Retrieval Tool. When given a protein query sequence, CDART displays the functional domains that make up the protein and lists proteins with similar domain architectures. The functional domains for a sequence are found by comparing the protein sequence to a database of conserved domain alignments, CDD using RPS-BLAST.

CDD: Conserved Domain Database. This database is a collection of sequence alignments and profiles representing protein domains conserved during molecular evolution.

cDNA: complementary DNA. A DNA sequence obtained by reverse transcription of a messenger RNA (mRNA) sequence.

CDS: coding region, coding sequence. CDS refers to the portion of a genomic DNA sequence that is translated, from the start codon to the stop codon, inclusively, if complete. A partial CDS lacks part of the complete CDS (it may lack either or both the start and stop codons). Successful translation of a CDS results in the synthesis of a protein.

CEPH: Centre d'Etude du Polymorphism Humain

CGAP: Cancer Genome Anatomy Project. CGAP is an interdisciplinary program to identify the human genes expressed in different cancerous states, based on cDNA (EST) libraries, and to determine the molecular profiles of normal, precancerous, and malignant cells. The project is a collaboration among the NCI, the NCBI, and numerous research labs.

CGH: Comparative Genomic Hybridization. CGH is a fluorescent molecular cytogenetic technique that identifies chromosomal aberrations and maps these changes to metaphase chromosomes. CGH can be used to generate a map of DNA copy number changes in tumor genomes. CGH is based on quantitative two-color fluorescence *in situ* hybridization (FISH). DNA extracted from tumor cells is labelled in one color (e.g., green) and mixed in a 1:1 ratio with DNA from normal cells, which is labelled in a different color (e.g., red). The mixture is then applied to normal metaphase chromosomes. Portions of the genome that are equally represented in normal and tumor cells will appear orange, regions that are deleted in the tumor sample relative to the normal sample will appear red, and regions that are present in higher copy number in the tumor sample (because of amplification) will appear green. Special image analysis tools are necessary to quantitative the ratio of green-to-red fluorescence to determine whether a given region is more highly represented in the normal or in the tumor sample.

CGI: Common Gateway Interface - a mechanism that allows a Web server to run a program or script on the server and send the output to a Web browser.

Cluster: A group that is created based on certain criteria. For example, a gene cluster may include a set of genes whose similar expression profiles are found to be similar according to certain criteria, or a cluster may refer to a group of clones that are related to each other by homology.

Cn3D: "See in 3-D" is a structure and sequence alignment viewer for NCBI databases. It allows viewing of 3-D structures and sequence–structure or structure–structure alignments. Cn3D can work as a helper application to the browser or as a client–server application that retrieves structure records from the Molecular Modelling Database (MMDB, see below) directly from the internet. The Cn3D homepage provides access to information on how to install the program, a tutorial to get started, and a comprehensive help document.

Codon: Sequence of three nucleotides in DNA or mRNA that specifies a particular amino acid during protein synthesis; also called a triplet. Of the 64 possible codons, 3 are stop codons, which do not specify amino acids.

COGs: Clusters of Orthologous Groups (of proteins) were delineated by comparing protein sequences from completely sequenced genomes. Each COG consists of individual proteins or groups of paralogs from at least three lineages and thus corresponds to an ancient conserved domain.

Consensus sequence: The nucleotides or amino acids found most commonly at each position in the sequences of homologous DNAs, RNAs, or proteins.

Contig: A contiguous segment of the genome made by joining overlapping clones or sequences. A clone contig consists of a group of cloned (copied) pieces of DNA representing overlapping regions of a particular chromosome. A sequence contig is an extended sequence created by merging primary sequences that overlap. A contig map shows the regions of a chromosome where contiguous DNA segments overlap. Contig maps provide the ability to study a complete and often large segment of the genome by examining a series of overlapping clones, which then provide an unbroken succession of information about that region.

Coriell: Coriell Institute of Aging Cell Repository

CPU: Central Processing Unit. The CPU is the computational and control unit of a computer, the device that interprets and executes instructions.

CSS: Cascading Style Sheets. CSS specify the formatting details that control the presentation and layout of HTML and XML elements. CSS can be used for describing the formatting behaviour and text decoration of simply structured XML documents but cannot display structure that varies from the structure of the source data.

Cubby: A tool of Entrez, the Cubby stores search strategies that may be updated at any time, stores LinkOut preferences to specify which Link Out providers have to be displayed in PubMed, and changes the default document delivery service.

DCMS: Data Creation and Maintenance System

DDBJ: DNA Data Bank of Japan

Definition line: A sequence in FASTA format begins with a single-line description, followed by lines of sequence data. The definition line or description line is distinguished from the sequence data by a "greater than" (>) symbol in the first column also DEFLINE, as in a flat file.

DNA: Deoxyribonucleic acid is the chemical inside the nucleus of a cell that carries the genetic instructions for making living organisms. DNA is composed of two anti-parallel strands, each a linear polymer of nucleotides. Each nucleotide has a phosphate group linked by a phosphoester bond to a pentose (a five-carbon sugar molecule, deoxyribose), that in turn is linked to one of four organic bases, adenine, guanine, cytosine, or thymine, abbreviated A, G, C, and T, respectively. The bases are of two types: purines, which have two rings and are slightly larger (A and G); and pyrimidines, which have only one ring (C and T). Each nucleotide is joined to the next nucleotide in the chain by a covalent phosphodiester bond between the 5' carbon of one deoxyribose group and the 3' carbon of the next. DNA is a helical molecule with the sugar–phosphate backbone on the outside and the nucleotides extending toward the central axis. There is specific base-pairing between the bases on opposite strands in such a way that A always pairs with T and G always pairs with C.

Domain: A "domain" refers to a discrete portion of a protein assumed to fold independently of the rest of the protein and which possesses its own function.

Draft sequence: Draft sequence refers to DNA sequence that is not yet finished but is generally of high quality (i.e., an accuracy of greater than 90%). Draft sequence data are mostly in the form of 10,000 base pair-sized fragments, the approximate chromosomal locations of which are known. The following keywords are associated with draft sequence: phase 0, light-pass coverage of a clone, generally only 1× coverage; phase 1, 4–10× coverage of a BAC clone (order and orientation of the fragments are unknown); and phase 2, 4–10× coverage of a BAC clone (order and orientation of the fragments are known). Phase 3 refers to the completely finished.

DTD: Document Type Definition. The DTD is an optional part of the prolog of an XML document that defines the rules of the document. It sets constraints for an XML document by specifying which elements are present in the document and the relationships between elements, e.g., which tags can contain other tags, the number and sequence of the tags, and attributes of the tags. The DTD helps to validate the data when the receiving application does not have a built-in description of the incoming data.

DUST: A program for filtering low-complexity regions from nucleic acid sequences.

E-value: Expect value. The E-value is a parameter that describes the number of hits one can "expect" to see by chance when searching a database of a particular size. It decreases exponentially with the score (S) that is assigned to a match between two sequences. Essentially, the E-value describes the random background noise that exists for matches between sequences. For example, an E-value of 1 assigned to a hit can be interpreted as meaning that in a database of the current size, one might expect to see one match with a similar score simply by chance. This means that the lower the E-value, or the closer it is to "0", the higher is the "significance" of the match. However, it is important to note that searches with short sequences can be virtually identical and have relatively high E-value. This is because the calculation of the E-value also takes into account the length of the query sequence. This is because shorter sequences have a high probability of occurring in the database purely by chance. For more information, see the following tutorial.

EC number: A number assigned to a type of enzyme according to a scheme of standardized enzyme nomenclature developed by the Enzyme Commission of the Nomenclature Committee of the International Union of Biochemistry and Molecular Biology (IUBMB). EC numbers may be found in ENZYME, the Enzyme nomenclature database, maintained at the ExPASy molecular biology server.

EMBL: European Molecular Biology Laboratory

Entrez: Entrez is a retrieval system for searching several linked databases. It provides access to the following NCBI databases: PubMed, GenBank, Protein, Structure, Genome, PopSet, OMIM, Taxonomy, Books, Probe Set, 3D Domains, UniSTS, SNP, and CDD. (See the Entrez chapter or the Entrez web page.)

Entrez Gene: (formerly known as LocusLink). Entrez Gene provides tracked, unique identifiers for genes (GeneIDs) and reports information associated with those identifiers for unrestricted public use. See the Entrez Gene chapter or web page.)

EST: Expressed Sequence Tag. ESTs are short (usually approximately 300–500 base pairs), single-pass sequence reads from cDNA. Typically, they are produced in large batches. They represent the genes expressed in a given tissue and/or at a given developmental stage. They are tags (some coding, others not) of expression for a given cDNA library. They are useful in identifying full-length genes and in mapping.

e-PCR: Electronic PCR is used to compare a query sequence to mapped sequence-tagged sites (STSs) to find a possible map location for the query sequence. e-PCR finds STSs in DNA sequences by searching for subsequence that closely match the PCR primers present in mapped markers. The subsequence must have the correct order, orientation, and spacing that they could plausibly prime the amplification of a PCR product of the correct molecular weight.

epub citation: "A head-of-print" citation. PubMed now accepts citations from publishers for articles that have been published electronically ahead of the printed issue. PubMed displays the category "[epub ahead of print]" in the part of the citation where the volume and pagination would ordinarily display. For example: Proc Natl Acad Sci U S A. 2000 May 2 [epub ahead of print].

ExoFish: Exon Finding by Sequence Homology. Exofish is a tool based on homology searches for the rapid and reliable identification of human genes. It relies on the sequence of another vertebrate, the puffer fish *Tetraodon nigroviridis* (similar to Fugu), to detect conserved sequences with a very low background. The genome of *T. nigroviridis* is eight times more compact than the human genome and has been used in the comparative identification of human genes from the rough draft of the human genome (Roest Crollius et al., Nat Genet 25:235-238; 2000).

Exon: Refers to the portion of a gene that encodes for a part of that gene's mRNA. A gene may comprise many exons, some of which may include only protein-coding sequence; however, an exon may also include 5' or 3' untranslated sequence. Each exon codes for a specific portion of the complete protein. In some species (including humans), a gene's exons are separated by long regions of DNA (called introns or sometimes "junk DNA") that often have no apparent function but have been shown to encode small untranslated RNAs or regulatory information. (See also splice sites.)

Exon-trapped: Exon trapping is a technique for cloning exon sequences from genomic DNA by selecting for functional splice sites, relying on the cellular splicing machinery. The genomic DNA containing the putative exon(s) is cloned into an exon-trap vector, which has a promoter, polyadenylation signals, and splice sites, and then transfected into a cell line. If there are functional splice sites in the genomic DNA fragment, the segments of DNA between the splice sites will be removed. Total RNA is isolated and reverse-transcribed. After cDNA synthesis and PCR amplification, the exon of interest is cloned.

ExPASy: Expert Protein Analysis System is a proteomics server of the Swiss Bioinformatics Institute (SIB).

FASTA: The first widely used algorithm for similarity searching of protein and DNA sequence databases. The program looks for optimal local alignments by scanning the sequence for small matches called "words". Initially, the scores of segments in which there are multiple word hits are calculated ("init1"). Later, the scores of several segments may be summed to generate an "initn" score. An optimized alignment that includes gaps is shown in the output as "opt". The sensitivity and speed of the search are inversely related and controlled by the "k-tup" variable, which specifies the size of a "word" (Pearson and Lipman). Also refers to a formatfor a nucleic acid or protein sequence.

Fingerprint: The pattern of bands on a gel produced by a clone when restricted by a particular enzyme, such as *Hin*dIII.

Finished sequence: It is high-quality, low-error DNA sequence that is free of gaps. To qualify as a finished sequence, only a single error out of every 10,000 bases (i.e., an accuracy of 99.999%) is allowed.

FISH: Fluorescence *in situ* hybridization. In this technique, fluorescent molecules are used to label a DNA probe, which can then hybridize to a specific DNA sequence in a chromosome spread so that the site becomes visible through a microscope. FISH has been used to highlight the locations of genes, sub chromosome regions, entire chromosomes, or specific DNA sequences. It has been used for mapping and the detection of genomic rearrangements, as well as studies on DNA replication.

Flat file or flat file: A flat file is a data file that contains records (each corresponding to a row in a table); however, these records have no structured relationships. To interpret these files, the format properties of the file should be known. For example, a database management system may allow the user to export data to a comma-delimited file. Such a file is called a flat file because it has no inherent information about the data, and interpretation requires additional information. Files in a database management system have more complex storage structures.

Freeze: To copy changing data so as to preserve the dataset as it existed at a particular point in time, also used to refer to the resulting set of frozen data.

FTP: File Transfer Protocol. A method of retrieving files over a network directly to the user's computer or to his/her home directory using a set of protocols that govern how the data are to be transported.

Gap: A gap is a space introduced into an alignment to compensate for insertions and deletions in one sequence relative to another. To prevent the accumulation of too many gaps in an alignment, introduction of a gap causes the deduction of a fixed amount (the gap score) from the alignment score. Extension of the gap to encompass additional nucleotides or amino acid is also penalized in the scoring of an alignment. (See the figure for more information.)

GB: gigabytes

GBFF: GenBank Flat File refers to a format gbff.

GenBank: GenBank is a database of nucleotide sequences from more than 100,000 organisms. Records that are annotated with coding region features also include amino acid translations. GenBank belongs to an international collaboration of sequence databases that also includes EMBL and DDBJ. [See the GenBank chapter (Chapter 1) or the GenBank web page.]

GeneID: GeneID is a unique identifier that is assigned to a gene record in Entrez Gene. It is an integer and is species specific. In other words, the integer assigned to dystrophin in human is different from that in any other species. For genomes that had been represented in Locus Link, the GeneID is the same as the LocusID. The GeneID is reported in RefSeq records as a 'db_xref' (e.g. /db_xref="GeneID: 856646", in GenBank format).

genetic code: The instructions in a gene that tell the cell how to make a specific protein. A, T, G, and C are the "letters" of the DNA code; they stand for the chemicals adenine, thymine, guanine, and cytosine, respectively, that make up the nucleotide bases of DNA. Each gene's code combines the four chemicals in various ways to spell out three-letter "words" that specify which amino acid is needed at every position for making a protein.

GenomeScan: A gene identification algorithm that is used to identify exon–intron structures in genomic DNA sequence.

Genotype: The genetic identity of an individual that does not show as outward characteristics. The genotype refers to the pair of alleles for a given region of the genome that an individual carries.

GEO: Gene Expression Omnibus. GEO is a gene expression data repository and online resource for the retrieval of gene expression data from any organism or artificial source. Many types of gene expression data from platform types, such as spotted microarray, high-density oligonucleotide array, hybridization filter, and serial analysis of gene expression (SAGE) data, are accepted, accessioned, and archived as a public dataset. [See the GEO chapter (Chapter 6) or the GEO web page.]

GI: The GenInfo Identifier is a sequence identification number for a nucleotide sequence. If a nucleotide sequence changes in any way, a new GI number will be assigned. A separate GI number is also assigned to each protein translation within a nucleotide sequence record, and a new GI is assigned if the protein translation changes in any way. GI sequence identifiers run parallel to the new accession. (For Version system of sequence identifiers see the description of Version).

GSS: Genome Survey Sequences are analogous to ESTs except that the sequences are genomic in origin, rather than cDNA (mRNA). The GSS division of GenBank contains (but is not limited to) the following types of data: random "single-pass read" genome survey sequences, cosmid/BAC/YAC end sequences, exon-trapped genomic sequences, and *Alu*-PCR sequences.

Heterozygosity: The probability that a diploid individual will have two different alleles at a particular genome locus. These individuals are defined as heterozygous, whereas individuals who have two identical alleles at the locus are defined as homozygous. The probability can be estimated by sampling a representative number of individuals from the population and dividing the number of heterozygotes by the total number sampled.

HIV: Human Immunodeficiency Virus. HIV-1 is a retrovirus that is recognized as the causative agent of AIDS (Acquired Immunodeficiency Syndrome).

HNPCC: Hereditary non polyposis colon cancer

Homogeneously staining region: A region of the chromosome identified cytologically by DNA staining or the FISH technique because of the presence of multiple copies of a sub chromosomal region resulting from amplification.

Homologous: The term refers to similarity attributable to descent from a common ancestor. Homologous chromosomes are members of a pair of essentially identical chromosomes, each derived from one parent. They have the same or allelic genes with genetic loci arranged in the same order. Homologous chromosomes synapse during meiosis.

HTGS: High-Throughput Genomic Sequences. The source of HTGS are large-scale genome sequencing centers; unfinished sequences are in phases 0, 1, and 2, and finished sequences are in phase 3.

HTGS_CANCELLED: A keyword added to GenBank entries by sequencing centers to indicate that work has stopped on a clone and that the existing sequence will not be finished. Sequencing centers may stop work because the clone is redundant or for various other reasons.

HTGS_PHASE0, HTGS_PHASE1, HTGS_PHASE2, HTGS_PHASE3: Keywords added to GenBank entries by sequencing centers to indicate the status (phase) of the sequence (see phase definitions described under draft sequence).

HTML: Hypertext Mark-up Language. HTML is derived from SGML. It is a text-based mark-up language and is used to primarily display information using a web browser and to link pieces of information via hyperlinks. The tags used in an HTML document provide information only on how the content is to be displayed but do not provide information about the content they encompass.

HUP: Hold Until Published. HUP refers to the category for data that is electronically submitted for when it should be released to the public.

ICBN: International Code of Botanical Nomenclature

ICD: International Classification of Diseases

ICD-O-3: International Classification of Diseases for Oncology, 3rd edition

ICNB: International Code of Nomenclature of Bacteria

ICNCP: International Code of Nomenclature for Cultivated Plants

ICTV: International Committee on Taxonomy of Viruses

ICVCN: International Code of Virus Classification and Nomenclature

ICZN: International Code of Zoological Nomenclature

Ideogram: A diagrammatic representation of the karyotype of an organism.

IMAGE Consortium: Integrated Molecular Analysis of Genomes and their Expression. It is a consortium of academic groups that share high-quality, arrayed cDNA libraries and place sequence, map, and expression data of the clones in these arrays into the public domain. With the use of this information, unique clones can be rearrayed to form a "master array", with the aim of ultimately having a representative cDNA from every gene in the genome under study. To date, human, mouse, rat, zebra fish, and *Xenopus laevis* genomes have been studied.

Intron: Refers to that portion of the DNA sequence that is present in the primary transcript and that is removed by splicing during RNA processing and is not included in the mature, functional mRNA, rRNA, or tRNA and also called an intervening sequence. (See also splice sites.)

ISAM: Indexed Sequential-Access Method. ISAM is a database access method. It allows data records in a database to be accessed either sequentially (in the order in which they were entered) or randomly (using an index). In the index, each record has a unique key that enables its rapid location. The key is the field used to reference the record.

ISCN: International System for Human Cytogenetic Nomenclature

ISO: International Organization for Standardization

ISSN: International Standard Serial Number. The ISSN is an eight-digit number that identifies periodical publications, including electronic serials.

Karyotype: The particular chromosome complement of an individual or a related group of individuals, as defined by both the number and morphology of the chromosomes, usually in mitotic metaphase, and arranged by pairs according to the standard classification.

LANL: Los Alamos National Lab

LIMS: Laboratory Information Management Systems. LIMS comprise software that helps biological and chemical laboratories handle data generation, information management, and data archiving.

LinkOut: A registry service to create links from specific articles, journals, or biological data in Entrez to resources on external web sites. Third parties can provide a URL, resource name, brief description of their web sites, and specification of the NCBI data from which they would like to establish links. The specification can be written as a valid Boolean query to Entrez or as a list of identifiers for specific articles or sequences. Entrez PubMed users can then select which external links are visible in their searches through the NCBI Cubby service (see above). (See the LinkOut chapter or web page.)

Locus: In a genomic contect, locus refers to position on a chromosome. It may, therefore, refer to a marker, a gene, or any other landmark that can be described.

MACAW: Multiple Alignment Construction and Analysis Workbench. MACAW is a program for locating, analyzing, and editing blocks of localized sequence similarity among multiple sequences and linking them into a composite multiple alignment.

Map Viewer: The Map Viewer is a software component of Entrez Genomes that provides special browsing capabilities for a subset of organisms. It allows one to view and search an organism's complete genome, display chromosome maps, and zoom into progressively greater levels of detail, down to the sequence data for a region of interest. If multiple maps are available for a chromosome, it displays them aligned to each other based on shared marker and gene names and, for the sequence maps, based on a common sequence coordinate system. The organisms currently represented in the Map Viewer are listed in theEntrez Map Viewer help document, which provides general information on how to use that tool. The number and types of available maps vary by organism and are described in the "data and search tips" file provided for each organism.

MB: megabytes

MEDLINE: MEDLINE is NLM's database of indexed journal citations and abstracts in the fields of biomedicine and healthcare. It encompasses nearly 4,500 journals published in the United States and more than 70 other countries. (For more information, see the Fact Sheet.)

MegaBLAST: MegaBLAST is a program for aligning sequences that differ slightly as a result of sequencing or other similar "errors". When larger word size is used, it is up to 10 times faster than more common sequence-similarity programs. MegaBLAST is also able to efficiently handle much longer DNA sequences than the blastn program of the traditional BLAST algorithm. It uses the GREEDY algorithm for a nucleotide sequence alignment search.

Mesh: Medical Subject Headings. MeSH refers to the controlled vocabulary of NLM used for indexing articles in PubMed. MeSH terminology provides a consistent way to retrieve information that may use different terminology for the same concepts. (See the MeSH homepage.)

Metathesaurus: Metathesaurus is a National Cancer Institute browser containing different biomedical vocabularies, including the International Classification of Diseases for Oncology ICD-O-3.

MFASTA: Multi-FASTA format.

MGC: Mammalian Gene Collection. MGC is a project of the NIH to provide a complete set of full-length (open reading frame) sequences and cDNA clones of expressed genes for human and mouse.

MGD: Mouse Genome Database. MGD contains information on mouse genetic markers, molecular segments, phenotypes, comparative mapping data, experimental mapping data, and graphical displays for genetic, physical, and cytogenetic maps.

MGI: Mouse Genome Informatics. MGI houses a database that provides integrated access to data on the genetics, genomics, and biology of the laboratory mouse.

Microsatellite: Repetitive stretches of short sequences of DNA used as genetic markers to track inheritance in families (e.g., CC[TATATATA]CCCT). Also known as short tandem repeats (STRs).

MIM: Mendelian Inheritance in Man. First published in 1966, *Mendelian Inheritance in Man (MIM)* is a genetic knowledge base that serves clinical medicine and biomedical research, including the Human Genome Project.

Minimal tiling path: An ordered list or map that defines the minimal set of overlapping clones needed to provide complete coverage of a chromosome or other extended segment of DNA (compare with tiling path).

MMDB: Molecular Modeling Database. MMDB is a database of three-dimensional biomolecular structures derived from X-ray crystallography and nuclear magnetic resonance (NMR) spectroscopy.

MMDB-ID: Molecular Modelling Database Accession number.

mRNA: messenger RNA. mRNA describes the section of a genomic DNA sequence that is transcribed, and can include the 5' untranslated region (5'UTR), CDS, and 3' untranslated region (3'UTR). Successful translation of the CDS section of an mRNA results in the synthesis of a protein.

Mutation: A permanent structural alteration in DNA. In most cases, DNA changes have either no effect or cause harm, but occasionally a mutation can improve an organism's chance of surviving, and the beneficial change is passed on to the organism's descendants. Typically, mutations are more rare than polymorphisms in population samples because natural selection recognizes their lower fitness and removes them from the population.

NCBI: National Center for Biotechnology Information

NCBI Toolkit: Contains supported software tools from the Information Engineering Branch (IEB) of the NCBI. The NCBI Toolkit describes the three components of the ToolBox: data model, data encoding, and programming libraries. It provides access to documentation for the DataModel, C Toolkit, C++ Toolkit, NCBI C Toolkit Source Browser, XML Demo Program, XML DTDs, and the FTP site.

NCI: National Cancer Institute

NEXUS: NEXUS refers to a file format designed to contain data for processing by computer programs. NEXUS files should end with .nxs or .nex for purposes of clarity (Maddison et al., Syst Biol 46:590-621; 1997).

NIH: National Institutes of Health

NLM: National Library of Medicine

NMR: Nuclear Magnetic Resonance. NMR is a spectroscopic technique used for the determination of protein structure.

nr-PDB: non-redundant Protein Data Bank

OMIM: Online Mendelian Inheritance in Man. OMIM is a directory of human genes and genetic disorders, with links to literature references, sequence records, maps, and related databases.

Ortholog: Orthology describes genes in different species that derive from a single ancestral gene in the last common ancestor of the respective species.

Orthology: Orthology describes genes in different species that derive from a common ancestor, i.e., they are direct evolutionary counterparts.

Paralog: A paralog is one of a set of homologous genes that have diverged from each other as a consequence of gene duplication. For example, the mouse α-*globin* and β-*globin* genes are paralogs. The relationship between mouse α-*globin* and chick β-*globin* is also considered paralogous.

Paralogy: Paralogy describes the relationship of homologous genes that arose by gene duplication.

PCR: Polymerase Chain Reaction, - a technique for amplifying a specific DNA segment in a complex mixture. Also present in the DNA mixture are short oligonucleotide primers to the DNA segment of interest and reagents for DNA synthesis. PCR relies on the ability of DNA to separate into its two complementary strands at high temperature (a process called denaturation) and for the two strands to anneal at an optimal lower temperature (annealing). The annealing phase is followed by a DNA synthesis step at an optimal temperature for a heat-stable DNA polymerase. After multiple rounds of denaturation, annealing, and DNA synthesis, the DNA sequence specified by the oligonucleotide primers is amplified.

PDB: Protein Data Bank. The PDB is a database for 3D macromolecular structure data.

Pfam: Pfam is a database housing a large collection of multiple sequence alignments and hidden Markov models covering many common protein domains.

Phenotype: The observable traits or characteristics of an organism, e.g., hair color, weight, or the presence or absence of a disease. Phenotypic traits are not necessarily genetic.

PHRAP: A computer program that assembles raw sequence into sequence contigs (see above) and assigns to each position in the sequence an associated "quality score", on the basis of the PHRED scores of the raw sequence reads. A PHRAP quality score of X corresponds to an error probability of approximately $10^{-X/10}$. Thus, a PHRAP quality score of 30 corresponds to 99.9% accuracy for a base in the assembled sequence.

PHRED: A computer program that analyses raw sequence to produce a "base call" with an associated "quality score" for each position in the sequence. A PHRED quality score of X corresponds to an error probability of approximately $10^{-X/10}$. Thus, a PHRED quality score of 30 corresponds to 99.9% accuracy for the base call in the raw read.

phyletic pattern: Pattern of presence–absence of a cluster of orthologs (COG) in different species.

PHYLIP: PHYLogeny Inference Package, - a package of programs for various computer platforms to infer phylogenies or evolutionary trees, freely available from the Web.

PIR: Protein Information Resource

PMC: PubMed Central - NLM's digital archive of life sciences journal literature.

PMID: PubMed ID number

PNG: Portable Network Graphics. An extensible file format for the lossless, well-compressed storage of raster images (images that are composed of horizontal lines of pixels, such as those created by a computer screen). Compression of image, media, and application files is necessary to reduce the transmission time across the web. The technique of lossless compression reduces the size of the file without sacrificing any original data, and the image after expansion is exactly as it was before compression.PNG overcomes the patent issues of GIF (Graphic Interchange Format) and can replace many common uses of TIFF (Tagged Image File Format). Several features such as indexed color, grayscale, and truecolor are supported, as well as an optional alpha-channel. PNG is designed to work well in online viewing applications and is supported as an image standard by the WWW.

poly A: A string of adenylic acid residues that are added to the 3' end of the primary mRNA transcript. Poly(A) polymerase is the enzyme that adds the poly A tail, which is between 100 and 250 bases long.

Polymorphism: A common variation in the sequence of DNA among individuals. Genetic variations occurring in more than 1% of the population would be considered useful polymorphisms for genetic linkage analysis.

Polypeptide: Linear polymer of amino acids connected by peptide bonds. Proteins are large polypeptides, and the two terms are commonly used interchangeably.

PRF: Protein Research Foundation

Private polymorphism: Variations those are only common in specific populations. Usually such populations are reproductively isolated from other, larger groups. These variations may be completely absent in other groups.

ProtEST: A database of protein sequences from eight organisms: human (*Homo sapiens*), mouse (*Mus musculus*), rat (*Rattus norvegicus*), fruitfly (*Drosophila melanogaster*), worm

(*Caenorhabditis elegans*), yeast (*Saccharomyces cerevisiae*), plant (*Arabidopsis thaliana*), and bacteria (*Escherichia coli*). (See the ProtEST web page.)

PROW: Protein. An online resource that features PROW Guides—authoritative, short, structured reviews on proteins and protein families. The Guides provide approximately 20 standardized categories of information (abstract, biochemical function, ligands, references, etc.) for each protein.

Pseudogene: A sequence of DNA that is very similar to a normal gene but that has been altered slightly so that it is not expressed. Such genes were probably once functional but, over time, acquired one or more mutations that rendered them incapable of producing a protein product.

PSI-BLAST: Position-Specific Iterated BLAST. PSI-BLAST (Altschul et al., J Mol Biol 215:403-410; 1990) is used for iterative protein–sequence similarity searches using a position-specific score matrix (PSSM). It is a program for searching protein databases using protein queries to find other members of the same protein family. All statistically significant alignments found by BLAST are combined into a multiple alignment, from which a PSSM is constructed. This matrix is used to search the database for additional significant alignments, and the process may be iterated until no new alignments are found.

PSSM: Position-Specific Score Matrix. The PSSM gives the log-odds score for finding a particular matching amino acid in a target sequence.

PubMed: retrieval system containing citations, abstracts, and indexing terms for journal articles in the biomedical sciences. It includes literature citations supplied directly to NCBI by publishers as well as URLs to full text articles on the publishers' web sites.PubMed contains the complete contents of the MEDLINE and PREMEDLINE databases. It also contains some articles and journals considered out of scope for MEDLINE, based on either content or on a period of time when the journal was not indexed and, therefore, is a superset of MEDLINE.

PXML: PubMed Central XML file

QBLAST: A queuing system to BLAST that allows users to retrieve their results at their convenience and format their results multiple times with different formatting options.

QTL: Quantitative Trait Locus. A QTL is a hypothesis that a certain region of the chromosome contains genes that contribute significantly to the expression of a complex trait. QTLs are generally identified by comparing the linkage of polymorphic molecular markers and phenotypic trait measurements. The density of the linkage map is important in the accurate and precise location of QTLs; the higher the map density, the more precise the location of the putative QTL, although there is increased likelihood that false positives will be detected. Once QTLs have been mapped to a relatively small chromosomal region, other molecular methods can be used to isolate specific genes.

RCSB: Research Collaboratory for Structural Bioinformatics. RCSB is a nonprofit consortium that works toward the elucidation of biological, macromolecular, 3-D structures.

Reciprocal best hits: Reciprocal are proteins from different organisms that are each other's top BLAST hit, when the proteomes from those organisms are compared to each other. For example, proteins A–Z in organism 1 are compared against proteins AA–ZZ in organism 2. If protein A has a best hit to protein RR, and RR's best hit, when it is compared to all the proteins in organism 1, also turns out to protein A, then A and RR are reciprocal best hits. However, if RR's best hit is to B rather than to A, then A and RR are not reciprocal best hits.

RefSeq: RefSeq is the NCBI database of reference sequences; a curated, non-redundant set including genomic DNA contigs, mRNAs and proteins for known genes, and entire chromosomes.

RepeatMasker: Program that screens DNA sequences for interspersed repeats and low-complexity DNA sequences.

RFLP: Restriction Fragment Length Polymorphism - Genetic variations at the site where a restriction enzyme cuts a piece of DNA. Such variations affect the size of the resulting fragments. These sequences can be used as markers on physical maps and linkage maps. RFLP is also pronounced "rif lip".

RH map: Radiation Hybrid map. A genome map in which STSs are positioned relative to one another on the basis of the frequency with which they are separated by radiation-induced breaks. The frequency is assayed by analyzing a panel of human–hamster hybrid cell lines. These hybrids are produced by irradiating human cells, which damages the cells and fragments the DNA. The dying human cells are fused with thymidine kinase negative (TK−) live hamster cells. The fused cells are grown under conditions that select against hamster cells and favor the growth of hybrid cells that have taken up the human *TK* gene. In the RH maps, the unit of distance is centirays (cR), denoting a 1% chance of a break occurring between two loci.

RNA: Ribonucleic Acid. A single-stranded nucleic acid, similar to DNA, but having a ribose sugar, instead of deoxyribose, and uracil instead of thymine as one of its bases.

RPS-BLAST: Reverse Position-Specific BLAST. A program used to identify conserved domains in a protein query sequence. It does this by comparing a query protein sequence to position-specific score matrices (PSSM)s that have been prepared from conserved domain alignments. RPS-BLAST is a "reverse" version of position-specific iterated BLAST (PSI-BLAST); however, RPS-BLAST compares a query sequence against a database of profiles prepared from ready-made alignments, whereas PSI-BLAST builds alignments starting from a single protein sequence.

SAGE: Serial Analysis of Gene Expression. An experimental technique designed to quantitatively measure gene expression.

Sequin: Sequin is a stand-alone software tool developed by the NCBI for submitting and updating entries to the GenBank, EMBL, or DDBJ sequence databases. It is capable of handling simple submissions that contain a single, short mRNA sequence and complex submissions containing long sequences, multiple annotations, segmented sets of DNA, or phylogenetic and population studies.

SGD: Saccharomyces Genome Database - A database for the molecular biology and genetics of *Saccharomyces cerevisceae*, also known as baker's yeast.

SGML: Standard Generalized Markup Language - The international standard for specifying the structure and content of electronic documents. SGML is used for the mark-up of data in a way that is self-describing. SGML is not a language but a way of defining languages that are developed along its general principles. A subset of SGML called XML is more widely used for the mark-up of data. HTML (Hypertext Mark-up Language) is based on SGML and uses some of its concepts to provide a universal mark-up language for the display of information and the linking of different pieces of that information.

SKY: Spectral Karyotyping. SKY is a technique that allows for the visualization of all of an organism's chromosomes together, each labelled with a different color. This is achieved by using chromosome-specific, single-stranded DNA probes (each labeled with a different fluorophore) to hybridize or bind to the chromosomes of a cell; resulting in each chromosome being painted a different color. This technique is useful for identifying chromosome abnormalities because it is easy to spot instances where a chromosome painted in one color has a small piece of another chromosome, painted in a different color, attached to it. (Also see FISH, CGH.)

SKYGRAM: 1. A software tool to automatically convert the short-form karyotype into an image representation of a cell or clone, with each chromosome displayed in a different color, with band overlay. The program will also incorporate the number of cells for each structural abnormality, which is displayed in brackets. 2. The full ideogram or a cell or clone, with each chromosome displayed in a different color, with band overlay.

SMART: Simple Modular Architecture Research Tool. A tool to allow automatic identification and annotation of domains in user-supplied protein sequences. For example, the SWISS-PROT database is an extensively annotated and non redundant collection of protein sequences. SWISS-PROT annotations have been mined for SMART-derived annotations of alignments.

SMD: Stanford Microarray Database. SMD stores raw and normalized data from microarray experiments, as well as their corresponding image files. In addition, the SMD provides interfaces for data retrieval, analysis, and visualization. Data are released to the public at the researcher's discretion or upon publication.

SNP: Common, but minute, variations that occur in human DNA at a frequency of 1 every 1,000 bases. An SNP is a single base-pair site within the genome at which more than one of the four possible base pairs is commonly found in natural populations. Several hundred thousand SNP sites are being identified and mapped on the sequence of the genome, providing the densest possible map of genetic differences. SNP is pronounced "snip".

SOFT: Simple Omnibus Format in Text. SOFT is an ASCII text format that was designed to be a machine-readable representation of data retrieved from, or submitted to, the Gene Expression Omnibus (GEO). SOFT is also a line-based format, making it easy to parse, using commonly available text processing and formatting languages. (For examples of SOFT, see the guide.)

splice sites: Refers to the location of the exon-intron junctions in a pre-mRNA (i.e., the primary transcript that must undergo additional processing to become a mature RNA for translation into a protein). Splice sites can be determined by comparing the sequence of genomic DNA with that of the cDNA sequence. In mRNA, introns (non-protein coding regions) are removed by the splicing machinery; however, exons can also be removed. Depending on which exons (or parts of exons) are removed, different proteins can be made from the same initial RNA or gene. Different proteins created in this way are "splice variants" or "alternatively spliced".

SSAHA: Sequence Search and Alignment by Hashing Algorithm. SSAHA is a software tool for very fast matching and alignment of DNA sequences and is used for searching databases containing large amounts (gigabases) of genome sequence. It achieves its fast search speed by converting sequence information into a "hash table" data structure, which can then be searched very rapidly for matches (Ning et al., Genome Res 11:1725-1729; 2001).

SSLP: Simple Sequence Length Polymorphisms. SSLPs are markers based on the variation in the number of short tandem repeats in DNA.

STS: A short DNA segment that occurs only once in the human genome, the exact location and order of bases of which are known. Because each is unique, STSs are helpful for chromosome placement of mapping and sequencing data from many different laboratories. STSs serve as landmarks on the physical map of the human genome.

Substitution matrix: A substitution matrix containing values proportional to the probability that amino acid i mutates into amino acid j for all pairs of amino acids. Such matrices are constructed by assembling a large and diverse sample of verified pair wise alignments of amino acids. If the sample is large enough to be statistically significant, the resulting matrices should reflect the true probabilities of mutations occurring through a period of evolution. (See also BLOSUM 62.)

SWISS-PROT: SWISS-PROT is a curated protein sequence database that provides a high level of annotation (such as the description of protein function, domain structures, post-translational modifications, variants, etc.), a minimal level of redundancy, and high level of integration with other databases.

Sybase: A trademarked family of products that include databases, development tools, integration middleware, enterprise portals, and mobile and wireless servers.

Synteny: On the same strand. The phrase "conserved synteny" refers to conserved gene order on chromosomes of different, related species.

Tax BLAST: BLAST Taxonomy Reports page. Tax BLAST groups BLAST hits by source organism, according to information in NCBI's Taxonomy database. Species are listed in order of sequence similarity with the query sequence, the strongest match listed first.

Tax ID: Taxonomy Identifier. The taxID is a stable unique identifier for each taxon (for a species, a family, an order, or any other group in the taxonomy database). The taxID is seen in the GenBank records as a "source" feature table entry; for example, /db_xref="taxon:<9606>" is the taxID for *Homo sapiens*, and the line is therefore found in all recent human sequence records.

Taxid: See taxID.

Termination codon or stop codon: One of three codons that do not specify any amino acid and hence causes translation of mRNA into protein to be terminated. These codons mark the end of a protein coding sequence.

TIGR: The Institute for Genomic Research

Tiling path: An ordered list or map that defines a set of overlapping clones that covers a chromosome or other extended segment of DNA.

TPA: Third-Party Annotation

TPF: Tiling Path Format. A table format used to specify the set of clones that will provide the best possible sequence coverage for a particular chromosome, the order of the clones along the chromosome, and the location of any gaps in the clone tiling path. Also used to refer to a file (Tiling Path File) in which the minimal tiling path of clones covering a chromosome is specified in Tiling Path Format or to the minimal tiling path of clones so defined.

Translation start site: The position within an mRNA at which synthesis of a protein begins. The translation start site is usually an AUG codon, but occasionally, GUG or CUG codons are used to initiate protein synthesis.

UID: Unique Identifier Digit

UMLS: Unified Medical Language System - A project of the National Library of Medicine for the development and distribution of multipurpose, electronic "Knowledge Sources", and associated lexical programs. The purpose of the UMLS is to aid the development of systems that help health professionals and researchers retrieve and integrate electronic biomedical information from a variety of sources and to make it easy for users to link disparate information systems, including computer-based patient records, bibliographic databases, factual databases, and expert systems.

Unfinished sequence: See draft sequence.

UniGene cluster: ESTs and full-length mRNA sequences organized into clusters such that each represents a unique known or putative gene within the organism from which the sequences were obtained. UniGene clusters are annotated with mapping and expression information when possible (e.g., for human) and include cross-references to other resources. Sequence data can be downloaded by clusterthrough the UniGene web pages, or the complete dataset can be downloaded from the repository/UniGene directory of the FTPsite.

UniSTS: UniSTS presents a unified, non-redundant view of sequence-tagged sites (STSs). UniSTS integrates marker and mapping data from a variety of public resources. If two or more markers have different names but the same primer pair, a single STS record is presented for the primer pair, and all the marker names are shown.

UNIX: UNIX is an operating system that was developed by Dennis Ritchie and Kenneth Thompson at Bell Labs more than 30 years ago. It allows multitasking and multiuser capabilities and offers portability with other operating systems. It comes with hundreds of programs that are of two types: integral utilites, such as the command line interpreter; and tools such as email, which are not necessary for the operation of UNIX but provide additional capabilities to the user. It is functionally organized at three levels: the kernel, which schedules tasks and manages storage; the shell, which connects and interprets user's commands, calls programs from memory, and executes them; and tools and applications, which offer additional functionality to the operating system, such as word processing and business applications. UNIX® was registered by Bell Laboratories as a trademark for computer operating systems. Today, this mark is owned by The Open Group.

URL: Uniform Resource Locator. It is the address of a resource on the Internet. URL syntax is in the form of protocol://host/localinfo, where "protocol" specifies the means of fetching the object (such as HTTP, used by WWW browsers and servers to exchange information, or FTP), "host" specifies the remote location where the object resides, and "localinfo" is a string (often a file name) passed to the protocol handler at the remote location, also called Uniform Resource Identifier (URI).

UTF-8: UCS (Universal Character Set) Transformation Format - An AscII-preserving encoding method for Unicode (a standard to provide a unique number for every character irrespective of the platform, program, or language).

UTR: Untranslated Region. The 3' UTR is that portion of an mRNA from the position of the last codon that is used in translation to the 3' end. The 5' UTR is that portion of an mRNA from the 5' end to the position of the first codon used in translation.

VAST: Vector. A computer algorithm used to identify similar protein 3D structures.

Weight: An assignment of importance to a term in a search query. If a term in a search query is found to match a word in a document, that word is given a "weight". The exact weight of the word will depend on the emphasis given to the word by the author or its position in the document. For example, a word that occurs in a chapter title will have a higher weight than the same word if it occurs in the body of the chapter. Similarly, words that occur in data collections are also assigned weights, depending on how frequently the terms occur in the collection.

WGS sequence: Whole Genome Shotgun sequence. In this semi-automated sequencing technique, high-molecular-weight DNA is sheared into random fragments, size selected (usually 2, 10, 50, and 150 kb), and cloned into an appropriate vector. The clones are then sequenced from both ends. The two ends of the same clone are referred to as mate pairs. The distance between two mate pairs can be inferred if the library size is known and has a narrow window of deviation. The sequences are aligned using sequence assembly software. Proponents of this approach argue that it is possible to sequence the whole genome at once using large arrays of sequencers, which makes the whole process much more efficient than the traditional approaches.

WHO: World Wide Web - A consortium (W3C) that develops technologies such specifications, guidelines, software, and tools for the internet.

XML: Extensible Mark-up Language. XML describes a class of data objects called XML documents and partially describes the behavior of computer programs that process them. XML is a subset of SGML, and XML documents are conforming SGML documents. XML documents are made up of storage units called entities, which contain either parsed or unparsed data. Parsed data is made up of characters (a unit of text), some of which form character data, and some of which form mark-up. Mark-up includes tags that provide information about the data, i.e., a description of the structure and content of the document. Character data comprises all the text that is not mark-up. XML provides a mechanism to impose constraints on the storage layout and logical structure.

XSL: Extensible Style sheet Language. XSL is used for the transformation of XML-based data into HTML or other presentation formats, for display in a web browser. This is a two-part process. First, the structure of the input XML tree must be transformed into a new tree (e.g., HTML), allowing reordering of the elements, addition of text, and calculations—all without modification to the source document. This process is described by XSLT. Second, XSL-FO (XSL Formatting Objects, an XML vocabulary for formatting) is used for formatting the output, defining areas of the display page and their properties. In this way, the source XML document can be maintained from the perspective of "pure content" and can be separated from the presentation. An XML document can be delivered in different formats to different target audiences by simply switching style sheets.

XSLT: Extensible Style sheet Language: Transformations. XSLT is a language for transforming the structure of an XML document. XSLT is designed for use as part of XSL, the style sheet language for XML. A transformation expressed in XSLT describes a sequence of template rules for transforming a source tree into a result tree; elements from the source tree can be filtered and reordered, and a different structure can be added. A template rule has two parts: a pattern that is matched against nodes in the source tree; and a template that can be instantiated to form part of the result tree. This makes XSLT a declarative language because it is possible to specify what output should be produced when specific patterns occur in the input, which distinguishes it from procedural programming languages, where it is necessary to specify what tasks have to be performed in what order. XSLT makes use of the expression language defined by XPath (a language for addressing the parts of an XML document) for selecting elements for processing, for conditional processing, and for generating text.

YAC: Yeast Artificial Chromosome - Extremely large segments of DNA from another species splices into the DNA of yeast. YACs are used to clone up to one million bases of foreign DNA into a host cell, where the DNA is propagated along with the other chromosomes of the yeast cell.

ZFIN: Zebra fish Information Network. ZFIN is a database for the zebra fish model organism that holds information on wild-type stocks, mutants, genes, gene expression data, and map markers.

Source: http://www.ncbi.nlm.nih.gov

-------------------- E N D --------------------

www.ingramcontent.com/pod-product-compliance
Lightning Source LLC
Chambersburg PA
CBHW070217190526
45169CB00001B/3